GW00482903

Antiquities
of
Rural Ireland

Antiquities
— *of* —
Rural
Ireland

Muiris Ó Súilleabháin
Liam Downey
Dara Downey

Word*well*

First published in 2017
Wordwell Ltd
Unit 9, 78 Furze Road, Sandyford Industrial Estate, Dublin 18
www.wordwellbooks.com

Cover image: an early church site on St Mac Dara's Island, Co. Galway
(courtesy of Brendan Riordan).

ISBN 978-0-9933518-9-1

British Library Cataloguing-in-Publication Data.
A catalogue record for this book is available from the British Library.

The authors and publisher gratefully acknowledge the generous assistance of Teagasc and the
Heritage Council in the publication of this volume.

Typeset in Ireland by Alicia McAuley Publishing Services: www.aliciamcauley.com
Copy-editors: Emer Condit, Alicia McAuley
Cover design by Wordwell Ltd

Printed by Gráficas Castuera, Pamplona

Contents

Preface

Professor Gerry Boyle, director of Teagasc

Teagasc is delighted to be associated with the publication of this collection of review articles, which synopsises current knowledge on the many archaeological features associated with the evolution of Ireland's farming economy and landscapes. The articles, which were originally published in *Archaeology Ireland*, help to raise our awareness and understanding of our rich farming heritage and of how farming through the generations has shaped, and will continue to shape, our rural landscape.

As the current managers of the land, present-day Irish farmers can trace a long lineage back to the earliest farmers, the first people to actively tend the land. Prehistoric farming has been revealed at Céide, Co. Mayo, where Ireland's earliest agricultural landscape has been preserved beneath the blanket of peat for over 5,000 years. Ancient farming, dating from the early Christian period (AD 500–1200), is most visible on the landscape in the many thousand ringforts, whose circular enclosures were essentially protected farmyards. Medieval monastic orders and Anglo-Norman settlers in the twelfth century brought considerable change and new technology to agriculture. They cleared woodland and founded towns, villages and medieval field systems.

In the sixteenth and seventeenth centuries, land ownership in large areas of the country was redistributed to English planters and others. The 'agricultural revolution' involved the introduction of new crops, vegetables, trees, improved breeds of sheep and cattle and new systems of crop rotation. The agricultural boom of Napoleonic times, when there was a shift from pasture to tillage, helped fuel the population explosion in the century up to the 1840s.

Most of the lowland landscape we see today was laid out in the eighteenth and nineteenth centuries, when common land was enclosed by establishing earth banks, stone walls and hedgerows. The enclosure of millions of hectares of land created the patchwork-quilt appearance of the present rural landscape.

These and many other landscape features are presented in this excellent series of articles and the authors highlight their importance in seeking to understand today's farming landscape. Teagasc and its predecessor organisation, An Foras Talúntais (AFT), also identified strongly with the need to understand the past in order to change and improve the future. AFT recognised that present-day farming could not be understood, and progress could not be achieved, in the absence of a full understanding of the biological and physical aspects of agricultural systems, but also their social and historical context. It was this belief that prompted the publication by AFT in the 1960s, for example, of the monumental resource studies of west Cork and west Donegal—*West Cork resource survey* (1963); *West Donegal resource survey* (1969). Teagasc is building on this intellectual foundation through its support for, among many other examples: *The living farmland: a guide to farming with nature in Clare* (Shannon, 2008); the Burren LIFE Project (http://ec.europa. eu/environment/life/project/Projects/index.cfm?fuseaction=search. dspPage&n_proj_id=2661); the Royal Irish Academy's *New survey of Clare Island* (https://www.ria.ie/research-projects/new-survey-clare-island); and a number of joint projects with the UCD School of Archaeology.

In supporting the publication of this comprehensive collection, I trust that the excellent scholarship reflected in the various articles will reach a wider audience and create a broader understanding of how our farming and rural landscape emerged. I also hope that the publication will strengthen consensus around the critical need to ensure that Ireland retains across the country viable and sustainable farms, which are necessary to maintain the economic and social wellbeing of rural communities and the integrity of our countryside.

Foreword

Michael Starrett, CEO of the Heritage Council

It is a pleasure on behalf of the Heritage Council to provide a foreword for this publication on the monuments of our rural landscapes. I am particularly delighted to collaborate with Teagasc on the funding of the publication, as over the years the Heritage Council and Teagasc have enjoyed a unique relationship as two state agencies with ostensibly vastly differing responsibilities. Our first sense of common ground was found in research and followed publication by the Heritage Council in 2001 of a research paper entitled *The archaeological features at risk project.* This highlighted the ongoing role that archaeological survey played in understanding risks for the preservation of field monuments. Liam Downey, then director of Teagasc, immediately grasped the significance of the work. The Heritage Council and Teagasc also, uniquely for state agencies, shared the same chairman from 2000–8 (Dr Tom O'Dwyer). The provider of the preface to this book, Professor Gerry Boyle (now director of Teagasc) contributed to the publication of *Proposals for Ireland's landscapes* by the Heritage Council in 2010. The basis for all of these links has been the importance of people and place, the links and connections between our major land use and the value we attach to our natural and cultural heritage.

As such, two of the authors of this publication, Professor Liam Downey and Professor Muiris Ó Súilleabháin, have helped the Heritage Council over many years through wise counsel and membership of statutory committees and working groups. Since 2016, Muiris has done so as a member of the Heritage Council. And, since 2003, and amidst the achievements of busy professional lives, they have found the energy, commitment and expertise to produce short state-of-knowledge papers in *Archaeology Ireland* on subjects as diverse as rundale farming, megalithic tombs and medieval monuments. They have done so to share knowledge and ensure access to information that enhances understanding and enjoyment of these significant aspects of our national heritage. This is what we are celebrating here.

James Joyce once pointed out that 'places remember events', and in this we can recognise how deeply time has become embedded within place, and might be said to have become one of its dominant characteristics. The monuments described in this book are vital pieces of the Irish rural landscape and this work helps to return these monuments to the important place they once occupied in our consciousness.

While this publication sets out the importance of cultural-heritage landscapes, we should not lose sight of the fact that historic places and monuments are important ecological habitats and that extensive traditional farming regimes are also good for the maintenance of cultural landscapes. Traditional farming practices have been shown to be beneficial not just for biodiversity but also for the preservation of archaeological monuments, especially in upland and marginal areas, for maintaining the character of traditional field systems and for continuing the usage of vernacular farm buildings. The Heritage Council's work on high nature value farming and the development of the Traditional Farm Buildings Grant Scheme serve to emphasise this point.

Many of Ireland's finest historic landscapes are located, as is now acknowledged, in economically marginal areas, particularly uplands and semi-natural areas. Accordingly, these present opportunities for learning, recreation and rural diversification. The continued survival of monuments such as those described in this publication is an important, and often overlooked, indicator of the sustainability of our farming and general land-use practices.

We see this publication as an important step in the ongoing care and understanding of our archaeological heritage and in the recognition of the cultural landscapes in which it sits. Through the Heritage Council's Heritage Officer Network with local authorities, its grant programmes for local communities, online digital information resources, field monument advisors and the Adopt a Monument Scheme, local communities can engage in projects that help reconnect people with their landscapes. This publication will help this ongoing reconnection.

Acknowledgements

The research-based contributions of a wide range of individuals and organisations in both the public and private sectors have been of central importance in compiling the articles contained in this book. Every effort has been made to acknowledge photographs and drawings used in the original articles. We apologise if we have made any errors or omissions in this regard. Any such errors will be rectified in subsequent editions of this book.

A gratifying feature of this knowledge-dissemination initiative is the open access provided in respect of information, sometimes prior to its publication. Our appreciation of this collaboration and also the assistance received from various colleagues in providing photographs or diagrams for publication is reflected in the acknowledgements attached to the individual articles. Particular gratitude is due to Connie Murphy for his generosity in sharing field knowledge and images from the Beara Peninsula.

Behind the scenes, ongoing technical assistance from Conor McDermott of the UCD School of Archaeology has been invaluable, not least in preparing the book.

Special thanks are due to the National Monuments Service for providing images illustrating many of the entries here, and also access to the data in the Archaeological Survey of Ireland database. The information brought to our attention by the Heritage Council is also much appreciated.

Generous sponsorship provided by Teagasc (together with the Heritage Council) towards the publication of this book is most gratefully acknowledged.

Introduction

For half a century after its publication in 1942, Seán P. Ó Ríordáin's *Antiquities of the Irish countryside* was the unmatched authority on archaeological monuments in Ireland. Updated a few times, most recently in the 1970s, it stood the test of time until being overtaken by a flood of new discoveries, colourful publications and spectacularly illustrated web sites during the past few decades. However, it has not been fully superseded. This volume does not claim to be a comprehensive heir, but it begins the process of creating a worthy modern successor.

The task Ó Ríordáin faced three quarters of a century ago was significant and the challenge of replacing his book today would be herculean, owing to a flood of new information and a broadening of archaeological horizons. An old French drain, still functioning underground in some remote corner of a field, may not be quite as noticeable as a great megalithic tomb, but it too was built by someone whose anonymous handiwork captures a moment in time and preserves a detail of farming life in the past. The megalithic tomb is intriguing, but the drain, like an old photograph of people saving hay by hand a hundred years ago, is closer to home.

In 2003 we began a series of articles for *Archaeology Ireland* under the banner 'Know your monuments'. More than 50 articles have now been produced, each devoted to a specific topic, and this book is a compilation of those articles, assembled to shed light on Ireland's agricultural and rural past. It does not pretend to be comprehensive, but we hope it will prove interesting and eye-opening. The articles attempt to collect reasonably up-to-date information about the various archaeological traces, supported by images, summaries of diagnostic features and lists of publications where additional information may be sourced. The contributions have proved to be useful for landowners wishing to check on specific features they have encountered, for students and teachers seeking a quick and reliable introduction to specific topics, for archaeologists trying to contextualise discoveries in the field, and for dilettantes, in providing a miscellany of old reliables and unexpected treats. Some of the articles were originally produced more than ten years ago, and we apologise for any resultant omissions.

Many readers will jump directly to those articles that are of specific interest to them and, for that reason, each article is preceded by a summary to indicate its contents. For those wishing to read more systematically, the volume is divided into seven thematic sections, each with its own introduction. The following overview is accompanied by an indicative timeline presented in two illustrations, devoted respectively to prehistoric (Fig. 1) and historical (Fig. 2) features.

Setting the scene

Sections I & II—Agriculture & Food processing

The evolution of agriculture from the Neolithic period (Fig. 1) is reflected in the occurrence of prehistoric field boundaries and plough-marks in the landscape. With reference to these early beginnings, the prominence of corn and milk products in the staple diet of the population at large is signalled by the introduction of quern stones into Ireland during the Neolithic period and, as outlined below, the discovery of milk-fat residues embedded in the matrix of pottery vessels from the same period. The protracted time-span of quern-stone use, even into the past century, as well as the finds of bog-butter with dates ranging between the seventeenth century BC and the eighteenth century AD, indicate the primacy of corn and milk products throughout the ages.

Wedge tombs are key monuments for understanding life and death in Bronze Age Ireland. They reflect the practical, symbolic and cultural concerns of the communities that built them and are important secondary indicators of agricultural activity, especially in western areas. The prevalence of *fulachta fiadh* during the Bronze Age may be another proxy, attributable to livestock production gaining momentum during that period.

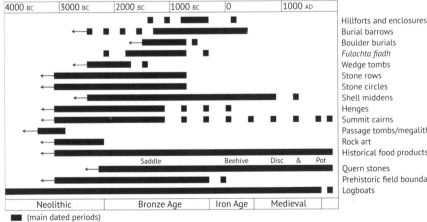

Fig. 1— Indicative timelines: predominantly prehistoric times.

In early medieval Ireland, ringforts were predominantly enclosed farmsteads in an environment where the management of livestock was a primary preoccupation. Cows at that time were much valued for their milk and associated dairy products. In essence, Ireland had a predominantly dairy-based economy during this period, although the production of cereals appears to have increased in importance towards the end of the first millennium AD. Evidence suggests that cereal production and processing became more widespread from the eighth century AD, and involved innovations seemingly introduced by ecclesiastical communities. Corn-drying kilns and watermills, representing the two characteristic technologies in post-harvest cereal processing, became common features of the agricultural landscape (Fig. 2).

In the Anglo-Norman period, field enclosures and ridge-and-furrow cultivation became more widespread (Fig. 2). With the further intensification of agricultural production in the post-medieval period, underground drainage was more widely adopted, and farm lime kilns became ubiquitous during the late nineteenth and early twentieth centuries.

An interesting aspect of the evolution of farming and food production outlined above is the prevalence of archaeological features associated with more arable farming and grain processing (Figs 1 and 2). However, livestock production, apparently practised in Ireland over the millennia, is much less obvious in the archaeological record. This may be because crop cultivation and processing required the progressive adoption of an array of support features, including secure field boundaries, quern stones for grinding grain, drainage systems, corn-drying kilns, watermills, windmills and lime kilns, which generally left characteristic archaeological remains (Figs 1 and 2). Conversely, livestock-farming in previous centuries involved much less infrastructural hardware. Cattle were mainly outwintered and the provision of animal housing would have been limited on most farms and not especially distinctive in the archaeological record. Thus, archaeological remains indicating livestock would be less common than crop-related features.

In many respects the most enduring impact of farming systems, both crop and livestock, on the landscape may be their influence on settlement patterns (Fig. 2).

Section III—Settlement

From the late Bronze Age to the Iron Age, the construction of hillforts and hill enclosures occupying elevated defensive positions appears to have become prevalent. While crannogs also appear to have been built as early as the late Bronze Age, these man-made islands continued to be erected and used as defensive and possibly high-status lake settlements up until the late medieval period, with a noticeable surge in early medieval times.

In early medieval Ireland, ringforts and church sites were prominent nodes of dispersed settlement in the landscape. Both were associated with farming and were common locations for souterrains. The introduction of corn-drying kilns and watermills during the period (Fig. 2) indicates the growing importance of grain production.

Beginning in the twelfth century AD in areas under Anglo-Norman control, notably in eastern counties, the widespread development of mottes and moated sites—and the establishment of manors, tower-houses and medieval towns—underlines the continuing link between agriculture and settlement. This relationship continued into the post-medieval period, as indicated by clusters of houses, generally termed clachans (Fig. 2), which were usually associated with the rundale farming system.

Section IV—Getting around

Logboat usage in Ireland began as early as the Mesolithic or very early Neolithic period (Fig. 1) and was still evident up until the latter part of the seventeenth century, which underlines the historical importance of waterways in everyday transport. Currachs appear to have emerged in the Iron Age and both types of craft coexisted through the medieval period. The early decades of the 1800s heralded a transition to more modern currachs. Plank-built boats, used on European waters from the Bronze Age if not earlier—and, famously, the craft of choice in Viking trade and predatory activity—have not yet featured in the 'Know your monuments' series.

Early writing in Ireland during the first millennium AD mentions a wide variety of routeways, leading modern scholars to infer the likely corridors of travel at the time. By the early decades of the eighteenth century, with a roadway infrastructure connecting towns around the country, most of the principal rivers appear to have been bridged at important crossings.

Section V—Local enterprises

While agriculture and food production continued to be of central importance, the establishment of local enterprises such as charcoal production, kelp production, salt-making and turf-harvesting made sizeable contributions to the progressive development of greater diversification in local economies from the post-medieval period onward.

Section VI—Coastal features

From the Neolithic period and earlier, coastal areas were exploited for their food resources, as may be seen from the wide distribution and scale of shell middens around the seaboard (Fig. 1). Remains of promontory forts are located in strategic positions around the coast. They were

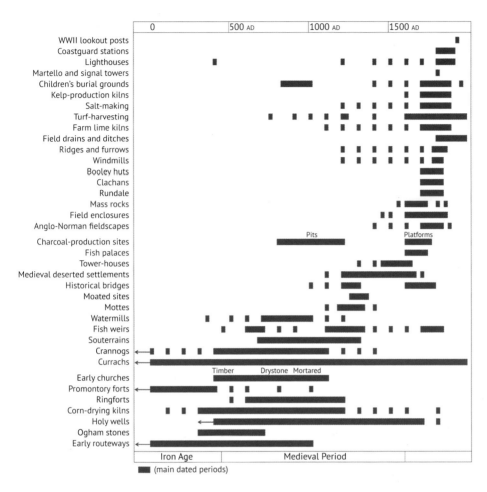

Fig. 2—
Indicative
timelines:
predominantly
historical
times.

constructed for defensive purposes and may date from the Iron Age, with some possibly older and some occupied in later times (Fig. 2).

Fish weirs constructed in coastal waters, particularly estuaries, testify to the intensity of medieval fishing and its continuation through later centuries. In the seventeenth and eighteenth centuries, large shoals of pilchard captured around the south and south-west coasts were preserved by salting in curing stations, known in some localities as fish palaces.

From the 1800s, various types of buildings were progressively constructed at key locations around the coast—notably Martello towers, signal towers, Coastguard stations and lighthouses, culminating in the erection of lookout posts with the onset of World War II (Fig. 2).

Section VII—Ritual and ceremony

Archaeological features are clues to Ireland's past, their construction and usage reflecting the marked changes that occurred in cultural and social practices through time (Figs 1 and 2). Passage tombs, for example, were primarily Neolithic monuments, while henges are associated with the progression from the Neolithic into the Bronze Age and beyond. Many summit cairns are linked with clusters of passage tombs—and some in fact contain passage tombs—but others are known to contain only early Bronze Age structures or apparently no internal structures, which highlights the difficulty of interpreting unopened summit cairns. A specialised form of rock art is associated with passage tombs, while a more universal form of rock art, associated primarily with boulders and rock faces located in their natural landscape setting, may have originated in the Neolithic period, but seems to have continued into the Bronze Age. Certain motifs—notably the circle and cupmark—are common to both forms of rock art. Henges were enclosures used apparently for ritual purposes and have been likened to amphitheatres where people could have assembled.

From the threshold of the Bronze Age, and earlier in some instances (Fig. 1), a complex of monument types—stone circles, stone rows and pairs, single standing stones, wedge tombs and boulder burials—became gradually more prevalent in the Irish landscape, sometimes in isolation and sometimes closely associated. Assemblages of these monuments in south Munster are sometimes linked with the discovery of Bronze Age copper mines in the region. Conversely, wedge tombs appear to have formed an integral part of a change in settlement throughout Ireland, brought about by an increasing dependency on agriculture. In mid-Ulster, the layout of the stone circles and rows is striking. Built of smaller structural stones than equivalent monuments in Munster, the assemblage at Beaghmore, Co. Tyrone comprises a multiplicity of rings and adjoining rows as well as cairns and other features. At least some of the stone circles in mid-Ulster may have been built during the Neolithic period.

Astronomical orientations built into many megalithic monuments are among their most debated features. They have been recorded at various stone circles, stone rows and pairs, wedge tombs and even individual standing stones with oblong cross-sections. However, this common feature is balanced by marked differences in architecture as well, presumably, as function and meaning. Wedge tombs and occasionally stone circles were used as repositories of human remains and as places of associated community gatherings. However, given their relatively simple structure, the functions of stone rows and stone pairs may have been different, as seasonal calendars associated with critical agricultural practices and the scheduling of time.

In the transition from the later Bronze Age into the Iron Age (Fig. 1), burial barrows were prominent funerary monuments and it appears that the burials placed in them were generally cremations. They frequently occur in clusters with other monuments from the later prehistoric period.

The record of barrows has increased dramatically, arising from the greater availability of aerial photography in recent decades.

The advent of Christianity in the fifth century AD resulted in religious practices blending imported features with the native heritage. Many holy wells are thought to have originated as prehistoric shrines; ogham stones feature a distinctive form of Gaelic writing seemingly inspired by the Roman script; while the rectangular shape of early churches often stands in marked contrast to the circular huts located beside them. Early and later medieval church sites were multi-purpose settlements in which religious functions went hand in hand with agriculture, craftworking and scholarship. From penal times and possibly a century earlier, Mass rocks became ceremonial locations in remote areas, reflecting the religious, social and political tensions of post-medieval Ireland. Children's burial grounds were another prolific feature of the post-medieval Irish landscape.

Section I
Agriculture

Although the number of people making their living directly from the land has fallen sharply over the past 50 years, there were half a million people doing just that in the republic alone around 1950. Farming is ingrained in the heritage of Ireland and has been practised on the island for approximately 6,000 years. Céide Fields, sealed beneath the blanket peat of north Mayo, is probably the most famous ancient agricultural landscape in western Europe. The ingrained association with farming in Ireland makes it difficult to imagine that three and a half thousand years of human settlement, well over a hundred successive generations of people, lived a non-farming lifestyle, from the end of the Ice Age until the arrival of agriculture around 4000 BC.

Once begun, the production of livestock, particularly cattle, and the cultivation of crops have continued to be practised to the present day. They have left us with an intriguing array of archaeological evidence.

During the Middle Ages, two broad geographical farming regions began to emerge on the island of Ireland. In many parts of the east and south, productive farmland comprised large stretches of open two- and three-field farming systems. In western Ireland, rundale infield/outfield farming with booleying of livestock on commonages was widely practised by the late eighteenth century.

Land enclosure was increasingly undertaken in eastern Ireland from the seventeenth century, with ridge-and-furrow cultivation becoming more prevalent. Enclosure took place later in western areas, apparently from the earlier part of the nineteenth century. The application of lime to farming land became widespread in the eighteenth and nineteenth centuries, and farm drainage systems were adopted during the 1800s. During the period 1780–1840, more land appears to have been cultivated in Ireland than ever before or since.

Ancient fields

In north Mayo, at the Céide Fields and Belderrig, stone walls have been found under the blanket peat that began to cover the Neolithic farmed landscape in the fourth millennium BC. The pre-bog walls at Céide appear to form a coaxial pattern of relatively large rectangular fields, which may have been associated mainly with cattle-, sheep- and even conceivably deer-farming. At Belderrig, tillage plots were located beside a Bronze Age cabin built around 1500 BC, on the floor of which were found a number of saddle querns (discussed elsewhere here). Further south in County Mayo, at Carrownagloch, excavations have revealed cultivation ridges, stone walls and, again, a circular cabin, representing tillage farming at the beginning of the first millennium BC.

Field boundaries from the Neolithic period and Bronze Age have been recorded in a number of other counties, including Kerry, Down and Clare. Systematic investigation of abandoned field walls still visible on the surface in upland areas like the Blackstairs Mountains or the mountains of south County Dublin promise a more comprehensive understanding of the farming systems practised in Ireland in earlier times.

Fig. 1 — Exposed section of pre-bog wall with Céide Fields Visitor Centre in the background. The line of the wall is shown by the white posts.

Prehistoric field boundaries

Field boundaries are probably the most common archaeological features in the Irish countryside. The current patchwork is the product of evolving social norms, political interventions, regional preferences, developments in farming techniques and a variety of initiatives by generations of individual farmers. The evidence may be less comprehensive in the case of prehistoric field boundaries, but there is enough to suggest that ancient land-management strategies were influenced by similar forces, as well as—there being a considerably longer time-span involved—the effects of changing climatic conditions.

Recognising prehistoric field boundaries

The best-known ancient field boundaries in Ireland are those found sealed beneath blanket peat along the western seaboard. In north Mayo, Séamus Caulfield's research has shown that the stone walls at Céide Fields and Belderrig are resting on the underlying soil and are covered by peat that began to cover the farmed landscape in the fourth millennium BC. Associated surveys, by Noel Dunne and Greta Byrne, have demonstrated that pre-bog landscapes are not confined to the core area around Céide but rather extend over a larger expanse of north Mayo. Michael Herity's excavations at Carrownaglogh, further south in County Mayo, revealed an interesting complex of Bronze Age cultivation ridges and stone walls.

Systematic multidisciplinary scrutiny of the type carried out in north Mayo has not occurred elsewhere and the evidence is consequently more ambiguous. Some of the best examples occur on the Kerry peninsulas, where stone walls are again known beneath the cut-away peat, as are other features that until recently were regarded as classic early Bronze Age monuments. The date assigned traditionally to these 'diagnostic' features can no longer be taken for granted, as Blaze O'Connor's work at the Drumirril rock-art complex in County Monaghan emphasises, but the main effect of the evidence assembled over the past 20 years is to demonstrate that field walls associated with such monuments might date from as early as the Neolithic period and as late as the late Bronze Age. Radiocarbon evidence suggests that a pre-bog field system known on Valentia Island, Co. Kerry, dates from the late Bronze Age. At Millin Bay, on the tip of the Ards Peninsula in County Down, a stretch of field wall was found to be preserved beneath a Neolithic monument.

In the instances described above, the various field boundaries are unambiguously ancient. It remains to be seen how many of the abandoned boundaries that are visible on the surface in various pockets of the Irish landscape, especially in marginal or pastoral farming land, can be assigned to the prehistoric period. There has been a tendency to regard these as the remains of post-medieval or medieval systems. This is an issue that needs to be reviewed, as emphasised by Carleton Jones's association of field boundaries with mainly Bronze Age monuments on the Burren, Co. Clare.

Types of field boundaries

The stone walls at Céide and Belderrig appear to have been well built, although today they survive in a semi-collapsed state. By comparison with more recent field walls, there is a certain blandness about them in the sense that they seem to lack access gaps of the type that are standard in more recent field boundaries. The evidence here is incomplete since only a tiny fraction of the walls have been fully exposed, the remainder having been surveyed by probing at intervals, but there is nevertheless a marked absence of open gaps, in-filled gaps and repairs of the type that are a common feature of today's field boundaries. This may be due to the intended function of the boundaries, with less emphasis on the passage of animals and people from one field to another, and it may also indicate that the walls had a relatively short life-span before the land became sealed beneath the peat, leaving insufficient time for the accumulation of ongoing repairs and alterations.

Fig. 2— Stone wall exposed beneath the cut-away bog at Belderrig, Co. Mayo, a Neolithic/Bronze Age complex excavated by Seamus Caulfield.

Fig. 3—Greta Byrne, manager of the Céide Fields Visitor Centre, demonstrates the technique of tracking the profile of a wall lying hidden beneath the peat.

A variety of field-boundary styles are known from the Bronze Age. In north Mayo some earthen boundaries are known. At Belderrig a landscape previously farmed in the Neolithic period was reclaimed around 1500 BC, and new stone walls as well as wooden fencing were used. The remains of field boundaries made from organic material, whether constructed with posts and wattle or grown naturally, are more difficult to identify on the ground than stone walls. The existence of palisades under and near megalithic tombs, as at Knowth and Tara, for example, may suggest that wooden boundaries may have been the norm since Neolithic times in areas where stone was less readily available. Although the Stone Age enclosures at Donegore Hill and Lyles Hill in County Antrim are not fields in the conventional sense, they indicate that palisades could easily have been used as field boundaries.

In any case, stone walls and to a lesser extent earthen banks are the most obvious evidence at our disposal today. At the late-Bronze Age farm in Carrownaglogh the enclosed area appears to have been extended once or twice, the stones from the existing wall apparently being stolen in each instance. The ancient boundaries identified in the townland of Fanygalvin, Co. Clare, have been described as **mound walls** because of their low, grass-covered appearance. They are particularly important because they are not sealed beneath peat. In other words, the search for prehistoric field boundaries should not be confined to peat-covered areas of Ireland.

Field patterns and land use

As anyone who studied under Séamus Caulfield will know, the pre-bog walls at Céide form a coaxial pattern of large rectangular fields extending across the landscape. These appear to reflect a system of pastoral farming. Cattle would have been the mainstay of this economy, but sheep and perhaps deer might also have played a role.

There is evidence for tillage in the Irish Neolithic period, as at Beaghmore in County Tyrone, but it has not been associated with any of the known field systems from the period. At Belderrig, however, a number of tillage plots were located beside a Bronze Age hut (dated to *c*. 1500 BC), on the floor of which were found a number of saddle querns, used in the grinding of grain. The plots survived in the form of parallel ridges, rather like those for growing potatoes in more recent times, the furrows providing good drainage in a damp climate. Evidence for the use of an ard was revealed beneath the plots.

The excavations at Carrownaglogh demonstrated that extensive areas of ridge-and-furrow cereal cultivation took place in the second half of the Bronze Age, even in this relatively mountainous setting. It seems that a deterioration in the Irish climate some time around 2000 BC led to a rapid expansion of bogland, with a resultant constriction of arable land. From about 1400 BC, however, tillage seems to have become increasingly important in the economy. After peaking early in the first millennium BC, arable farming seems to have declined in the Iron Age.

Conclusion

The dramatic discoveries at Céide and a small number of other sites have created the impression that field boundaries and early Irish farming in general are well understood. This is an illusion. Some British scholars, for instance, argue seriously that society in the Neolithic of Ireland and Britain was essentially nomadic. The evidence from Céide and Belderrig seems to challenge this interpretation but is open to being dismissed as a localised aberration. We may argue that the Neolithic landscape of north Mayo is unusual only in its preservation, but the best way to demonstrate something is to fill out the record. It is interesting that the recent motorway and gas-pipeline excavations have achieved this in the case of rectangular houses. Although the excavated corridors are too narrow to trace broad networks of ancient fields, they would have been expected to reveal some evidence of prehistoric field boundaries.

As in County Clare, it is possible that some of the relict field systems that are visible in the mountainous landscapes of Cork and Kerry, for instance, may date from prehistoric times. Likewise, can we assume that all the abandoned field systems in the landscape are post-medieval unless proven otherwise? This is justified where evidence exists for a later date, as in the case of the relict field system that clearly post-dates the construction of the ringforts and other early medieval enclosures at Rathcroghan, Co. Roscommon. In other instances, where boundaries and even cultivation ridges are visible, the assumed post-medieval date should perhaps be re-examined.

This article was originally published in the Autumn 2004 issue of Archaeology Ireland.

Fieldscapes

Medieval farming in many parts of eastern and southern Ireland appears to have involved large stretches of open arable land, especially during the thirteenth century, and peasant holdings were divided into strips scattered throughout large common fields. Enclosure of arable strips seems to have started in the Middle Ages and the process was well under way, at least in certain areas, by the early eighteenth century—for instance, on the former Anglo-Norman land associated with the medieval town of Fethard, Co. Tipperary. The enclosure of manor land can be seen on an early eighteenth-century map of lands around Gowran, Co. Kilkenny, represented by the formation of two different types of fields. Fields shown to be long, narrow and curved seem to represent the enclosure of several ridges in the former open field; larger fields embody the enclosure of furlongs comprising a number of contiguous strips.

Fig. 1—Ridge and furrow cultivation at Tousist, Co. Kerry (courtesy of Brendan Riordan).

Anglo-Norman footprints

Recognising the contribution that the Anglo-Normans made to shaping the modern farmed landscape of Ireland requires an understanding of how the land was farmed, laid out and subsequently enclosed. Medieval ploughing has left its footprints on the landscape. As outlined below, this impact is much more marked in England.

England

The midlands of England are characterised by corrugated fieldscapes of wide and high ridges, extending for up to 200m in length. These are the relict remains of long-lived, sinuous ridges and furrows, some of which were repeatedly ploughed for over 500 years (Upex 2004).

As further detailed by Professor Tadhg O'Keeffe (2000; pers. comm.), the classic system for the organisation of agricultural land in the twelfth and thirteenth centuries in England was the open-field system. Farmland was generally divided into two or three sectors, each containing large fields. Within these sectors, rotation of arable crops was commonly practised. The land in one section was left fallow. Animals grazed the fallow land and fertilised the ground. Land newly released from fallow was generally sown in winter with wheat (or, less frequently, rye), and oats (or sometimes barley) in the spring of the second cycle of crops.

Individual farmers often held their land in strips, comprised of several contiguous plough runs, which are described in the landscape as 'selions'. The ridges and furrows are usually 'reverse S' in plan, as explained below. Contiguous strips formed furlongs, which were blocks of land. Grouped together, these furlongs constituted fields (Fig. 2). Individual farmers often held their land in strips that were scattered across fields in each of the sectors and were fairly equitably distributed between good and less productive land.

The furlongs within a field were ploughed in unison by groups of farmers and sown with the same crop. Consequently, few permanent enclosing boundaries were required. The plough teams moved backward and forward along the length of the furlongs but stopped short of reaching the ends, in order to give the team room to turn. This left bands of uncultivated ground at the ends of the furlongs. Some of the soil dragged along the furrows accumulated in these areas. This led to the build-up of substantial banks, known as headlands, at the ends of the furlongs. To facilitate turning, plough

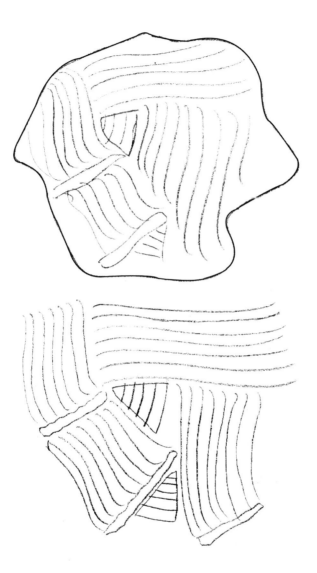

Fig. 2—
Contiguous
strips formed
furlongs,
and furlongs
grouped together
constituted fields
(courtesy of
Tadhg O'Keeffe).

teams appear to have been driven at an angle into the ends of strips, resulting in the 'reverse S' curvature of ridges and furrows mentioned above.

Ireland

Corrugated landscapes of medieval ridge and furrow, comparable to those in the midlands of England, are much less extensive and accentuated in Ireland. Most ridges found in many parts of the country are relatively narrow (less than 1–2m wide) and are usually lazy-beds, used in potato cultivation. Wider ridges more associated with corn production are less frequently recorded. Whether this is due simply to under-recording or to the fact that corn ridges in Ireland were used for much shorter periods and hence are not as sharply defined as those in England is open to conjecture. It is also possible that ridges narrower than those that characterise the midlands of

England were preferred in medieval Ireland. It is interesting to note that, in terms of length, some of the ridges found in Ireland are comparable to those in England.

Notwithstanding the limited amount of archaeological landscape research undertaken on medieval farming in Ireland, the generally held view, as further elaborated by O'Conor (1998), is that open-field farming, involving crop rotation, was introduced into eastern Ireland by English settlers. O'Conor envisages many parts of eastern and southern Ireland as comprising large stretches of open, arable land, especially during the thirteenth century. Peasant holdings were divided into strips of land scattered throughout large common fields. An implication of this perspective of medieval farming is that the Anglo-Normans brought along a marked shift in the prevailing balance between livestock and crop production.

Although it may previously have been practised by the Irish, open-field rotational crop production was predominantly undertaken in areas of Anglo-Norman manors. Indeed, its adoption in Ireland could be seen as what is referred to by O'Keeffe (pers. comm.) as an Anglo-Norman phenomenon.

To illustrate the contribution of Anglo-Norman settlement to the shaping of the modern farmed landscape, some important archaeological features of medieval farming that are progressively being identified are outlined below.

Fig. 3—An early eighteenth-century map of the Anglo-Norman borough of Gowran, Co. Kilkenny (courtesy of the National Library of Ireland).

Anglo-Norman footprint

Closed fields

Two different types of earlier fields, formed in one instance by the enclosure of several ridges and in the other by the enclosure of furlongs (totally or in part), are recorded on post-medieval maps of the manor lands of south-east Ireland (O'Keeffe 2000). Both can be seen on an early eighteenth-century map of lands around Gowran, Co. Kilkenny (Fig. 3), which shows the partial and piecemeal enclosure of fields around the settlement. The long, narrow, curved fields represent the enclosure of several ridges in the former open fields. The larger fields represent the enclosure of entire furlongs or parts of furlongs. The closed fields may have resulted from the amalgamation of multiple strips under the ownership of one individual. While the land in Gowran appears to have been held in strips, O'Keeffe points out that in many cases the large, closed fields may simply preserve parcels of land that had never been subdivided into arable strips that were farmed by different farmers.

A case-study of the former Anglo-Norman land associated with the medieval town of Fethard, Co. Tipperary, recently completed by O'Keeffe (pers. comm.), identifies two long strip fields with the shape and orientation found in open-field systems, as well as possible areas of permanent common grazing and woodland. The layout of the system may conceivably pre-date the Anglo-Norman arrival. By the late 1700s, at least, members of the Fethard community whose ancestors had worked cooperatively in the open fields began to regard their strips as private property and to enclose them. There were increasing levels of enclosure around the town over a period of half a century. By 1708 the process was well under way, and may indeed have commenced much earlier, perhaps in the fifteenth century.

This study by O'Keeffe demonstrates the potential of cartographic records for elucidating the nature of open-field farming in Anglo-Norman Ireland and its subsequent enclosure in the late medieval period, leading to the type of field-enclosure pattern that is well represented in eastern Ireland. While enclosures in the modern landscape are considered to be predominantly post-medieval, further mapping studies would make valuable contributions to identifying extant boundaries that could be medieval in origin.

Headlands

As previously indicated, headlands are formed by the turning of medieval ploughs in the Anglo-Norman open-field system. Such features have been identified in the two adjacent manors of Oughterard and Castlewarden, Co. Kildare (Hall *et al*. 1985). No ridge-and-furrow remains were found between the headlands. This is interpreted as suggesting that in these manors the preference may have been for flat ploughing—essentially the ploughing of one season's ridge back into the previous season's furrow.

Ridge and furrow

A number of relatively wide ridges are progressively being identified, some on what were Anglo-Norman manors (O'Sullivan and Downey 2007). Ridges ranging in width from approximately 7m to 10m have been found on a medieval manor at Moyaliff, Co. Tipperary (Mark Hennessy, pers. comm.). These are of comparable width to the medieval ridges found extensively in England.

Evidence of widespread ploughing has been found by Charles Mount on the Anglo-Norman manor of Ballysax, south of the Curragh. Furrows detected were up to 170m long, and the space between the furrows extended from 1.5m to 6.5m. Since the geophysics may not have detected some intervening furrows, however, the actual metre width of the ridges is unclear.

Ridges over 2m wide and in some instances up to 3m or more in width have been recorded recently at a number of sites in the Beara Peninsula (Connie Murphy, pers. comm.). A site at Tousist (Co. Kerry) is characterised by ridges extending along the lower hillside, in some instances for an estimated 150–200m (Fig. 1). It is interesting to speculate as to the possible association of this ridge-and-furrow site with the Petty / Lansdowne estate established in the later seventeenth century.

Extensive ridge-and-furrow cultivation has recently been recorded in the Curragh, Co. Kildare, by John Feehan (2007). The ridges range from 2m to over 4m in width, but are generally around 2.5m wide. One of the best-preserved systems has well-defined ridges extending for some 170m. The ridges reflect earlier arable cultivation of as yet uncertain date(s). Some of the ridged fields pre-date the late seventeenth century. Feehan considers that they may conceivably be much older.

Conclusion

As noted by O'Keeffe (pers. comm.), perusal of the cartographic records reveals how widespread enclosed open fields were prior to 1900, including areas in the immediate hinterland of Dublin.

The making of field boundaries, and of maps depicting them, reflects a shift away from the collectivism that characterised open-field farming to a more capitalist society. This involved the recognition of land as private property, the status of which could be secured by enclosure. Further to this, O'Keeffe concludes that the enclosure of arable strips is likely to have started in Ireland in the Middle Ages. In this regard, he puts forward for consideration the research hypothesis that the enclosure of the landscape and the emergence of tower-houses may have been simultaneous and related phenomena in the late 1300s and 1400s.

Diagnostic features

- Corrugated landscapes of wide ridges (typically 2–4m wide but up to 10m in width) and furrows, often curving as a 'reverse S'.

- Long, narrow fields formed by the enclosure of several medieval ridges, and larger fields formed by the enclosure of entire furlongs or parts of furlongs.
- Substantial banks of soil (known as headlands) accumulated at the end of plough runs.

Acknowledgements

This article draws extensively on the publications of and additional information provided by Professor Tadhg O'Keeffe, School of Archaeology, UCD, who also made available to us a copy of the paper he was preparing for publication.

References

Feehan, J. 2007 *Cuirrech life: the Curragh of Kildare, Ireland*. Dublin.

Hall, D.N., Hennessy, M. and O'Keeffe, T. 1985 Medieval settlement and agriculture at Oughterard and Castlewarden, Co. Kildare. *Irish Geography* **18**, 16–25.

O'Conor, K.D. 1998 *The archaeology of medieval rural settlement in Ireland*. Discovery Programme Monograph 3. Dublin.

O'Keeffe, T. 2000 *Medieval Ireland—an archaeology*. Stroud.

O'Sullivan, M. and Downey, L. 2007 Ridges and furrows. *Archaeology Ireland* **21**, 34–7.

Upex, S. 2004 A classification of ridge and furrow by an analysis of cross-profiles. *Landscape History* **26**, 59–75.

This article was originally published in the Winter 2007 issue of Archaeology Ireland.

Post-medieval fieldscapes

The rundale system of farming appears to have been adopted extensively in the seventeenth century, especially in disadvantaged farming areas in the west and north. Usage of the system increased sharply in the late eighteenth century, so that by the beginning of the nineteenth century it was widely practised in western Ireland as well as in several eastern areas.

The rundale farming area typically comprised an infield, an outfield and commonage. Rundale was primarily a livestock and grazing system. Summer grazing was undertaken on the commonage, where the animals were herded mainly by young people staying in booley huts (discussed elsewhere). In the post-harvest period, livestock were grazed in the infield and apparently outwintered in the outfield. The infield was the core food-cropping area and maintenance of its fertility was of fundamental importance.

Consolidation of holdings and land enclosure spread quickly in Ireland during the 1830s, so that after 1850 rundale was found only in the most remote areas.

Fig. 1—Rundale farming in Erris, Co. Mayo, photographed in 1955 (courtesy of the National Museum of Ireland).

Rundale

R undale farming was extensively practised in the pre-Famine period by communities of small farmers who typically resided in **clachans**. These characteristic rundale settlements are detailed in Part 1 of this article on post-medieval fieldscapes (see Spring 2008 issue of *Archaeology Ireland*).

Rundale farming was an integrated infield/outfield crop- and livestock-production system, where the landholding was communal. Several joint tenants were involved, often with extensive kinship ties. The system was largely regulated by the farmers themselves; they worked cooperatively and were responsible for the joint rent of the holding (Yager 2002). The land involved in a rundale holding lay mainly within a single townland (Buchanan 1973). Where the townland was large, it was sometimes divided among several rundale groups, each holding its land separate from the others. Joint holdings varied in size; most of those at Lecale (Co. Down) had between 50 and 100 acres of arable land in the 1730s. While the holdings were larger at the end of the eighteenth century, more recent rundale communities rarely included more than nine or ten farmers.

Farm layout

In addition to small enclosed gardens and haggards alongside the clachan houses, the rundale farms typically included three land uses (Fig. 2).

The **infield** was the core of the rundale farm (Buchanan 1973). It was located around the clachan, and was frequently bounded by a high earthen bank. As it included the best land available, the infield was used primarily for crop production (Fig. 3). It was divided into unfenced strips, usually some 50–250yds in length and not more than 20yds in width. Plots were demarcated by low earthen banks known variously as **mearings**, **ribs**, **roddens**, **keelogues** and **bones**. As further detailed below, individual landholders cultivated a number of strips distributed throughout the infield. In twentieth-century rundale, the infield strips were demarcated by permanent boundaries and held by individuals who had a right of inheritance (Buchanan 1973).

The **outfield** was a larger area of more marginal land outside the infield and sometimes extended to the booleying grounds (see below). It was generally separated from the infield by a surrounding wall (Whelan 1997). The outfield was used largely for grazing livestock but sections might be cultivated periodically (Buchanan 1973). The land was sometimes divided into plots, scattered as in the infield.

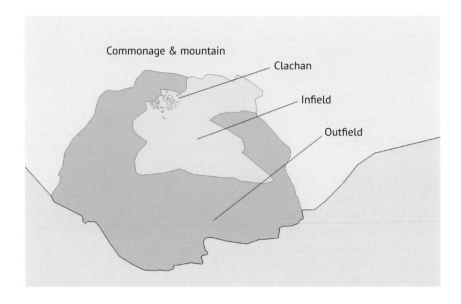

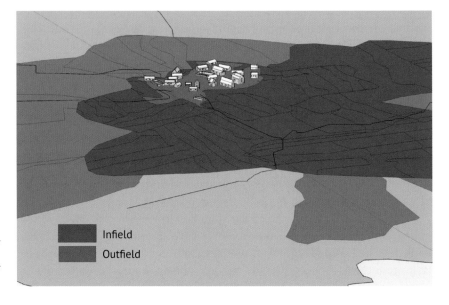

Fig. 2— Reconstruction of a rundale holding, comprising the infield around the clachan, outside of which was the outfield and beyond this the commonage extending to the mountain area (courtesy of Tadhg O'Keeffe, UCD School of Archaeology).

The **commonage** lay beyond the outfield and generally made up the rest of the townland or the lease-holding (Whelan 1997). To prevent overgrazing, the amount of land that each farmer was allowed to graze was limited, using the old Gaelic measure of **collup** or **sum**. This corresponded to the amount of grass needed to feed a cow, with appropriate equivalents for other livestock (Buchanan 1973; Whelan 1997).

Farming system

As further detailed by Whelan (1997), the rundale farming system of cooperative management, agreed land use and a joint labour system for certain tasks was a sustainable response to a situation where technology and capital were limited but labour was unrestricted.

Rundale farming had a strong bias towards stock grazing. Crop production, although important, was a subsidiary farm enterprise, but seems to have been more developed in the south-east than in the north and west (McCourt 1971). The sustainability of rundale farming required the effective integration of the crop and livestock dimensions of the system. In particular, a dynamic ecological equilibrium had to be maintained between the livestock-carrying capacity of an individual holding and the optimisation of crop production. Cultivation intensity had to be controlled to ensure the sustainability of the infield cropping system. Maintaining the fertility of the infield was fundamentally dependent upon the availability of animal manure, its single most important nutrient component (Whelan 1997). This in turn was determined by the number of livestock grazed on a holding, which again had to be controlled to avoid overgrazing and pasture damage.

Individual families were allocated separate plots of varied size, scattered throughout the infield (Yager 2002). This, together with periodic reallocation of the plots, was intended to equalise the share of different-quality land between tenants (Buchanan 1973). This system, termed **changedale**, seems to have been common in the eighteenth century. In most of the nineteenth-century rundale settlements recently surveyed in the Glens of Antrim, however, changedale did not operate (Bell 2007). Families might keep the same strips for several generations, which could lead to extreme fragmentation of holdings.

The infield was kept in continuous cultivation, often leading to a loss of soil fertility and reduced crop yields. According to Buchanan (1973), several communities used an oats/potatoes cropping cycle, usually without any fallow and with an application of manure annually or every second year. Throughout the seventeenth century oats were the main cereal grown on rundale farms, but by the early nineteenth century barley had become an

Fig. 3—Rundale farming in Erris, Co. Mayo, photographed in 1955 by A.T. Lucas (courtesy of the National Museum of Ireland).

important cash crop in the drier east and also in the west. In the pre-Famine period, a potato-dependent rundale was extensively used on the poorer lands, especially in western Ireland (Whelan 1997).

After the crops were harvested, the arable fields were opened to the animals. They grazed the stubble, and the entire landscape in some districts seems to have become a commonage until around St Patrick's Day (Yager 2002). The manuring of the fields by the cattle and sheep was supplemented by dung accumulated in the clachans. As the population grew, the demand for manure intensified, leading to the extensive use of lime and seaweed (Whelan 1997). When required, parts of the outfield were also cultivated, especially for potatoes, involving a cropping cycle of several years (Buchanan 1973).

Natural meadows along rivers or lakes were carefully regulated to give each farmer a proportion of hay and grazing, calculated according to his share of the infield. Where the land was divided into plots, scattered as in the infield, they were worked in severalty and grazed by herding the animals, each on its own plot. Most of the grazing, however, had to be undertaken elsewhere. In particular, the effective operation of the rundale system required the movement of livestock away from the arable fields during the period between sowing and harvesting the crops (Evans 1957). Especially in the west and north, and other mountainous districts in the east, livestock were moved to seasonal pastures in the summer. This practice, known as **booleying**, was, as further detailed by Bell (2007), an integral part of the rundale system. In addition to protecting the crops from the livestock, it extended the grazing area available to the rundale settlement. During the day, the cattle were herded in the upland grazing areas, usually by young people staying in rudimentary shelters known as **booley huts**. In some areas, such as the Glens of Antrim, cattle were brought down for milking in walled enclosures beside the booley huts (Bell 2007).

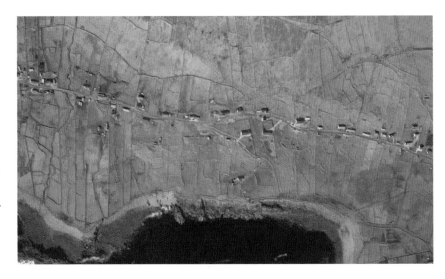

Fig. 4—
Ladder fields
superimposed on
existing arable
ridges, Aphort,
Arranmore
(courtesy of
the National
Coastline
Survey, Marine
Institute).

Location

At the beginning of the nineteenth century rundale was widely practised in western Ireland, extending from Donegal and Derry in the north, through Sligo, Mayo and Galway, to Kerry and west Cork, as well as in several eastern areas, including Kilkenny, Wicklow and eastern Ulster (Buchanan 1973). In the pre-Famine period, communities of small farmers were extensive along the Atlantic seaboards and the drumlin belt. Even at their maximum development in the mid-nineteenth century, however, the overall extent of such farm communities was limited and they were never the dominant settlement type nationally (Whelan 1997). Although not necessarily the same, the overall geographical distribution of rundale farming may not have been markedly different from that of clachans, shown in the Spring 2008 issue of *Archaeology Ireland*.

Dating/origin

When rundale farming was first practised in Ireland is uncertain. It appears to have been adapted more extensively, especially in the west and north, when population growth began in the seventeenth century, increasing sharply in the late eighteenth and early nineteenth centuries. Following the seventeenth-century privatisation of communal pastures, upland areas, especially in western Ireland, were extensively colonised by communities of small farmers engaged in a potato-dependent rundale system, which seems to have become practically universal in the poorer lands in the pre-Famine period (Whelan 1997). Consolidation of holdings and land enclosure spread quickly in the 1830s, and after 1850 rundale was found only in the most isolated and worst-managed estates (Buchanan 1973). The system survived, however, on the islands of Inishkea (Co. Mayo) until 1906 (Yager 2002). Also, as recently reported by Bell (2007), rundale persisted in Antrim much later than the nineteenth century. On Rathlin Island it seems to have been continued in some form in 1908, and possibly as late as the 1970s at the Brockey clachan.

As further detailed by Yager (2002), communally regulated farming systems were common in Europe in the Middle Ages. The farming system known as **runrig**, formerly practised in Scotland and still surviving in parts of the Outer Hebrides, is closely related to the rundale system (Bell 2007). Rather than an indigenous Irish innovation, therefore, rundale may be an adaptation of previous European developments. In much of northern Europe there was a shift from single fields attached to individual farms to common field systems in the Middle Ages, and the division into infield and outfield is well documented for many villages in England from the thirteenth century (Faith 1997). Infields with entitlement to land in the common fields were characteristic features of villages in various parts of England in the thirteenth and fourteenth centuries. The outfield consisted of an area of much freer tenure liable to be rented. Further to this, Faith (1997) adds that the vocabulary of infield and outfield is late medieval, but the structure itself looks earlier.

Prevailing fieldscapes

The layout of rundale farms has been largely eliminated in many districts. With some exceptions, the remains of infield and outfield seldom survive in existing fieldscapes. Conversely, many clachans continued to exist but in radically transformed fieldscapes. Little evidence of infield remains was found at the clachan sites recently surveyed in the Glens of Antrim (Bell 2007). Rundale outfields rarely survive as unenclosed land, but may be found as a girdle of small regular fields occupying the outfield area (Buchanan 1973). Moreover, by the beginning of the nineteenth century commercial grazing had largely replaced booleying, except in some remote areas.

Evidence for the nineteenth-century enclosure of fields can be seen in the field boundaries around many clachans. Where the clachan was surrounded by land of roughly the same altitude, more recently enclosed fields can be identified by their overall regularity of layout (Bell 2007). In sloping or more mountainous areas the land was often reorganised into long narrow farms running from the better lowland to the poorer land, and in some districts extended from near the coast back into the surrounding hills. This process, known as **stripping**, created the **ladder fields** (Fig. 5) that are prevalent in the Glens of Antrim (Bell 2007). They are also found elsewhere in different parts of the west and north, including some of the islands off the north coast of Ulster, where, as further detailed by Forsythe (2006), more recently enclosed fields were also laid out in a **fan pattern**. They comprise strips with boundary walls radiating out from a central point on the island. This is well exemplified on Tory Island (Fig. 5), where the clachan has a rare surviving infield with a surrounding stone wall separating it from the outfield (Whelan 1997).

Diagnostic features

- Rundale farms were typically located around clusters of houses/ buildings known as clachans (further detailed in the Spring 2008 issue of *Archaeology Ireland*).
- Often little physical evidence remains of the infield and outfield; they may have been incorporated into more recently enclosed fields laid out in regular/quadrilateral form and, in some districts, in a ladder or fan pattern, depending on the topography of the land around the clachan.
- They are located mainly around the seaboard and hill margins in the west and north, and also in hilly districts of Kilkenny and Wicklow.

Acknowledgements

Dr Jonathan Bell kindly made available to us, in advance of publication, his article based on the Glens of Antrim Historical Society's Clachan Project, which involved a survey undertaken in conjunction with Mervyn Watson and with members of the Glens Society. We are also grateful to Dr Wes Forsythe, University of Ulster, and Críostóir Mac Cárthaigh, University College Dublin, for providing the photographs, and to Professor Tadhg O'Keeffe, University College Dublin, for the reconstructions of a rundale holding.

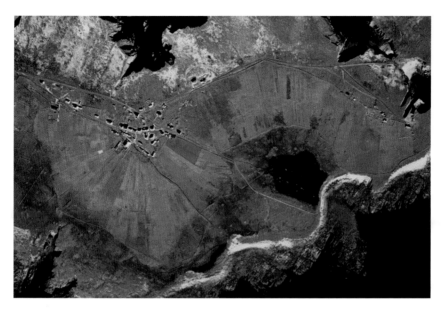

Fig. 5—Fan-shaped field pattern extending from East Town, Tory Island, with surrounding wall separating the infield from the outfield (courtesy of the National Coastline Survey, Marine Institute).

References

Bell, J. 2007 Rundale in the Glens of Antrim. *Ulster Folklife* **52**.

Buchanan, R.H. 1973 Field systems in Ireland. In A.R.H. Baker and R.A. Butlin (eds), *Studies of field systems in the British Isles*. Cambridge.

Evans, E.E. (ed.) 1957 *Irish folk ways*. London.

Faith, R. (ed.) 1997 *The English peasantry and the growth of lordship*. London and Washington.

Forsythe, W. 2006 Improving insularity: an archaeology of the islands off the north coast of Ireland in the Later History Period, 1700–1847. Unpublished Ph.D thesis, University of Ulster.

McCourt, D. 1971 The dynamic quality of Irish rural settlement. In R.H. Buchanan, E. Jones and D. McCourt (eds), *Man and his habitat: essays presented to Emyr Estyn Evans*. London.

Whelan, K. 1997 The modern landscape: from plantation to present. In F.H.A. Aalan, K. Whelan and M. Stout (eds), *Atlas of the Irish rural landscape*. Cork.

Yager, T. 2002 What was rundale and where did it come from? *Béaloideas* **70**, 153–86.

This article was originally published in the Autumn 2008 issue of Archaeology Ireland.

Booleying

Relatively small, unimposing enclosures found in many upland landscapes, especially in disadvantaged farming areas, are often presumed to be the remains of booley huts associated with the movement of cattle and other livestock to summer grazing on commonages.

Some form of booleying appears to have been practised in Ireland in medieval times and possibly from as far back as the Neolithic period. Because few of the upland sites have been systematically excavated, the time-span represented by booley huts is uncertain. However, in post-medieval times, booleying was an integral part of the rundale farming system, which was widely practised in disadvantaged farming areas in the late eighteenth and early nineteenth centuries. Indeed, the survival of booleying into recent centuries may to a considerable extent be a legacy of rundale farming.

The distinction between booley huts and various forms of more ancient settlement is seldom obvious on the ground without archaeological excavation, but it is likely that they account for a proportion of ancient mountain hut sites.

Fig. 1 —Booley huts, visible left of the two hikers, are often located on grassy platforms in peat-covered mountain terrain. This example is from west Cork.

Booley huts

L arge numbers of huts, enclosures and field networks are known on the peat-covered mountain slopes of Ireland. An unmeasured but significant proportion of these are considered to be booley huts. Whether the majority were built specifically as booley huts or simply reused as such on an *ad hoc* basis is another matter.

Booleying

Buailteachas, anglicised to 'booleying', is the Irish term for transhumance, a form of farming involving the summer grazing of cattle on upland and mountain pasture. It survived up to recent times in various mountainous regions of Europe, such as Switzerland, southern Germany and Spain, as well as Ireland, where it was widely practised until the mid-nineteenth century.

Traditionally, on 1 May, the cows, dry cattle, sheep and goats from the farm settlement were driven to the summer grazing in the hills, returning to the settlement in October. It seems that each settlement had a particular tract of mountain, and during the summer the livestock were moved from place to place within this tract. Where the summer grazing was located at a distance from the settlement, members of the families moved with the livestock and lived for a couple of months in temporary dwellings, termed booley huts, tending the older cattle, making and salting butter, feeding the calves and pursuing various other pastoral activities. The booley huts lay vacant during the greater part of the year. At least two contemporary accounts of the practice survive, one from the sixteenth century (by Edmund Spenser, 1596) and one from the seventeenth (by Roderic O'Flaherty, 1684).

How old are booley huts?

In Ireland booleying appears to have been a central feature of the agricultural economy between the sixteenth and eighteenth centuries. Its decline was brought about by many factors, notably the agrarian revolution of the eighteenth century, the land-enclosure movement, the breakup of the rundale village system, the reclamation and cultivation of hilly land as the population expanded, and the increasing prevalence of sheep-farming.

Much more difficult to chart, however, is the origin of the tradition. Brehon Law glosses speak of 'going out about May from the green of the old (winter) residence to the summer pasture (*airge*)' and of 'leaving the grassland for the old residence about November Day'. A number of references in medieval manuscripts suggest that some form of booleying was being practised at that time also. The relevant evidence from prehistoric times is inconclusive, but it is possible (even probable) that a form of booleying was practised from Neolithic times onward.

The antiquity of booleying is one matter; the antiquity of the physical remains, the booley huts, is another matter entirely. The problem is that huts and associated field networks, presumed by many to be the remains of temporary booleying settlements, have not been systematically examined on an extensive scale. It is even debatable whether booley huts exist as a definable archaeological class.

Is it possible to recognise a booley hut?

The structures that are presumed to be the remains of booley huts are circular, oval, rectangular or square enclosures, measuring 2–5m across in west Cork and even more elsewhere. They are often visible as wall footings, usually one or two courses high but occasionally as much as 1m or more in height. It is tempting to consider that those with reasonably well-preserved walls or banks may be of more recent vintage, while those consisting of low platforms or barely visible banks or walls may date from earlier times. Booley huts tend to occur singly or in clusters on patches of better-drained mountain pasture near small streams or springs, and are often sited on grassy knolls or small, naturally occurring terraces. It is a matter of conjecture whether booleying is the only type of settlement that would have produced such structures in these settings. The occurrence of these huts on patches of especially green grass, often noticeable from a considerable distance, may be significant. Such greenness might be the result of cattle droppings over many generations.

Regional variations

Anyone who has visited the Dingle Peninsula, or consulted the archaeological survey of the area, will be aware that exceptionally large numbers of drystone huts, constructed in the corbel fashion and known as clochans, occur on the slopes of the hills, sometimes in association with enclosed plots of ground. Although some may be normal domestic habitations, dating from any time between the Bronze Age and the later medieval period, others may be the remains of booley huts.

Hut sites of various shapes are extensively scattered throughout the Caha Mountains and other parts of west Cork. To the east of the Healy Pass, on the north-facing slopes of Knockowen, a number of hut sites occur on fairly level grassy platforms in rough rocky pasture. Lower down to the north, clusters of seven or eight hut sites, sometimes conjoined, can be found in the Fehanagh area. Further down again, another cluster is obscured by ferns. As elsewhere, the hut sites are frequently associated with enclosures and are sometimes located within larger oval enclosures, an acre or more in size, defined by mainly collapsed field walls. It is tempting to speculate on

Fig. 2—Cluster of booley huts, visible left of the hikers, located within an oval enclosure on the slopes of the Caha Mountains.

whether such enclosures were linked with the management of farm animals and the daily round of milking and feeding.

On Achill Island oval huts recorded at a booley centre in 1943 were over 5m long and 3.5m wide, with surrounding walls that were over 1m high. In the Mourne Mountains traces of oval and circular huts are known. Like those on Achill Island, they appear to have been larger than the ones in west Cork.

Comment

As the foregoing suggests, it is difficult to provide the reader with a neat set of criteria that might be used in deciding whether any particular complex of huts in rocky or peat-covered hilly land were built for booleying. It is even difficult to identify those that might have been used secondarily for this purpose. In itself, the lack of certainty draws attention to an important archaeological resource that has barely been studied. Many of the regions where so-called booley huts occur feature evidence of intensive settlement from both the Bronze Age and the past 1,500 years. It is remarkable that we probably know more archaeologically about Bronze Age farm activity in some of these regions than we do about the farming activity of recent centuries.

References

Aalen, F.H.A. 1964 Clochans as transhumance dwellings in the Dingle Peninsula, Co. Kerry. *Journal of the Royal Society of Antiquaries of Ireland* **94**, 39–45.

Evans, E.E. 1963 *Irish heritage—the landscape, the people and their work* (Chapter VI, 'Village and booley'). Dundalk.

Ó Moghrain, P. 1943 Some Mayo traditions of the Buaile. *Béaloideas* **13**, 161–72.

Ó Moghrain, P. 1944 More notes on the Buaile. *Béaloideas* **14**, 45–52.

This article was originally published in the Winter 2003 issue of Archaeology Ireland.

Post-medieval farming

Two principal fieldscapes became common in Ireland from the seventeenth century onward. Productive farmland in the east was characterised by two- or three-field systems. In the west the rundale infield/outfield system was apparently more prevalent, especially in marginal farming areas.

Widespread enclosure of land took place from the seventeenth century, through the eighteenth century and into the nineteenth century. In particular, land that was more productive was progressively enclosed from the beginning of this period, leading to the formation of rectilinear fieldscapes over much of eastern Ireland. In western areas, enclosure took place later, seemingly from around the early to mid-nineteenth century. In rundale areas, the enclosure of strips cultivated by individual farmers may have brought about narrow fields. Small, regular fields may have been formed in the outfield, with ladder fields running from the lower ground to hill margins.

Fig. 1—Parallel fields running uphill from a clachan in Fuhir townland, overlooking Ballydonegan Bay, Beara Peninsula, west Cork (courtesy of Connie Murphy).

Field enclosure

In the early seventeenth century much of the farmed landscape of Ireland was, as further detailed by Duffy (2007), largely characterised by unenclosed, open-field systems. In many places these overlay earlier historical field systems and associated settlements, now being increasingly revealed (O'Sullivan and Harney 2008). During the eighteenth century a frontier of settlement change appears to have moved across Ireland from east to west, resulting in clustered settlements (**clachans**: see Spring 2008 issue of *Archaeology Ireland*) being gradually replaced by dispersed farmsteads (Duffy 2007). From the seventeenth century and throughout the eighteenth century there was widespread enclosure of fields, footprints of which can still be found in some prevailing fieldscapes.

From subsistence to commercial farming

The landscape was transformed from the seventeenth century by the shift from subsistence to commercial farming (Buchanan 1973). The pervasive influence of cattle production on the rural economy has been a major force in shaping Ireland's fieldscapes. The export of surplus livestock expanded substantially and dominated Anglo-Irish trade prior to the mid-eighteenth century. Livestock-rearing became a dominant enterprise, especially in the large farm areas of Leinster and Munster. Most of the large, regular fields of eastern Ireland discussed below seem to have been formed about that time (Buchanan 1973). The characteristic Ulster pattern of small, regular fields seems to have evolved mainly in the nineteenth century. As the demand for grazing increased, some landlords began to enclose land that had provided grazing for rundale farmers. By the beginning of the nineteenth century commercial grazing had, apart from in some remote areas, largely replaced booleying, which was an integral part of the rundale farming system.

Enclosure for livestock-rearing was generally preceded by consolidation of holdings, undertaken by landlords and their substantial tenants. Further to this, Buchanan (1973) points out that enclosure was also undertaken for tillage, often by small farmers. As grazing expanded, there was an increasing shortage of home-grown grain. By 1720 English grain had become cheaper in the Dublin market than the home-grown product. This led to greater emphasis on tillage in the second half of the eighteenth century; government subsidies were provided for grain transport and export, and tariffs were placed on grain imports. As a result, farmers in the eastern counties found tillage

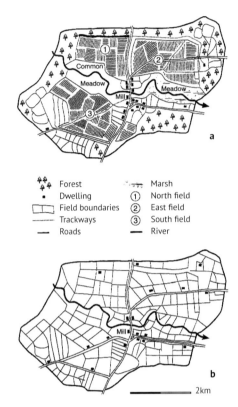

Forest
Dwelling
Field boundaries
Trackways
Roads

Marsh
① North field
② East field
③ South field
River

Fig. 2—
(a) Medieval open
three-field system;
(b) modern
enclosed
landscape
(courtesy of
P. Duffy).

2km

more profitable than cattle-rearing (Buchanan 1973). For those holding land in severalty (ownership of real estate by a single individual), more land could be devoted to cash crops—mainly barley before 1760, and thereafter wheat. For rundale farmers, however, spring-sown wheat is reported to have disrupted the traditional practice of wintering stock in the infield. Thus enclosure became more common in the second half of the eighteenth century, wherever common fields had previously survived enclosure for grazing (*ibid.*). Enclosure seems to have begun earlier in parts of south Leinster and County Down.

Continuous cropping on rundale farms was maintained by liberal use of the soil-conditioner known as marl. As noted by Buchanan (1973), however, sustained production was only achieved by the encroachment of arable production on common pastures. Marling practices apparently also stimulated enclosure of infield plots. This had already progressed a long way when wheat became a principal crop in the later 1760s. A final stimulus to enclosure was the introduction about that time of a new rotation in place of marl, based first on peas and later on clover.

Field enclosure

Two principal types of fields were common from the seventeenth century (Duffy 2007). The east of the country was characterised by a two- or three-field system involving crop rotation (Fig. 2), with associated commons in woodland, marsh and meadows. In the west, the rundale infield/outfield system was more common, especially in marginal farming areas. The infield seems to have been kept in continuous cultivation, and in response to population growth in the nineteenth century the outfield may also have been cultivated.

From the seventeenth century the landscape was progressively fenced, especially on the more productive lands of the east and the planted lands in Ulster and Leinster (Buchanan 1973; Duffy 2007). In general, enclosure was implemented more systematically through the landed estate system, leading to relatively uniform, rectilinear fieldscapes over much of eastern Ireland. Residual common land in east Leinster was enclosed by acts of parliament in the late eighteenth century. Tenants were required to fence boundaries, for instance on the Kingston estate in south Tipperary in 1727. Some estates employed agriculturalists and established model farms to demonstrate the advantages of enclosure.

In western areas enclosure took place later, occurring from around the early to the mid-nineteenth century on estates in Sligo, Cork and Monaghan (Duffy 2007). Landscape reorganisation in the west accelerated through the second half of the century especially, with the passing in 1848/9 of the Encumbered Estates Acts. In some cases the remains of fragmented rundale landscapes were fossilised in the new enclosed fieldscapes.

Consolidation and enclosure were undertaken through the initiative of individual farmers or as a result of landlord intervention. Where subdivision of holdings had not reached extreme proportions, it was sometimes possible to arrange an exchange of strips to form more compact holdings, which could then be enclosed. As further noted by Buchanan (1973), the resultant pattern was often characterised by a series of narrow strips enclosed from the former infield and surrounded by a girdle of small rectangular fields occupying the outfield. Such farms were rarely compact, consisting of scattered blocks of fields interspersed with those of neighbouring holdings and often with clachans surviving among the dispersed farmsteads.

Reorganisation became more common as holdings were increasingly repossessed by landlords in the 1830s. In an estate in southern Donegal, square fields were laid out and arranged in compact holdings, which were allocated to the tenants by drawing lots (Buchanan 1973). Later in the nineteenth century the government assumed responsibility for the consolidation of holdings. The Congested Districts Board and its successor, the Land Commission, played a central role in the rearrangement of farm holdings. In many instances **square farms** were laid out or, where appropriate, **ladder farms** or **stripped holdings**, which were often preferred by rundale farmers (*ibid.*). Stripping of holdings began in the west of Ireland in the early nineteenth century and was continued by the Congested Districts Board into the twentieth century (Bell 2007). Narrow strips of land, subdivided into fields roughly proportionate to an individual farmer's rundale plot, were allocated to each farmer, including a share in the mountain commonage (Duffy 2007). In many cases a new house was built on the roadside adjacent to the allocated holding. Such rearrangements were facilitated by local migration, migration to the midlands or emigration of selected householders (*ibid.*).

Reformed fieldscapes

Ireland's fieldscapes have been radically transformed during recent decades, especially by the intensification of farming. This is clearly evident from the baseline perspective (Buchanan 1973), outlined below, of field types and their regional distribution in the mid-twentieth century, shortly before Ireland joined the EU, or the EEC, as it was then known (Table 1; Fig. 3).

Table 1	Main field types, mid-twentieth century			
Important features	Regular fields—roughly quadrilateral			Irregular fields
	Large	Small & medium	Ladder	
Shape	Straight-sided	Straight-sided	Slightly curved, long & narrow	Parallel boundary walls with cross-fences	Small, irregular
Distribution	Large farm areas	Predominant type, wide prevalence	Limited	Running from valley bottoms to hill margins	Small proportion of fields in an area
Regional location	Eastern central lowlands	Ulster, Leinster, Munster	Leinster, Munster, Connacht	Ulster, Connacht & elsewhere	South-west —mountain areas
Possible origin	Anglo-Norman	Ulster: seven-teenth-century Plantation	Leinster & Munster: Anglo-Norman; Connacht: possibly native	Rundale farming	Early nineteenth-century enclosure
Farming system	Store cattle production	Mixed farming on small holdings	Arable production important		Marginal farming

The fields existing by that time may be placed in two broad categories: those with a regular and those with an irregular shape. Regular fields were the most common. They were straight sided, roughly quadrilateral in shape and with a length some one and a half times their breadth. Regular fields comprised three main types, namely large, small/medium and ladder fields.

Large, regular fields occupied a core area in the eastern half of the central lowlands. The area was at that time associated with large farms engaged in the production of store cattle. It was formerly an important Anglo-Norman area.

Small and medium rectangular fields were the predominant field type, occurring in Ulster, Leinster and Munster. They were most prevalent in Ulster, where they constituted a remarkably uniform field type, associated perhaps with the seventeenth-century Plantation (Buchanan 1973). Areas in which small fields occurred were primarily engaged in mixed farming on relatively small holdings. Small and medium-sized regular fields included a sub-category of **slightly curved, long, narrow fields**, which resembled the common field strips of the English midlands. Strip fields occurred in Munster but were mainly concentrated in east Connacht, south Leinster and the vicinity of Dublin, where they may have been enclosures from common fields. In Leinster and Munster they occurred in areas where Anglo-Norman influence was strong. The strip fields found

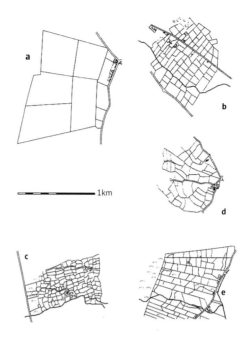

Fig. 3—Fields in the mid-twentieth century: (a) regular fields—Jordanstown, Co. Meath; (b) small, regular fields—Ballykine Lower, Co. Down; (c) small, irregular fields—Glinsmouth, Co. Kerry; (d) curved strip fields—Nicholastown, Co. Kilkenny; (e) ladder farms—Foriff, Co. Antrim (courtesy of R. Buchanan).

in Connacht may perhaps represent a native common field system that was adopted by the Anglo-Normans (*ibid.*).

Ladder fields were a distinct type of regular enclosures found frequently in hill lands and running from valley bottoms to hill margins. They consisted of a series of parallel boundary walls divided by cross-fences to form fields of about two or three acres. Ladder fields were found mainly in Ulster and Connacht. Their characteristic straight lines and precise angles reflect a proficiency in survey, suggesting that they may have been enclosed in the relatively recent past, possibly from a former rundale farm (or farms). Buchanan (1973) points out that, if this was so, rundale farming must have been more widespread than generally thought in the western districts and hills of Ulster and Munster. In this regard, elongated fields with parallel boundary walls and divided by cross-fences, which are prevalent in the Beara Peninsula (Fig. 4, marked on the 1841 OS map) and are also found elsewhere in south-west Munster, may reflect the locations of former rundale farms.

Small, irregular fields were the other main category of field types. They rarely accounted for more than a small proportion of fields found in an area. They occurred mainly in mountain areas of the south-west and seem to have represented the piecemeal enclosure of marginal land by farmers (Buchanan 1973). Many were presumably formed in the early nineteenth century at the height of the population pressure, but some could be older.

The landscape of Ireland will be reshaped fundamentally in the decades immediately ahead by the restructuring of agriculture, response to energy demands and increasing climate change. To track these changes and quantify their impacts, a baseline record of prevailing fieldscapes needs to be compiled as a matter of urgency. In the meantime, we might ask what the extensive

*Fig. 4—
Elongated fields
with parallel
boundary walls,
divided by
cross-walls and
running up to
the hill margin
from the clachan
located at Fuhir,
overlooking
Ballydonegan
Bay in the Beara
Peninsula, west
Cork (marked
on the 1841 OS
map) (courtesy of
Connie Murphy).*

removal of field boundaries under archaeological supervision during the past 20 years has contributed to our knowledge of these archaeological features.

Diagnostic features

- Regular, large, straight-sided fields found mainly in eastern central lowlands.
- Regular, small/medium-sized fields, the predominant type, found mainly in Ulster, Leinster and Munster.
- Slightly curved, long, narrow fields, with limited distribution in Leinster, Connacht and Munster.
- Ladder fields with parallel boundary walls running from valley bottoms to hill margins, and with cross-fences, found mainly in Ulster, Connacht and elsewhere.
- Small, irregular fields, found in the south-west mountain areas.

Acknowledgements

The insights provided by Professor Martin Downes, National University of Ireland, Maynooth, are much appreciated. We are also grateful to Professor Patrick Duffy, National University of Ireland, Maynooth, and Professor Ronald Buchanan, formerly of Queen's University, Belfast, for their permission to use Figs 2 and 3 respectively.

References

Bell, J. 2007 Rundale in the Glens of Antrim. *Ulster Folklife* **52**.

Buchanan, R.H. 1973 Field systems in Ireland. In A.R.H. Baker and R.A. Butlin (eds), *Studies of field systems in the British Isles*. Cambridge.

Duffy, P.J. 2007 Cultural landscapes. In P.J. Duffy (ed.), *Exploring the history and heritage of Irish landscapes*. Dublin.

O'Sullivan, A. and Harney, L. 2008 Early Medieval Archaeology Project (EMAP): Investigating the character of early medieval archaeological excavations, 1970–2002. Unpublished report for the Heritage Council. UCD School of Archaeology, Dublin.

This article was originally published in the Winter 2008 issue of Archaeology Ireland.

Cultivation

Striking ridge-and-furrow cultivation patterns from prehistoric times have been found underneath blanket bog at Céide Fields and Carrownaglogh in County Mayo. From medieval times onward, ridge-and-furrow cultivation with the plough became especially prevalent.

Corrugated ridge-and-furrow landscapes have been recorded in many places across Ireland, examples being the Curragh in County Kildare and some marginal farmland such as the Beara Peninsula in County Cork and upland slopes now more commonly used for grazing. Some of the best-preserved systems have ridge and furrow of extensive length (up to 150m) and curved outline, each ridge ranging from 2m to 4m in width to 10m or more. However, the ridges most commonly found in the countryside tend to be relatively narrow (about 1.5m to 2m wide) and seemingly typical of potato cultivation in recent centuries.

In the period 1780–1840, more land appears to have been cultivated in Ireland than ever before or since, leaving us with numerous expanses of pre-Famine ridge-and-furrow land, presumably the traces of former corn and potato ridges. In some areas along the Atlantic coast, the traces derive from cultivation extending well into the twentieth century.

Fig. 1 — Ridge-and-furrow cultivation at Tousist, Co. Kerry (courtesy of Connie Murphy).

Ridges and furrows

Ridge cultivation appears to have been well known in ancient and medieval Ireland. Ridges are frequently mentioned in old Irish texts, where ridges and tillage are almost synonymous (Ó Danachair 1970). Ridge-and-furrow cultivation with the plough became notably more prevalent from medieval times. In the period 1780–1840 in particular, more land was under cultivation in Ireland than ever before or since, and evidence of intensive pre-Famine cultivation can be seen in the landscape today as traces of former corn and potato ridges.

Ridge cultivation, on a large scale, declined in the later nineteenth century with the advent of effective underground drainage systems and mechanical drill husbandry and harvesting (Bell 1984). In the midlands of England, where land was taken out of arable farming from the fourteenth century, ridge-and-furrow cultivation, with characteristic wide and high ridges, is preserved as corrugations in the fieldscape.

The following outline provides an overview of the principal types of ridge-and-furrow cultivation recorded in Ireland, mainly for corn and potato production, as well as details of construction, dimensions and possible periods of use.

Functions

Ridge-and-furrow cultivation was undertaken to aid drainage, by providing raised seedbeds that protected the seed and crop from excessive moisture, especially on soils that were poorly drained or subject to high levels of rainfall.

As detailed below, most of the ridges recorded in Ireland are relatively narrow (Fig. 2). From an ergonomic perspective, narrow ridges are likely to reflect spade cultivation, especially of potatoes on what are generally known as 'lazy-beds'. The potatoes were sometimes grown in rotation. After two years of potato cultivation, ridges were sometimes rebuilt for the growing of corn, with narrowed furrows being used (Bell 1984). The wider ridges recorded in Fig. 2 are more generally associated with corn production. Ridges comparable in width to those used in medieval England are not widely recorded in Ireland. As discussed below, however, a number of important examples of medieval arable farming systems have come to light in recent decades. Long, curvilinear (reverse S-shaped) ridges are generally identified with medieval open-field tillage systems in Europe (Parry 1976). Curved ridges were recorded in Ireland in the nineteenth century (Doyle 1844).

Construction

Ridges were made in Ireland with either the spade or the plough, or a combination of both. Their construction varied, depending on the location, soil type, crops grown, rotation and harvesting methods.

The practices used since the eighteenth century in ridge-making in Ireland are extensively documented by Bell (1984), including detailed reconstruction drawings of the lazy-beds. This form of ridge-and-furrow cultivation involved building up ridges on strips of untilled land, and is regarded as being particularly associated with Ireland. The term 'lazy' seems to have been derived from a Middle English usage meaning 'untilled'. The ridges were constructed on strips of untilled land by ploughing or digging the furrows and turning the sods onto the untilled strips. The ridges were then built up with further soil from the furrows.

Where ridges and furrows were constructed on tilled land, the surface was first broken up by ploughing and cross-ploughing. As described by Ó Danachair (1970), wide ridges for corn were formed by turning several furrows from each side with the plough and finishing with the spade and shovel. Annual splitting of ridges occurred where potatoes were planted in successive seasons, as illustrated by the following verse (Ó Danachair 1970):

> In the place where the furrow is this year
> The ridge shall be next year
> In the place where the ridge is next year
> The furrow shall be the year after.

When a corn crop followed potatoes, the usual practice was to reshape the ridges for their new purpose.

Ploughing the same furrow in successive seasons, often for decades and generations, led to the formation of greatly raised ridges, bounded by deep

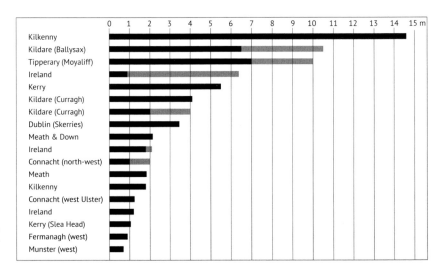

Fig. 2—Widths of a number of ridges recorded in Ireland.

Fig. 3a (top)—Ridges on the north-east margin of the Curragh on Racehorse Hill (courtesy of John Feehan).

Fig. 3b—Ridges on the western edge of the Curragh on the Cill Dara Golf Course (courtesy of John Feehan).

furrows. The characteristic corrugated fieldscape preserved in the midlands of England is the relict remains of long-lived plough ridges, some of which survived in use for over 500 years (Upex 2004). In some places the ridges and furrows have a height difference of half a metre or more, conferring a strongly rippled effect on the fieldscape.

Dimensions

As indicated by Bell (1984), the dimensions of ridges varied in response to soil conditions, tillage practices and the crops cultivated. The shape or profile of ridges in cross-section was also influenced by topographic and weather conditions.

The widths of a number of ridges recorded in Ireland are shown in Fig. 2. Although not intended to be exhaustive, the measurements compiled here indicate that most ridges were less than 1.5–2m wide (including the lower limits of some width ranges recorded).

Eight broader ridges are also shown in Fig. 2. Seven of these range in width from 2m to 10m. The other example is exceptionally wide (14.6m) and was noted in 1802 as being associated with ploughing 'in balk' for corn crops (Tighe 1802). As was pointed out by Ó Danachair (1970), the 4.1m-wide ridges found in the Curragh, Co. Kildare, were the widest hitherto observed by him. John Feehan (2007) recently established the widespread occurrence in the Curragh of ridges ranging from 2m to over 4m in width, but generally in the region of 2.5m. One of the best-preserved systems had well-defined ridges extending for some 170m (Fig. 3). Furrows of similar length have also been recently detected at Ballysax, south-east of the Curragh, by Charles Mount (pers. comm.). Geophysics and excavation indicate that the spaces between the furrows ranged from approximately 1.5m to 6.5m in width. Where large gaps occurred between the furrows, the geophysics may have missed intervening furrows and hence the actual metre width of the ridges is uncertain. Ridges ranging in width from approximately 7m to 10m have been found at Moyaliff, Co. Tipperary, by Mark Hennessy (pers. comm.).

Apart from the exceptionally broad type (14.6m) recorded in the early 1800s in Kilkenny, of the 18 ridges shown in Fig. 2 only those at Moyaliff, Co. Tipperary, are comparable in width to the medieval ridges found in England. These are typically about 8m wide, although wider and narrower ridges are known (Mark Hennessy, pers. comm.). The other six broad ridges shown in Fig. 2 have widths intermediate in size between the wide ridges typical of

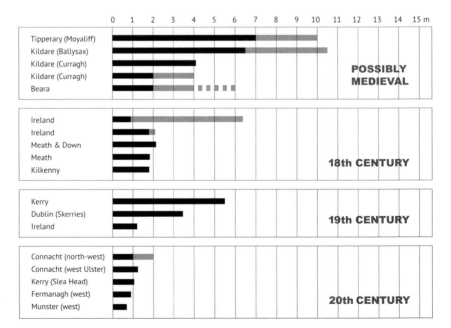

Fig. 4—
Comparative
ridge widths
from different
periods.

medieval England and the narrow (some 1.5–2m wide) ridges recorded in Ireland. Thus it is possible that ridges narrower than those used in England were preferred in medieval Ireland.

The relatively low number of wide ridges in Ireland may of course simply reflect under-recording. It is not likely, however, that such ridges were ploughed out to a substantially greater extent in areas of medieval arable farming in Ireland than in the midlands of England. Wide ridges may have been in use in Ireland for a much shorter period and hence were not as sharply defined as the characteristic medieval ridges found in England. Alternatively, flat ploughing may perhaps have been preferred in Ireland, as evidenced by the medieval agricultural landscape of County Kildare at Oughterard and Castlewarden (Hall *et al.* 1985).

Dating

What are possibly primitive plough-marks that could have belonged to Neolithic farmers have been found at the prehistoric settlement in the Céide Fields. Ridge cultivation considered to be Bronze Age has been reported both at the Céide Fields and at Carrownagloch, Co. Mayo.

Four of the ridges shown in Fig. 4 may be associated with the medieval period. The widest ridges (4.1m) recorded by Ó Danachair (1970) are in the Curragh, Co. Kildare. These are located on what he suggests may be old monastic land, not cultivated since the middle of the sixteenth century. As previously mentioned, John Feehan (2007) has recently identified well-preserved ridge-and-furrow cultivation in the Curragh. Some of these ridged fields pre-date the late seventeenth century. He suggests that the ridges reflect the productive base of an earlier economy of as yet uncertain date. They are possibly medieval and some perhaps much older. Further to this, evidence of widespread ploughing on the Anglo-Norman manor of Ballysax, south-east of the Curragh, has been produced by Charles Mount. Furrows were detected up to 170m long and similar in lateral extent to those ridges identified recently in the Curragh. The records show that in 1282 the manor of Ballysax supplied substantial quantities of wheat and oats to the Earl Marshall. Mount has also identified extensive areas of medieval or post-medieval plough cultivation at Lackanamona near Mallow, Co. Cork, as well as evidence in the historical record for the growing of corn in the thirteenth century in other parts of Cork. The wide ridges found at Moyaliff, Co. Tipperary, are on a medieval manor (Mark Hennessy, pers. comm.).

When the other ridges shown in Fig. 4 were used in crop cultivation is not certain. The majority are relatively narrow (from less than 1m to about 2m wide). According to Arthur Young (Hutton 1892), the growing of corn on ridges had virtually disappeared in the 1770s and ridge cultivation was generally used for potatoes. The pre-eminence of narrow ridges in the records made in the eighteenth, nineteenth and twentieth centuries seems to be consistent with this observation. As shown in Fig. 4, the majority of ridges recorded in the twentieth century are somewhat narrower than those of the eighteenth century. In this regard, Doyle (1844) noted that the 'common Irish' practice in the mid-nineteenth century was to make 'extremely narrow' ridges about 4ft (1.2m) wide. This suggests that the narrow ridges, especially those under 1m wide, were used for potato cultivation.

Given the limitation of the existing records, caution is clearly necessary in comparing ridge widths from different periods. Although speculative, the presentation in Fig. 4 may be indicative of a narrowing of ridge widths over time, perhaps reflecting the aforementioned shift in the eighteenth century from corn to predominantly potato cultivation. It may also be partially due to the move to reclaim marginal, poorly drained land.

Diagnostic features

- Corrugated relict fieldscape of raised ridges bounded by furrows.
- Ridges may range from under 1m to some 10m in width and the furrows from about 0.5m to 0.75m or more in width.
- The ridges less than 1–2m wide may be more associated with potato cultivation than the wider ridges used in corn production.

Acknowledgements

The information provided by Dr John Feehan, Dr Mark Hennessy, Dr Charles Mount, Dr Mick Monk, Dr Martin Downes and Professor Tadhg O'Keeffe is greatly appreciated. Dr Feehan kindly made available to us a copy of the paper he was preparing for publication, and his permission to use some of the illustrations is gratefully acknowledged.

References

Bell, J. 1984 A contribution to the study of cultivation ridges in Ireland. *Journal of the Royal Society of Antiquaries of Ireland* **114**, 80–97.

Doyle, M. 1844 *A cyclopedia of practical husbandry* (ed. W. Rham). London.

Feehan, J. 2007 *Cuirrech life: the Curragh of Kildare, Ireland*. Dublin.

Hall, D.N., Hennessy, M. and O'Keeffe, T. 1985 Medieval agriculture and settlement in Oughterard and Castlewarden, Co. Kildare. *Irish Geography* **18**, 16–25.

Hutton, A.W. (ed.) 1892 *Arthur Young's Tour in Ireland (1776–1779)*. Dublin.

Ó Danachair, C. 1970 The use of the spade in Ireland. In R.A. Gailey and A. Fenton (eds), *The spade in northern and Atlantic Europe: the use of the spade in Ireland*. Belfast.

Parry, M.L. 1976 A typology of cultivation ridges in southern Scotland. *Tools & Tillage* **3**, 3–19.

Tighe, W. 1802 *Statistical observations relative to the county of Kilkenny*. Dublin.

Upex, S. 2004 A classification of ridge and furrow by an analysis of cross-profiles. *Landscape History* **26**, 59–75.

This article was originally published in the Summer 2007 issue of Archaeology Ireland.

Agricultural drainage systems 1

A s the enclosure of land proceeded, a network of ditches developed, which functioned as both land boundaries and field drains. Indeed, ditches are reported to have been the most important features of early field-drainage systems.

Introduced by improving landlords in the late eighteenth and early nineteenth centuries, drains with built-in water conduits began to be used by some ordinary farmers, perhaps most widely in the main tillage areas.

Three forms of drains were constructed on farmland in Ireland during the nineteenth century:

- **Stone-filled drains** of various forms, reported from the earlier part of the century, were part-filled with small stones and often covered with tough sods before earth was put over them.
- **Stone-built ducts**, allowing a freer passage of water, were introduced during the early decades of the century. The earlier stone-built ducts were triangular structures, while those assembled in later years were rectangular in form. Drains were part-filled with stones, covered with turf and completed with earth.
- **Sod-built ducts** were used in drains constructed in parts of Ireland where stones were scarce and are said to have served the purpose quite well, when properly fashioned.

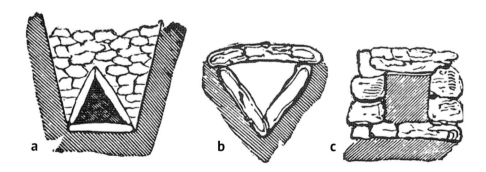

Fig. 1—Traditional drains constructed with stone ducts as depicted by Martin Doyle in A cyclopedia of practical husbandry *(1839) (courtesy of Jonathan Bell).*

Traditional drains and ditches

Drainage systems were, by the Roman period, known to be important in increasing food production from agricultural land (Box 1). By the eighteenth/nineteenth centuries, sometimes referred to in the UK as the 'Golden Age of Agriculture', drainage was being strongly advocated by knowledgeable commentators as the first step in agricultural improvements, and as particularly crucial in land being prepared for crop production (Doyle 1839; Stephens 1847).

Box 1   **Roman field drainage**

'If the land is wet it should be drained with trough-shaped ditches dug three feet wide at the surface and one foot at the bottom and four feet deep. Blind these ditches with rock ... In stiff soils open ditches should be used and in loose soils the drains should be covered ... drains in orchards four feet deep and in corn fields three feet ...'

—Quotation from Cato (234–149 BC), Roman farmer/soldier.

The abolition of the Corn Laws (1846) and consequent concerns over free trade in corn gave a major impetus to land drainage and heralded the development of early modern drainage systems. Henry Stephens, a leading nineteenth-century authority on agricultural drainage in the United Kingdom, pointed out in *A manual of practical drainage* (1847) that abolition of protective duties would 'necessitate the practice of draining in every part of the kingdom. ... To compete therefore with the foreigner, there exists ... the most powerful incentive for increasing the permanent fertility of the soil ... by pursuing a substantial system of drainage.' Further to this, he added that 'where the ground is under the plough covered drains are requisite' and 'when properly formed are best adapted even for sheep pasture'.

The major drainage forms developed over many centuries can, as shown in Fig. 2, be differentiated into ditches, traditional drains and early modern drains. The term 'ditch' as used in this article (see below) applies to those drainage systems which functioned both as land enclosures or boundaries and as field drains, and which tended to be larger than those specifically designed for drainage purposes only. Traditional drains, the main subject of the article, are stone-filled drains and drains constructed with water-channels or ducts built with stones or sods. These were progressively replaced by early

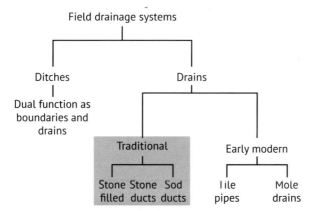

*Fig. 2—
Schematic
differentiation
of field-drainage
systems, with
drains discussed
in detail here
indicated by
shading.*

modern drains, of which the two important forms, tilepipe drains and mole drains, are dealt with in the Summer 2010 issue of *Archaeology Ireland*.

Having outlined some important features of ditches, an overview is presented below of a number of recent excavations pertaining to the medieval period, with particular regard to the main drainage features revealed. Following this, a detailed perspective is given of the forms of traditional drains. The article draws extensively on the invaluable publications kindly provided by Austin O'Sullivan from the Agricultural Museum at Johnstown Castle, Co. Waterford.

Ditches are, as indicated in the comprehensive textbook on agriculture edited by Robinson (1962), the most important feature of field-drainage systems. In relation to early drainage systems, Robinson noted that as the enclosure of land proceeded a network of ditches developed, to the increasing benefit of field drainage. Many of the ditches were natural watercourses, but from them were dug side ditches at convenient intervals to divide the land into suitable plots for working and, at the same time, to bring drainage water from the plots to the watercourses.

Medieval drainage systems

The technologically advanced water-management systems developed by the medieval period and their application in post-harvesting food-processing can be seen, as outlined below, from the important case-studies received from Matthew Seaver (CRDS Ltd). An agricultural complex excavated at Raystown, Co. Meath, comprised fields, water-management systems, kilns and mills centred on a burial ground and associated settlement areas, and dated from between the fifth and twelfth centuries AD. Arable and pastoral agriculture was carried out at the site, and the grain was processed in the corn-drying kilns and mills. As shown in Fig. 3, the site is characterised by complex arrangements of boundary ditches and drains.

Boundary ditches excavated at Raystown were consistently more than 2m deep and 2m wide. Some were repeatedly redug over time—a characteristic requirement for ditches. As noted by Seaver, they were at different times tied into the milling system, so as to prevent overflow in a millpond or to allow tail-race water to exit to a stream which feeds the Broad Meadow River.

Large drains (1.5m deep and at least 2m wide) excavated at the site served to remove water from the hill slopes; they were relatively narrow and shallow at the upper part of the slope and wider and deeper at the base. Seaver observed that it can be difficult to distinguish these large drains from the boundary ditches. The recutting of the latter, however, indicates a wider agricultural function than just drainage.

Smaller drains (less than 0.5m deep and less than 1.5m wide) in general provided localised drainage for threshing areas and kiln sites, as well as other important areas of activity, and often fed into larger ditches.

Ditches that functioned both as field boundaries and as drains were also found in an early medieval field system excavated by Seaver in Laughanstown townland, south Co. Dublin. The boundaries of a long, curving field (500m long and 100m wide) comprised sequences of ditches. One section of the ditch system was shallow at either end and had a stone revetment that was fed by a drain. The revetment may have acted as a sump for water, presumably for local use. The ditches were still in use in the eleventh–twelfth century, when charcoal from a nearby production site was being thrown into the southern boundary ditch.

The occurrence together of different forms of drainage features in part of an early medieval landscape is evident from an excavation of a ringfort and attached field system in the neighbouring Glebe townland. Some field boundaries fed into the ringfort ditch and a drain exited the ringfort, allowing water to pass into the natural shallow valley below.

Many other detailed excavations undertaken in the Dublin region in recent years have also provided important insights into medieval drainage features. As further detailed in the compilation of a number of these

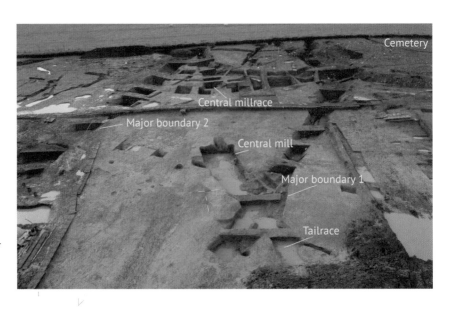

Fig. 3— Agricultural complex excavated at Raystown, Co. Meath, showing boundary ditches and their juxtaposition relative to a central mill and millraces (courtesy of Matthew Seaver (CRDS Ltd); photo: Hawkeye).

excavations provided by Michael Potterton, these are variously described as boundary ditches and small ditches, or as gullies and trenches.

Traditional drains

By the early decades of the 1800s, covered drains under the surface were being used in Britain, especially in cultivated land and also in grassland (Stephens 1847). Underground drainage seems not to have been used in many parts of Ireland until the late 1800s and early 1900s (Gailey and Fenton 1969). The system was introduced by improving landlords, who by the late 1700s and early 1800s were, as further detailed by Bell and Watson (2008), constructing hollow or French drains, with stone-built and sod-built ducts. This system was also used by some ordinary farmers.

Stone-filled drains: Stephens noted in 1847 that 'stones have hitherto been the most common material employed for filling drains'. Drains part-filled with stones continued to be used during the 1800s and, in parts of Ireland, well into the 1900s. Doyle (1839) described the different forms of stone-filled drains seen in Ireland in the early decades of the 1800s. They were constructed with small stones to a height of some 15–18in. about the bottom. Before the earth was put over them, the stones were often covered with some dry materials such as tough sods. Other materials used included coarse grass and straw.

Stone-built ducts: Stephens (1847) strongly advocated that 'All deep drains should be furnished with built conduits' and that 'an open duct will afford a freer passage for water than a mass of loose stones'. He stressed that it 'is requisite to have a duct in every drain for the water to pass quickly away'. Triangular ducts were formed from three flat stones, with sides measuring around 6in. (Stephens 1847). These were placed against each other at the bottom of the drain, resting either on the apex of the triangle or on a

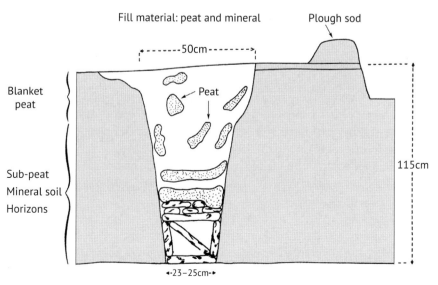

Fig. 4— Diagrammatic representation of an underground drain with a well-built rectangular stone duct excavated at Rossmore Forest, Co. Laois (courtesy of Michael Conry).

flat base lying on the bottom. The side stones were held in position by small stones. The drain was filled to a height of 18in. with small stones, covered with turf or other dry materials, and completed with earth.

The various forms of drains with stone ducts built in Ireland in the early decades of the 1800s were described by Doyle (1839), and three of them are depicted in Fig. 1. More recently constructed rectangular stone ducts seem to have been more securely built, as evidenced by the drain excavated in Rossmore Forest, Co. Laois, by Conry (1973), which was built in the 1800s as part of a famine-relief scheme. As shown in Fig. 4, it had a rectangular duct built with flagstones and with a diagonal cross-stone, presumably to provide greater stability.

Sod-built ducts: Where stones were scarce and fields had to be drained of surface water, sod-built ducts were constructed (Doyle 1839). They are said to have served the purpose well, if properly made, in particular the form with supporting shoulders. These were constructed by digging a trench (14–16in. wide and 2ft or 3ft deep) and taking out from the bottom a 'split' or channel, leaving a small shoulder on each side. The first sod taken from the trench was wedged in until it rested, with the grass side downwards, on the small shoulders of the trench, thus forming a duct over the narrow channel left at the bottom of the drain (Doyle 1839; Stephens 1847). The trench was filled with loose earth to a few inches above the surface.

The dimensions of the three forms of traditional drains were, in many respects, not markedly different. They were around 24–36in. deep, and the height of the stones covering the stone ducts or those used in stone-filled drains was some 15–18in. The width of the drains constructed with stone- or sod-built ducts fell within the range of 14–20in. The stone-filled drains, however, were somewhat narrower, measuring around 8–12in. at the top of the stones.

Diagnostic features

The main characteristics of ditches and traditional drains often found in farmland are summarised below.

- **Ditches** that served as both boundaries and drainage features tended to be appreciably larger than drains, usually over 1m deep, some 2m wide, with evidence of having been repeatedly redug, and often U shaped.
- **Drains** were traditionally dug to a depth of 2–3ft with sloping sides, and were either part-filled with small stones or were constructed with stone-built ducts at the bottom.
- Stone-filled drains tended to have relatively narrow bases (around 3–9in. wide), covered with small stones to a height of 15–18in. and the trench filled with earth.
- Drains with ducts were generally stone-built (some were originally made with sods), placed on a flat bottom (upwards of 15–20in. or more wide) and covered with small stones to a height of 18in.; the trench was filled with earth.

Acknowledgements

The excavation case-studies received from Matthew Seaver are gratefully acknowledged, as are the details of recent excavations in the Dublin region provided by Michael Potterton. We also much appreciate the invaluable publications and practical information kindly provided by Austin O'Sullivan, Michael Conry, Tim Gleeson, Brendan Riordan, Martin Downes, John Sweeney, Derry O'Donovan, Paddy Cunningham, Tomas Cummins, Finola O'Carroll, Jerry O'Sullivan and Gordon Purvis.

References

Bell, J. and Watson, M. (eds) 2008 *A history of Irish farming, 1750–1950*. Dublin.

Conry, M.J. 1973 Dating old stone drains in Rossmore Forest. *Carloviana* (1973), 22–5.

Doyle, M. (ed.) 1839 *A cyclopedia of practical husbandry*. Dublin.

Gailey, A. and Fenton, A. (eds) 1969 *The spade in northern Atlantic Europe*. Belfast.

Robinson, D.H. (ed.) 1962 *Fream's elements of agriculture*. London.

Stephens, H. (ed.) 1847 *A manual of practical drainage*. Dublin.

This article was originally published in the Spring 2010 issue of Archaeology Ireland.

Agricultural drainage systems 2

The 1840s saw a transition from traditional stone drains to early modern drains, three types of which were used over the subsequent century:

- **Tilepipe drains**, current in Ireland during the early decades of the nineteenth century, resulted from the development of clay tiles and pipes in the late eighteenth century. They were made by placing horseshoe tiles over flat 'sole' tiles to form underground culverts. Subsequently, a singled fabricated unit comprising both the horseshoe and sole was introduced.
- **Cylindrical tilepipe drains** largely superseded the horseshoe-and-sole version. By 1870 they were regarded as the most common type of tilepipe drain, so that in the early years of the twentieth century the horseshoe-and-sole was said to have been 'a thing of the past'.
- **Mole drains**, possibly not used in Ireland until the second half of the nineteenth century, consisted of underground channels cut into dense subsoil using the mole plough, an implement developed in the mid-nineteenth century. Such drains were formed in areas with clay subsoil that was free from stones or veins of sand or gravel. They had many of the advantages of tilepipe drains but were less costly.

Cylindrical tilepipe drain at Johnstown Castle, Co. Wexford (detail from Fig. 2).

Early modern drains

The 1840s were a watershed in the development of agricultural drainage systems, characterised by the transition from traditional stone drains to early modern drains. Part 1 of this article dealt with traditional drains and ditches. An overview is given below of tilepipe drains and mole drains, the two predominant forms of early modern field-drainage systems (Fig. 1). Following a brief outline of some recently excavated post-medieval land-drainage features, the chronology of underground field-drainage developments is presented, including an indicative timeline for the main period of use of the different forms of drains. In compiling the article, the publications kindly provided by Austin O'Sullivan from the Agricultural Museum at Johnstown Castle have been most helpful.

Post-medieval drainage systems

Agricultural drainage features pertaining to the post-medieval period have been found in development-led excavations undertaken throughout the country. Ditches, which are the most important feature of field-drainage systems, functioned both as field boundaries and as drains and outfalls for the main field drains. A number of the post-medieval drainage features recorded in *Excavations* (2009) seem to have been ditches constructed to serve both purposes. Others may have been provided for drainage purposes only.

Stone drains and stone-filled drains (Part 1) were found in a number of excavations dated to the post-medieval period. Features of early modern

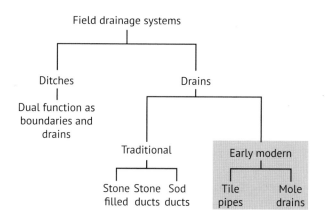

Fig. 1—Schematic differentiation of field-drainage systems, with drains discussed in detail here indicated by shading.

*Fig. 2—
Cylindrical
tilepipe drain
excavated at
Johnstown
Castle, Co.
Wexford
(courtesy
of Austin
O'Sullivan).*

drains were also recorded. As shown in Fig. 2, a cylindrical tilepipe drain was excavated at Johnstown Castle, Co. Wexford. It comprised socketed pipes placed on the soil at the bottom of a trench (18in. deep and 12in. wide), with a single line of red bricks on either side and covered with flat stones (Austin O'Sullivan, pers. comm.).

Overall, the excavations mentioned above underline the continued use of traditional drains into the period when early modern drainage was being more widely used.

Early modern drains

Tilepipe drainage

The development of clay tiles and pipes in the late 1700s in Britain and their widespread use from the mid-1800s constituted an important technological innovation in underground drains, heralding the development of modern drainage systems. The term 'tilepipes' applied to these features is derived from the semicircular or crescent shape of the early tiles used to form underground culverts and their similarity to the familiar ridge tile (Harvey 1980).

Mole drainage

In clay subsoils, mole drainage, properly undertaken, was a satisfactory and economic alternative to tilepipe drainage. Farmers with seasonally wet land have for centuries exploited the plasticity and tenacity of clay in their drainage operations to produce underground channels (Robinson 1962). The mole ducts were near-circular in cross-section, often some 3–4in. in diameter. They were cut through the subsoil, usually at a depth of upwards of 15–20in. and 3–5yds apart (Watson and More 1945; Robinson 1962).

Mole drainage had many of the advantages of tilepipe drains but was less costly. It could only be practised, however, where there was a clay subsoil free from stones or veins of sand or gravel and where a good fall was assured (Watson and More 1945). Accordingly, archaeological remains of mole drains are likely to be confined mainly to areas with clay subsoil.

Chronology of drainage developments

Important insights into the transition from traditional to early modern drains may be derived from Stephens's *A manual of practical drainage* (1847), detailing developments in the UK, and from Doyle's (1839) description of drainage practices in Ireland during the early decades of the 1800s. These publications show that developments in underground drainage systems in Ireland broadly tracked those in Britain (Fig. 3).

As evidenced by the extensive specifications and other technical details provided by Stephens, the construction of drains with stone-built ducts appears to have received considerable attention in Britain in the early decades of the 1800s. Stone-filled drains were also made, but seemingly to a much lesser extent from the mid-1800s. In this regard, Stephens noted that 'stones have hitherto been the most common material employed for filling drains'. Perhaps they were at that time being superseded by drains with stone ducts, which were being strongly advocated, for example by Stephens, who stressed that 'an open duct will afford a freer passage for water than a mass of loose stones'.

The mid-1800s saw a sea change in drainage technology, with the development of clay tiles and pipes and the construction of tilepipe drains (Fig. 3). Drains constructed with tiles were first laid down in Britain in the late 1700s, and the early 1800s saw the local development and use of a variety of such tiles, then generally known as horseshoe tiles (Harvey 1980). By the 1840s, tile-making machines were producing various forms of tiles, including a horseshoe and sole in a single prefabricated unit. As further detailed by Harvey, tiles and pipes marked 'Drain' date from between 1826 and 1850. This reflects the tax levied during the period on bricks and tiles, and from which tiles made for 'the sole purpose of draining marshy land' were exempt in 1826. Pipes of 1in. diameter, known as pencil pipes, were also used for a rather short period, from the 1840s to the 1870s, when they were finally abandoned because of silting and blockage.

Timeline of advances in field-drainage systems

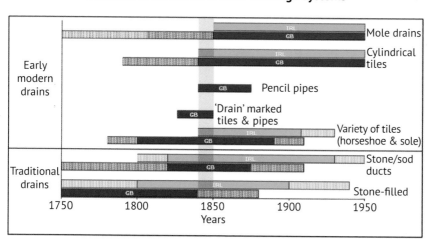

Fig. 3— Chronology of underground field-drainage developments and an indicative timeline for the main periods of use.

Predecessors of the modern cylindrical tilepipes were introduced in Britain at the end of the 1700s but were not widely used until the development in the 1840s of machines for their cheap mass production (Harvey 1980). The new form of pipes won rapid acceptance and by 1870 had largely superseded the tile and sole. As noted by Bell and Watson (2008), a British text published in 1909 declared that the horseshoe drains were 'a thing of the past'.

Mole drainage has been described as 'tilepipe drainage without tilepipes' (Harvey 1980). The practice was not widely used until the development of the mole plough in the mid-1800s, when mole drainage seems to have been largely 'confined to some parts of England, where grassland on a clay subsoil abounds' (Stephens 1847).

Stone-filled drains and drains constructed with stone-built ducts were, as described by Doyle (1839), used in Ireland in the early decades of the 1800s. They may perhaps have been most widely used in the main tillage areas. Underground drains were not common in many parts of the country until much later (Gailey and Fenton 1969). Commenting, it seems, on drains with stone-built ducts, Doyle (1839) contended that 'none of these contrivances are half as good … as filling with small stones which can never close and therefore secure an uninterruptedly free channel for water to filter through'. His views on the effectiveness of such drains in Ireland are the converse of those of Stephens (1847), referred to above. The apparently poor performance of stone-built ducts may have prolonged the construction of stone-filled drains in Ireland beyond the 1800s (Fig. 3). In the late 1880s, drains with well-built stone ducts were, as further detailed by Conry (1973), constructed throughout the country to relieve famine distress. The drain with a rectangular duct excavated at Rossmore Forest, Co. Laois, was markedly different and apparently more securely built than the triangular stone ducts detailed by Doyle in the early decades of the 1800s (see Spring 2010 issue of *Archaeology Ireland*).

Tilepipe drainage systems were used in Ireland in the early decades of the 1800s, and the horseshoe and cylindrical forms depicted by Doyle (1839) are shown in Fig. 4. Relative to the details recorded on traditional stone drains, the information provided by Doyle on tilepipe drains is much less comprehensive. Whether this reflects the later advent of such drainage systems in Ireland compared to Britain is open to question. As further detailed by Bell and Watson (2008), however, clay tiles and pipes were increasingly used in Ireland from around the mid-1800s, and by 1870 cylindrical pipes were regarded as the most common type of tilepipe drainage.

Mole drainage, the other form of early modern drainage system, is not referred to by Doyle (1839) and may not have been practised in Ireland until the second half of the 1800s. It was a cost-effective system of drainage, well known in the 1900s and still used today for particular drainage operations, often stone filled (Fig. 5).

Conclusions

Traditional drains were constructed in Ireland in the early 1800s and before, and continued to be made until the late 1800s and into the 1900s, when early modern drains had become the most common form. As shown in Fig. 3, there is considerable overlap in the chronology of advances made in drainage developments since the 1700s. The following indicative timeline can, however, be discerned in terms of the main period of use of the different forms of field-drainage systems in Ireland. Traditional drains were the predominant type up to the mid-1800s. Those with stone-built ducts seem to have become the more common form in the second part of the century, and continued to be used into the 1900s. Early modern drains were predominantly used from around the mid-1800s. Cylindrical tilepipe drains superseded tiles and soles as the century advanced, to become the most prevalent form of field drain constructed. The main period of use of mole drains seems to be somewhat later and, indeed, they may not have been as widely used in clay subsoils as might be expected.

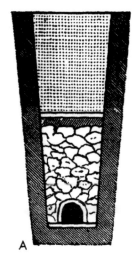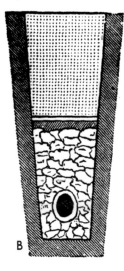

Fig. 4—Tilepipe drainage systems recorded in early nineteenth-century Ireland: (A) horseshoe tiles placed on flat 'sole' tiles; (B) cylindrical pipetiles as depicted by Doyle (1839) (courtesy of Jonathan Bell).

A   B

The development of a more definitive timeline for the main periods of use of the different forms of field drainage practised in Ireland will require more systematic analysis of the records of field drains and ditches found in excavations undertaken throughout the country.

Diagnostic features

The main characteristics of early modern drainage systems found in farmland are outlined below.

- **Ditches** often served as both field boundaries and important drainage features, and may be found with outfalls from the main field drains. They tend to be sizeable U-shaped culverts (1m and more deep and some 2m wide) with characteristic evidence of having been repeatedly redug.
- **Tilepipe drains** contain the remains of tiles or cylindrical pipes laid on the bottom of a narrow trench, dug to around 2ft deep and covered with small stones, or perhaps just earth, to a height of around 15–20in.
- **Mole drains** were largely confined to areas with clay subsoil and comprised near-circular water channels formed at a depth of upwards of

Fig. 5 —
Twentieth-
century mole
drain discovered
during
excavations at
Knowth, Site M
(courtesy of
Matthew Stout).

15–30in. and 3–4yds or more apart. Some of those formed more recently may be gravel filled.

Acknowledgements

We gratefully acknowledge the informative publications and practical knowledge of historical field-drainage systems kindly provided by a number of agriculturalists, including Austin O'Sullivan, Tim Gleeson, Michael Conry, Martin Downes, Derry O'Donovan, Thomas Cummins, Jim Collins, Brendan Riordan, John Feehan, Paddy Cunningham, Michael McGrath and other colleagues. The archaeological and background information and other contributions received from Geraldine and Matthew Stout, Brian Shanahan, Donald Murphy, Linda Clarke and John Sweeney are also much appreciated.

References

Bell, J. and Watson, M. (eds) 2008 *A history of Irish farming, 1750–1950*. Dublin.

Conry, M.J. 1973 Dating old stone drains in Rossmore Forest. *Carloviana* (1973), 22–5.

Doyle, M. (ed.) 1839 *A cyclopedia of practical husbandry*. Dublin.

Gailey, A. and Fenton, A. (eds) 1969 *The spade in northern Atlantic Europe*. Belfast.

Harvey, N. (ed.) 1980 *The industrial archaeology of farming in England and Wales*. London.

Robinson, D.H. (ed.) 1962 *Fream's elements of agriculture*. London.

Stephens, H. (ed.) 1847 *A manual of practical draining*. Dublin.

Watson, J.A.S. and More, J.A. (eds) 1945 *Agriculture: the science and practice of British farming*. London.

This article was originally published in the Summer 2010 issue of Archaeology Ireland.

Making lime

Farm line kilns are prominent surviving traces of eighteenth- and nineteenth-century agriculture. During this period there may have been as many as a quarter of a million in the country. The application of lime to soil was commonly practised between the twelfth and seventeenth centuries and became widespread in the eighteenth century.

Two types of farm lime kiln were in use, namely the **draw kiln**, which burnt limestone in a continuous process, and the **flare kiln**, which operated discontinuously on a batch basis.

Lime neutralises the acidity of soil, releases its nutrients, promotes the breakdown of organic matter in the soil and makes the ground more workable. However, many early experiences with the practice highlighted the damage that over-liming can do by exhausting soil nutrients. This is captured in the old Irish saying, 'Lime enriches the father but impoverishes the son.'

Farm lime kilns became less prevalent in the late nineteenth century and gave way to the industrial manufacture of lime, which began to be combined with commercial salt production.

Fig. 1 — Kiln at Gorteen, Co. Offaly (courtesy of Declan Quinlan).

Lime kilns

Lime kilns—sometimes pronounced 'lime kills'—were furnaces used to produce lime by heating limestone at temperatures of up to 1,000°C. Burning the limestone, as the process is generally known, decomposed the limestone and converted it to lime, frequently known as **quicklime** or **burnt lime**. This was used extensively in building, agriculture and related purposes. Farm lime kilns, which existed in their thousands in the countryside in the eighteenth century and especially the early nineteenth century, are the main focus of this article. Industrial lime and brick works, which largely replaced them in the second half of the nineteenth century, are also touched upon.

Two types of permanent kilns were generally used in the production of lime for agricultural purposes. These were the **draw kilns** and the less popular **flare kilns**. The draw kilns burnt limestone in a continuous process. The flare kilns operated on the basis of a discontinuous batch process. These different methods of operation involved, in particular, differences in the fire-box or fireplace systems deployed in the two kilns. Otherwise both kilns had a number of common structural features.

Principal components

The two types of farm kiln were generally of roughly similar dimensions; both were loaded from the top and had their furnaces (fire-boxes) at the bottom. Based on descriptions provided by Quain (1984) and more recently by Quinlan (2004), the two kiln types contained the following four main structural components.

Furnace shaft

This consisted of a roughly cylindrical shaft built of sandstone or sometimes of the same limestone as was being burnt in the kilns (the heat generated in the kiln was only sufficient to affect limestone broken into small lumps). This shaft was the container in which the entire burning operation took place.

Masonry casing

Lime kilns were usually built into a bank of rising ground and enclosed on the other sides by a stone-built structure, usually rectangular in shape. The space between the furnace shaft and the enclosing structure was filled in with broken stones, clay, sand and other non-combustible material, which provided support, expansion and insulation for the kilns.

Draw-hole or stoke-hole

This was located at the front of the kiln base. In addition to providing draught and access to the fire, the draw-hole was also the means by which the lime was withdrawn from the kilns. The stoke-hole in draw kilns was often built to accommodate one or two men, and sometimes a cart. Some have an arch built in stone or brick, and are flared inwards to meet the working aperture of the furnace.

Kiln head

This was the flat top of the kiln, above the furnace shaft, on which the final breaking of the limestone and the loading into the kiln took place. The kiln top had cast-iron covers to serve as dampers and to moderate the draught. Because this area was frequently enveloped in smoke, a wall was usually built around the edge of the kiln head for protection against accident to man or draught animal.

Draw kilns

Draw kilns, the more common type, burned limestone in a continuous process, as previously noted. Hence they were also known as **continuous, perpetual** or **running kilns**.

The characteristic feature of draw kilns was a permanent grate fixed over the fire-box/place. Alternating layers of limestone and fuel were stacked on top of the grate. As the fuel burned and decomposed the limestone, the lime dropped through the draw/stoke-hole. Further layers of fuel and limestone were added at the top, and the process continued sometimes for weeks or months until the required amount of lime was produced. The draw kilns had the capacity to produce large amounts of lime and were also fuel efficient. However, they had the disadvantage of allowing the lime to mix with the ash from the burnt fuel. Also, the limestone had to be broken into small pieces prior to burning.

Flare kilns

The main alternative to the draw kiln was the flare kiln, also known as an **arch**, **standing** or **French kiln**. In loading this type of kiln, a rough arch of limestone was built over the fire-box/place using the same limestone as that burnt in the kiln. This supported the rest of the single charge of limestone overhead. The fire was lit through the stoke-hole at the bottom of the kiln. It was kept stoked for several days by adding fuel as required, until all the limestone was burnt. When the kiln cooled down, the lime was unloaded. Flare kilns had the advantage of being able to burn large flags and boulders of limestone, and they also kept the lime separate from the fuel ash. Despite these advantages, flare kilns were much less popular in Ireland than draw kilns because they were considered to be much less profitable. As well as consuming more fuel, they required the constant labour of several men, often for three days and nights, while burning a single charge of limestone.

*Fig. 2—
Glenregan
lime kiln at
Kinnitty, Co.
Offaly (courtesy
of Declan
Quinlan).*

Shape and size

The general requirement of a lime kiln was that it should be as high as possible—some 20ft was desirable and 30ft preferable. The dimensions for an improved draw kiln developed in the early nineteenth century had a total height of 26ft (*c*. 8m). The middle section was 14ft (4m) high and 8ft (2.5m) wide. The funnel-shaped drawing and top sections were each 6ft (2m) high.

The 11 lime kilns recently surveyed by Quinlan (2004) in the Slieve Bloom area were generally rectangular in shape and the majority were of roughly comparable size (Fig. 2). The heights and lengths of the majority were 2–4m. Two were only about 1m high but were up to 2.4–3.6m long. The largest and most impressive of the lime kilns surveyed was 5.1m high and 6.6m long (Fig. 3). This is located at Glenregan, Co. Offaly (site no. 2437-036-00).

Fuelling the kilns

Because of the need to generate temperatures in the region of 1,000°C for protracted periods, lime kilns required large quantities of fuel. They tended to burn roughly equal amounts of fuel and limestone. However, this was largely dependent on the fuel type/mix used. One estimate indicates that the production of one ton of lime in a draw kiln requires some ten times more peat than coal. Prior to the destruction of Irish woods in the fifteenth–sixteenth centuries, timber was widely used in the burning of limestone. Peat was also used with coal and **culm** in later periods. In a number of locations in Munster, furze was a main fuel source in the late nineteenth century. Elsewhere, furze was used to start the fire or was mixed with other fuels.

The quality of lime produced depended upon the know-how and skills of the lime-burner in maintaining the required temperature in the kilns and determining the rate and length of the burning process. The control of the firing temperature depended upon observing the colour of the fire. This was affected by the amount of carbon dioxide released during the conversion of limestone to lime, as well as that produced by the fuel. Also, vapour produced by feeding kilns with wet limestone or fuel soaked in water facilitated the production of good lime. It was important to ensure that the gas-flow through the kiln was evenly distributed. This required considerable know-how when placing and selecting the kiln fill. Also, the size of the broken limestone was important. If too small, the gas-flow was impeded, while large lumps of limestone increased the burning time.

*Fig. 3—
Glenregan
lime kiln, Co.
Offaly (courtesy
of Declan
Quinlan).*

Chemistry of lime production and use

Lime may be best described as a soil-improver/conditioner rather than a fertiliser. Also, the term 'lime-burning' is an over-simplification. A number of discrete chemical changes are involved in the conversion of limestone to lime and in its subsequent use in agriculture and building.

Burning

Calcium carbonate is the main constituent of limestone. When burnt in a kiln, the calcium carbonate decomposes and on releasing carbon dioxide is converted into calcium oxide (CaO), which is lime, or **quicklime**, as it is more commonly known. The importance of this simple chemical change is that, unlike the calcium carbonate, the lime produced is much more reactive with and soluble in water. To produce good-quality lime requires limestone containing upwards of 50–90% calcium carbonate that can be broken into evenly sized lumps for complete burning.

Slaking

When exposed to water, the calcium oxide (lime) is converted into calcium hydroxide $(Ca(OH)_2)$. This process is termed **slaking**, and hence the calcium hydroxide produced is commonly called **slake lime** or **hydrated lime**. When sufficient water is present, the process is attended by the release of heat, often in the form of vapour bubbles and steam, and the mixture tends to become quite hot. It was because of its heat-generating capacity, when mixed with water, that lime became known as quicklime.

Calcium hydroxide, or slake lime, with its characteristic caustic or alkaline attributes, is the active ingredient responsible for the many uses of lime in agriculture, building and related uses.

Soil neutralisation

The enhancement of soil fertility following the application of lime is principally due to the alkalinity of the slake lime produced when lime is exposed to moisture. The slake lime neutralises the acidity of the soil. This promotes the breakdown of soil organic matter, and also releases the limited quantity of nutrients contained in the topsoil. Especially in areas with acidic soils, application of lime has made major contributions to raising soil productivity and making the ground more workable.

Because it was considered more beneficial to the land, farmers commonly took lumps of lime straight from the kiln, while still hot, to the fields. This incurred the risk of the lime/quicklime picking up moisture or indeed getting wet during transport, and the resultant heat generation setting fire to the cart. The lumps of lime, spread out in small, evenly spaced heaps, absorbed moisture and broke down into powdered slake lime (calcium hydroxide), which could be easily spread with a shovel.

The benefits of liming lasted for a number of years. However, as many early experiences showed, over-liming can be harmful, by exhausting soil nutrients. Hence the old Irish saying, 'Lime enriches the father but impoverishes the son.'

Mortar hardening

Lime slaked with excess water and mixed with sand produces mortar for stone building. When exposed to air, the mortar hardens by losing water, and because of its alkalinity the slake lime ($Ca(OH)_2$) absorbs carbon dioxide and reverts to calcium carbonate, the predominant component of the limestone from which it was originally derived.

Historical perspective

The majority of farm lime kilns surviving today are monuments to eighteenth- and early nineteenth-century agriculture. However, the production of lime by the burning of limestone is a very ancient technology.

Lime-based mortars were extensively used in construction and related activities by various societies for thousands of years. It is reported that they were deployed by the Egyptians in the construction of the pyramids, by the Greeks as plasters on rough stone and by the Romans in making concrete, plaster, washers and in internal decorations.

In Ireland the burning of limestone may be traced to pagan times, when lime is said to have been used on the outer defences surrounding homesteads (duns) and on the hides of covered shields. The use of limestone for building and related uses probably goes back to at least the first millennium, when limestone technology may have been introduced in the early medieval period. The early monks were presumably familiar with the Roman technology of limestone-burning and the use of lime in building, and applied this knowledge in the construction of churches and round towers.

The burning of limestone for the specific purpose of using the lime produced in agriculture may be a later development. No reference to the use of burnt limestone for agricultural purposes has been found in the ancient law-tracts (Kelly 1997). However, the burning of limestone for the specific purpose of applying the lime produced to soil was commonly practised between the twelfth and seventeenth centuries. It became widespread in the eighteenth century, when many new technical developments were introduced into Irish farming.

In the mid-eighteenth and early nineteenth centuries, farm lime kilns were ubiquitous in the rural landscape, especially in limestone areas and where the soil was acidic. For instance, the 1842 Ordnance Survey 6in. maps for County Cork show thousands of lime kilns spread especially densely in the limestone areas of the river valleys. The hinterland of the Bride River and Upper River Lee had a high concentration of lime kilns, with many located adjacent to peat sources in the proximity of bogs (Collins 2004). In the Blackwater area, 53 lime kilns were concentrated within a 2-mile area around Mallow (Sleeman 1990). A similar situation prevailed in many other parts of the country, such as the Slieve Bloom area, which had 818 lime kilns in the 1840s (Quinlan 2004). Assuming that each limestone operation (quarrying, transport, breaking and burning, etc.) involved a cluster of some three or four landowners, there may have been something in the region of a quarter of a million or more lime kilns in Ireland in the eighteenth and early nineteenth centuries.

Home burning of limestone became less prevalent in the late nineteenth century and did not survive for long after the Famine in many areas. The small-scale farm lime kilns gave way to the industrial manufacture of lime by quarries with a convenient supply of limestone and fuel and access to public transport.

Extensive industrial-scale lime-manufacturing works were established at strategic locations throughout Ireland. A number of these introduced the recently invented Hoffman Kiln for the manufacture of lime and bricks. This new process did not require the limestone to be broken prior to being

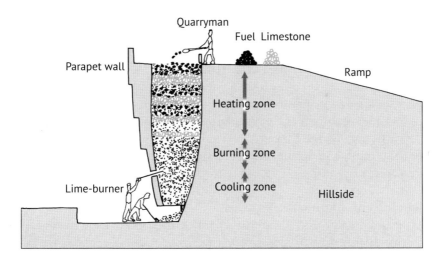

Fig. 4—Diagram of a working kiln (courtesy of Ursula Mattenberger).

loaded into the kiln and thus provided considerable improvements in labour productivity. It also provided substantial fuel savings compared to earlier kilns.

A very extensive lime and brick works employing the Hoffman process was commenced in 1866 at Castle Espie, Co. Down (*The Irish Builder*, 1 June 1867). The kilns, which had a chimney 172ft high, comprised 24 compartments, each capable of containing 100 tons of limestone and with the capacity to manufacture 600 tons of lime per week.

To meet the large demand for lime in the area, the Munster Brick and Lime Company commenced in 1873 the erection of a Hoffman Kiln at Clonmel, where it had access to cheap limestone and fuel (*The Irish Builder*, 15 May 1873). The company was located beside a siding from the Southern Railway, which enabled lime to be sent by rail all over the country.

A large works located in Cork city in the late nineteenth century used the enormous heat generated by the kiln to produce salt as well as lime, as is evident from the name—the Salt and Lime Works, Leitrim Street (*Southern Industry* **2** (1), January 1889). Rock salt was dissolved in water and, following filtration, the resultant solution was placed in large shallow pans in a large chamber above the furnace, where the water was carefully evaporated off to yield salt. Depending on whether the evaporation of the salt was carried out quickly or slowly, salt of coarse or fine texture could be produced. The salt was of a high quality and suitable for butter-making.

Lime was extensively used in agriculture in the first half of the nineteenth century but the practice of burning limestone on farms declined in the second half of the century. The availability of natural and artificial fertilisers such as imported **guano** and **superphosphate**, allied with the displacement in the twentieth century of lime by crushed limestone, led to the final demise of the lime-kiln operations.

Attractive ruins of permanent lime kilns still exist throughout the countryside, but the overwhelming majority of those recorded in the 1840s have been destroyed. Only 8 of the 53 lime kilns recorded around Mallow in the 1840s survived in reasonable condition in 1990 (Sleeman 1990). Similarly, in the Slieve Bloom area, of the 818 lime kilns recorded in the 1840s less than 20% were listed in 1909. In 1994 only 27 lime-kiln sites were identified in the area, of which 13 have since been destroyed (Quinlan 2004). This represents a destruction rate of some 37% in the past decade.

Lime kilns played a central role in the development of agriculture in Ireland and are an important element of our heritage. To prevent the further destruction of lime kilns and other archaeological features of recent centuries, the practice of operating a cut-off date of AD 1700, after which sites are not normally considered for inclusion in SMRs and as a result are not offered adequate legal protection, needs to be discontinued.

Checklist of diagnostic features

- Stone structures usually built in a bank of rising ground and enclosed on the exposed sides by stone walls with an opening in the front of the kiln.

- Generally rectangular in shape and of different dimensions—typically perhaps 2–4m in height and length, with many smaller and larger types.
- Found in various locations, most frequently in fields and sometimes on roadsides or in farmyards, often in close proximity to fuel sources, such as peat bogs.

Acknowledgements

This article has drawn extensively on a thesis entitled 'A study of lime kilns in the Slieve Blooms' (UCD, 2004) by Declan Quinlan, whose cooperation is gratefully acknowledged. This and other sources are listed below. We are also grateful to Dr Colin Rynne of the Department of Archaeology, UCC, for providing invaluable information.

References

Birthistle, D. 1974 Lime and lime-kilns. *Old Kilkenny Review* **46**, 75–7.

Collins, J.F. 2004 The immense furnace of Anachally and the parsimony of the landlord: aspects of burning and using Muskerry limestone. *Bandon Historical Journal* **19**, 36–54.

Kelly, F. 1997 *Early Irish farming*. Dublin.

Quain, J.T. 1984 Lime kilns of Ardmore and Grange. *Ardmore Journal* **1**, 14–17.

Quinlan, D. 2004 A study of lime kilns in the Slieve Blooms. Unpublished M.Arg.Sc. thesis, University College Dublin.

Sleeman, M. 1990 A lost tradition—the forgotten kiln. *Mallow Field Club Journal* **5**, 95–100.

This article was originally published in the Summer 2005 issue of Archaeology Ireland.

Section II
Food processing

The availability and provision of food are fundamental requirements of existence. Today, as society becomes more remote from the production process and people often take it for granted that food just *arrives* on supermarket shelves, the general population has a diminished connection to the various stages of production. Up until quite recently, however, food production was a more local undertaking, on the family farm or even in the cottage garden. Specialised equipment required for certain stages of the process was often communal in nature, even when controlled by a specific family or other interest, and it is easy to imagine a *meitheal* (or neighbourly work party) assembling to participate in the work and any associated activities. It is likely that the features presented below were the location or outcome of such cooperation.

Dairy and cereal were the predominant **historical food products** consumed in Ireland from the medieval period up to recent centuries. They could have provided many of the nutrient requirements of the general population apart from during periods of perennial and episodic shortages.

Traditionally envisaged as places designed to cook meat, *fulachta fiadh* are now increasingly considered to have been multi-purpose sites. The grinding of grain from prehistory was attended by intermittent progressive advances in **quern-stone** design. Saddle querns, introduced into Ireland in the Neolithic period, were the original grinding implements and they later gave way to rotary querns. **Corn-drying kilns** represented a notable innovation in Irish agriculture during the medieval period. Up until the mid-1800s they were an important feature of virtually every townland. **Watermills**, another advanced technology of early medieval agriculture, are the most extensively dated structures of the period. **Windmills**, seemingly introduced into Ireland by the Anglo-Normans, became prominent features with the intensification of cereal production in the period AD 1770–1815.

Diet and production

D airy products and cereals have been important components of the Irish diet from prehistory through to the Middle Ages and on into more recent centuries. Butter appears to have been a significant foodstuff from prehistoric times. Samples of butter from bogs date from the early seventeenth century BC up until the late eighteenth century AD, representing a time-span of some 3,400 years. The amount of meat, particularly beef, generally eaten by the population at large seems to have been quite limited. Also, the consumption of fish in Ireland never seems to have been especially high. Indeed, before the Famine, both meat and fish appear to have been eaten in very small quantities by the general population. However, a wide range of fruits and vegetables, both wild and cultivated, were ordinarily consumed in Ireland from deep in prehistoric time.

Fig. 1—Figure-of-eight corn-drying kiln excavated at Mullanstown, Co. Louth (courtesy of Fintan Walsh, IAC).

Historical food products

Corn and milk were, according to Lucas (1960–2), the mainstay of the historical diet of the general population of the country. A number of notable advances pertaining to earlier food sources have been published during the past decade (McCormick 2007; 2013; Synnott 2014; Smyth and Evershed 2015; Peters 2015). The main conclusions of these studies are integrated in this article, with an overview just recently published (Stuijts and Downey 2016) of Lucas's perspective on the food products predominantly consumed by the wider population from earlier times.

Milk and dairy products

From the Neolithic and on through medieval times, cattle were a predominant feature of agriculture in Ireland (Lucas 1960–2). Notably, the vast bulk of the cattle population consisted of cows. Butter appears to have been an important part of the Irish diet from prehistoric times. As stated emphatically by Lucas (1960–2), 'virtually every kind of source of every age, ancient, medieval and recent, substantiates the evidence for the importance of butter'. Over the past 300 years, upwards of some 500 finds of bog-butter have been unearthed in Ireland, as well as some in Scotland.

As shown in Fig. 2, 17 samples of bog-butter finds from Ireland were radiocarbon dated in 2006. The majority were from the Iron Age. A number dated from AD 765 to 1660. A further 20 samples were dated more recently (Synnott 2014). This shows that the time-span during which butter was deposited in bogs extended from the Bronze Age (early seventeenth century BC) up to the late eighteenth century AD, a range of some 3,400 years.

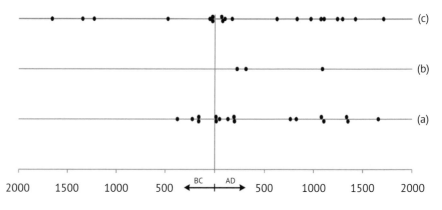

Fig. 2—Mean radiocarbon dates for bog-butter samples: (a) 17 Irish samples dated in 2006, (b) three Scottish samples and (c) 20 recently dated samples (courtesy of C. Synnott).

Scientific analysis published in 2015 by Smyth and Evershed established that the fat residues adhered to and absorbed into the clay matrix of Neolithic pottery vessels contained fatty acids typical of milk fat. Indeed, milk-fat derivatives were the dominant fat residues detected in solvent extracts from vessels dating from all phases of the Neolithic. Further to this, Smyth and Evershed stated that the results of the analysis 'provide the first unequivocal evidence that dairying in Ireland began in the Neolithic and that it was being practised by some of the very earliest farming communities on the island'. Pottery assemblages of early, middle and late Neolithic date yielded the same strong dairy signal, as did assemblages from different parts of the country and from different site types. These chemical analyses, taken together with the radiocarbon dates of bog-butter summarised in Fig. 2, are consistent with the perspective advanced by Lucas (above) concerning the primacy of milk and dairy products, especially butter, among the foods generally consumed in Ireland from prehistory, down through the medieval period and on into modern times.

Fats from meat, as well as very low levels of plant-derived lipids, were also detected in the residues extracted from the Neolithic pottery vessels. Just over 10% of the vessels appear to have contained meat fats predominantly, or a mixture of milk and meat fats. Accordingly, while the extent to which meat was typically cooked in Neolithic pots is uncertain, Smyth and Evershed (2015) concluded that the analysis undertaken provided overwhelming evidence for the processing of milk and dairy products in Ireland during the Neolithic era.

Meat products

Drawing on a wide range of documentary sources, including the accounts of visitors and settlers, Lucas reviewed the composition of the general diet, virtually item by item, and concluded that:

- 'beef seems to have been most commonly consumed by the higher ranks of society';
- '[b]y far the most important kind of flesh meat eaten in ancient, medieval and later times seems to have been pork or bacon';
- 'mutton was only a casual item in the menu'.

Further to this, the informative discourse on patterns of food consumption in Ireland published by Clarkson and Crawford (2001) noted that between the seventeenth and early twentieth centuries beef and mutton were eaten by the wealthy and that dairy foods remained dominant among the indigenous population. They draw attention in particular to what they describe as the best-known seventeenth-century account of Irish diets, which was written by Sir William Petty in 1672. According to Petty, the Irish

'feed chiefly upon Milk and Potatoes … The Diet of these people is Milk, sweet and sower, thick and thin, which is also their Drink in Summer-

> time, in Winter Small-Beer or Water … Their Food is Bread in Cakes … Potatoes from August till May … Mussels, Cockles and Oysters near the Sea; Eggs and Butter made rancid by keeping in Bogs … As for Flesh they seldom eat it, notwithstanding the great plenty thereof, unless it be a one of the smaller Animals, because it is inconvenient … to kill a Beef, which they have no convenience to save. So as 'tis easier for them to have a Hen or Rabbit, than a Beef of equal substance.'

Livestock production was, as further detailed by McCormick (2013), the dominant system of farming in early medieval Ireland. Cattle were the principal livestock kept during the period, representing approximately 40–50% of the species present in early medieval assemblages. Pigs were generally the second most prevalent species present, ranging from about 20% to upwards of 30% of the total. Sheep/goats appear to have generally accounted for around 20% or more of the livestock in the assemblages.

Dairying is generally accepted as the most widespread system of cattle production in early medieval Ireland. Cows were of exceptional importance, highly valued for their capacity to produce milk for consumption and for use in making dairy goods. The majority of male animals were seemingly killed off for their meat around three years of age. Accordingly, McCormick (2007) postulated that Ireland had in 'the Early Medieval Christian period … a country-wide livestock economy based on dairying …'.

Meat in substantial amounts would have been produced by the livestock systems outlined above, especially during the seasonal slaughtering of excess animals in the later part of the year (Stuijts and Downey 2016). Much of this meat, however, in particular the beef, may have been consumed at communal feasting events/large gatherings, which were seemingly common in earlier times. In addition, some of the meat produced could have been included in the food rent that client farmers were required to pay their lords as part of the prevailing clientship arrangements. In such circumstances the amount of meat, and particularly beef, available for consumption by the general population on a regular basis would have been substantially curtailed.

The extent to which meat contributed to the regular diet of the general population has been further questioned by an extensive review recently published by Peters (2015) on the food entitlements of peasants and commoners in early medieval Ireland. Based on a wide range of information from Old and Middle Irish law, combined with literary, ecclesiastical and archaeological sources, Peters concluded that, 'At its core, the diet of peasants and commoners consisted mainly of *prima facie* cereals and dairy products', and that '[m]eat, furthermore … considered by historians to be the reserve of the nobility, was also a part, albeit minor, of the diet of commoners'. He added, however, that there is some evidence to indicate that peasants and commoners were likely to consume beef on special occasions. Pigs were kept solely for consumption and appear to have been the main dish served at most feasts during the festival of *Samain*.

Fig. 3—Early eleventh-century corn-drying kiln excavated at Haynestown, Co. Louth (VJK).

Cereals

Many strands of evidence have identified the late seventh/eighth century as a period of change. In particular, the production of cereals appears to have grown in importance from the eighth century (McCormick 2013). There was a sizeable increase in the use of corn-drying kilns, rising to a peak in the sixth century, as further detailed by M. Monk and O. Power (*Archaeology Ireland*, Summer 2012). Large numbers of 'figure-of-eight kilns' gave way to a reduced number of larger and better-built 'keyhole-type kilns' (Figs 1 and 2). The use of watermills increased from the eighth century AD onwards, with the highest concentration being built between 750 and 850.

These changes may perhaps indicate a move away from subsistence farming towards the production of agricultural surplus controlled by the political élite (McCormick 2013). Such a shift in agricultural production would have had important implications for the availability of food products, particularly the cereals that were, according to Lucas (1960–2), a mainstay of the diet of the general population in earlier times.

Fruits and vegetables

The wide range of fruits and vegetables, both wild and cultivated species, commonly eaten in Ireland from earlier times would have provided the general population with important sources of nutrients, including vitamins, antioxidants, minerals, dietary fibre etc. (Stuijts and Downey 2016).

Fish

Reports compiled during the medieval period by Giraldus Cambrensis and Don O'Sullivan Beare testify to the abundance of fish around the coast, as well as in the rivers and lakes (Stuijts and Downey 2016). Notwithstanding their abundance, fish appear not to have been greatly consumed in Ireland. They were essentially a *supplement* to the diet. In this regard, Clarkson and Crawford (2001) wrote that 'the consumption of fish has never been high in Ireland'. In a similar vein, Peters (2015) recently stated that the importance of fish in the diet of peasants and commoners in early medieval Ireland should not be overstated. While these resources were controlled by lords and the church, they are likely to have allowed for some consumption of fish by local groups.

Dietary information gathered from the early decades of the nineteenth century, particularly the Poor Law Inquiry of 1835–6, showed that fewer than 7% of the parishes in Ireland recorded the consumption of fish other than herrings. Clarkson and Crawford assert that 'Before the famine, meat and fish were eaten only in tiny quantities …'.

As distinct from the impressive array of highly valued fish species mainly associated with the consumption patterns of the upper classes, herrings and pike, together with a number of low-valued shellfish, were prominent features of the fish diet of the wider population, particularly the poorer classes.

Conclusion

The staple food products that were the mainstay of the Irish diet from earlier times, as outlined above, could have provided many of the main nutrient requirements of the general population, subject to perennial seasonal and episodic food shortages (Stuijts and Downey 2016).

Fig. 4—Late-dated stone-lined keyhole-type kiln excavated at Ballintemple, Co. Cork (courtesy of T. Cummins, S. Lane and A. Purcell Ltd).

Acknowledgements

The contributions of Mick Monk, Ronan Gormley, Brendan Riordan, Connie Murphy, Bob Lawlor and Gordon Purvis to this article are much appreciated. We are most grateful to Teagasc for undertaking the publication of the booklet entitled *Historical farm and fish food products predominantly consumed by the general Irish population from earlier times* (Carlow).

References

Clarkson, L.A. and Crawford, R.M. (eds) 2001 *Feast and famine: food and nutrition in Ireland, 1500–1920*. Oxford.

Lucas, A.T. 1960–2 Irish food before the potato. *Gwerin* **3**, 8–43.

McCormick, F. 2007 Mammal bone studies from prehistoric Irish sites. In E.M. Murphy and N.J. Whitehouse (eds), *Environmental archaeology in Ireland*. Oxford.

McCormick, F. 2013 Agriculture, settlement, and society in early medieval Ireland. *Quaternary International* **30**, 1–12.

Peters, C.N. 2015 'He is not entitled to butter': the diet of peasants and commoners in early medieval Ireland. *Proceedings of the Royal Irish Academy* **115**C, 79–109.

Smyth, J. and Evershed, R.P. 2015 The molecules of meals: new insights into Neolithic foodways. *Proceedings of the Royal Irish Academy* **115**C, 27–46.

Stuijts, I. and Downey, L. 2016 *Historical farm and fish food products predominantly consumed by the general Irish population, some from earlier times*. Carlow.

Synnott, C. 2014 Bog butter—what is it, where was it found, and when and why was it put there? In P. Foynes, C. Rynne and C. Synnott (eds), *Butter in Ireland from earliest times to the 21st century*. Cork.

This article was originally published in the Summer 2016 issue of Archaeology Ireland.

Fulachta fiadh

As well as the cooking of meat, a range of activities might have been carried out at *fulachta fiadh*, including textile processing, clothes-washing and dyeing, brewing and bathing. They could even have functioned as saunas and sweat-houses.

The vast majority of *fulachta fiadh* were in use during the Bronze Age, especially in the centuries from 1800 to 800 BC. They appear to have been used for activity of a communal or ritual nature.

An intriguing aspect of these monuments is their profusion and striking concentrations in certain locations. They are estimated to be the most common prehistoric monuments in Ireland, but their geographic distribution is quite uneven. For instance, the most intense concentrations are known in County Cork, while the number recorded in Kerry is comparatively low.

Fulachta fiadh are associated with particular landscape features and tend to be found in wet, marshy locations, often beside a stream or even a lake.

Fig. 1—A fulacht fiadh in the townland of Cappanaparka, Adrigole, west Cork (courtesy of Niamh O'Donoghue).

Ancient cooking places

*F*ulachta fiadh or burnt mounds survive as low-lying man-made mounds of charcoal-enriched soil and heat-shattered stones, some of which are easily broken by hand. Classic examples of these mounds are typically crescent or horseshoe shaped, sometimes over 1m in height and ranging up to 30m in diameter. Other examples are circular, oval or D shaped, possibly as a result of weathering and erosion. They are normally grass covered. In ploughed fields *fulachta fiadh* show up as noticeable black spreads in the otherwise brown soil, often in an area that is wet and marshy or beside a stream/streamlet.

Structural features

Large numbers of *fulachta fiadh* have been excavated in recent years by archaeologists working on various motorway projects. In addition to the mound of discarded stones, some other core features identified many years ago by the late Michael J. O'Kelly tend to recur. The first of these is a pit at the 'centre' of the crescent-shaped mound. The pit is lined with wooden planks (occasionally the remains of a dugout canoe) or stone slabs, forming a trough up to 2m long and 1m wide and deep. One of the best preserved of these troughs consisted of two to three individual pieces of timber hollowed out from a single oak trunk. Its capacity was *c*. 264 litres (58 gallons) of water. Other recurring features are: a hearth in which the stones were heated before being lowered into the trough of water; arrangements of post-holes, possibly

Fig. 2—Sketch showing a typical view of a reasonably intact fulacht fiadh. *The mound forms a penannular ring around the location of the water-trough. Notice the stream in the foreground and the wetland plants in the centre of the monument (drawing by Margaret Kennedy).*

the remains of huts or other shelters; and an adjacent water source, usually a small stream, the course of which is sometimes lost in marshy ground.

Function and usage

It is assumed that the trough was filled with water, possibly by diverting the stream along a small artificial canal, and that the heated stones were then added until the required temperature was reached. Experiments suggest that the trough of water can be brought to the boil very quickly and that a joint of meat, wrapped in straw, can then be cooked following the normal formula used today (20 minutes per pound, followed by a final 20 minutes). Afterwards, the remnants of the heat-shattered stones would have been removed, and the characteristic horseshoe-shaped mound is interpreted as the result of the repeated dumping of these discarded stones from the trough.

The assumption that the *fulacht fiadh* was designed to cook meat does not emerge directly from the archaeological evidence. On the contrary, the expected discarded animal bones are rarely found at these sites and finds of any type are sporadic, apart from the features described above. It is from literary sources and folklore that the notion of cooking arises. The word *fulacht* may originally have meant 'recess' or 'cavity', extended in this case to 'pit' and subsequently 'cooking-pit'. The second element might be *fiadh* ('of the deer' or 'of the wild') or *fion* (related to a roving band of hunters or warriors, or even the Fianna of legend or Fionn MacCumhail himself). In the background is the heroic world of legend, where Fionn and his band lived a healthy outdoor life, roving freely through the countryside, hunting deer for sustenance and eating communally. The so-called *fulachta fiadh* were seen as the physical remains of such communal feasting. However, apart from notable exceptions such as the *fulacht fiadh* at Fahee South in the Burren, discarded animal bones showing possible butchering marks are not found as a matter of course at these sites. Accordingly, archaeologists have considered other possibilities requiring considerable amounts of heated water, such as textile-processing, clothes-dyeing, leather-working and brewing, or activities involving bathing, saunas and sweat-houses. In order to put some distance between the accumulating archaeological evidence and the traditional assumptions, some archaeologists avoid the term '*fulacht fiadh*' in favour of the more neutral 'burnt mound'.

One of the intriguing aspects of these monuments is the profusion in which they occur at specific sites. Archaeologists on motorway projects have sometimes found themselves excavating considerable numbers of *fulachta fiadh* within an area of no more than a hectare or two. In some cases the mounds crowd along both sides of a stream over a considerable distance. It is doubtful whether occasional or seasonal usage could lead to such intense clustering. The occurrence of hut sites adjacent to complexes of *fulachta fiadh* may also point to a more prolonged use of individual sites. Such huts might have served as meat stores, temporary shelters, sleeping-huts, private ritual spaces or even as permanent domestic structures, depending on the activity taking place at the site.

To summarise, it is generally accepted that *fulachta fiadh* reflect communal activity of an industrial or ritual nature. The scarcity of finds and the occasional reuse of boat fragments as troughs has been taken as a possible indicator in favour of some long-forgotten ritual activity. This is supported by the location near water, an element to which spiritual significance has been assigned in many places through the ages. The mixing of two symbolically powerful elements, fire and water, might have been seen to be especially meaningful.

Fig. 3—A fulacht fiadh in marginal land between the sloped hillside to the left and the marshy floor of the valley to the right. The figure wearing a striped top stands at the centre of the monument and the other figure is standing on the mound. The course of a stream passes the large rocks immediately beyond the mound (photo: Niamh O'Donoghue).

Distribution

Fulachta fiadh are estimated to be the most common prehistoric monuments in Ireland, a significant claim considering the large numbers of ringforts, ring-barrows and ring-ditches that are known. By the mid-1980s, over 4,000 burnt mounds had been recorded. Since then, large numbers have continued to emerge annually and it is likely that the majority of sites remain undetected. The geographical distribution as currently known is very uneven. The most intense concentrations are known in County Cork (2,000+), while large numbers are also known from Counties Clare (400+), Kilkenny (250+), Mayo and Waterford. Motorway excavations, notably along the N11 in County Wicklow, have revealed considerable numbers of these monuments during the past decade.

In some counties, such as Kerry, the number of recorded sites is comparatively low. Within individual counties, too, there is variation. In County Cork, for instance, they are preferentially concentrated in the east Muskerry and Duhallow areas. Similarly, in County Kilkenny clusters of *fulachta fiadh* appear to be concentrated in the north-west and south of the county. Whether this uneven distribution is due partly to variations in fieldwork coverage is an issue that cannot be dismissed. Geographically, however, it is a feature of the monument type that it tends to occur close to streams or streamlets, often in isolated pockets of marginal, wet and marshy land. Particular parts of the landscape may have been especially conducive to the construction and use of *fulachta fiadh*. If you have a copy of the Discovery map for your area, you will be able to check whether any *fulachta fiadh* have been noted in the locality. Likewise, the County Archaeological Inventory for

Fig. 4—A rare example of an artefact from a fulacht fiadh. This carved stone bowl was recovered from the surface of a ploughed site east of Slievenamon in south County Tipperary. The farmer noticed it in the freshly ploughed soil (photo: Muiris Ó Súilleabháin).

your county or area, if it has been published, may contain descriptions of known *fulachta fiadh* in your area.

When were they constructed?

Scientific dating of excavated sites indicates that the overwhelming majority were in use during the Bronze Age, concentrating in the period 1800–800 BC, although some have produced even earlier dates while others appear to be later. In general, science does not support the idea that these monuments might be the physical evidence of a heroic proto-historic era, the mythical world of the traditional legends.

Diagnostic features

- Low-lying mound, up to 1m or more in height and generally not more than 30m in diameter, typically crescent or horseshoe shaped but sometimes circular, oval or D shaped.
- Beneath the sod, the mound comprises charcoal-enriched soil and heat-shattered stones, some of which may be easily broken by hand. Other subsurface features may include the trough, hearth and possibly some post-holes.
- Often found in a wet, marshy part of a field, or beside a stream, streamlet or even a lake.
- In ploughed ground, the site may show as a very dark patch, with lots of charcoal and burnt stones.

Further information

Ó Drisceoil, D. 1988 Burnt mounds: cooking or bathing? *Antiquity* **62**, 671–80.
O'Kelly, M.J. 1954 Excavations and experiments in ancient Irish cooking-places. *Journal of the Royal Society of Antiquaries of Ireland* **84**, 105–55.
Waddell, J. 1998 *The prehistoric archaeology of Ireland*, pp 174–8. Galway.

This article was originally published in the Spring 2004 issue of Archaeology Ireland.

Grinding grain

Quern stones were used for grinding grain. Saddle querns, the earliest form, appeared during the Neolithic period and seem to have been in use mainly during the Bronze Age. Their use declined during the Iron Age as they were progressively replaced by rotary querns. This change represented a striking technological advance in the processing of cereals.

The rotating motion of beehive querns, the earliest form of rotary quern in Ireland, required less physical effort in grinding than the back-and-forth motion of saddle querns. Beehive querns date from the Iron Age and are mainly associated with the northern half of the country. Over time in the early centuries AD they gave way to disc querns, which were to survive in use until the twentieth century.

Disc querns were extensively used in Ireland throughout the past 2,000 years and are the form of quern to be found extensively in ringforts and crannogs of the early medieval period. Pot querns may have been introduced into Ireland in the Norman period. They were used not only for grinding grain but also for refining flour and for grinding seeds, herbs, spices etc.

Querns used in more recent times could be adjusted to produce different grades of flour by placing leather washers around their spindles. They were also used extensively to grind malt for *poitín*-making.

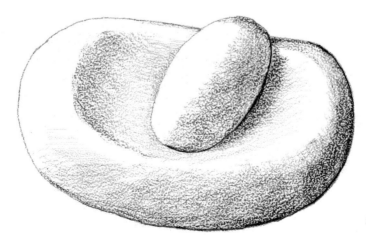

*Sketch of a saddle quern
(detail from Fig. 1).*

Quern stones

Prior to the emergence of advanced industrial technology in modern times, cereal-processing relied heavily on the use of querns or mills, both using stone as the grinding agent. The original grinding implement was the saddle quern, but for much of the past 2,000 years various improved technologies have been in use, as outlined below. Querns were worked manually by individuals, so the surviving stones are naturally smaller in scale, whereas mills utilised heavier stones and were driven by water or other means. A quern or mill invariably consisted of two stones and, even today, examples can be seen in rural areas, frequently as garden ornaments. Leaving mills to one side for another occasion, the four main categories of querns found in Ireland are **saddle, beehive, disc and pot querns** (Fig. 1).

A synoptic overview of the four quern categories is presented in Table 1, including their structure/characteristic features, dimensions, constituent types, main periods of use, geographical distribution and usual find sites. The reciprocal motion of the saddle quern distinguishes it from the other three, which employ the more advanced mechanical principle of continuous rotary motion and hence are generically termed rotary querns.

In an in-depth and comprehensive study of rotary querns completed in 1966, Caulfield examined, measured, classified and catalogued over 500 quern stones; he also detailed the decorations, in particular the crosses, found on a number of them. This article draws extensively on the invaluable information provided by Caulfield's study, which also describes a specific type of disc quern characterised by a knob on one side, by which the upper stone is rotated, and hence termed a 'knobber quern'. The number of such querns is very small and their use in Ireland seems to be limited, both geographically and chronologically.

As evidenced by the large number of querns found in the course of the Harvard excavations at Lagore (43), Cahercommaun (35), Ballinderry 1 (7) and Ballinderry 2 (10), as well as other excavations, many of which were not preserved, Caulfield reckoned that the total number of querns could well have exceeded 1,000. That was 40 years ago. In view of the exponential growth in excavations, especially in the past decade, early attention needs to be given to developing an up-to-date catalogue of querns found in Ireland. It would also be interesting to know whether the chronological, spatial and general contextual framework summarised here requires any adjustments in the light of subsequent discoveries.

Parameters	Saddle querns	Beehive querns	Disc querns	Pot querns
Structure/ characteristic features	Bed stone— large Rubber stone D shaped/egg shaped	Dome-shaped upper stone Funnel-shaped hopper with narrow feed pipe	Two flat disc-shaped stones Upper stone with central narrow per-foration and handle hole(s)	Pot-shaped lower stone
Dimensions: upper stones (general range)	–	Diameter 28–36cm Thickness 9–19cm	Diameter 30–60cm Thickness 5–10cm	Large-diameter stones, 50–60cm Small-diameter stones, 15–25cm
Main quern types	Ovoid Elongated	Handle holes Horizontal slotted Upright rounded	A, D, C	Large flat-bottomed Small mortar type
Main period of use	Late Bronze Age (also Neolithic and early Bronze Age)	Iron Age (from second century BC and not beyond fourth century AD)	A: first millennium AD D: AD 500–1000 C: second millennium AD	Post-Norman period Up to recent decades
Geographical distribution of finds	South-east: highest density North: sizeable number	North of Dublin to Galway line	Widespread	–
Usual find sites	Crannogs Houses and burial sites	Bogs (not found on habitation sites)	Ringforts Crannogs	–

Table 1 — Synoptic overview of querns

Saddle querns

Saddle querns are usually quite large, comprising an upper stone, termed the 'rubber stone', and a lower stone, termed the 'bed stone'. The shape of the bed stone was seen in the nineteenth century as resembling a saddle and the use of the term today applies specifically to the bed stone (Fig. 2).

The bed stone is usually wide enough to contain the rubber and of sufficient length to allow the rubber to be drawn to and fro on its surface, which was deliberately prepared so as to facilitate the grinding process. While saddle querns seem to have been introduced into Ireland in Neolithic times, they were, as outlined below, mainly used in the late Bronze Age.

A variety of other names have been used to describe saddle querns, including 'oblong querns', 'grain grinders', 'corn crushers', 'grain rubbers' and 'mealing stones'.

Types of saddle querns

As further detailed in Connolly's (1994) comprehensive review of saddle querns in Ireland, two broad forms have been identified, namely ovoid and elongated querns. The ovoid saddle querns have been further differentiated into oval and pear-shaped types, and the elongated form into trapezoidal and subrectangular querns. In terms of functionality, the grinding area of the stone is of more significance than its actual shape. As the active component of saddle querns, however, the rubber stone is of paramount importance. Two main types have been identified. The most common is the plano-convex stone, which in cross-section is D shaped, with a smooth grinding area (which may be somewhat convex) and a rounded top. The other type is egg or ovoid shaped, without any pronounced flat areas.

The motion by which the rubber stone was applied to the bed stone during the grinding process is uncertain, especially in view of the different shapes of the rubber stone. A rocking and grinding motion has been suggested, whereby the dried grain was simultaneously crushed and ground (Connolly 1994). A convex rounded rubber stone used in conjunction with a concave grinding area appears to be most effective. However, a flat or slightly convex

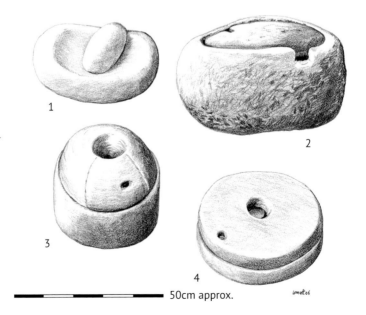

Fig. 1—Types of querns discussed here: (1) saddle quern, (2) pot quern, (3) beehive quern, and (4) disc quern.

1

2

3

4

50cm approx.

rubber stone would be more effective with querns that were not, or were only slightly, concave.

Connolly catalogued 228 saddle querns (186 of which were provenanced) and 65 rubber stones, and drew attention to a further 20 finds. The two stones are seldom found together—only three of the saddle querns were found with rubber stones. Recent excavations have produced a number of saddle querns or quern fragments additional to those catalogued by Connolly. In total, several hundred saddle querns have been found in Ireland. While local resources were exploited in the production of the querns, certain stone types were preferred. In Ireland granite and sandstone appear to have been the most widely used. Some of the northern querns were made from dolerite or basalt. A quern from County Clare was made from limestone.

Main period of use

The earliest evidence for the use of saddle querns in Ireland comes from the Neolithic period. Excavation records show a greater incidence of saddle querns on sites datable to the Bronze Age, and they occur more frequently on late Bronze Age sites than on early Bronze Age sites. Their use seems to have declined during the Iron Age, when they appear to have been progressively replaced by the rotary quern, which was a major technological innovation in the processing of cereals, as outlined below.

Distribution

The highest incidence of saddle querns recorded in the 1990s was in the eastern half of the country, with pockets of high density in Carlow, Wicklow and south Kildare, and in Westmeath, Offaly, Laois and Meath. A sizeable number of saddle querns were also recorded in the northern counties, as well as in coastal locations north of a line from Dublin to Limerick (Connolly 1994). Conversely, there has been a distinct lack of saddle-quern finds in the south-west and also in the west, apart from some coastal locations. The geographical distribution of finds of saddle querns is markedly different from that of beehive querns.

Location

Saddle querns occur on a variety of sites, such as crannogs, house sites and burial sites.

Beehive querns

As indicated by their name, beehive querns have dome-shaped upper stones. They are also characterised by a central funnel-shaped hopper with a narrow feed pipe. Grain was poured into the hopper and percolated gradually down the feed pipe onto the grinding surface of the bottom stone. The rotary motion of the upper stone, in use, was easy to maintain and involved less physical strain than the back-and-forward rolling of the rubber stone on the saddle quern. A further benefit was that no downward pressure was needed.

As detailed further below, beehive querns were in use in Ireland during the Iron Age.

Caulfield (1977) has catalogued 215 beehive quern stones found in Ireland but noted that the total number is likely to be appreciably higher. With some exceptions, the diameters of beehive querns generally range between 28cm and 36cm, and the thickness usually falls within the range of 9–19cm. They are relatively heavy objects, generally weighing over 20–40kg. The feed pipe is usually 2–3cm wide. The relatively narrow feed pipe, combined with the weight of the upper stone, points to the use of narrow iron spindles around which the upper quern stone was rotated. Also, to provide the necessary purchase, metal rather than wooden handles may have been used. Beehive querns have two main types of handle holes: horizontal slotted holes and upright rounded holes.

Main period of use

Beehive querns are dated to the Iron Age (Caulfield 1977). They may have been in use for a considerable period, from the second century BC to the fourth century AD, giving way progressively to disc querns.

Distribution

Beehive querns are predominantly found in the area north of a line from Dublin to Galway. The coincidence of their geographical distribution with that of the La Tène metalwork tradition points to a cultural association between these two most common classes of Iron Age artefacts (Caulfield 1977). More recent studies in this regard (Warner 2002) suggest that the La Tène metalwork may have been associated with the wealthy rancher-warriors and the beehive querns with the poorer corn-growers.

Location

The provenance of half of the beehive querns catalogued by Caulfield is known. Contrary to what would be expected for such domestic artefacts, they are not found on habitation sites such as ringforts, hillforts or crannogs. Beehive querns are most commonly found in bogs, often under peat.

Disc querns

Disc querns consist of two flat disc-shaped stones, an upper stone with a central cylindrical perforation and handle hole(s) or depression and a lower stone with a central spindle hole. As detailed further below, disc querns were used over an extended time period of some 2,000 years, ranging from the early first millennium, and surviving in some places up to recent decades.

Dimensions

As shown by Caulfield, disc querns have defined diameter limits of some 30–60cm, with thicknesses generally ranging from some 5cm to 10cm. They have a high diameter/thickness ratio, generally greater than four to one.

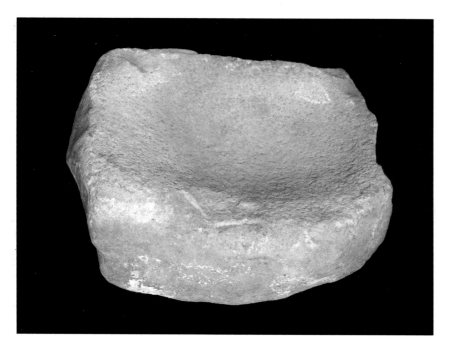

Fig. 2—Lower stone of a saddle quern, measuring 37.5cm in length, 33cm in width and 14cm in height.

With some exceptions, quern weights fall roughly within the region of 20–30kg. Stones that exceed 60cm in diameter were considered more likely to be millstones.

Quern types

Based on the arrangement of holes for the handles used to turn the upper stone, Caulfield differentiated disc querns into three types, each with different usage periods.

In the A-type querns (16%), the handle hole enters the upper surface of the stone at an angle and emerges at the edge of the stone. The C-type querns (65%) had a short handle set upright into a perforation in the upper stone, midway between the central perforation and the edge of the stone. The D-type (21%) are querns with a small depression in the upper stone into which was inserted a loose handle that revolved in the hand as the stone was turned.

Main periods of use

A-type querns are considered to have replaced saddle querns in the pre-Roman period and seem to have been widely used in Ireland during the first millennium AD. D-type querns are represented on a number of excavation sites in Ireland and seem to have been most widely used from AD 500 to 1500. C-type querns were rare in the first millennium in Ireland but are well represented in medieval contexts. They seem to have been widely used in the second millennium AD. This is reflected in the predominance of C-type querns in many collections.

Location
Disc querns have a widespread distribution in Ireland. In contrast to beehive querns, they are often found in habitation sites and seem to be the dominant form found in ringforts and crannogs.

Pot querns
These querns derive their name from the characteristic pot-shaped lower stone, which has a cylindrical hollow inside which the upper stone was revolved.

Quern types
Two types of pot querns have been described by Kelly (1984). The larger type are flat-bottomed querns, the upper stones of which range in diameter from 50cm to 60cm. The smaller pot querns have upper stones ranging in size from 15cm to 25cm. While some of these have square, flat-bottomed lower stones, most are circular and are supported on three short legs.

The two types of pot querns may have had different functions (Kelly 1984). The larger querns were suitable for grinding grain. It has been suggested that two operators facing each other were deployed in operating the pot querns. The smaller querns may have been used to refine flour, or perhaps as mortars for grinding seeds, herbs, spices etc.

Main period of use
Pot querns were used in Britain in the Middle Ages and may have been introduced into Ireland in the Norman period. They continued in use up until recent decades.

Modern querns
Querns used in Ireland in the recent past had a bridge of wood or iron fitted to the underside of the upper stone across its central perforation to accommodate the spindle, around which the upper stone could revolve. The spindles were upright pieces of iron or wood, which respectively were either fitted directly into the hole in the bottom stone or set in a peg of wood wedged into the hole. Iron spindles were fitted into an opening in the bridge and served to keep the revolving upper stone central. Wooden spindles were fitted into a socket in the underside of the bridge. The weight of the upper stone rested directly on the spindle upon which it revolved.

The upper stone of the querns used in Ireland in the recent past was turned by means of a fixed handle inserted in a hole in the stone. To produce different grades of flour, leather washers were inserted around the spindle so as to lighten the weight of the upper stone on the lower. In some instances, bridges of varying shoulder thickness were used to raise and lower the upper stone so as to produce either coarse or fine flour.

Before being ground, the grain had to be dried and hardened by semi-roasting at the fire. The hardened grain was fed in pinches almost continually into the central hole in the quern. If the hole was filled with grain, it emerged unground at the edge. A clean white sheet was placed on the floor and the quern was either placed directly on top of the sheet or on a form placed on the sheet, with a vessel containing the grain on a stool beside the workers.

In addition to the production of flour, querns were extensively used in the recent past to grind malt barley for *poitín*-making, which was a sizeable component of the economy of many rural areas. Indeed, the decline in the use of querns in rural Ireland has been attributed to the availability of treacle, which eliminated the necessity for grinding malt barley, rather than to the availability of milled flour.

References

Caulfield, J.J. 1966 The rotary quern in Ireland. Unpublished MA thesis, University College Dublin.

Caulfield, S. 1977 The beehive quern in Ireland. *Journal of the Royal Society of Antiquaries of Ireland* **107**, 104–38.

Connolly, A. 1994 Saddle querns in Ireland. *Ulster Journal of Archaeology* **57**, 26–36.

Kelly, E.P. 1984 Two quernstones from Co. Meath. *Ríocht na Mide* **7** (3), 103–11.

Warner, R. 2002 Beehive querns and Irish 'La Tène' artefacts: a statistical test of their cultural relatedness. *Journal of Irish Archaeology* **11**, 125–30.

This article was originally published in the Summer 2006 issue of Archaeology Ireland.

Drying grain in days of old

Corn-drying kilns were used mostly to dry grain in order to reduce its moisture content prior to storage or grinding. They were also used for other crops that had to be dried during processing, notably flax.

The basic kiln, which was inserted in the ground, comprised four main structural components, namely a **bowl**, **flue**, **stoke-hole** and **drying platform**. It functioned somewhat like a large tobacco-pipe. The majority of corn-drying kilns have been dated to between the fourth and thirteenth centuries AD, with a large number of figure-of-eight kilns giving way to a more effective and larger keyhole design, which was required to dry larger quantities of grain. Drying and hardening grain in corn-drying kilns was a prelude to grinding in watermills.

Fig. 1—The kiln at Haynestown, Co. Louth. The stoke-hole (with large boulder) is located in the centre of the photograph; the covered flue runs uphill from there to the drying chamber; and a ditch runs out of the stoke-hole in the lower right corner.

Corn-drying kilns

Corn-drying kilns were a key element of Irish agriculture for at least a thousand years. They are mentioned in early texts, medieval examples have been excavated along motorway routes, and identifiable kilns have survived in certain parts of the countryside to the present day.

These kilns were used for a number of purposes, mostly related to the drying of cereals and other crops. In Ireland, the two basic purposes for which they were constructed seem to have been to dry grain and to harden it prior to grinding. Up to the mid-1800s virtually every townland seems to have had a drying kiln. The emergence of drying kilns in Ireland stretches back to early historical times, but the essential technology changed little from one century to another, at least until the advent of mechanised systems in modern times.

Structural components

As illustrated in Figs 1 and 2, the small corn-drying kilns found in the Irish countryside are in plan frequently keyhole or dumb-bell shaped. The basic kiln was inserted into the ground and comprised four main structural components, namely a bowl, a flue, a stoke-hole and a drying platform.

While kilns vary in size, the typical **bowl** is a curvilinear drystone-built chamber, with a typical diameter of some 1.5–2m. It is usually built of drystone walling and sometimes has a stone-built platform surrounding its top.

A long, straight **flue**, sometimes tapering, and defined also by drystone walling with a lintelled roof, extends out from the bottom of the bowl. The flues are of varying length, ranging from 1.8m in some cases to 3.6m in others, and both the width and height are in the region of 40cm. The longer flues tend to be about two and a half times the length of the base of the bowl. They are sometimes wider at the outer end than at the junction with the bowl, and often run slightly uphill to facilitate the flow of the draught.

A **stoke-hole** (either a natural depression or a cut feature), in which the fire was burned to effect the drying, occurs at the mouth of the flue. Kilns were often sited to take maximum advantage of the prevailing wind and were used mainly on days when the wind direction assisted the convection of air through the flue to the drying platform. A kiln functioned somewhat like a large tobacco-pipe.

The **drying platform**, overlying the bowl, typically consisted of heavy timber supports overlaid with wattles, carrying a layer of straw and/or straw mat, through which the heat was able to pass quite easily from below to the grain, which in more recent times was placed on a sheet of cloth lying on top of the straw. Some kilns are reported to have had conical or sometimes flat roofs. These were placed over the bowl when grain-drying had to be carried out in wet or damp conditions. The roof usually had a small door, which was located over the position of the flue, presumably to control the draught.

Corn-drying kilns were frequently built into banks or slopes for stability. In these cases, a large part of the structure was below the ground surface, with just the stone platform or a few courses of the wall of the bowl protruding above ground level. However, on flat ground, *built-up* kilns were erected, especially in situations where the land was shallow and where there were no steep slopes or hill banks into which the kilns could be excavated.

Drying process

Kilns were usually for communal use. They were presumably worked by the individual owners of the corn as and when the occasion demanded, and cooperatively when it was necessary to dry a large quantity of grain, such as for malting. In more recent times the fuel used seems to have been mainly turf, which was supplied by the owner(s) of the corn.

Well-lighted shovelfuls of red-hot turf embers were inserted into the flue and withdrawn when quenched. The suction inwards and upwards through the flue drew the heat into the bowl and up through the drying platform on which the corn was placed. An even, moderate heat over an extended period was required to dry the corn. This was a slow process and could take up to 24 hours. However, a new type of kiln, which dried a hundredweight of corn in one hour, came into use in the early 1800s. It required the corn to be burned more frequently.

The removal of the dried corn from a kiln in County Mayo is described as follows. 'When the malt was hardened sufficiently, a man went down into the kiln with a quilt and spread it all around the bottom of the kiln, and up along the sides, and the straw under the malt was then separated and the malt fell through it on to the quilt. The quilt was then tucked around the malt and lifted up and brought home to be ground.'

Because of the distance between the fire at the outer end of the flue and the drying platform over the top of the kiln, and also because peat, the commonly used fuel, burns with a fairly low flame and with a minimum of sparks, the risk of accidental burning was reduced (references in the annals point to the fire hazards associated with kilns). Only red peat embers, rather than fresh burning peat, were shovelled into the flue. Furthermore, a baffle stone placed at the bowl end of the flue would have prevented hot embers from being swept up the flue by the wind and coming too close to the drying platform. A baffle stone was still in place in a corn-drying kiln excavated near Castleisland, Co. Kerry, in 1991; examples are also known from a number of sites in Britain.

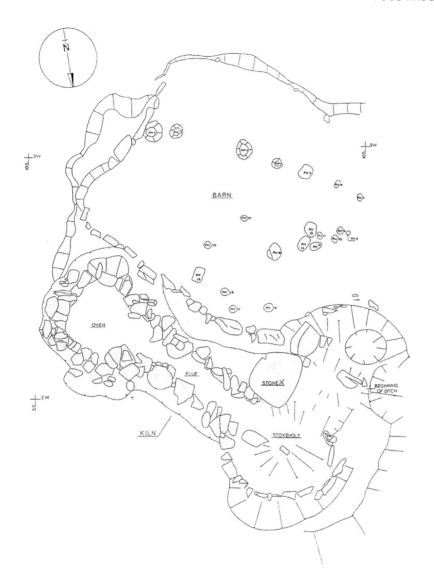

Fig. 2—Plan of a dumb-bell-shaped eleventh- or twelfth-century corn-drying kiln and associated barn, Haynestown, Co. Louth, excavated in 1993.

Geographical location

The distribution pattern of corn-drying kilns revealed by the 1830s Ordnance Survey maps is predominantly one of survival in the north-west and west. This may be a reflection of the fact that the rural economy of which the corn-drying kiln was an integral part survived longest in the northern and western parts of Ireland. The small number found outside these areas may be due to the earlier loss of the socio-economic system to which they belonged.

Time-span

In Britain corn-drying kilns seem to have been part of the rural economy since Roman times, and examples of a general keyhole shape have been dated to between approximately AD 900 and 1600.

Few Irish corn-drying kilns have been definitively dated. A keyhole-shaped kiln in the bank of a ringfort at Rathbeg, Co. Antrim, may have dated from the thirteenth or fourteenth century. A late thirteenth- or early fourteenth-century date is also suggested for the period of use of a keyhole-type kiln excavated in 1981/2 at Kilferagh, Co. Kilkenny (Fig. 1). A dumb-bell-shaped kiln (Fig. 2) and associated barn excavated in 1993 at Haynestown, Co. Louth, were constructed in the eleventh century. Various ditches, including one associated directly with the kiln, were cut into the hillside at this time. Two human burials found in one of the ditches appeared to date from this phase in the establishment of a medieval agricultural complex at Haynestown.

Corn-drying kilns similar to the later Irish types, and often excavated into a hillside, were in use in parts of Highland Scotland and the Hebrides in the twelfth century. The distinctive characteristic of this type of kiln is the long flue. Linguistic evidence points to the possibility that this type of kiln was known in both countries at about the same time. It has been suggested that corn-drying kilns of the late thirteenth or early fourteenth century may have represented a response to the climatic deterioration that took place in that period.

Corn-drying kilns were, of course, a feature of Irish agriculture in early Christian times and are referred to in early laws and the lives of the saints.

Wider uses

While the kilns in Ireland seem to have been constructed primarily for the drying and hardening of grain, they also fulfilled a number of other functions.

In Britain kilns were used to dry grain prior to threshing, following a damp harvest or a short growing season, and to reduce moisture levels in grains before storage. They also seem to have been used (i) to fumigate for insect infestation, such as grain weevil, (ii) to prepare seed grain for winter sowing, and (iii) to facilitate removal of the tight-fitting glumes of hulled wheat, particularly emmer and spelt. Kilns were also used for other crops that had to be dried during processing.

Flax kilns were used, in Tyrone for instance, to dry flax, which was extensively grown in the nineteenth century. Following retting, the flax had to be absolutely dry before scutching. Corn-drying kilns were also converted to lime kilns by disconnecting the flue and constructing a furnace box at the bottom of the corn bowl (for further details on lime kilns see the Summer 2005 issue of *Archaeology Ireland*). Such conversions—which seem to have been fairly widely carried out, for instance in north-west Donegal and south Tyrone, and presumably elsewhere—may explain the failure to find more of the old corn-drying kilns. However, another extensive use to which they were put, namely the illicit distillation of *poitín*, is said to be responsible for the survival of much knowledge about the construction, method of working and terminology of small corn-drying kilns.

Checklist of diagnostic features

- Long, straight, narrow, occasionally tapering flue, usually running slightly upslope and built of closely set walling, and often with considerable evidence of burning at the outer end.
- Bowl frequently built into a bank of sloping ground, with the curvilinear top protruding above ground, surrounded possibly by a stone platform.
- Sometimes found on flat ground as a built-up structure.
- Surviving examples predominantly found in the north-west and west of Ireland.

Acknowledgements

In preparing this article, extensive use was made of the sources listed below. The invaluable information provided by Dr M.F. Monk, Department of Archaeology, UCC, and M.F. Hurley, Archaeologist, Cork County Council, is gratefully acknowledged.

References

Byrne, M. 1991 A report on the excavation of a cashel at Ballyegan near Castleisland, Co. Kerry. *Journal of the Kerry Archaeological and Historical Society* **24**, 6–16.

Gailey, A. 1970 Irish corn drying kilns. *Ulster Folklife* **15/16**, 52–71.

Hurley, M.F. 1987 Kilferagh, Co. Kilkenny. In R.M. Cleary, M.F. Hurley and E.A. Twohig (eds), *Archaeological excavations on the Cork–Dublin gas pipeline (1981–82)*. Cork.

This article was originally published in the Autumn 2005 issue of Archaeology Ireland.

Watermills

Watermills were usually built on or adjacent to lesser streams that flow into larger rivers. Some mills were driven by tidal power. Two types of watermills predominated, namely those with horizontal millwheels, which were the majority, and those with vertical millwheels.

A notable feature of the dating profile of watermills is the prominence of construction dates in the period AD 700–1000. Indeed, almost half of the dated mills were constructed in the hundred years from AD 750 to 850, corresponding to the so-called 'Golden Age' of early Ireland. The later construction of watermills in the twelfth and thirteenth centuries has been attributed to the coming of the continental monastic orders and Anglo-Norman colonisation.

The range of early medieval watermills found in Ireland, notably the complex milling sites at Nendrum (Co. Down) and Little Island (Co. Cork) point to an arable farming base in Ireland that was well developed by the tenth century. This is further underlined by the comprehensive excavations recently undertaken at Raystown (Co. Meath).

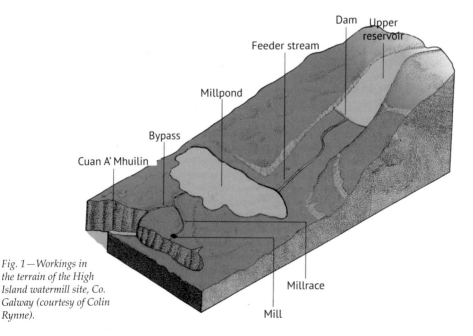

Fig. 1—Workings in the terrain of the High Island watermill site, Co. Galway (courtesy of Colin Rynne).

Energy from nature

Water-powered mills and their associated water-supply systems, comprising mill-dams, races and ponds, were among the most advanced technological developments of early medieval agriculture. While they greatly improved the grinding of grain, a large proportion of the meal and flour for domestic consumption continued to be produced by means of hand-operated rotary querns. This overview of watermills, combined with those on corn-drying kilns and quern stones published in the Autumn 2005 and Summer 2006 issues of *Archaeology Ireland* respectively, helps to provide an archaeological perspective on arable farming and grain-processing in ancient Ireland.

Construction

Watermills consisted of two main structural entities, namely the mill building and the water-supply system. Considerable expertise, including surveying skills, was required in the construction of the water-supply system, so as to ensure a steady flow from the millpond through the millrace to the millwheel.

The watermill on High Island (Fig. 1), off the coast of Galway, is the best-preserved early medieval mill site (Rynne *et al.* 1996). As illustrated in Fig. 1, its operation involved (i) an upper dam, which was the reservoir for the mill, (ii) a feeder stream leading downhill from the upper dam to (iii) the millpond, (iv) the millrace or headrace, which directed the water to the mill, (v) a bypass channel to divert excess water during periods of heavy rainfall, and (vi) the mill building.

Horizontal- and vertical-wheeled mills

As shown in Rynne's (1998) conjectural reconstructions (Fig. 2), two types of watermills were widely used, namely those with horizontal millwheels and those with vertical millwheels. The vast majority, including the one on High Island, were horizontal-wheeled mills, operated with a single water-delivery chute or flume. Some had two delivery chutes, however—for instance, the early medieval mills found at Little Island in Cork Harbour (Rynne 1992). The milling complex at Little Island used tidal power to drive a large double horizontal-wheeled mill and a small vertical-wheeled mill.

Number and location

The number of mill sites now known amounts to 97, of which the bulk are horizontal-wheeled mills (Brady 2006). Just nine vertical-wheeled watermills are known, but they appear to have become more numerous in the later Middle Ages. The early mills generally were not built on main river channels. While there are exceptions, most sites are located on or adjacent to lesser streams that flow into a larger river. Some mills, such as the milling complexes at Nendrum (Co. Down) and Little Island (Co. Cork), were driven by tidal power. Since such watermills were often situated in exposed locations, they required sturdy buildings and constant maintenance.

As further detailed by Brady (2006), the highest geographical concentrations of early medieval watermills are in the south and east of the country (Fig. 3). There are 27 sites in County Cork alone, where they tend to be situated along the main river valleys, aligned east–west, and also along the coast. There are more scientifically dated mill sites of the first millennium in the province of Munster than in the rest of Europe (Rynne 1998). The second concentration of early medieval watermills (Fig. 3) is in Leinster, along the River Nore—there are 12 sites in County Kilkenny. Most of the remaining mill sites are in the midland counties and in the north-east. Few mill sites have been found in the western half of the country, especially in those areas with poor soil and high rainfall. Brady (2006) notes that the concentration of watermills in the south and east of Ireland highlights the areas where arable farming and grain-processing were most intensive in the early medieval period. Cereal production was not limited to the south and east of the country, however, as evidenced by the wide geographical distribution of quernstones found on early medieval sites. Nonetheless, it may be noted that because of the drier and sunnier climate and more suitable soils, cereal production in Ireland is today largely confined to the south and east, including those areas with the highest concentration of early medieval watermills.

A high concentration of mills (135, mainly watermills) from the later medieval period (*c.* 1100–1650) has been identified within the Dublin region (Brady 2006). Their distribution follows centres of population and they are concentrated on the coastal areas, particularly to the north of the city, within the city itself, and along the Liffey and other main river valleys.

Dating profile

The early Irish law-tracts relating to watermills and watercourses are concerned with horizontal-wheeled mills. As already indicated, the bulk of the 97 surviving sites are horizontal-wheeled watermills. As Rynne has shown, however, both horizontal- and vertical-wheeled watermills were used in Ireland in the early medieval period.

Forty-three mill sites have been closely dated (Brady 2006) and, according to Rynne (1989), watermills are now the most accurately dated structures of early medieval Ireland. The chronological spread of dates ranges from the earliest site at Nendrum, Co. Down (AD 340–600), to the latest dated site at Patrick Street, Dublin (1243 ± 9). A noteworthy feature of the dating profile is the predominance of construction dates between AD 700 and 1000. Indeed, almost half (19) of the 43 dated mills were constructed in the hundred-year

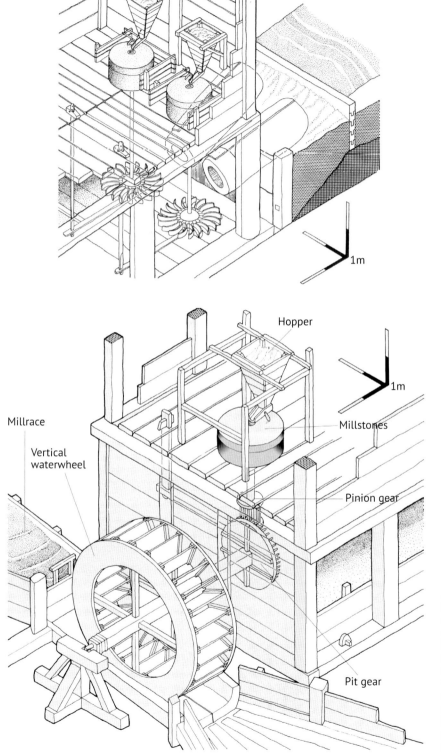

1m

1m

Hopper

Millstones

Millrace

Vertical
waterwheel

Pinion gear

Pit gear

*Fig. 2 —
Conjectural
reconstructions
of (top) the
horizontal-
wheeled
watermill and
(bottom) the
vertical-wheeled
watermill at
Little Island, Co.
Cork (courtesy of
Colin Rynne).*

period between 750 and 850, corresponding to the so-called 'Golden Age' of early Ireland. The twelfth- and thirteenth-century construction of watermills is attributed to the coming to Ireland of the continental monastic orders, followed by the Anglo-Norman colonisation (Brady 2006). While there are frequent references in the late medieval period to specific mills, relatively few sites dating from this time have been located. Both horizontal- and vertical-wheeled watermills continued to be used, however. The horizontal mill excavated by Rynne (1997) at Patrick Street in Dublin was extensively rebuilt in the later fourteenth century and continued in use until the early seventeenth century.

The range of early medieval watermills found in Ireland, and particularly the complex milling sites at Nendrum and Little Island, point to a well-developed arable farming base in Ireland by the tenth century. This is further underlined by the recent excavation conducted by Matthew Seaver at Raystown, Co. Meath, of what could perhaps be described as an industrial-scale agricultural development (Fig. 4), comprising the remains of six

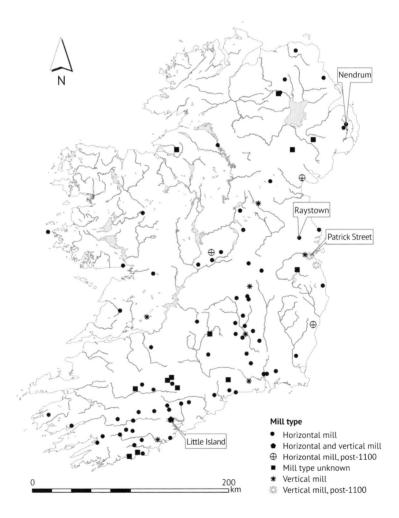

Fig. 3—The distribution of early medieval and other dated mills in Ireland (courtesy of Niall Brady).

Mill type

● Horizontal mill
⬟ Horizontal and vertical mill
⊕ Horizontal mill, post-1100
■ Mill type unknown
✳ Vertical mill
▒ Vertical mill, post-1100

0   200 km

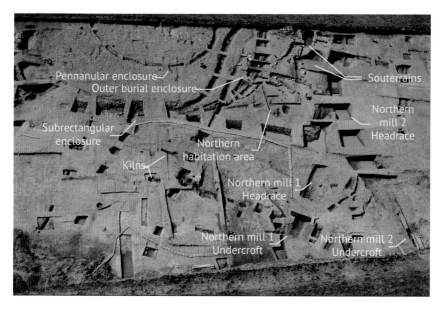

*Fig. 4—
Excavation at
Raystown, Co.
Meath, showing
the remains
of a series of
six horizontal
watermills
and associated
millraces, five
corn-drying
kilns, furnaces,
hearths and
multiple ditches,
as well as
burials (courtesy
of Matthew
Seaver).*

horizontal watermills, with finely engineered millraces, and five corn-drying kilns, along with bowl furnaces, hearths and multiple ditches, as well as burials.

Checklist of diagnostic features
- Usually only the basal workings of watermills survive, such as timberwork associated with troughs, sluices, dams, penstocks and occasionally the wheel-house. Sometimes the remains of water-supply systems are found, such as dams, feeder streams and millponds.
- The remains of watermills are mostly found at a remove from main river channels and are usually located on or adjacent to feeder streams or along intertidal foreshores. Early medieval mills are mainly concentrated in the south and east of the country.

Acknowledgements
This article draws extensively on the publications, listed below, by Dr Colin Rynne of the Department of Archaeology, UCC, and Dr Niall Brady of the Discovery Programme. Their permission, and also that of Matthew Seaver of CRDS Ltd, to use the illustrations contained in this article is much appreciated. Dr Niall Brady kindly made available to us a copy of a paper that was yet to be published.

References
Brady, N. 2006 Mills in medieval Ireland: looking beyond design. In S. Walton (ed.), *Wind and water, the medieval mill*. University Park, Pennsylvania.

Rynne, C. 1989 The introduction of the vertical watermill into Ireland: some recent archaeological evidence. *Medieval Archaeology* **33**, 21–31.

Rynne, C. 1992 Milling in the seventh century—Europe's earliest tide mills. *Archaeology Ireland* **6** (2), 22–4.

Rynne, C. 1997 The Patrick Street watermills. In C. Walsh (ed.), *Archaeological excavations at Patrick, Nicholas and Winetavern Streets, Dublin*. Dingle.

Rynne, C. 1998 The craft of the millwright in early medieval Munster. In M.A. Monk and J. Sheehan (eds), *Early medieval Munster: archaeology, history and society*. Cork.

Rynne, C., Rourke, G. and White-Marshall, J. 1996 An early medieval monastic watermill on High Island. *Archaeology Ireland* **10** (3), 24–7.

This article was originally published in the Autumn 2006 issue of Archaeology Ireland.

Windmills

Early windmills known as post mills were wooden buildings whose entire structure could be rotated to face their sails into the wind. Tower mills became relatively common the early decades of the seventeenth century AD. These were fixed masonry towers with a rotating cap section on top containing the sails and drive shaft. With the expansion of cereal production, large, powerful windmills became more prevalent from around AD 1770. The height of these technologically advanced mills allowed larger sails to be used to drive four sets of millstones at a time.

Major concentrations of windmills were erected in Counties Down and Wexford, which were important cereal-growing areas. Industrial-scale millstone-quarry sites have been recorded at Waterford Harbour, in the Mourne Mountains (Co. Down) and at Lough Eske (Co. Donegal).

The capless shells of former windmills are prominent hilltop features in some coastal areas and many are remembered in local placenames.

Fig. 1—Tacumshin windmill (Co. Wexford), built in the 1840s. Its thatched cap and tail-pole were formerly common features of Irish windmills (courtesy of Austin O'Sullivan).

Harnessing the wind

Windmills were apparently introduced into Ireland by the Anglo-Normans. Over the succeeding centuries they were used on a large scale to harness wind to grind corn, by means of millstones manufactured from stone specifically selected and fashioned for that purpose (Rynne 2006; Hamond 2011; Colfer 2015).

There was a substantial increase in the number of mills erected after 1770. While many fell into disuse over the following half-century, some 250 are shown on the first editions of the Ordnance Survey maps compiled between the 1830s and 1842. With the intensification of cereal cultivation between 1770 and 1815 windmills became prominent hilltop features, especially along the east coast, with notable concentrations in Counties Wexford and Down.

In essence, windmills comprised three principal functional components, namely the tower, sails and millstones, and, as outlined below, they underwent considerable developments in terms of their architecture and technology over the centuries.

Windmill types

The early windmills were known as **post mills** (Box 1). They comprised a wooden building supported by a vertical post around which the windmill was pivoted to face the sails into the prevailing wind. The entire structure could be rotated through 360 degrees by means of a tail-pole. This enabled the miller to adjust the position of the sails to accommodate changes in wind direction, by the expedient of rotating the mill building. The mill machinery was contained in a wooden framework. The entire structure was usually erected on high ground, often on a specially prepared mound adjacent to a township.

As observed by Rynne (2006), the earliest wind-powered mill in Ireland was at Kilscanlan, near Old Ross, Co. Wexford. It was at work in 1281 and is generally thought to have been a post mill, a number of which are known to have been in existence in the seventeenth century outside some of the walled towns. A number of possible later or earlier post-medieval windmill mounds have been identified in County Meath (Rynne 2006). Further to this, Rynne observed that post mills appear to have been no longer built in Ireland after the seventeenth century, and that there are no surviving examples of post mills in Ireland. Their former existence can, however, be confirmed from early maps.

> ### Box 1   Diagnostic features
>
> **Post mills**
> Wooden building supported on a vertical post, around which the structure could be rotated by means of a tail-pole to face the sails towards the wind.
>
> **Tower mills**
> Towers built before 1770 were typically cylindrical, three- or four-storey, masonry-built, fixed structures. A rotating cap section on the top contained the sails, which had the power to drive two pairs of millstones.
>
> **Large, powerful, cylindrical, tapered towers**
> These were equipped with sails with the capacity to drive four sets of millstones and with a staging built at the first-floor level to enable the miller to adjust the sails.
>
> **Ancillary buildings**
> These could include corn-drying kilns and storehouses, which were often erected nearby the windmill.
>
> Sources: O'Sullivan 1984; Hamond 2011; Rynne 2006; Colfer 2015

Tower mills became relatively common from the early decades of the seventeenth century in Ireland's main grain-producing counties on the eastern seaboard, and also began to appear in the midlands. They typically comprised a cylindrical masonry tower (Box 1). This was a fixed entity with a rotating cap section set on top, containing the sails and drive-shaft (Figs 1–4). A tail-pole connected to the cap enabled the miller to turn it, and thus the sails, into the prevailing wind.

The tower mills built before *c.* 1770 in Ireland tend to be cylindrical, three- or four-storey rubblestone structures, around 3–4m in internal diameter and about 6–7.5m high, with just enough power developed from the sails to drive two pairs of millstones (Rynne 2006). A good example of this type of mill at Elphin, Co. Roscommon, built about 1750, has been restored to working order. The remains of this type of mill generally survive in the landscape as a shell. Its gearing would have been of wood, and its moveable cap portion would have had a wooden roof covered with thatch.

As detailed below, the small tower mill at Tacumshin (Co. Wexford) (Fig. 1), with tail-pole and thatched cap, retains many of the features of early eighteenth-century examples, although it was built in 1848.

Large, powerful windmills (Figs 2–4), associated with the expansion in cereal production, were cylindrical, tapered towers (akin to a truncated cone), around 5–8m in diameter and about 10m high (Box 1). They became more common from around 1770. Towards the close of the Napoleonic Wars the cultivation of cereals in Ireland became a very profitable enterprise. To

Fig. 2 (left)— Guinness windmill, Thomas Street, Dublin (courtesy of Colin Rynne).

Fig. 3 (right)— Multi-storey tower windmill at Dundalk, Co. Louth (courtesy of Colin Rynne).

satisfy the emerging larger markets, the newer mills were architecturally and technologically more advanced. Many had four or five floors, and their increased height allowed larger sails to be used to drive four sets of millstones. As the sails no longer extended to the ground, a wooden staging was provided at first-floor level to enable the miller to adjust them.

As further detailed by Rynne (2006) and Hamond (2011), the well-known Guinness windmill (Fig. 2) on Thomas Street (Dublin) appears to have been built in the period 1790–1810. It is one of the tallest mills in Europe. The multi-storey tower windmill in Dundalk (Fig. 3) typifies the largely similar windmills built around the same time, including the restored examples at Blennerville (Co. Kerry) (Fig. 4) and Ballycopeland (Co. Down), built *c*. 1880.

Geographical distribution

As previously noted, some 250 windmills are recorded on the first editions of the Ordnance Survey maps compiled between the 1830s and 1842. The vast majority are clustered in notable concentrations in Counties Down and Wexford. Both counties were important cereal-producing areas, and wind speeds along the eastern coast favoured the construction of windmills.

Windmills were often used to supplement watermills, particularly on watercourses that tended to dry up during the summer months. Where practicable, however, water power, which could be stored in millponds and regulated by means of sluices or inlet control gates, was preferred to wind power (Rynne 2006). With windmills, the speed of the sails could be regulated by altering the area of the canvas spread.

The demand for milled cereals contracted at the end of the Napoleonic Wars in 1815, and many windmills had become disused by the early 1830s. In addition, the increasing concentration of mills in the ports to process imported grain in newly erected steam-powered mills accentuated the decline in smaller water- and wind-powered grain mills.

Functionality

A well-informed perspective on the mode of operation of earlier tower mills is provided in the detailed account of the windmill at Tacumshin, Co. Wexford (Fig. 1), published by O'Sullivan (1984). Although erected in the mid-nineteenth century (1846, carved on doorway lintel), it retains many of the key functional features of the earlier type of three-storey tower mills (Box 1).

Tacumshin was a tower mill comprising a fixed tower building containing the machinery; only the roof or cap could be turned to face the sails into the wind (O'Sullivan 1984). The revolving cap is straw thatched, with a weatherboarded dormer for the wind-shaft. Interestingly, virtually all the timber in the mill, and seemingly also much of that in other windmills of south Wexford, was driftwood or was obtained from shipwrecks occurring in the Carnsore area (*ibid.*). The ground floor is paved with limestone flags.

The roof or cap is a conical thatched framework of rafters and cross-battens. A large wooden tail-pole, extending from the back of the cap framework and linked to a large cartwheel running on the ground, functioned as a lever to turn the sails into the wind.

Tacumshin windmill has, as noted by O'Sullivan, two pairs of millstones of Leinster granite, each 4ft in diameter. They became thinner, lighter and more brittle as they wore; a set lasted about 30 years. One pair of millstones was dressed for grinding barley, beans and wheat, and the other for shelling and grinding oats. The former had radial hand-cut grooves, which were deepest at the centre of the stone and tapered off towards the edges. The whole surface of the latter pair was covered with small holes. The oats were run through twice, and then hand-winnowed on the ground floor to become groats.

When the mill was in use, full sacks were lifted by means of a hoist on the

Fig. 4 — Blennerville windmill near Tralee, Co. Kerry (courtesy of Colin Rynne).

top floor and emptied into hoppers over the millstones. The grain was then channelled through the stones and down into a receiving sack on the ground floor. The mill had a grain-drying kiln and grain storehouse nearby.

Millstone manufacture

The importance of mills in the broader economy of rural areas in the late medieval period is highlighted by the following indicators. Over 4,000 examples of mills have been noted on the Ordnance Survey maps of Ireland of the 1820s and 1840s (Hogg 2008). Further to this, Colfer (2015) has recorded over 50 quarries throughout the island (Box 2).

Box 2	Millstone quarries in post-medieval Ireland

This research represents the first detailed study of post-medieval millstone quarries in Ireland, locating them within a wider social, historical and European context. The transformation of natural stone into cultural artefacts as monolithic millstones was a decisive component in the local economy of regions with a suitable geology. Millstones were transported to areas where the indigenous bedrock was unsuitable for grinding cereals. Over 50 quarries have been recorded throughout the island of Ireland, which has enabled the identification of methods of millstone manufacture and transportation, along with a typology of both millstones and millstone quarries. Areas with both physical and historical evidence for industrial-scale millstone quarry sites include Waterford Harbour, the Mourne Mountains, Co. Down, and Lough Eske, Co. Donegal.

Sources: Niall Colfer, pers. comm.; Colfer 2015

Fig. 5—The cutting of a millstone 'rough-out' from granite bedrock, overlooking Newcastle, Co. Down (courtesy of Niall Colfer).

Niall Colfer's research on post-medieval millstone quarries in Ireland has provided a fuller appreciation of the importance of mills in the rural economy of previous centuries, as well as of the technological requirements of millstone manufacture (Box 2). Notable areas with both physical and historical evidence for industrial-scale millstone-quarry sites include Waterford Harbour (Fig. 5), the mountains of Mourne, Co. Down (Fig. 6), and Lough Eske, Co. Donegal.

The fashioning of natural stone into monolithic millstones was a skilful process. The rock types commonly employed in millstone manufacture included sandstone conglomerate, granite and quartzite bedrock (Colfer 2015). Colfer observed that the main feature common to all stone types is the presence of quartz. This would have provided a durable cutting edge for a face-grinder millstone used in the processing of cereals.

The stone selected for millstone manufacture was required to be hard and free of any flaws that would cause it to fracture when in use. In addition, it had to have the right texture to provide a cutting surface that would not become polished too quickly. The large quantities of broken and unfinished stones often found at millstone quarries (Figs 5 and 6) testify to the difficulty involved in sourcing a flawless piece of stone.

Time-span

As previously indicated, windmills appear to have been introduced into Ireland by the Anglo-Normans and reached their zenith in the post-industrial period. In the later 1800s working windmills would have been a rare sight (Rynne 2006; Hamond 2011; Colfer 2015). Capless shells of former windmills are still prominent hilltop features in certain coastal areas, although many are

Fig. 6 — A coastal millstone quarry at Waterford Harbour, showing several abutting and overlapping 'dishes' from where millstones have been removed (courtesy of Niall Colfer).

remembered only in placenames (Hamond 2011). Nevertheless, some wind-powered devices continued to be used for land drainage and for pumping well water to dwelling houses.

Acknowledgements

Niall Colfer kindly made available to us information from sections of his Ph.D thesis (funded by the Irish Research Council). The invaluable contributions on windmills received from Fred Hamond, Franc Myles, Austin O'Sullivan and Colin Rynne are much appreciated. Thanks are also due to Conor McDermott for drawing our attention to some recently excavated windmill sites.

References

Colfer, N. 2015 Turning stone into bread: millstone quarries in post-medieval Ireland. Unpublished Ph.D thesis, University College Dublin.

Hamond, F. 2011 Windmills. In F.H.A. Aalen, K. Whelan and M. Stout (eds), *Atlas of the Irish rural landscape*. Cork.

Hogg, W. 2008 *Mills of Ireland: a list dated about 1850*. Dublin.

O'Sullivan, A.M. 1984 Tacumshin windmill—its history and mode of operation. *Journal of the Wexford Historical Society* **9**, 66–73.

Rynne, C. (ed.) 2006 *Industrial Ireland, 1750–1930: an archaeology*. Cork.

This article was originally published in the Summer 2015 issue of Archaeology Ireland.

Section III
Settlement

I n modern Ireland, habitation refers to a spectrum of settlement types, from the single, isolated house in the countryside to large-scale urban sprawl in the cities. Such extremes did not occur in the primeval past, but there was variety then as now. In the Neolithic period, for example, there were isolated houses as well as small clusters of houses, but there may also have been less-sturdy tent-like structures, relatively easy to erect or demolish.

The constructions featured in this section represent an eclectic collection, ranging from settlement enclosures within which traces of houses have been found and primarily defensive enclosures in which domestic habitation might not have been the key concern, to strong tower-houses of the late medieval period and intriguing souterrains of the first millennium AD.

Hillforts are sprawling defended enclosures focused on the summits of hills. They could have been used for a variety of purposes, such as refuge, communal assembly and strategic control of territorial boundaries. They appear to date generally from the late Bronze Age, with suggestions of a beginning in the thirteenth century BC, but some may have been constructed in the Iron Age. It should also be noted that a small number of settlement enclosures on elevated sites are known from the Neolithic period. Smaller hilltop enclosures are also known, typically located at lower altitudes, the vast majority surrounded by a single, substantial rampart. The dating and function of these hilltop enclosures is mainly inferred from comparisons with hillforts or occasionally ringforts.

Better known is the **ringfort** (known variously as a rath, lios, cashel or even fairy fort), the classic domestic enclosure of early medieval times, beginning in the middle of the first millennium AD. Ringforts were enclosed settlements, mostly farmsteads, that flourished during the second half of the first millennium (mostly AD 600–900) and tapered off before the coming of the Anglo-Normans. Differences in the structural form of ringforts and aspects of their functional positioning in the landscape have been taken to reflect the hierarchical nature of settlement in the early medieval period, as well as their purpose for agricultural production or another gainful activity. In some areas, ringforts are located on top of knolls or small hillocks. This leads to confusion in the case of hilltop enclosures of smaller spatial extent, which may manifest aspects of both the hillfort and ringfort and may be difficult to categorise without archaeological excavation.

Souterrains are generally found in or adjacent to ringforts and other settlements of the same period. **Crannogs**, traditionally seen as island strongholds or defensive refuges, are now thought to have been used for a much wider range of activities by different social classes across various time phases from the late Bronze Age to the late medieval period. In many ways, **church sites** of the period mirrored their secular equivalents and engaged in many of the same food-producing practices.

Mottes were the predominant location of early tower-like castles in Anglo-Norman Ireland, and the centres of manorial demesne farms. **Moated sites** are generally considered to have been the protected farmsteads of the Anglo-Normans, although some may have been constructed for other purposes, and are amongst the most numerous surviving earthworks from the high medieval period. It was in the century following the Anglo-Norman invasion that most of the towns in Ireland emerged. They typically emerged around a juxtaposition of castle and church and can be seen in their most original form in the archaeology of **deserted medieval towns**.

Tower-houses, often found standing in isolation as ivy-clad ruins occasionally enclosed by a bawn, are the most visible secular medieval buildings in the modern landscape. The term **clachan** refers to a compact cluster of houses without urban elements such as churches, shops, pubs or schools. Dating predominantly from post-medieval times, clachans are located along country roads or down narrow by-roads and laneways and are usually associated with rundale farming, although they also exist independently. Many of these settlements were decimated by the effects of the Famine, but their remains are still to be seen in certain rural areas today. They are occasionally still inhabited, although reduced to a handful of houses at most.

Hillforts

Hillforts were largely defended enclosures located strategically to overlook the adjoining landscape. Those built on accessible sites may have been focal settings where ceremonial business and other communal activities were undertaken, involving periodic occupation for these events. They may also have been places of refuge in times of danger. High-altitude hillforts with panoramic fields of vision overlooking well-defined historic routeways could possibly have played a role in the strategic control of territorial boundaries.

The construction of large hillforts occupying defensive locations may have developed in the late Bronze Age with the emergence of powerful local individuals and tribal formations. While hillforts appear to date generally from the late Bronze Age, some may belong to the Iron Age.

Smaller hilltop enclosures are also known. They are typically less than a hectare in area and marked by impressive defences, usually a single surrounding bank. Located on relatively low but prominent hills or knolls, these may have substantial ramparts and may have been used as high-status residential centres. Their relationship with hillforts on the one hand and ringforts on the other is ambiguous and remains to be more fully clarified. Radiocarbon dates from the ditch of the substantial enclosure at Clenagh, Co. Clare indicate that the site was abandoned during the Iron Age.

Fig. 1—Trivallate hillfort, Mooghaun, Co. Clare (photo: Con Brogan, National Monuments Service, Department of Arts, Heritage and the Gaeltacht).

Hilltop enclosures

Fortified enclosures, built in elevated positions, appear to have become more prevalent in the late Bronze Age. Hillforts, the primary focus of this article, were typically large enclosures surrounded by substantial ramparts, and deliberately sited in generally strategic positions overlooking the local landscape (Box 1). Hilltop enclosures are, as outlined below, distinguished from hillforts by their comparatively smaller size and are usually located on significantly lower eminences.

Functions

Hillforts were defended enclosures, built of earth, timber or stone, with paramount importance being attached in their construction to the choice of an easily defended position and to the scale and deposition of the ramparts (Raftery 1994). Outside of Ireland, hillforts were often occupied on a permanent or semi-permanent basis by a substantial number of people, and in certain areas they approached the status of towns.

As outlined below, various different functions have been ascribed to hillforts in Ireland (Grogan 2005). Not all such enclosures may have served the same purpose, however.

House sites have been identified in a number of hillforts, such as Mooghaun, Co. Clare (Fig. 1), or immediately outside the defences. The limited excavation information for hillforts in Ireland suggests that many were occupied but that the scale of occupation was limited to a few families, too few for hillforts to be seen as conventional defended settlements (Grogan 2005).

Accessibility was probably an important determinant of the primary purpose of different hillforts. High-altitude hillforts on exposed mountains, as opposed to hilltops, are unlikely to have been used for everyday domestic settlement. The majority of hillforts have panoramic fields of vision over parts of the surrounding landscape. Some high-altitude sites occur along well-defined prehistoric routeways and may, as further detailed by Grogan, have been used for the strategic control of territorial boundaries. For instance, the impressive group of large, closely spaced hillforts around Baltinglass (Co. Wicklow) may be indicative of their siting in relation to neighbouring territories and potential confrontations. The strategic control of routeways does not, however, fully accord with the relatively large size (below) of an appreciable number of high-altitude hillforts. It is difficult to envisage why such large defended enclosures would have been required for lookout posts that were perhaps occasionally occupied by small groups of defenders engaged in territorial control.

Some hillforts, in particular the more accessible sites, may have been constructed as places of short-term refuge in times of danger for the communities who built them. Certain hillforts may have been focal points within tribal areas, built for communal gatherings where at certain times of the year important functions were carried out, such as ceremonial, business and commercial activities, perhaps involving periodic occupation.

The construction of large hillforts occupying defensive locations may reflect fundamental social changes arising in the late Bronze Age, when society seemingly became more hierarchical, leading to the emergence of powerful local individuals and tribal formation (Waddell 1998). It may not be a coincidence that hillforts began to emerge towards the end of the second millennium BC, a period when seismic changes were occurring further afield, notably in the Mediterranean region, and there was a proliferation of bronze weaponry in Ireland, including the first appearance of swords.

Excavation at Clashanimud hillfort (Figs 2 and 3) in Innishannon parish, north of Bandon (Co. Cork), revealed important evidence of the conflicts that appeared to have arisen among regional powers in the early stages of the late Bronze Age (O'Brien 2012). Shortly after the hillfort was built (around 1100 BC), its palisaded bank-and-ditch defences were deliberately destroyed by fire, possibly in the course of a direct attack or battle in the vicinity. The hillfort was not rebuilt or occupied in the Bronze Age, nor was it used in later periods.

Fig. 2—Aerial view of Clashanimud hillfort, in the parish of Innishannon, north of Bandon, Co. Cork (courtesy of W. O'Brien).

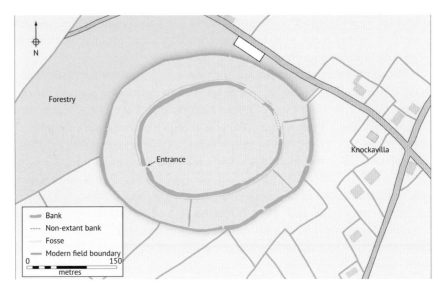

Fig. 3—Plan of Clashanimud hillfort, Co. Cork (courtesy of W. O'Brien).

Typology

Irish hillforts vary considerably in size, ranging from a small number less than 1ha in area to several enclosing more than 10ha (Grogan 2005). Some 70% are up to 5ha in area, with a further 18% between 5ha and 10ha, and some appreciably larger in size—notably the exceptionally large complex at Spinan's Hill, Co. Wicklow, which covers over 130ha.

Hillforts in Ireland have been differentiated into three classes, based on the number of defensive ramparts and site location (Raftery 1994; Waddell 1998; Grogan 2005).

Class 1 are univallate hillforts with a single line of defence (Fig. 4). They are a common type, representing almost two thirds of hillforts. They are usually less than 3.5ha in extent, but some are much larger. One of the largest known is Knocknashee, near Ballymote (Co. Sligo), where the remains of a rampart enclose an entire hilltop in an area of some 22ha (Waddell 1998).

Class 2 are multivallate hillforts, usually with two or three surrounding ramparts, which may be closely or widely spaced (Fig. 5). They are generally larger than those defended by a single rampart. The impressive Clashanimud hillfort recently excavated by O'Brien (2012) extends over an area of 8.9ha, with two concentric and widely spaced enclosures (Figs 2 and 3). The defences of the inner enclosure included an external ditch and an inner bank, topped with a palisade of oak timbers. Several thousand oak posts would have been used in the construction of the timber palisade. Mooghaun, Co. Clare (Fig. 1), is one of the largest known multivallate hillforts, with its three stone ramparts encompassing almost 12ha (Waddell 1998).

Class 3 hillforts are inland promontory forts, fewer than a dozen of which have been recorded. The variation in size and defensive construction is considerable, from Lurigethan, Co. Antrim (13ha), to Castle Gale, Co. Limerick, with an enclosed area of only 1.4ha.

Fig. 4—
Univallate
hillfort,
Courthoyle
(photo: Con
Brogan, National
Monuments
Service,
Department of
Arts, Heritage
and the
Gaeltacht).

Dating

Hilltop locations have been in use as settlement sites in Ireland since the Neolithic era. The first construction of substantial ramparts on hilltop sites appears to date generally from the late Bronze Age. Very few of the substantial number of hillforts recorded in Ireland (some 74) have been excavated.

Late Bronze Age material recovered at Rathgall (Co. Wicklow) and Freestone Hill (Co. Kilkenny) dates the hillforts to this period, and the calibrated radiocarbon dates from Rathgall in particular indicate sustained activity from the thirteenth century BC, corresponding to the evidence from the cliff-top fort at Dún Aonghasa (Inis Mór, Co. Galway), occupied from the thirteenth century BC. Further evidence for the construction and occupation dates of hillforts has been produced by excavations at Mooghaun (Co. Clare) and Haughey's Fort (Co. Armagh). At Mooghaun hillfort, radiocarbon evidence suggests that the ramparts were built in the final decades of the tenth century BC, followed by occupation down to the late ninth century BC. Haughey's Fort seems to have been built around 1100–1080 cal. BC, and Clashanimud (Co. Cork) c. 1100 BC (O'Brien 2012).

Given the relatively few excavated and dated examples, it may be premature to extrapolate a late Bronze Age date for the sizeable number of other hillforts recorded in Ireland. O'Brien's (2012) suggestion that there were two main periods of hillfort construction in Ireland—those with a single enclosure corresponding generally to the Iron Age and at least some multivallate sites to the later Bronze Age—is a neat distinction which, if sustainable, will prove invaluable.

The chronology of hillforts in Ireland is being progressively elucidated, as illustrated by the excavation undertaken by Warner (2009) at Clogher (Co. Tyrone). Based on the excavation and associated evidence, including the presence within the surrounding earthworks of an Iron Age ring-barrow (see

Archaeology Ireland, Winter 2012), Warner concluded that the Clogher site is likely to be a univallate hillfort of Iron Age date.

Hilltop enclosures

These sites share characteristic morphological features with hillforts, but are distinguished from them in particular by their comparatively small size (Grogan 2005). Hilltop enclosures range in size from 0.13ha to 1.97ha; they are typically less than 1ha in area and enclosed by generally impressive defences. An estimated 134 hilltop enclosures have been identified in Ireland, of which the vast majority (over 80%) are univallate sites. Like their hillfort counterparts, multivallate hilltop enclosures may have closely or widely spaced ramparts. Very substantial defences comprising three or four closely spaced massive ramparts characterise a distinct group of hilltop enclosures, including Tlachtga, Rathra and Ringestown. Some univallate sites also have sizeable ramparts, such as Clenagh (below).

Most hilltop enclosures are located on low but prominent hills or knolls, and many with substantial ramparts do not make the same defensive use of summit contours as hillforts (Grogan 2005). This, and their significantly lower elevations than hillforts, makes their use as high-status residential sites more plausible.

Assessment of the date and function of hilltop enclosures is almost entirely dependent on their very close similarities to hillforts (Grogan 2005). Very few hilltop sites have been excavated. At Clenagh (Co. Clare), the substantial defences consisted of a bank with a very large ditch and an outer bank. While occupation debris was recovered, the interior of the enclosure had been extensively damaged by later agricultural activity. Radiocarbon dates from the ditch indicate that the site had been abandoned during the Iron Age.

Fig. 5— Multivallate hillfort, Rathgall, Co. Wicklow (photo: Con Brogan, National Monuments Service, Department of Arts, Heritage and the Gaeltacht).

Hilltop enclosures in Munster are located mainly in fertile, low-lying terrain, comprising the largest swathe of good agricultural land in the province (Grogan 2005), suggesting that agriculture in the form of crop and livestock production was a mainstay of the associated economy. Grain-storage pits are commonly found in the interiors of hillforts in Britain. The radial banks connecting the inner and outer enclosures of the Clashanimud hillfort (Fig. 3) created small fields that were used for cultivation and animal grazing in the early modern period (O'Brien 2012).

Box 1	Diagnostic features

Hillforts
- Typically large enclosures with one or more lines of earthwork defences, timber palisades or stone walling, which usually follow the contours of the hill summit.
- Positioned to take advantage of naturally defensible topography and strategically positioned with panoramic views of the local landscape.
- Vast majority of sites are located in elevated positions, ranging from easily accessible slopes to higher altitudes and remote sites, and to almost inaccessible peaks; some are located on inland promontories.

Hilltop enclosures
- Defences similar to hillforts but smaller in size, typically less than 1ha in area.
- Mostly located at significantly lower elevations than hillforts, many on low but prominent hills or knolls.
- Not positioned to make the same defensive use of hilltop contours as is commonly the case with hillforts.

Acknowledgements

The background information provided by Gabriel Cooney and Paul Walsh is gratefully acknowledged.

References

Grogan, E. 2005 *The North Munster Project, Vol. II. The prehistoric landscape of north Munster*. Discovery Programme Monograph 6. Bray.

O'Brien, W. 2012 Hillforts. In W. O'Brien, *Iverni: a prehistory of Cork*. Cork.

Raftery, B. 1994 Hillforts. In B. Raftery, *Pagan Celtic Ireland: the enigma of the Irish Iron Age*. London.

Waddell, J. 1998 Elusive settlements and ritual sites. In J. Waddell, *The prehistoric archaeology of Ireland*. Galway.

Warner, R. 2009 Clogher in late prehistory. In G. Cooney, K. Becker, J. Coles, M. Ryan and S. Sievers (eds), *Relics of old decency: archaeological studies in later prehistory. Festschrift for Barry Raftery*. Bray.

This article was originally published in the Spring 2013 issue of Archaeology Ireland.

Rath, lios and cashel

Ringforts were enclosed residential locations, usually farmsteads, constructed throughout the early Christian period in Ireland, predominantly between AD 600 and 900.

Univallate ringforts appear to have been associated mainly with cattle-farming systems, perhaps with some crop production, while platform ringforts were apparently associated with arable farming.

Multivallate ringforts are generally considered to have been high-status sites. They were centrally located in prominent positions, reflecting the hierarchical organisation of society during the heyday of ringfort-building.

Fig. 1 – Aerial view of univallate rath (top left) and rath with bank, ditch and counter-scarp bank (bottom right) at Deenodes, Co. Sligo (from Ursula Egan et al., Archaeological inventory of south Sligo, Plate 33 (photo: Archaeological Survey of Ireland).

Ringforts

R ingforts are circular enclosures, ranging from small univallate forms to larger raised enclosures and more complex multivallate examples (Fig. 2). In presenting an overview of ringforts, this article, which focuses mainly on their central function in agriculture, has drawn on the comprehensive reports published by Matthew Stout (1997) and more recently by Thomas Kerr (2007), and on the invaluable insights provided by Aidan O'Sullivan.

Location

Ringforts are among the most numerous domestic archaeological monuments in Ireland, amounting to over 45,000 (Stout 1997). As shown in Fig. 3, they are generally more prevalent in the western half of the country. The areas of highest ringfort density are centred on Sligo Bay, the Burren and central County Limerick. Low-density areas include most of Leinster, north-west Ulster and the western extremities of Counties Donegal, Mayo and Galway, as well as parts of west Kerry and Cork.

*Fig. 2—
Multivallate
ringfort at
Rathealy,
Co. Kilkenny
(from E.R.
Norman and
J.K. St Joseph,
The early
development
of Irish society:
the evidence
of aerial
photography,
Plate 23).*

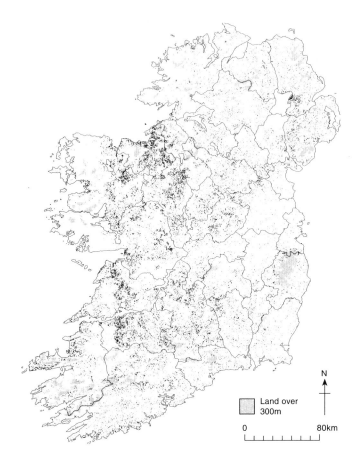

Fig. 3—
Distribution
map of ringforts
in Ireland (from
Stout 1997).

Land over 300m

N

0   80km

Ringfort types

Univallate ringforts, which are by far the most numerous (80% of the total in some areas), are circular enclosures, some 20–40m wide, with a single earthen bank and an external ditch. **Cashels** are ringforts with a stone-built enclosing wall. They are generally smaller than univallate ringforts, with an average internal diameter of 25m (and in some locations much less). **Counterscarp ringforts** have an additional low bank surrounding an internal bank and ditch. **Platform ringforts** have large, flat-topped central areas, raised some 2m or more above the surrounding countryside. Raised ringforts have been defined as having 'a perimeter bank around the top area' (Jope 1966). Platform ringforts may have been built by altering the natural landscape to develop a raised profile; alternatively, they may have been created by the accumulation of debris over a long period of occupation, so as to raise the enclosed area above the water-table and alleviate waterlogging. Kerr (2007) points out that relatively few platform ringforts seem to have been deliberately constructed; a number appear to have evolved from pre-existing univallate forms. **Multivallate ringforts** are larger and more complex structures, with two (bivallate) or three (trivallate) series of enclosing banks and ditches, and with central areas comparable in size to the univallate forms.

As further detailed by Kerr (2007), the majority of univallate ringforts date from *c.* AD 600–900. Multivallate and counterscarp ringforts show a similar dating distribution but may have a slightly earlier starting date. Platform ringforts seem to date from a later period, between the mid-eighth and mid-tenth centuries AD. The construction and occupation of ringforts appear to have tapered off before the coming of the Anglo-Normans (Stout 1997).

Farming

Ringforts were predominantly enclosed farmsteads, dispersed throughout the early Christian landscape. Some may have been built as cattle enclosures, or may have been subsequently used for this purpose, having originally been farmsteads.

The management of livestock, especially cattle, was the primary preoccupation of farmers in early Christian Ireland. Hay seems not to have been commonly made. Cattle appear to have been outwintered, involving some form of transhumance or booleying, as it is more commonly known in Ireland.

The practice of moving cattle and other livestock to summer grazing had a number of important economic benefits. As well as protecting crops from damage by livestock, it allowed some home pastures to be closed off to conserve grass for winter feeding. In addition, by availing of the summer growth of grass in upland areas, where it is likely to have been more abundant in earlier times, more stock could be maintained throughout the year. It may also have been seen as essential, as otherwise the animals could become prone to disease owing to the continual use of local water. The change of location and pasture may have reduced the parasite infestation cycle.

Milk production was the principal element of the farming systems. Dairying and dairy products, including cream, butter, buttermilk and various cheeses, are well attested to in early Christian Ireland. Conversely, there are few references to beef cattle in the period (Kerr 2007). Sheep-rearing was widely practised. Pigs were kept for their meat and lard; pork was traditionally used for feasting.

Cereal production was important in early Irish farming, especially from the fifth century, catalysed by the establishment of monastic settlements. By the late eighth century, sufficient quantities of grain were being produced to require the construction of watermills. Tillage appears to have been undertaken in small fields adjoining the ringforts. It seems, as outlined below, to have been associated in particular with the advent of platform ringforts.

In response to the occupants' needs, manufacturing also took place within ringforts. Indeed, a number seem to have been permanent centres of craftsmanship and manufacture, as evidenced by the presence of furnaces.

Spatial and hierarchical configuration

The comprehensive studies published by Stout (1997) and Kerr (2007) have made important contributions to our understanding of the chronology of ringforts, their functioning, and the spatial and hierarchical organisation of ringfort settlements. These comprised a complex array of social classes, ranging from the king through a hierarchy of nobles/lords to a hierarchy of farmers, below which were the ranks of the unfree or *doer*, who were the most numerous.

Land ownership was not vested in an individual farmer but was held commonly by a family grouping descended from a shared ancestor. Similarly, livestock were not held outright. Cattle in particular could be borrowed by certain farmer grades from a noble or the king. This noble–farmer clientship system is reflected in the spatial and hierarchical configuration of ringfort settlements.

Stout (1997) has developed a model for the juxtapositioning, hierarchical operation and functional interdependence of the different ringfort types in the south-west midlands. Multivallate ringforts are envisaged as being centrally located in a prominent situation with a commanding view of the countryside and close to a road or other artery of communication. They appear to have been the dwellings of the lord, the *aire forgaill*, who is understood to have had a holding of approximately six *tír cumail* (*c.* 83ha), much of which may have been rented to the *ócaire*, the sons of nobility or other landless freemen. Large, well-defended univallate ringforts tend to be located in strategically important positions on the lower slopes near the boundaries of ringfort settlements. They appear to have been the farmsteads of a lower grade of noble, known as *aire déso*. In addition to farming three quarters of their holding directly, the *aire déso* class appear to have had interterritorial military functions.

Medium-status univallate ringforts were situated on good agricultural land, located along less strategically significant but well-drained slopes at some distance from the lord's multivallate ringfort. They may have been the farmsteads of the lowest grade of independent farmer, the *bóaire*, whose families owned their lands outright but rented cattle from the lord. The boundaries of those farms may possibly correspond roughly with modern townland boundaries. Small, low-status univallate ringforts tend to be located in close proximity to the high-status multivallate sites. They were poorly defended and may have been the farmsteads of the *ócaire*, who rented land from the *aire forgaill*. The livestock managed by the *ócaire* may have been composed of seven cows (plus a bull), seven pigs (plus a boar) and seven sheep, as well as a horse and ox.

Outside the ringfort settlement, large uninhabited regions may have included land farmed in common or retained as extensive woodlands.

Stout's (1997) spatial–hierarchical model outlined above provides an innovative perspective on the functioning of ringfort settlements. It fits with the pattern of ringfort settlement in the south-west midlands and also in Roscommon. Whether it is equally applicable to other regions of Ireland remains to be established, however.

Fig. 4—Platform rath at Dún na Sciath, on the shores of Lough Ennell, Co. Westmeath (photo: Richard Warner).

Functions of the different ringfort types

The sitings, in terms of altitude and soil preferences, of the different ringfort types in north-west Ulster have been extensively investigated by Kerr (2007). The altitude preferences of the different ringfort types in Counties Donegal and Monaghan are atypical, apparently reflecting those counties' particular topographies. In the other four counties the univallate ringforts show a preference for an altitude range of 30–150m. Cashels, as would be expected, exhibit a preference for a higher altitude (150–210/300m) in four of the counties. Conversely, the altitude preference of both platform and counterscarp ringforts is lower—less than 100m in a number of the counties. The four ringfort types, with some exceptions, show a preference for better-quality soils with grazing for 35–45 animals. Multivallate ringforts, unlike the other four ringfort types, show few preferences for altitude ranges and soil quality.

The altitude and soil preferences presented by Kerr are consistent with the prevailing understanding of the function of univallate ringforts as pastoral farmsteads engaged primarily in livestock-farming, especially cattle grazing, perhaps with some arable production. Cashels seem to have fulfilled a similar function, within the constraints imposed by their location at higher altitudes or on poor-quality soils.

Platform ringforts were also predominantly agricultural structures. Their ramped/sloping structure, however, allied to the relatively confined central area, indicates that they were not purposefully designed for cattle-rearing (Kerr 2007). As they date from a later period (*c.* mid-eighth to mid-tenth centuries) than the other ringfort types (*c.* AD 600–900), Kerr concludes that the emergence of platform ringforts may have heralded a transition from the predominantly cattle-based farming systems that characterised univallate ringforts to a more arable-oriented agriculture. Notwithstanding the marked climatic downturn in the early and mid-ninth century, the expansion of arable production is further evidenced by a major period of mill construction in AD 800 ± 20, coinciding with the emergence of platform ringforts. Arable farming appears to have been a determining feature of platform ringforts, some of which may have been constructed for reasons of status and prestige, as lordly dwellings, during the ninth century. About 19% of ringforts in the south-west midlands have been identified as platform ringforts (Stout 1997), and a lower proportion (around 10%) in north-west Ulster (Kerr 2007). Thus it is uncertain whether arable production actually exceeded livestock agriculture in areas where platform ringforts were constructed.

Counterscarp ringforts may have had a similar agricultural focus to platform ringforts. In some counties the preferred altitude and soil type are those that would be expected of agricultural structures. Since this is not the situation in all cases, however, farming may not necessarily have been the main reason for the construction of counterscarp ringforts. Kerr (2007) considers that they may also have had an alternative function that appears to relate more to political geography than to the physical environment.

Multivallate ringforts were high-status sites. Unlike the other ringfort types, farming is unlikely to have been the primary occupation of their builders. Their location seems to have owed more to local political geographies than to the physical environment (Kerr 2007).

Acknowledgements

The detailed information, insights and illustrations provided by Dr Aidan O'Sullivan are most gratefully acknowledged.

Fig. 5—Stone cashel at Leacanabuaile, Kimego West, Co. Kerry (from Ann O'Sullivan and J. Sheehan, The Iveragh Peninsula: an archaeological survey of south Kerry, Plate XIa).

References

Jope, E.M. 1966 *The archaeological survey of County Down*. Belfast.

Kerr, T.R. 2007 *Early Christian settlement in north-west Ulster*. British Archaeological Reports, British Series 430. Oxford.

Lee, J. and Diamond, S. 1970 *The potential of Irish land for livestock production*. Dublin.

Stout, M. 1997 *The Irish ringfort*. Dublin.

This article was originally published in the Autumn 2007 issue of Archaeology Ireland.

Souterrains

These underground man-made structures consisting of one or more chambers linked by narrow creepways are frequently found in or adjacent to ringforts, cashels and other settlements, including ecclesiastical sites and some promontory forts. A considerable number feature structural evidence to suggest they may have been built to provide temporary refuge in times of danger. They might also have been used as ongoing repositories for food, the lower temperature allowing milk and other products to last longer.

The main period of souterrain usage in Ireland was from around AD 750 to 1250, with some earlier examples (mostly in the south) and possibly some later survivals in more remote areas. Ogham stones have been recorded in the fabric of many souterrains, sometimes functioning as roof lintels.

Fig. 1—Souterrain at Benagh, Co. Louth.

Underground passages

Children of all ages visiting the great Neolithic complex at Knowth enjoy living life on the edge by crawling through the souterrain on the northern side of the cairn. Likewise, at Dowth, in the days of reasonably open access, it was as much the souterrains as the megalithic tomb that stayed in the memory of visitors. As these examples illustrate, souterrains hold a special fascination for people, and here we try to encapsulate the principal features of this monument type.

Description

As illustrated in Figs 2 and 3, souterrains are underground man-made structures comprising one or more chambers linked by tunnels called creepways and with the entrance or entrances more or less concealed at ground level. Some examples are relatively simple in design, with a passageway leading to a drystone chamber. Others are more complex, with two or more interlinked chambers. It is as well to acknowledge that, besides known souterrains, there are likely to have been many that were uncovered in the past and not publicised for a variety of reasons.

Construction

Two basic methods were employed in the building of souterrains. The vast majority are drystone structures, formed by digging a series of trenches and then building drystone walls against their sides. These were then capped with flagstone roofs. Some souterrains were built by digging a construction shaft, tunnelling down into clay and rock, the shaft being subsequently backfilled. In some instances both methods were employed. A small number of souterrains were constructed of timber. Based exclusively on the construction method predominantly employed, it has been suggested that souterrains might

Fig. 2—Detail of Gallery 6 at Newtownbalregan with capstones on; note the use of field-collected stones (© StudioLab).

be classified as follows: (i) drystone-built, (ii) earth-cut, (iii) rock-cut, and (iv) wooden.

Location

Upwards of 3,500 souterrains have been discovered to date. While they have been found throughout the country, their geographical distribution is very uneven. West Cork, Kerry, north Antrim, south Galway and north Louth have the highest concentrations of these structures. Conversely, large tracts of the more central and northern regions of the country have very few souterrains, including most of Leinster, north Munster, Longford, Cavan, Monaghan, Fermanagh and Armagh. Earth-cut souterrains are predominantly confined to south Cork, while rock-cut souterrains are concentrated in the extreme south and north of the country.

Settlement context

Souterrains are generally found in locations associated with settlement sites, including open settlements, enclosed settlements (especially ringforts and cashels), ecclesiastical sites and some promontory forts.

At Knowth in the Boyne Valley excavations have revealed evidence of a settlement complex of souterrains and houses dating from the second half of the first millennium AD, the period in which the site may have functioned as a seat of regional power. Stones decorated with megalithic art about 4,000 years earlier were incorporated into the drystone fabric of the walls or used as lintels. The occurrence of half-uncial and ogham inscriptions in the megalithic tombs suggests that these too may have functioned as souterrains at the time.

Ogham stones have been recorded in the fabric of many souterrains in the south of Ireland, notably Counties Cork and Kerry, where they sometimes act as roof lintels. Likewise, the souterrain at Oweynagat in the Rathcroghan complex, Co. Roscommon, appears to incorporate two ogham stones. At Aghacarrible, near Lispole on the Dingle Peninsula, there was a cross-slab as well as some ogham stones in the structure of the souterrain associated with a ringfort.

Fig. 3— Newtownbalregan souterrain under excavation in its ringfort context (© StudioLab).

Function

Two basic functions have been ascribed to souterrains: (i) temporary refuges in times of danger, and (ii) storage cellars where dairy and other food products were stored at a cool temperature (perhaps *c.* 10°C). The balance of

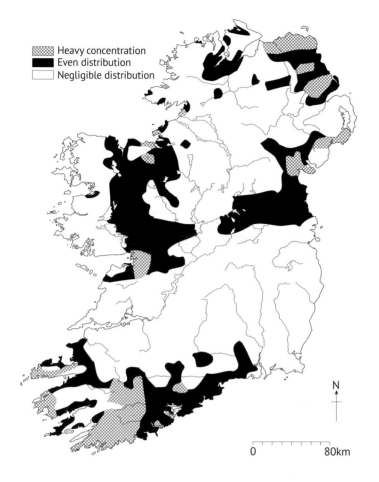

*Fig. 4 —
Distribution of
souterrains in
Ireland (after
Clinton 2001).*

Heavy concentration
Even distribution
Negligible distribution

N

0   80km

opinion currently favours the view that at least a considerable proportion
of souterrains were built to provide secure places of refuge. On a day-to-
day basis, however, they may also have functioned as food repositories,
and experience suggests that they are especially effective in keeping dairy
products reasonably fresh in warm weather. The storage view is supported
by the occurrence of cubby-holes and other storage features. It has also been
suggested that souterrains located at ecclesiastical sites may have fulfilled
the same functions as round towers.

The refuge interpretation derives from a number of factors, not least
the efforts apparently made to render access difficult in many cases. It has
been suggested, for example, that the purpose of the zigzag line of many
souterrain complexes, involving abrupt changes of direction in some cases,
was to make it difficult for raiders to dig down from above in order to break
into the souterrain. In rare instances, access by means of the souterrain
entrance was rendered awkward by the incorporation of low-set lintels,
obstructive sill-stones, obstructive jamb-stones or murder holes. There are
also suggestions that souterrains were sometimes designed in such a way
that occupants could not be smoked out by fires lit at the entrance.

Age

Souterrains found in Ireland are dated generally to the second half of the first millennium AD and to the earlier centuries of the second millennium. Recent research indicates that the main period of souterrain usage in Ireland was from *c.* AD 750 to 1250, with some earlier examples, mostly in the south, and possibly some later survivals in more remote areas. Many of the artefacts found in souterrains are from the core area of usage.

Checklist of diagnostic features

- Underground man-made structure.
- Drystone-built and tunnelled.
- Narrow concealed entrance(s) at ground level.
- Located in or adjacent to settlement sites of the early medieval period.
- Dated, by means of radiocarbon dating and diagnostic objects, to between the latter half of the first millennium AD and the earliest centuries of the second millennium AD.

Further information

Readers with an interest in souterrains might profitably read Mark Clinton's *The souterrains of Ireland*, published by Wordwell in 2001. Dr Clinton provides a detailed overview of this monument type and reviews the type of material that has been found in souterrains. Much of the information provided here has been culled from this source. Individual souterrain complexes have been discussed in previous issues of *Archaeology Ireland*.

This article was originally published in the Winter 2004 issue of Archaeology Ireland.

Crannogs

Besides functioning as strongholds or defensive refuges, these man-made islands were used for a wide range of purposes—for example, as royal residences, ecclesiastical settlements, island hermitages and centres for metalworking and other crafts. Several crannogs were the homesteads of the 'middle classes' or the habitations of social groups or households with little appreciable wealth or power.

Crannogs are predominantly located in the northern half of the country and are mainly concentrated in the drumlin lakes of Counties Cavan, Monaghan, Leitrim and Fermanagh. They were built or occupied at various times in the past, including the late Bronze Age, the early Iron Age, the early Middle Ages and the later medieval period. However, the most intensive phase of the building, occupation and abandonment of crannogs took place in the early Middles Ages. While evidence of settlement is a predominant feature of crannogs, some may have been fishing or industrial platforms, or may indeed have been used for other purposes.

Fig. 1—View of Coolure crannog, Co. Westmeath, from the shore.

Lake dwellings

Crannogs are man-made islands, usually built in lakes. They are seen as small circular or oval islands along the shore, often tree clad, and built of stone, timber and soil.

Crannogs tend to be found in small lakes. They occur infrequently or rarely in the large midland lakes of the River Shannon system (Lough Ree and Lough Derg), and are also few in number in Lough Erne and Lough Neagh. They are most commonly located in small, sheltered bays of lakes with gently sloping shorelines. A small number have been found in rivers (e.g. the Boyle River), estuaries and coastal wetlands.

Estimates suggest that there were once some 2,000 crannogs on the island of Ireland. They have also been found in Scotland and Wales. Ireland currently has 1,200 registered sites. However, the actual number may be appreciably higher, given the lack of dedicated surveys and the ease with which these monuments can be obscured by wetland vegetation and shallow depths of water. While a large number of crannogs were examined during the lake-settlement research boom of the nineteenth century, only about five have been excavated to modern standards.

Geographic distribution

Crannogs are mostly found in the northern half of the country (Fig. 2), especially in the band of counties stretching from Mayo and Sligo across through Roscommon, Leitrim, Fermanagh, Cavan and Monaghan, and extending into County Down. They are mainly concentrated in the drumlin lakes of Cavan, Monaghan, Leitrim, Roscommon and Fermanagh. Particular concentrations are also found in Lough Carra and Lough Conn (Co. Mayo), Lough Gara (Co. Sligo), Drumhallow Lough (Co. Roscommon) and Lough Oughter (Co. Cavan). While crannogs are more dispersed across the west and north-west, concentrations occur in Lough Conn, Lough Cullin and around Castlebar Lough.

Crannogs occur in much lower numbers in the southern half of the country and also in the more northern counties, notably County Donegal. While this may be seen to reflect the lower prevalence of lakes in these counties, the geographical distribution of crannogs does not strictly parallel that of lakes. For instance, Counties Donegal and Clare have a sizeable number of lakes but do not have the density of crannogs that characterises Counties Cavan, Monaghan and Fermanagh.

The number of crannogs in small lakes in the high-density counties can range from just one or two to perhaps twenty or more, depending on how the term is defined (see below). Smaller lakes can have one or a group of crannogs, as in Lough Eyes and Drumgay Lough (Co. Fermanagh). On larger lakes they tend to be distributed along the shoreline at regular intervals.

Construction

While they are usually circular or oval in plan, crannogs vary widely in size and form. Most appear to have been built of layers of stone boulders, small to medium-sized cobblestones, branches and timber, lake-marl and other organic debris. They range in size from relatively large constructed islands 18–25m in

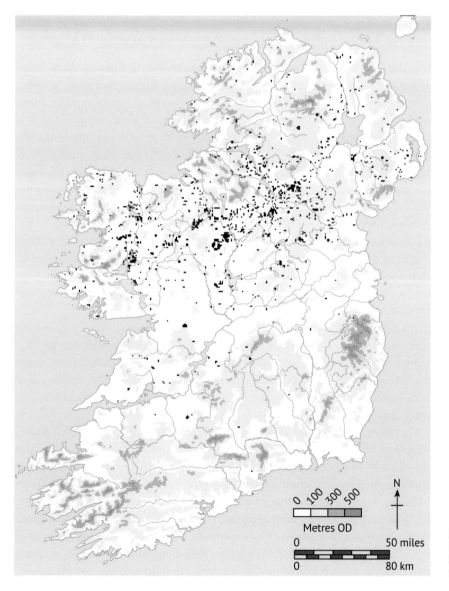

0 100 300 500
Metres OD

N

0   50 miles

0   80 km

Fig. 2—
Distribution of
known crannogs
in Ireland.

*Fig. 3—
Reconstruction
of a crannog
(courtesy
of Aidan
O'Sullivan).*

diameter to smaller mounds 8–10m in diameter and can have a wide range of other structural features, such as cairns, level upper platforms, wooden revetments, palisades and stone walls, houses, working spaces and middens, along with well-defined entrances, jetties, pathways and stone causeways.

A reconstruction drawing by Aidan O'Sullivan of a hypothetical early medieval crannog, based on evidence from sites in the north midlands, is shown in Fig. 3. This envisages the crannog as consisting of a cairn of stones laid over a wooden foundation, with sand and clay spread across this upper surface, and enclosed within an 'inner' round palisade. It shows remnants of a second palisade at the water's edge and another 'outer' palisade in the water surrounding the crannog. A stone causeway leads through the shallow water to the crannog entrance. Within the crannog are a roundhouse, an outer hearth and working spaces.

Functions

Crannogs have traditionally been seen as island strongholds or defensive refuges. However, depending on their size, location and history, they are known to have been used for a much wider range of functions—from royal residences to metalworking and other craft centres, the residences of ecclesiastical communities, safe havens for the storage of valuables, and occasionally island hermitages.

However, it is clear from archaeological surveys that most crannogs were just small islands or lakeshore dwellings that were built, used and occupied by various social classes. Small crannogs were the habitations of social groups or households with little wealth or power. Several crannogs were the homesteads of the 'middle class'. Others may have been fishing or industrial platforms, used seasonally or periodically for particular tasks. While evidence of settlement is a common feature of crannogs, some may not have been dwellings. Rather, they could have been boundary or route markers, cairns or burial mounds, or even a consequence of quarrying.

Age

Crannogs were built or occupied at various times in the past, in the late Bronze Age (*c.* 900–600 BC), the early Iron Age (600–200 BC), the early Middle Ages (AD 400–1100), and even the late medieval period (AD 1200–1400). However, the most intensive phases of crannog-building, occupation and abandonment took place in the early Middle Ages.

Artefacts

Crannogs have produced large assemblages of artefacts, including items of clothing (shoes and textiles), personal adornments (brooches, pins and rings), weaponry (swords, spearheads, axes and shields), domestic equipment (knives, chisels and axes) and ecclesiastical metalwork (hand-bells, crosses and book-shrines).

Definition and classification

The term 'crannog' was introduced in the thirteenth century; it traditionally refers to an artificially constructed island with a defensive palisade and built in the open water of a lake. The scope of the term is the subject of continuing debate among archaeologists. A broader definition of crannogs would include cairns without palisades and deliberately enhanced natural islands, as well as cairns, mounds and rock platforms situated along lakeshores and not necessarily surrounded by water (O'Sullivan 2004). By extending the scope of the term to include all largely man-made islands, regardless of age, crannogs in Lough Gara and other sites in Sligo, Roscommon and Mayo have been classified (Fredengren 2002), on the basis of their surface material, into **crannog cairns** (stony surface) and **crannog mounds** (grass, soil, wood

Fig. 4—Coolure crannog (photo: Aidan O'Sullivan).

surface). Based on their height above the bottom sediment, the two groups of crannogs have been further differentiated into **high** (2–3.5m), **low** (0.5–2m) and **platform** (0.1–0.5m) **crannogs**. In this classification system, an important criterion in identifying a site as a crannog is that its body is raised slightly above its surroundings, making it into an island. Sites with no body material of filling, either of cairn or mound material, that raises them above the water or wetland were excluded, such as circles of stones or posts/piles.

Checklist of diagnostic features

- Man-made small islands in lakes, usually circular or oval in shape and often tree clad.
- Built of layers of stone boulders, small to medium-sized cobblestones, branches and timber, lake-marl and other organic debris, and with a stony or grass/soil/wood surface.
- Structural timbers sometimes visible along the margins of the artificial island, especially during very dry summers.
- Found mainly in small sheltered bays of small lakes with gently sloping shorelines.
- Predominantly located in the northern half of the country, notably in the drumlin lakes of Cavan, Monaghan, Leitrim, Roscommon and Fermanagh, but also in other counties.

Acknowledgements

Extensive use was made of the sources listed below in preparing this article. The invaluable information provided by Dr Aidan O'Sullivan, School of Archaeology, UCD, is gratefully acknowledged.

References

Fredengren, C. 2002 *Crannogs: a study of people's interaction with lakes, with particular reference to Lough Gara in the north-west of Ireland*. Bray.

O'Sullivan, A. 1998 *The archaeology of lake settlement in Ireland*. Discovery Programme Monograph 4. Dublin.

O'Sullivan, A. 2004 The social and ideological role of crannogs in early medieval Ireland. Unpublished Ph.D thesis, National University of Ireland.

This article was originally published in the Winter 2005 issue of Archaeology Ireland.

Early church sites

The early Irish church was focused on a distinctive insular monastic system, wedded to the prevailing political dynamics of the day. Early ecclesiastical sites were multi-purpose settlements. In addition to the progressive development of churches and associated cemeteries, these settlements engaged in farming and food production, including the adoption of emerging innovations. Church settlements also functioned as important centres of craftworking. By the early centuries of the second millennium AD, the old ways had become archaic and were gradually renewed or replaced by a wave of continental influences.

Fig. 1—Early church site on St Mac Dara's Island, Co. Galway (courtesy of Brendan Riordan).

Building and farming

Recent decades have witnessed the emergence of a substantial body of knowledge on early ecclesiastical settlements in Ireland (AD 400–1100), as evidenced in particular by two recent INSTAR Heritage Council-funded projects (Ó Carragáin and Sheehan 2010; O'Sullivan *et al.* 2014). Building on this knowledge base, Lorcan Harney (2016) has recently compiled a comprehensive gazetteer of the archaeological excavations undertaken on 90 early medieval church settlements in Ireland.

Early stone churches were mainly concentrated south of a line stretching from County Dublin to County Mayo (Fig. 2). In addition to containing churches and cemeteries, these settlements engaged in farming and were important centres of craftworking (Box 1).

Box 1	Characteristic features of early medieval church sites

- These church sites were normally defined by one or more concentric, curvilinear enclosing elements, comprising ditches, banks, stone walls and palisades.
- Many small early medieval church sites contained a church and cemetery on the eastern side, and domestic and craft zones in the western quarters. Some sites had an innermost ritual core and less sacred outer enclosed spaces featuring domestic, craft and agricultural zones.
- Larger sites contained clusters of rectilinear timber-, post-and-wattle- or clay-built churches and curvilinear dwellings. At certain sites these were replaced between the tenth and twelfth centuries by larger, rectilinear and curvilinear stone dwellings and stone churches, with round towers added in some cases.
- Mills were often erected near the church sites, with corn-drying kilns typically within the outer precincts, and iron- and metal-working areas in sheltered locations.
- The original cemetery core was often sited to the south or east of the principal church or clustered around the tomb-shrine of the founding saint interred within the graveyard.

Source: Lorcan Harney, pers. comm.

Early churches

The early churches were typically single-cell buildings (Fig. 1), surrounded by a cemetery and situated within an enclosure (Figs 3 and 4). Early Christian churches erected between the fifth and ninth centuries were built primarily of timber, post-and-wattle and clay. Timber churches were by far the most common type (Ó Carragáin 2010). Around 20 organic-built churches (turf, timber and post-and-wattle) from the early medieval period have been revealed in excavations (Harney 2016).

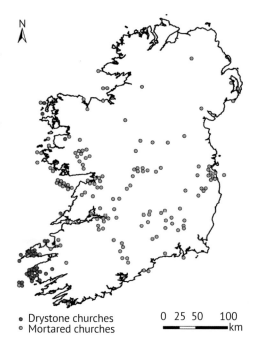

The earliest stone churches were drystone oratories, which are primarily concentrated on the Dingle and Iveragh Peninsulas of County Kerry and may represent a regional architectural form evolved from the 'beehive' corbelled

● Drystone churches
○ Mortared churches

0 25 50   100
━━━━━━━━━━km

Fig. 2— Geographical distribution of early church sites (based on Ó Carragáin and Sheehan 2010).

clochán. The drystone corbelled churches appear to be a peripheral west-coast form (Fig. 2), built from about the eighth century and probably mostly between 700 and 1100 (Ó Carragáin 2010).

Early medieval mortared churches (Fig. 2), approximately 140 of which have been recorded (Harney 2016), were primarily built between the tenth and early twelfth centuries. Further to this, Ó Carragáin (2010) observed that, until the eleventh century, most mortared stone churches had features known as antae—square-sectioned projections of the side walls beyond the end walls (Fig. 1).

Livestock production

The three main farm animals on early church sites, in order of importance, were cattle, sheep/goats and pigs. The faunal studies collated by Harney (2016) indicate, however, that the dominance of cattle was appreciably less than originally envisaged.

Other domesticated animals on church sites included horses and fowl, as well as dogs and cats. Horses are generally associated with men of rank, and the law-texts indicate that the *bóaire* farmer was expected to own two horses—one for riding and one for farm work. Domestic fowl were valued for their meat and eggs, with the latter forming an important part of the penitential diet of clerics.

Crops

The marked increase in evidence for crop cultivation arising from motorway excavations, in terms of field systems, corn-drying kilns, watermills, artefacts

Fig. 3—
Ecclesiastical
settlement on
Inishmurray, Co.
Sligo (courtesy
of the National
Monuments
Service,
Department of
Arts, Heritage,
Regional, Rural
and Gaeltacht
Affairs).

and archaeobotanical finds, highlights the importance of tillage in early medieval Ireland (Harney 2016). The central role of early church settlements in the introduction of a number of innovations in cereal production and processing has been underlined by Harney. Barley was the dominant cereal produced on early medieval sites, followed closely by oats, with much less wheat and rye. Barley and oats were important in the staple diets of the farming middle classes, and were crops suited to the prevailing climatic conditions. While barley may overall have been the most common cereal on early medieval sites, church communities cultivated a range of other crops to varying extents, in response to different economic, topographical or monastic/penitential dietary requirements.

Corn-drying kilns (Monk and Power 2012) and watermills (Rynne 2013), the two characteristic medieval technologies in post-harvesting cereal-processing, were common features of the agricultural landscape. Early medieval corn-drying kilns have been excavated on about 30 medium to large church sites (Harney 2016), sometimes in clusters located a short distance away from the site, apparently because of their potential as fire hazards.

Over 130 early medieval watermill sites are known in Ireland (Harney 2016). The most intensive mill-building phase (between the mid-eighth and mid-ninth centuries) coincided with the apparent increase in arable farming (McCormick and Murray 2014; O'Sullivan *et al.* 2014). Further to this, Harney adds that watermills appear to have been an agricultural innovation introduced into Ireland by Christian missionaries. The mills may have first appeared on church sites in the sixth century, and the upsurge in mill construction from the late eighth century could be related to the adoption of the technology by secular communities. The prominent association between ecclesiastical sites and mills is indicated by the discovery of millraces in close proximity to many early church sites, including Clonmacnoise (Harney 2016).

Food products

Bread, which has been described as the staple diet in most *Rules* and *Penitentials*, was apparently produced from oats, barley and sometimes wheat and rye (Harney 2016). Oats, which were deemed to be a low-value cereal, were closely associated with the lower farming *bóaire* and *ócaire* classes, and were also the diet of clerics of minor churches, particularly monasteries. Wheat bread was valued above other cereals and is tentatively associated with wealthy church sites that perhaps supported large monastic communities. All ecclesiastical communities may have included porridge, however, often produced from oat grain, as part of their wider diet.

The staple diet of bread at monastic sites like Tallaght was complemented by condiments of fish, butter, cheese or hard-boiled eggs, as well as herbs, vegetables and fruits, including cabbages, leeks and apples (Harney 2016). Domestic fowl appear to have been an almost ubiquitous feature of most early church sites, from small hermitages to important church sites such as Clonmacnoise. Their protein-rich eggs would have supplemented the penitential dietary and fasting regimes undertaken by communities, particularly on monastic sites.

Gardens were important in enabling communities to become largely self-sufficient in terms of foodstuffs. In particular, the range of vegetables, fruits and herbs grown would have complemented the staple diet of bread or porridge outlined above. Although vegetarian diets were generally favoured, the meats of wild pig and deer were also consumed at various church sites.

Overall, the information collated by Harney (2016) suggests that religious communities at early church sites typically had a varied diet, based mainly on cereal and milk products, supplemented seasonally with vegetables, fish and birds. The physical work commonly undertaken on early church settlements would have been difficult to sustain on strict monastic diets, however,

Fig. 4— Ecclesiastical settlement on Illaunloughan, Co. Kerry (courtesy of the National Monuments Service, Department of Arts, Heritage, Regional, Rural and Gaeltacht Affairs).

especially in exposed circumstances. Moreover, seasonal food scarcities would have been recurring problems compounded by protracted periods of inclement weather, especially during the spring. Indeed, the seasonal nature of both farming and fishing must have presented perennial challenges, requiring that food products be stored for consumption as required. Storage of food from one season for the next would have necessitated preservation.

During the Middle Ages, and seemingly earlier, salting was being used in the preservation of food, especially of meat and fish, and typically preceded drying or smoking processes. A number of monasteries in Ireland were involved in salt-making in the later medieval period, if not earlier (*Archaeology Ireland*, Winter 2016). With their sizeable communities, they would have required salt in considerable quantities. Further investigations of the records of monastic orders would help to address the prevailing gaps in our knowledge of salt-making and food preservation in medieval Ireland.

Feasting appears to have been an important communal activity on ecclesiastical sites, to celebrate Christian festivals and to mark saints' days, baptisms, marriages and funerals. Valued food products such as butter, honey and salted meats were usually added to monastic diets on Sundays, on the feasts of the Apostles, and particularly during Christmas, Easter and Pentecost (Harney 2016). Communal feasting appears to have occurred at secular as well as ecclesiastical sites, in the course of which important secular groups and clerics enjoyed a varied and meat-rich diet. In addition to its festive and hospitable attributes, communal feasting for large groups had the practical advantage of providing occasions for the consumption of the large quantities of fresh meat that became available when cattle or other large animals were slaughtered.

The archaeological excavations of church settlements outlined in the Early Medieval Archaeology Project (EMAP) (O'Sullivan *et al.* 2014) and extensively reviewed by Harney (2016) provide a comprehensive baseline

Fig. 5—
Ecclesiastical
settlement on
Skellig Michael,
Co. Kerry
(courtesy of
the National
Monuments
Service,
Department of
Arts, Heritage,
Regional, Rural
and Gaeltacht
Affairs).

for the further exploration of the foods typically consumed on early church settlements, relative to the general diet of contemporary secular communities in the surrounding landscape. It seems that the types of cereals and faunal food products consumed by the two communities were not markedly different, although the diets of ecclesiastical communities would have been more restricted than those of secular communities because of the more austere and ascetic food regimes associated with some monastics and penitents. Some interesting parallels may be drawn between the foodstuffs available on early church sites and the prominent historical food products that were the mainstay of the general diet of the Irish population at large from earlier times (*Archaeology Ireland*, Summer 2016). In both instances, the staple food products were mainly derived from cereals and dairy cattle, while the consumption of meat, particularly beef, was comparatively limited. Fish may, however, have made up a greater proportion of the foods consumed on many earlier church sites.

Acknowledgements

Lorcan Harney's Ph.D thesis has made an invaluable contribution to the compilation of this article. The information provided by Aidan O'Sullivan, Tomás Ó Carragáin, Conor McDermott, Derry O'Donovan, Ian Doyle and Paul Walsh is also much appreciated. The images received from Brendan Riordan, Tony Roche and Michael Corcoran have been most helpful.

References

Harney, L. 2016 Living with the Church in early medieval Ireland, AD 400–1100: archaeological perspectives on the sacred and profane. Unpublished Ph.D thesis, University College Dublin.

McCormick, F. and Murray, E. 2014 Excavations at an early church site at Struell Wells, Co. Down. In C. Corlett and M. Potterton (eds), *The church in early medieval Ireland in the light of recent archaeological excavations*. Dublin.

Monk, M.A. and Power, O. 2012 More than a grain of truth emerges from a rash of corn-drying kilns? *Archaeology Ireland* **26** (2), 38–41.

Ó Carragáin, T. 2010 *Churches in early medieval Ireland—architecture, ritual and memory*. New Haven, Connecticut.

Ó Carragáin, T. and Sheehan, J. 2010 *Making Christian landscapes: settlement, society, and regionality in early medieval Ireland*. Kilkenny.

O'Sullivan, A., McCormick, F., Kerr, T.R. and Harney, L. 2014 *Medieval Ireland AD 400–1100: the evidence from archaeological excavations*. Dublin.

Rynne, C. 2013 Mills and milling in early medieval Ireland. In N. Jackman, C. Moore and C. Rynne (eds), *The mill at Kilbegly: an archaeological excavation of an early medieval horizontal mill, and other investigations on the N6, Ballinasloe to Athlone road scheme*. Dublin.

This article was originally published in the Spring 2017 issue of Archaeology Ireland.

Mottes

Mottes were carefully engineered earthen mounds with a stone or wooden tower on top and a bailey attached to the base. Many, if not most, were erected in the late twelfth and early thirteenth centuries, with some built beyond AD 1300. They continued to be used both as residences and fortresses during the first quarter of the fourteenth century and some were used until they were abandoned or perhaps replaced by tower-houses in the fifteenth century.

In addition to defensive towers and palisades, mottes included a variety of residential, administrative and agricultural buildings, which may have been located in or adjacent to the bailey. A wide range of buildings associated with medieval farming have been recorded around mottes, including granaries, watermills, corn-drying kilns, dovecotes, sheepfolds and even a wooden dairy.

Fig. 1—Motte at Knockgraffon, Co. Tipperary (courtesy of the National Monuments Service, Department of Culture, Heritage and the Gaeltacht).

Anglo-Norman mounds

M ottes, with their characteristic upturned-flowerpot appearance, have a distinctive place in the traditional rural imagination, inspiring stories of ill luck befalling those who attempt to clear their sometimes lush coverage of deciduous trees. These imposing earthworks are relics of medieval timber-and-earth castles. They were the centres of medieval manors and the predominant type of early castle in Anglo-Norman Ireland. Mottes were built extensively throughout Europe.

A characteristic feature of mottes is the artificial, flat-topped earthen mound, generally circular in plan and encompassed by a deep fosse/ditch. On the summit of the mound originally stood a timber tower/building(s) enclosed by a protective wooden palisade, possibly with arrow-loops. Attached to the base of the mound was an enclosure, the bailey, surrounded by a bank and fosse. The entire complex is known as a motte-and-bailey (see Fig. 2).

What characterised a motte as a castle, as distinct from contemporary Irish structures, was the formidable complex of wooden or clay and timber defences and associated lordly residences (O'Conor 1998). The summit of the motte, as already indicated, was originally crowned by a wooden tower/ building(s) (known as a *bretêsche*), which commanded the perimeter and gateway of the entire complex. The residential, administrative, farm and other buildings essential to the successful operation of a motte castle may have been located in or adjacent to the bailey (O'Keeffe 2007), which in some instances may also have functioned as a fortification for a military garrison. The encircling banks of both the motte and the bailey were crowned with palisades of heavy timber. Access from the bailey to the motte was probably by some form of sloping wooden bridge or gangway, raised on stilts that may have been piled into the side of the mound.

Location

About 350 mottes are reported in the Irish countryside, with some estimates putting the original figure at 476 (O'Conor 1998). They are located mainly in the eastern half of the country. As shown on the map, mottes are heavily concentrated in north Leinster, notably in Counties Meath and Westmeath, and in east Ulster, particularly Counties Antrim and Down. While their distribution may reflect the general areas of Anglo-Norman colonisation, there are areas, such as east Cork and Limerick, with relatively few mottes

Fig. 2 —
Drawing
showing
reconstruction
of a motte-
and-bailey
(courtesy of
Kieran O'Conor,
National
University of
Ireland, Galway).

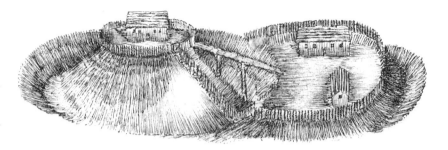

where the Anglo-Normans held power and where their impact was much greater than is suggested by the geographical distribution of mottes (Graham 1980).

Being defensive, mottes were usually constructed at sites that were easily defended and with commanding fields of vision, as well as at strategic locations such as crossing-points on major rivers. The existence of sizeable settlements, in particular the distribution of monasteries, may also have influenced the location of mottes, especially the larger, more important motte-and-baileys (Graham 1980).

Period of use

Many, if not most, mottes in Ireland were erected in the late twelfth and early thirteenth centuries, with some continuing to be built beyond 1300 (O'Conor 1998; 2002). It is now thought that mottes/motte-and-baileys began to be built after a full conquest had taken place and when individual lords were exploiting their new land grants.

Many mottes continued to be used as both residences and fortresses during the first quarter of the fourteenth century. Some seem to have remained in use until perhaps replaced by tower-houses in the fifteenth century or abandoned (O'Conor 1998; 2002). As noted by O'Keeffe (2007), several hundred mottes were provided with stoneworks and transformed into stone castles. The large earthworks associated with many of the prevailing stone castles are survivals from the original timber-and-earth castles. Many Anglo-Norman masonry castles in Ireland had ringwork (see below) rather than motte precursors, however (O'Conor 1998).

Functions

Mottes were very important functional centres in medieval rural Ireland. The majority were permanent castles, built by the Anglo-Normans as residences and marking the centres of manorial administration and of demesne farms—the lands within a manor retained by and farmed directly by the lord (O'Conor 1998). Some motte-and-bailey castles built in frontier areas of Anglo-Norman Ireland seem to have functioned solely or primarily as fortifications to hold garrisons. To protect the colony against Irish attacks, such fortified mottes were, as noted by O'Conor, built along the Ulster/Meath border, along the *de facto* border between the Anglo-Norman earldom of Ulster and Gaelic Ulster, and in the Laois/Offaly area of Leinster.

From an invasion perspective, while many mottes had a military function, their unsuitability as campaign fortresses is now being highlighted (O'Conor 1998; 2002). Large ringwork-type enclosures, another class of timber-and-earth castles, appear to have been better equipped for invasion purposes. Demanding less earth-moving in their construction, ringworks could be built more quickly than mottes and, in addition to

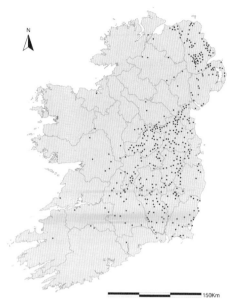

*Fig. 3—
Distribution
map of mottes in
Ireland (Kieran
O'Conor).*

accommodating a sizeable number of men, provided enclosures for barracks, warhorses and military equipment. While about 100 have been reported, the number of reliably identified Anglo-Norman ringworks in Ireland may be as low as 30, in contrast to the 350 or more mottes (O'Keeffe 2007). It is now felt that many so-called campaign castles associated with invasions were in the form of ringworks, and that, as previously indicated, mottes were built after a full conquest had taken place. In the relatively peaceful parts of Ireland, mottes sprang up at the centres of small, not-too-prosperous manors and may have extended relatively far down the social scale (Graham 1980).

Residential, administrative and farm buildings

Various aspects of Anglo-Norman control in areas of medieval Ireland were exercised from mottes. Thus, in addition to formidable defences such as timber towers and palisades, mottes featured a variety of residential, administrative and farm buildings (O'Conor 1998; 2002). Timber buildings used for accommodation as well as a hall, kitchen, chapel and watermills are known, and there were also administrative buildings, such as a manorial court to deal with disputes between tenants.

Farming was carried on from mottes, which, as previously indicated, were the centres of the manorial demesne farms. As described in more detail by O'Conor (1998; 2002), among the farm buildings around the motte castle at Inch, near Thurles, Co. Tipperary, were stables, a granary, a sheepcote and a malt kiln, as well as a garden. Associated with the motte castle at Knocktopher, Co. Kilkenny, were a grange and byre, a dovecote, fruit and herb gardens, and two mills. The motte at Cloncurry, Co. Kildare, had two eight-post barns, a cowshed, a corn-drying kiln, a threshing-house and a dovecote. The motte at Rathmore, Co. Kildare, is reported to have been attacked in 1305, when livestock and corn were taken away and farm equipment and agricultural and domestic buildings were destroyed. A granary, stables and sheepfold existed at the manorial centre at Lough Merans, Co. Kilkenny, which seems to have been a motte. The manor at Old Ross, Co. Wexford, the centre of which is marked by a motte, had a wooden dairy, a sheepfold or byre and two watermills. The motte at Callan, Co. Kilkenny, had beside it a farmyard or haggard with a wooden barn, a building for housing oxen, stone-built stables and two watermills.

Construction

Designed to support a habitable and defensive timber superstructure, mottes were carefully engineered structures. They were often built around natural topographical features, such as rock outcrops, low narrow ridges or eskers. They were also carved out of small gravel hills, as, for instance, the mottes of the drumlin belt around the Meath–Ulster border. In addition, pre-existing earthworks such as ringforts were adapted and made into mottes.

The technique sometimes described as ring-and-fill was often used in the construction of mottes (O'Keeffe 2007). The circumference of the mound was first marked out at ground level with two revetting walls or earthen banks. Within these rings, the motte was built up in carefully laid layers of soil, stabilised with alternate layers of turf and materials such as sand and gravel. Another technique was to pile up soil and other material around a specially constructed small mound or an existing prehistoric mound.

Mottes vary appreciably in height and spatial dimensions. An average-sized motte may be some 5m in height above ground level. The majority range in height from about 3m to over 10m, with some very large examples of more than 15m in height and 60m in overall diameter (O'Keeffe 2007). In County Meath, which has a high density of mottes, the height above the bottom of the surrounding fosse ranges from 4m to over 11m (Graham 1980). The area of the motte summits varies from less than 100m^2 to over 200m^2. The

Fig. 4—Motte at Killeshin, Co. Carlow.

ratio of the larger summit diameters to the height of individual mottes varies from 1.0 to 2.2.

Baileys vary markedly in shape, number and size. They are frequently crescent shaped, but other shapes occur and sometimes more than one bailey may be found (Leask 1986). The interior surface of the bailey could be at a higher level than the ground outside, and the size may range from some 20m across to an average of 30m (at the greatest dimensions), with larger ones reaching up to 45m. The width (at right angles to the axis of the motte-and-bailey) may range from some 20m to 45m. Baileys could be very extensive in area and were sometimes large enough to accommodate small village settlements (O'Keeffe 2007), as at Kilpeck in Herefordshire or St Mullins in Co. Carlow. As also noted by O'Keeffe, baileys of some description were a feature of the great majority of motte castles, if not all. About two thirds of all known mottes in Ireland have no visible baileys, however.

Checklist of diagnostic features
- Grassed, overgrown earthen mounds with no visible timber components.
- The mounds are artificial, flat-topped earthworks, generally circular in plan.
- A bailey may be attached to the base of the mound, but a substantial proportion of mottes in Ireland have none.
- Mottes generally range in height from about 3m to over 10m, with flat summits generally varying in area from under 100m^2 to over 200m^2.

Acknowledgements
The invaluable insights provided by Dr Kieran O'Conor (Department of Archaeology, National University of Ireland, Galway) and Professor Tadhg O'Keeffe (School of Archaeology, University College Dublin) in the preparation of this article are gratefully acknowledged. Some of the illustrations in the article were provided by Dr O'Connor, for which we are deeply grateful.

References
Colfer, B. 2002 *Arrogant trespass: Anglo-Norman Wexford, 1169–1400*. Wexford.

Graham, B.F. 1980 The mottes of the Norman liberty of Meath. In H. Murtagh (ed.), *Irish midland studies: essays in commemoration of N.W. English*. Athlone.

Leask, H.G. 1986 *Irish castles and castellated houses*. Dundalk.

O'Conor, K.D. 1998 *The archaeology of medieval rural settlement in Ireland*. Discovery Programme Monograph 3. Dublin.

O'Conor, K.D. 2002 Motte castles in Ireland: permanent fortresses, residences and manorial centres. *Château Gaillard* **20**, 173–82.

O'Keeffe, T. 2007 *Castles in Britain and Ireland: exploring the world of medieval lordship, 1050–1300*. London.

This article was originally published in the Spring 2007 issue of Archaeology Ireland.

Moated sites

Moated sites are found today as rectangular or sub-rectangular enclosures comprising a central platform with surrounding banks and ditches, which may be partly water filled.

As would be expected of farmsteads, moated sites are generally located in low-lying, fertile areas. They occur most frequently in the counties of Wexford, Kilkenny, Tipperary, Cork and Limerick. Significant clusters also occur in eastern Connacht, mainly on the borders between Anglo-Norman and Gaelic settlements. Conversely, counties such as Dublin, Meath and Louth—within the Anglo-Norman colonial heartland—contain very few moated sites. Although dating evidence is rather limited at present, this appears to indicate that moated sites were built in Ireland during the late thirteenth and early fourteenth centuries.

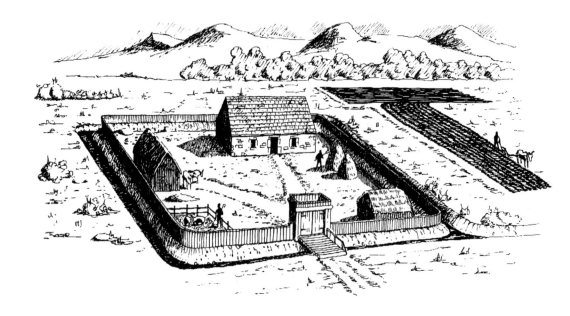

Fig. 1—Reconstruction drawing of a moated site.

Rectangular enclosures

Moated sites are among the most numerous extant earthworks of the medieval period and are usually regarded as Anglo-Norman protected farmsteads. As outlined below, however, the origins and functions of moated sites are more diverse than originally envisaged (O'Conor 1998; Barry 2003; O'Keeffe 2004).

Origin

A high proportion, and perhaps the majority, were built by the Anglo-Normans. Some moated sites, however, especially those in parts of the west that were not settled by the Anglo-Normans, were constructed and inhabited by Gaelic kings and lords (O'Conor 1998). Most of the moated sites in the northern part of Roscommon and some of those in Sligo and Leitrim appear to have been built by Irishmen. O'Conor further suggests that a similar situation may have prevailed in other parts of Ireland where Irish lords survived alongside Anglo-Norman knights, or in districts that lay in the margins between Gaelic lordships and the Anglo-Normans.

Functions

Moated sites are often associated with the movement onto marginalised lands, which in some instances were close to the territories of the Irish. Thus they are generally regarded as having been the protected farmsteads of free tenants who were taking new land into cultivation. Well-to-do settlers living out in the townlands that made up Anglo-Norman manors appear to have constructed moated sites, especially in districts that bordered on regions controlled by native Irish lords (O'Conor 1998). This would explain why moated sites are rarely situated at primary centres of Anglo-Norman settlements. The majority are more than 3.4km away from the nearest known nucleated settlement (Barry 2003). A significant minority are positioned in upland areas, where their inhabitants may have felt safer from possible threat. The ditches and banks around the isolated farmstead would have afforded some degree of protection.

While moated sites were protective in character and usually situated in non-strategic locations, such as low-lying floodplains or boggy areas, where their moats could be easily supplied with water, Barry (2003) points out that certain sites in Ireland do not conform to this model. He postulates that some examples may have had a military or strategic dimension to their function, as

Fig. 2—Moated site at Ogulla, near Tulsk (courtesy of the National Monuments Service, Department of Culture, Heritage and the Gaeltacht).

evidenced by what appear to be flanking terminals/towers at their corners. Also, those sited in upland commanding positions would have enjoyed a strategic advantage. The possible military or strategic function of moated sites is, however, an issue of ongoing debate. Indeed, the continued focus on defensibility as *the* function of Irish moated sites has been questioned (O'Keeffe 2004).

O'Conor (1998) notes that some moated sites may be the remnants of monastic granges, located on the scattered estates of medieval monasteries. A few may represent the remains of hunting lodges, especially those on marginal lands. Some moated sites may have contained gardens and fish-ponds, as is often the case outside Ireland (O'Keeffe 2004).

Structure

As shown in Fig. 2, the earthwork remains of moated sites are mostly found today as a single rectangular or subrectangular enclosure, comprising a central platform with surrounding banks and ditches, which may be partly water filled.

In 1977 Terry Barry conducted a comprehensive survey of the known moated sites in Counties Carlow, Kilkenny, Tipperary and Wexford, an area that contained over half of the total mapped sites. This showed that moated sites are generally rectangular in shape, with central platforms ranging in size from under 500m^2 to over 8,000m^2, and moats varying from 2m to 10m wide. The majority had platform areas of between 500m^2 and 2,500m^2 and moats of between 2m and 7m in width. Moated sites also vary greatly in the composition of the bank systems and in the height of the central platform above the surrounding ground level. Circular moated sites are rare and just a few wedge-shaped examples occur. In contrast to the situation in England, the vast majority of moated sites in Ireland have only one enclosure, and adjacent earthworks are not a common feature.

A relatively small proportion of moated sites in Ireland have evidence of entrances and/or internal structures on the central platform. As further documented by O'Conor (1998), the remains of such structures include (i) a large hall-like structure with a garderobe and the plinth of an unfinished gatehouse at Rigsdale (Co. Cork); (ii) dwelling-houses and farm buildings at Ballyveelish (Co. Tipperary); (iii) a corn-drying kiln, small house and outbuilding at Kilferagh (Co. Kilkenny); and (iv) a house and farm buildings at Kilmagoura (Co. Cork), as well as a stone pathway and the foundation timbers of a causeway/entrance across the ditch, which have been dated to between the twelfth and fourteenth centuries.

Fig. 3—
Distribution of moated sites in Ireland (courtesy of the Discovery Programme).

Number and location

With increasing numbers being identified annually, the total complement of moated sites in the Irish countryside has been estimated as 900–1,000 (O'Conor 1998). Given the difficulties of distinguishing denuded sites in heavily enclosed areas, however, the actual number may indeed be greater. Over half of the moated sites appear to have been destroyed since they were first mapped by the Ordnance Survey in the mid-nineteenth century (Barry 1979). Thus the original number of moated sites in Ireland may well have been some orders of magnitude greater than the actual number now known.

As would be expected of farmstead enclosures, moated sites are generally located in lowland fertile areas. Most occur in Counties Wexford, Kilkenny, Tipperary, mid-Cork and Limerick (Fig. 3). While those areas were heavily colonised in the late twelfth and early thirteenth centuries, counties such as Meath, Dublin and Louth, which constituted the core of the Anglo-Norman colony, contain almost no moated sites (O'Conor 1998). As previously mentioned, significant clusters of sites occur in eastern Connacht, mainly on the border between Anglo-Norman and Gaelic settlements. Very few moated sites occur in Ulster. This may reflect the tenuous military hold of the Anglo-Normans in that province, which may have required them to utilise mottes as protected settlement centres rather than the more lightly defended moated sites (Barry 1987).

Date range

Only a handful of the estimated 1,000 or more moated sites in Ireland have been excavated. Moreover, virtually no documentary records concerning these sites survive. Thus the overall date range for the construction and use of moated sites in Ireland cannot be stated definitively.

As further detailed by O'Conor (1998), Rigsdale (Co. Cork), the only firmly dated moated site, was built around 1300. Mylerspark (Co. Wexford), the only moated site with a surviving detailed account of its construction, was built in 1282–4. The moated site at Kilferagh (Co. Kilkenny) seems to have been built at some point in the thirteenth century and was occupied for the next century. The moated site at Ballyveelish (Co. Tipperary) may have been built some time in the thirteenth century and occupied into the fourteenth century. This rather limited dating evidence seems to indicate that moated sites in Ireland were built in the late thirteenth or early fourteenth century. This would concur with the date range of 1225–1325 originally proposed by Empey (1982).

A wide range of artefacts typical of medieval farmsteads have been found at moated sites. These include a late thirteenth/early fourteenth-century Edward I penny and a late thirteenth-century form of horseshoe at Rigsdale (Co. Cork). Sherds of locally produced thirteenth/fourteenth-century ware were found at the Ballyveelish moated site (Co. Tipperary).

Other artefacts found on moated sites include a wooden dish, disc-quern fragments, knives, iron nails, horseshoes, a rowel spur, small sheep shears, spindle-whorls, net-weights, stone hones, oyster shells, crop remains, and cattle, sheep, pig, horse and rabbit bones. Overall the numbers and range of artefacts found on the moated sites are remarkably similar to the finds recovered from excavations of undefended peasant houses located beside manorial centres (O'Conor 1998).

Fig. 4—
Remnants of a
moated site still
functioning as an
enclosure, with
trees growing
on the banks,
Mylerspark,
Co. Wexford
(courtesy of
the Discovery
Programme).

Diagnostic features

- Moats/ditches, generally rectangular or subrectangular in shape (sometimes with water) and enclosing a central platform, which may or may not be raised above the level of the surrounding land.
- Within this basic structural form, moated sites exhibit large variations in the width of the moats, the area of the central platforms and their height above the surrounding ground level, as well as the system of banks.
- The moats/ditches typically range from 2m to 7m in width, with some exceeding 10m.
- The central platforms typically range from 500m² to 2,500m², with some exceeding 8,000m².
- Occasionally, moated sites may be circular or wedge shaped.

Acknowledgements

The information provided by Professor Tadhg O'Keeffe (School of Archaeology, UCD) and Professor Terry Barry (Medieval History Department, TCD) has been most useful in compiling this article. Our thanks are also due to the National Monuments Service, Department of the Environment, Heritage and Local Government, and the Discovery Programme for permission to use their illustrations.

References

Barry, T.B. 1977 *Medieval moated sites of S.E. Ireland*. British Archaeological Reports, British Series 35. Oxford.

Barry, T.B. 1979 The destruction of Irish archaeological monuments. *Irish Geography* **12**, 111–13.

Barry, T.B. 1987 Anglo-Norman rural settlement. In T.B. Barry (ed.), *The archaeology of medieval Ireland*. London and New York.

Barry, T. 2003 The defensive nature of Irish moated sites. In J.R. Kenyon and K. O'Conor (eds), *The medieval castle in Ireland and Wales*. Dublin.

Empey, C.A. 1982 Medieval Knocktopher: a study in manorial settlement— Part 1. *Old Kilkenny Review* **2** (4), 329–42.

O'Conor, K.D. 1998 *The archaeology of medieval rural settlement in Ireland*. Discovery Programme Monograph 3. Dublin.

O'Keeffe, T. 2004 Were there designed landscapes in medieval Ireland? *Landscapes* **5** (2), 52–68.

This article was originally published in the Winter 2006 issue of Archaeology Ireland.

Deserted medieval towns

Many of the towns and villages that sprang up in the wake of the Norman invasion continue to flourish even now, but others were abandoned within a century or two for one reason or another. Two notable examples of deserted medieval towns are Rindown, situated on the peninsula on the western shore of Lough Ree, north of Athlone, and Newtown Jerpoint, located to the west of the Cistercian abbey of Jerpoint in County Kilkenny.

The standing remains of the town defences at Rindown consist of a particularly impressive stone wall stretching across the width of the peninsula and incorporating a gatehouse and three towers. The castle at the north-eastern point of the peninsula was one of the most important Anglo-Norman fortifications in Connacht in the thirteenth and fourteenth centuries. In the vicinity are the remains of the church and an adjacent fish-pond. This town was established in the 1220s and appears to have declined rapidly after the 1330s.

The standing remains of the deserted town of Newtown Jerpoint, which was apparently established in the 1190s, include the ruins of St Nicholas's Church (recently conserved) which dates from the thirteenth to the fifteenth century. The streets of the town survive as longitudinal hollows. Newtown Jerpoint declined in the late sixteenth century and became extinct in the early eighteenth century.

Fig. 1—Rindown town wall and associated tower defences (source: Heritage Council 2012).

Settlements that failed

Most inland towns in Ireland emerged in the century following the Anglo-Norman invasion. For one reason or another some failed after an initial period of success, and their physical remains in the countryside offer a poignant reminder of their glory days. The database compiled by the Department of Arts, Heritage, Regional, Rural and Gaeltacht Affairs (National Monuments Service) records 327 deserted medieval settlements, most prevalent in the midland counties (Fig. 2). Many failed during the fourteenth century but, as noted by O'Conor (1998), in certain areas in south Tipperary and Kilkenny—the counties where approximately one third of the deserted settlements have been recorded (Fig. 2)—they were less severely affected by the troubles of that century and survived up to the sixteenth century.

Rindown

The deserted town of Rindown, situated on the peninsula of St John's Point on the western shore of Lough Ree (north of Athlone), has one of the most important complexes of associated medieval monuments in the country. Rindown appears to have come to prominence during the high to late medieval period (1169–1600). The details of the array of archaeological features on the peninsula outlined below are based on the comprehensive Conservation and Management Plan compiled in 2012 by Blackwood Associates Architects, the lead consultants commissioned by St John's Heritage Group and funded by the Heritage Council.

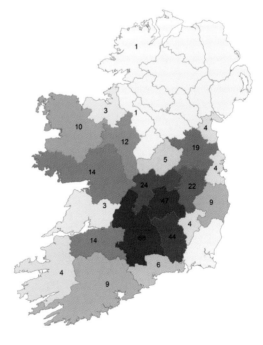

Fig. 2—
Geographical
density
distribution of
deserted medieval
settlements
recorded in
the database
compiled by the
Department of
Arts, Heritage,
Regional, Rural
and Gaeltacht
Affairs (National
Monuments
Service)
(courtesy
of Brendan
Ó Néill).

Town defences

The remains of the town defences consist of a particularly impressive stone wall (Fig. 1) that stretches for almost 700m across the entire width of the peninsula. It is a remarkable structure, considering the size of the settlement that it was intended to protect. It incorporates a gatehouse and three towers. In its original form, the gatehouse was the only point of entry through the wall to the town of Rindown, but three further openings were made subsequently, seemingly to facilitate farming. The gatehouse is likely to have originally been an arched structure.

Towers

The three towers in the town wall are rectangular at ground level, and at first-floor level each wall contains a splayed loop. In many parts of the wall there is evidence of a wall-walk, which would have been a timber structure along which the town's defenders could have moved.

Castle

Situated on a knoll at the north-eastern point of the peninsula, the castle is a large structure overlooking the harbour of Lough Ree and is separated from the town by an earthen bank and ditch. It was one of the most important Anglo-Norman fortifications in Connacht in the thirteenth and fourteenth centuries.

The castle consists of an ovoid curtain wall with a rectangular extension on the south-west. It was entered through a gatehouse, which is overlooked by the keep. A bridge spanned the ditch separating the castle from the town. The masonry piers that supported the castle drawbridge still survive, together with the foundations of the outer gate, which protected the bridge on the town side.

Fig. 3—Rindown castle and parish church, with fish-pond in the foreground (source: Heritage Council 2012).

Hospital of St John the Baptist

The hospital, which may have been founded much earlier, was described in 1596 as having a cloister and three decayed buildings. The ruins of the hospital are all that remain of what would have been an extensive medieval complex. It was located outside the town wall, about 200m to the north-west. Only the church survives, but undulations in the graveyard immediately east of the church indicate other former structures.

Parish church

The church is an important feature of the medieval settlement. It consists of a nave and chancel linked by a pointed arch. An ecclesiastical enclosure surrounds the church. As shown in Fig. 3, a fish-pond dating from the medieval settlement of the peninsula lies close to the church.

Street pattern and market-place

The site of the medieval town of Rindown lies in the fields between the castle and the town wall, a typical arrangement. The street pattern was almost certainly linear, seemingly running from the gatehouse on the town wall to the entrance to the castle.

There is now no trace of the whereabouts of the market-place, and there is practically nothing visible to the naked eye to indicate the pattern of streets within the medieval town. It is presumed that there was a direct road link between the gatehouse in the town wall and the bridge that spanned the ditch and led into the castle.

The precise location of the urban settlement has not been identified. The site between the town wall and the castle far exceeds in area any enclosed urban settlement in medieval Ireland.

Houses

The foundations of four houses have been recorded. The form of the stone walls and their location between the gatehouse and the castle suggest, however, that it is unlikely that they were the remains of medieval structures.

Quays

Safe Harbour, located on the northern shore of the promontory of Rindown, was a key feature of the infrastructure of the medieval settlement. A number of linear stone remains have been found on its foreshore. The largest feature is a slipway, which runs down beyond the low-water mark. The remains of a small wet-docking area run roughly parallel to the end of the slipway. A series of linear, narrow stone walls, possibly stone jetties, run out from below the slope upon which the castle wall stands.

Windmill

The mill is a well-preserved example of a seventeenth-century mill tower (see *Archaeology Ireland*, Summer 2015), located near the end of the peninsula.

Fig. 4—Aerial photograph of Newtown Jerpoint, showing plot boundaries to the north of the church and the roadway to the south-east (source: Heritage Council 2007, courtesy of Ian Doyle).

The surviving remains consist of a cylindrical stone tower, set on top of a round mound and surrounded by a ditch with an external bank. The tower had three floors and survives to its original height. The erection of such a substantial mill in the seventeenth century points to appreciable growth in grain production in the vicinity.

Newtown Jerpoint

The deserted medieval settlement of Newtown Jerpoint, Co. Kilkenny (Figs 4 and 5), located to the west of the Cistercian abbey of Jerpoint, was once an important town. Apparently established in the 1190s, it grew to the south of the bridge, now gone, over the shallow crossing point to the west of the junction of the Rivers Nore and Arrigle. The outline of the interesting remains of the deserted town presented below is based on the Heritage Conservation Plan produced in 2007 by Oxford Archaeology and commissioned by the Heritage Council.

The standing remains of the deserted town include the ruins of St Nicholas's Church (Fig. 6), which dates from the thirteenth–fifteenth century, and a small remnant of a secular, stone-built tower of medieval date, which may have been a small urban tower-house.

The surviving features of the thirteenth-century parish church of St Nicholas comprise the nave and chancel, along with a fifteenth-century rood-screen and gallery, which are considered to be unusual, and the residential tower added within the church. The churchyard contains a fine early fourteenth-century medieval slab effigy (Box 1; Fig. 7).

The streets survive as longitudinal hollows, bordered by rectangular terraces and the remains of burgage plots. The main north–south street, which is probably the 'Long Street' of the historical sources, is well defined, except where obscured by stone piles. The bridge, which was a crucial aspect of the infrastructure of the town, seems to have been beyond the northern end of the north–south road through the town, where two hollows have recently been located.

Box 1	Newtown Jerpoint: medieval graveslab

A medieval priest's graveslab (Fig. 7) was excavated in 2011 at Newtown Jerpoint, in the graveyard to the north of the parish church. It was located beside the fourteenth-century effigy known as the 'Nicholas slab', which local tradition records as marking the relics of St Nicholas of Myra (popularly associated with Santa Claus). It bears an extremely worn incised figure of an ecclesiastic and an inscription asking for God's mercy on the soul of Toris Colcnlev (probably Thomas Colclough). A fine collection of eighteenth/nineteenth-century gravestones may also be seen.

Source: Coilín Ó Drisceoil (Kilkenny Archaeology)

The east–west street, with house platforms on either side, is narrower and twisting, and loses definition beyond the western end of the churchyard. The T-junction between the two streets appears to have been marked by an ash tree, which is said to have been full of nails from the supplications pinned to it. The lower section and base of a stone cross contained in the graveyard of the church may originally have been located at the junction of the two streets.

Two well-defined buildings dating from the early thirteenth to the mid-fourteenth century were excavated at Jerpoint Church townland by Claire Foley for the Office of Public Works in 1973. As further detailed by O'Conor (1998), the first structure consisted of a rectangular mud-built peasant longhouse divided into two rooms, one of which may have been a byre. The

Fig. 5—Aerial photograph of Newtown Jerpoint, showing plot boundaries to the east of the road (visible left of centre) and the drainage channel running parallel to the River Nore (source: Heritage Council 2007, courtesy of Ian Doyle).

second structure was a more substantial stone building of at least two storeys and with a stone stairway leading to the first floor. It has been suggested that the building may represent the remains of a manor house, and that a contemporary circular, drystone-lined pit excavated at the site may perhaps have been either a well or a cold-storage area for hanging carcasses of meat or fowl.

Jerpoint Corn Mill is located outside the site of Newtown, on the east bank of the River Arrigle. The large four-storey building still contains remains of the wheels and mill machinery. There are various references to mills in Jerpoint, which could be on different sites or be parts of one mill complex. The remains of watermills on the west bank of the River Arrigle are likely to date from the origins of the town.

Newtown Jerpoint seems to have survived the traumatic fourteenth century. Petty's census of 1659 lists 29 inhabitants in 'Jerpoint', 27 Irish and two English. Newtown Jerpoint was in decline during the seventeenth century, and the great flood of 1763, which took out all the Nore bridges down to New Ross, could have led to its ultimate demise. The loss of its bridge and the consequent diversion of the road would have had more adverse consequences for Newtown Jerpoint than the dissolution of the abbey in 1540. As stated in the 2007 Heritage Conservation Plan referred to above, 'the most likely scenario is that the town declined in the late sixteenth century, surviving into the early seventeenth century as a hamlet, and finally becoming extinct in the early eighteenth century'.

Fig. 6—Church of St Nicholas at Newtown Jerpoint during conservation works in 2013, funded by the Heritage Council (courtesy of Ian Doyle).

Fig. 7—Medieval priest's graveslab excavated in 2011 at Newtown Jerpoint (courtesy of Coilín Ó Drisceoil, Kilkenny Archaeology).

Box 2   Diagnostic features

- Medieval settlement typically clustered around the remains of a church and manor house or castle, and may have surrounding earthworks of banks and ditches.
- Ground marked by earthworks, representing the remains of linear streets or roadways, burgage plots, boundaries and houses.
- Excavated houses typically consist of a two-roomed structure, with a living area at one end and a byre at the other end.
- Other standing features often found include the remains of towers and mills.

Acknowledgements

The historical context of Anglo-Norman settlements in Ireland provided by Kieran O'Conor has been most informative. The contributions of Ian Doyle, Paul Walsh, Coilín Ó Drisceoil and Maeve Connell are also much appreciated.

References

Heritage Council 2007 *Newtown Jerpoint, Co. Kilkenny: Heritage Conservation Plan*. Kilkenny.

Heritage Council 2012 *RinnDúin Conservation and Management Plan*. Kilkenny.

O'Conor, K.D. 1998 English peasant settlement on Anglo-Norman manors. In K.D. O'Conor, *The archaeology of medieval rural settlement in Ireland*. Discovery Programme Monograph 3. Dublin.

This article was originally published in the Autumn 2016 issue of Archaeology Ireland.

Tower-houses

Tower-houses were typically the defended residences of wealthy Anglo-Norman/English and Gaelic families in the later Middle Ages. They seem to have been erected predominantly beween AD 1450 and 1620. Many, however, were built before 1450 and some were built even before 1400. Tower-houses are generally three to five storeys in height, with the principal or more private rooms usually in the upper storeys. The living conditions, at least in some, appear to have been less than comfortable. Many originally had no regular fireplace or chimney, but these were often inserted later.

In many instances, the wealth required to support tower-houses was generated mainly from farming. They were built primarily in the most productive farming areas, with high concentrations in Counties Tipperary, Kilkenny, Cork and Limerick.

House and farm

Tower-houses are small, single-towered castles, three, four or five storeys in height and usually quite simple in plan. They are the most visible medieval secular buildings in the modern landscape. As many as 3,500 were built across the country in the medieval period, making Ireland by the 1600s the most heavily castellated part of these islands (Fig. 1). They are similar to the broadly contemporary peel towers built along the Anglo-Scottish border (Sweetman 2000).

Origins and locations

Tower-houses were typically the defended residences of wealthy Anglo-Norman/English and Gaelic families. The majority seem to have been erected between c. 1450 and 1620. Many, however, were built before the mid-1450s, and some before the end of the 1300s (Bradley and Murtagh 2003).

The areas with the highest concentration of tower-houses are those that experienced the greatest level of instability and changes in landownership, with, as discussed below, the more productive farmland being strongly favoured. Although many tower-houses were constructed by Anglo-Normans, they became very popular in Gaelic areas in the later Middle Ages, and more widespread. The majority are located south of a line from Galway to Louth (Fig. 2). They are most concentrated in Counties Tipperary and Kilkenny (the earldom of Ormond), County Westmeath (Old English/Gaelic marchlands) and in south Galway, east Clare and Limerick (Old English/Gaelic lordships). Relatively few are found in the northern and south-western areas of the country.

Fig. 1—
(a) Tower-house at Drishane and (opposite) (b) an unusually large example at Blarney, both in County Cork (courtesy of Colin Rynne).

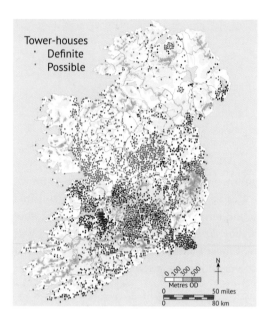

Tower-houses
· Definite
· Possible

Fig. 2—
Geographical
distribution of
tower-houses
(courtesy of
Matthew Stout).

Layout

Tower-houses were self-contained residences, with rooms stacked vertically and connected by winding stairs. The ground-floor room was poorly lit and usually served as a store or cellar. It frequently had a vaulted ceiling, a feature sometimes also found on other floors. Wicker mats were generally used in the preparation of the vaulting, and impressions of these can often still be seen in the mortar on the underside of the vaultings.

The principal rooms were generally located in the upper storeys. They were better lit, with larger ogee-headed windows and with punch-dressed stone for the jambs. Many tower-houses as originally built had no regular fireplaces. One or more were often inserted at a later date, usually at the expense of some windows. Where evidence for fireplaces remains, it is usually to be found on the upper floors. The interiors of the rooms were usually whitewashed or plastered, and evidence for this remains at many sites around the country.

The living conditions in tower-houses, at least in some instances, seem to have been less than comfortable. As further detailed by Leask (1986), some travellers in Ireland during the 1600s observed that 'They have little furniture and cover their rooms with rushes ...', and that 'When you come to yor. chamber, do not expect canopy and curtaines'.

Tower-houses were, as already indicated, defended residences, and many surviving examples have important defensive features such as double-stepped battlements, machicolations over doorways, slit windows at lower levels and murder holes at the entrance lobby. In a number of examples, grooves can be seen where a yett (iron grill) could be pulled across in front of the main door, which was always at ground level. From the late 1500s onwards, loops for guns became more common. The number of corner turrets varies, but one—usually above the stair—was sometimes higher than the others. A second turret often contained the garderobe or toilet. The roofs of tower-houses were slated, and some were thatched. Roofs of stone slats, oak timbers or shingles were also known.

Although often standing isolated today, most tower-houses were originally enclosed, at least partially, by a bawn or walled courtyard that sometimes had towers at the corners. Located within the bawn would have been the ancillary domestic buildings, as well as the buildings required for agriculture—a predominant occupation of many tower-house landowners.

Agriculture

Tower-houses occur in medieval towns and villages, but the bulk are dispersed throughout the countryside. In many instances the wealth required to support their occupants was generated mainly from farming. The close link between tower-houses in Ireland and agriculture is reflected in their location, which corresponds in large measure to what is known today to be the most productive farmland in the country. As shown in Fig. 2, high concentrations occur in Tipperary, Kilkenny, Cork and Limerick. Compared to the neighbouring counties of Dublin, Kildare, Carlow and Wexford, fewer tower-houses are found in the mountainous County Wicklow. While considerations of security, among other issues, influenced their location, unproductive farming areas were generally not favoured.

Excavations at Bremore Castle, Co. Dublin, by Finola O'Carroll of CRDS Ltd confirmed that the nearby area was used for agricultural purposes from the medieval period (O'Carroll 2009). Among the features uncovered were field drains, possible plough furrows, pits and boundary ditches. One of the pits, which produced medieval pottery sherds, may have been a former manure heap. Others could have been used as wells or cisterns to hold the water required for farming. Charred grain found within the furrows included wheat, barley and oats as well as legumes, which may have been part of the crop-rotation system employed. The layout of the field system suggests that it was part of a larger pattern of fields associated with laneways, at least one of which widened out into a yard-like area.

Information on the composition of agriculture in medieval Ireland is limited. Mixed farming, with cereal-growing predominant, seems to have been prevalent in the south-eastern and central regions of the country (Jager 1983). Within a relatively short period between c. 1200 and 1300, and coinciding with the maximum expansion of the Anglo-Norman colonisation, these regions seem to have experienced an increase in tillage said to be comparable with that of the main European cereal-growing areas. At that time, up to 75% of the utilised land in the south-eastern and central parts of Ireland was seemingly devoted to arable farming. As further detailed by Jager (1983), however, the area of arable production began to contract by the end of the 1200s, with the incursion of the native Irish into many Anglo-Norman-dominated areas of cultivated land. In the Pale, however, tillage was still dominant in the 1600s.

The recent comprehensive Medieval Rural Settlement Project undertaken by the Discovery Programme substantiates the dominance of arable farming in the wider Dublin region during the medieval period (Murphy and Potterton 2009). Analysis of surviving manorial documents providing land-use data from more than 20 manors in the Dublin region showed that the acreage of arable production amounted to almost three quarters (74%) of the total demesne land used in the area (Fig. 3), with some manors having almost their entire (over 90%) farmland in tillage. Conversely, the proportion of the land devoted to pasture (13%), and hence available for livestock production, was shown to be unexpectedly low. Analysis of later data recorded in the Civil Survey in the 1650s revealed a similar relative land-use pattern. Again, arable production was shown to be the predominant land use, averaging close on three quarters (74%) of all the farmland across the Dublin region (Fig. 3) and accounting for virtually the total farmland (over 90%) in some places. The proportion of the farmland devoted to pasture was strikingly low (14%) and similar to the level derived from the analysis of the data from around 1300.

The remarkable similarities found by Murphy and Potterton (2009) in the proportions of farmland in the Dublin region devoted to the different land uses between 1300 and 1650 (Fig. 3) does not imply that there was little or no change in the composition of agricultural production in the region over the 350-year period. As previously mentioned, tillage production in the south-eastern and central areas of Ireland seems to have reached a maximum around 1300 and then declined. Jager (1983) reported no such contraction within the Pale. By 1400, however, with a drop in population after a disastrous 50 years, there may have been a retreat from arable agriculture, and the 1650s figures may reflect the taking of pastureland back into arable production in response to demands from a resurgent population (Murphy and Potterton 2009).

The relatively low proportion of Dublin farmland devoted to pasture is, as already indicated, a somewhat surprising feature of the analysis summarised in Fig. 3. Whether this is due to under-recording of pasture relative to arable land and meadow, which seems to have occurred in the medieval period (Jager 1983), is uncertain. It may also reflect, at least in part, the stall feeding of livestock and the grazing of fallow land. Clearly, without sufficient livestock, the manure vital for maintaining the fertility of the arable land would have been in short supply. Dung from animals, especially pigs, within the city, as well as household and other wastes, was apparently used in the Middle Ages for manuring fields in the Dublin hinterland, as is further detailed by Corlett and Potterton.

In spite of any limitations inherent in the available data, the research undertaken by Murphy and Potterton (2009) clearly indicates that arable production was the most important farming enterprise across the Dublin region in the late medieval period. Indeed, a model of mixed farming, with cereal-growing predominant, may well have been the most prevalent farming system in the more productive landholdings during the period. As in recent centuries, however, and as is still a characteristic of Irish agriculture today, arable production in the medieval period is likely to have been predominantly concentrated in the east and south-east of the country. As shown in Fig. 3, mixed crops and livestock farms are currently largely concentrated in these regions (Crowley et al. 2008).

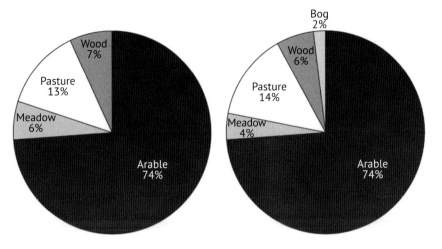

Fig. 3—Land use in the Dublin region, c. 1300 (left) (source: manorial extents) and c. 1650 (right) (source: Civil Survey) (courtesy of Margaret Murphy and Michael Potterton).

An alternative model of mixed farming with livestock predominant may have been the most prevalent farming system in much of the rest of the country during the medieval period, and indeed much earlier. The number of tower-houses in the fertile lowlands of County Limerick points to the importance of pastoral farming in generating wealth in medieval times (Donnelly 2001). Although an oversimplification, the quality of arable land may have been an important determinant of the location of tower-houses in the east and south-east of the country, whereas productive pastureland is likely to have been a more important determinant in areas west of the Shannon. Nevertheless, cereal production, sometimes on a considerable scale, seems to have been undertaken in the more productive farming areas in western counties, as evidenced by the occurrence of long (up to 170m or more), curvilinear, relatively wide (3m or more) ridges in such areas as the Beara Peninsula (O'Sullivan and Downey 2007). The period represented by such ridges needs, insofar as is possible, to be determined. Some of the wider ridges may be associated with the 'corn boom' of the late 1700s and early 1800s, or conceivably earlier grain cultivation. Apart from this period, livestock production seems to have been the dominant farming enterprise in Ireland over a long period of time. With the specialisation in farming over recent decades, this historical characteristic has become even more pronounced. Over 90% of the total farmed land is now devoted to livestock, with the Shannon acting as the main divide (Fig. 3) between the dairy-farming strongholds of Munster and the north-east and the specialised beef production concentrated in western counties (Crowley *et al.* 2008).

Diagnostic features
- Tall, generally square buildings, usually retaining some of the typical castle fortifications, such as battlements, narrow slit windows and machicolations.
- Often standing in isolation as ivy-clad ruins, but occasionally enclosed by a bawn.

- Later tower-houses of the sixteenth century had larger windows and more gun loops, chimneys and crenellations than earlier types. Many of the Irish tower-houses as originally built had no regular fireplaces or chimneys, but these were often inserted later.

Acknowledgements

Dr Michael Potterton kindly made available to us an article summarising the current state of knowledge about tower-houses. This is much appreciated, as is the information provided by Ian Doyle and Professor Tadhg O'Keeffe. The photographs of tower-houses were kindly provided by Dr Colin Rynne. We are grateful to Dr Matthew Stout, Dr Caroline Crowley, Professor Jim Walsh and David Meredith for permission to use the distribution maps of modern farming systems in Ireland.

References

Bradley, J. and Murtagh, B. 2003 Brady's Castle, Thomastown, Co. Kilkenny: a 14th-century fortified town house. In J.R. Kenyon and K. O'Conor (eds), *The medieval castle in Ireland and Wales: essays in honour of Jeremy Knight*. Dublin.

Corlett, C. and Potterton, M. (eds) (2009) *Rural settlement in medieval Ireland in the light of recent archaeological excavations*. Bray.

Crowley, C., Walsh, J. and Meredith, D. (eds) 2008 Crops, livestock and farming systems. In C. Crowley, J. Walsh and D. Meredith (eds), *Irish farming at the millennium—a census atlas*. Dublin.

Donnelly, C.J. 2001 Tower houses and late medieval secular settlement in County Limerick. In P. Duffy, D. Edwards and E. FitzPatrick (eds), *Gaelic Ireland c. 1250–c. 1650: land, lordship and settlement*. Dublin.

Jager, H. 1983 Land use in medieval Ireland: a review of the documentary evidence. *Irish Economic and Social History* **10**, 51–65.

Leask, H.G. (ed.) 1986 *Irish castles and castellated houses*. Dundalk.

Murphy, M. and Potterton, M. (2009) The Dublin region in the Middle Ages: settlement, land use and economy. In C. Corlett and M. Potterton (eds), *Rural settlement in medieval Ireland in the light of recent archaeological excavations*. Bray.

O'Carroll, F. (2009) A medieval and post-medieval farm landscape at Bremore, Co. Dublin. In C. Corlett and M. Potterton (eds), *Rural settlement in medieval Ireland in the light of recent archaeological excavations*. Dublin.

O'Sullivan, M. and Downey, L. 2007 Ridges and furrows. *Archaeology Ireland* **21** (2), 34–7.

Sweetman, D. 2000 *The origin and development of the tower house*. Cork.

This article was originally published in the Summer 2009 issue of Archaeology Ireland.

Clachans

Clachans were clusters of dwelling houses in rural Ireland, forming traditional villages without amenities such as shops, pubs, schools or churches. The occupants usually engaged in farming, especially rundale farming. However, clachans are also known in landscapes where there is no evidence of rundale farming. They may also have arisen in certain localities after rundale had given way to single tenancies. In addition to farming, clachan occupants engaged in fishing, weaving and spinning, while some may have been carpenters, blacksmiths etc.

Clachans varied markedly in size and typology. House clusters in the Glens of Antrim, for instance, appear to have been more substantial settlements, containing more well-built houses (some two-storey) and farm buildings, than the types of dwellings that characterised many clachans in the west of Ireland.

When the population was reaching its pre-Famine peak, a crescent of clachans existed around the seaboard in the north, west and south-west, and high densities also occurred in many mountain glens and hill margins. The main period of clachan development appears to have been the 1700s and early 1800s. They were widespread in the early nineteenth century but, with the marked decline in population following the Great Famine, many clachans were cleared and their associated farmland was enclosed. Likewise, while some clachans featured up to a hundred houses or more at their peak, most were reduced to a fraction of their pre-Famine size by the later part of the nineteenth century. This process continued more gradually through the twentieth century.

Fig. 1 (a)—General view of the Cruckincarragh clachan in the Glens of Antrim (courtesy of Jonathan Bell).

Clustered living

Compact farm clusters characterised both by their settlement form, known as **clachans**, and by their farming system, termed **rundale**, were most prevalent in the decades prior to the Great Famine. This article on post-medieval fieldscapes deals mainly with clachans. An associated article, in the Autumn 2008 issue of *Archaeology Ireland* (reprinted here on pp 22–9), focuses on the rundale farming system.

Clachans comprised a seemingly haphazard assemblage of houses and buildings (Fig. 1), often with a maze of narrow lanes and roads winding between them in an irregular manner. Absence of spatial order was not, however, a universal feature. In some clachans the houses had a distinctive parallel alignment, and in others they were arranged on each side of the road or, less frequently, around a small, ill-defined central space (Aalen 1978). Clachans generally have none of the buildings that typify a true village, such as a church, pub, shops or school. They were essentially concerned with farming, and are usually associated with the system of rundale farming, often involving families with close kinships (Yager 2002; Bell 2007).

Crops were mainly grown in the **infield** around the clachan. Cultivation, though important, was a subsidiary farming activity, but it may have been more developed in the south-east than in the north and west (McCourt

Fig. 1 (b) — General view of the Galboly clachan in the Glens of Antrim (courtesy of Jonathan Bell).

1971). Clachan farming had a strong bias towards stock-rearing. In many places, houses were shared with cows and other animals, and sanitation was generally rather basic. Some occupants of clachans may have engaged in weaving, spinning and fishing, while others may have been carpenters or blacksmiths. The clachan community was, however, primarily engaged in farming, in particular a level of subsistence farming involving a high degree of mutual interdependence.

Buildings

McCourt (1971) identified 150 clachans in parts of Derry, Antrim and Down, containing an average of 3.5 houses. Fifteen clachans had six or more houses, and the largest contained eleven houses. Clachans that appear to have had 20–40 houses/buildings, arranged in different spatial configurations, have been described by Aalen (1978). Some clachans became sizeable settlements. For instance, the clachan at Rathlackan, Co. Mayo, was in 1918 occupied by 50 families (Evans 1957) and appears to have comprised around 80 houses/ buildings. Many of the house clusters surveyed during the summer of 2006 in the Glens of Antrim were more substantial settlements than the disordered assemblages of dwellings that were typical of many clachans in the west of Ireland (Bell 2007). As elsewhere in Ireland, the clachans surveyed varied in size, with populations ranging from 33 up to 144. The houses in the clachan at Drumfresky had an attached garden and were arranged around a tiny patch of ground, known as the **common**, which was used to stack turf and to park carts. One of the houses was the home of the landlord's agent.

In addition to a number of well-built houses (some two storey), the clachans surveyed contained such farm buildings as a threshing barn, pigsties and cart houses. The clachan at Cullyvally had resident craftsmen, including a blacksmith and carpenter. The Galboly clachan had a sheepfold in 1800 and operated a shebeen until around 1880. On the evidence of the houses and range of farm buildings, Bell (2007) suggests that the clachans in the Glens of Antrim were developing a level of economic visibility distinct from the persistent poverty that prevailed in many clachans in the west of Ireland. A number of clachans in the Glens of Antrim continued to be inhabited when the associated rundale farming ceased in the early nineteenth century, and some are still occupied today.

Geographical location

The Ordnance Survey maps published between 1832 and 1840, when the population was reaching its Famine peak, showed (Fig. 2) a crescent of clachans around the seaboard and hill margins in the north, west and south-west (McCourt 1971). The distribution was dense in the mountain glens and hill margins of Antrim, the Sperrins, the west Wicklow Mountains, the Mournes, the Knockmealdown and Comeragh ranges of east Cork and Waterford, and also on the highland fringes of west Cork and Kerry. Marked concentrations were also recorded around rivers and lakes, sometimes in

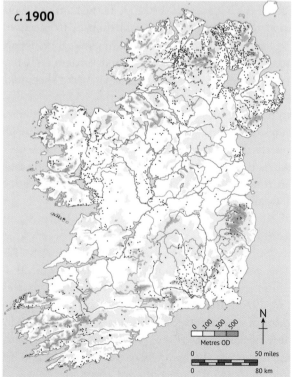

Fig. 2—Clachan distribution 1832–40 and 1900, mapped by McCourt (1971) (courtesy of Matthew Stout).

the floodplains. Clachans were densely concentrated on nearly all of the peninsulas and islands of Ulster, Connacht and Munster, and especially the southern tip of the Ards and in Lecale, Co. Down, as well as the coastal margins of the western and southern counties from Donegal to Wexford. In 1833 Rathlin Island had at least 12 clusters of houses, all apparently clachans (Bell 2007).

By 1900 clachan densities had declined sharply (Fig. 2) and had receded to the coastal margins of the north, west and south, with some remnants around the Shannon (McCourt 1971). Clachan losses were particularly marked in the south-western peninsulas, Clare and east Connacht.

Dating

There is no clear evidence that clachans were part of the medieval landscape (McCourt 1971; Aalen 1978). In this regard, the earlier view—of continuity in the existence of clachans as a settlement form for 1,000 years and more—is refuted in Doherty's (2002) comprehensive review of settlement in early Ireland. Some of those recently surveyed in the Glens of Antrim are located at prehistoric sites, where Mesolithic and Neolithic artefacts have been found in large numbers. Although not indicative of continuous occupation since these times, the attributes of the sites utilised by the clachan farmers may also have attracted earlier occupants (Bell 2007).

Clachans are now generally seen as predominantly post-medieval in date. Those mapped in the first part of Fig. 2 are of mid-nineteenth-century date, and many in west Connacht seem to be no earlier than the seventeenth century (McCourt 1971). The widespread occurrence of clachans is largely a consequence of the particular demographic, social and economic pressures affecting Ireland in the eighteenth and nineteenth centuries. They existed in Ireland during the seventeenth and eighteenth centuries and were widespread in the early nineteenth century (Aalen 1978), but declined in density in the decades following the Famine. Clachans are a feature of subsistence farming and are, as previously indicated, typically associated with rundale farming. As noted by McCourt (1971), however, clustered settlements existed in certain parts of Ireland independently of open-field cultivation, and seem to have arisen in certain locations after rundale had given way to single tenancies. A series of estate maps of the mid-eighteenth and mid-nineteenth centuries show clachans growing from the subdivision of single tenancies and from small settlement groups. The reverse process was equally common and especially rapid after the mid-nineteenth century. Because of the waxing and waning of settlement, townlands were in a continuous state of flux between the mid-eighteenth and mid-nineteenth centuries (McCourt 1971).

The far-reaching changes implemented by local landlords in the decade following the Famine resulted in the dispersal of many clachans and the general adoption of enclosure and hedging, which can still be seen in parts of Ireland today (Aalen 1978).

Diagnostic features

- Cluster of houses/buildings, some perhaps still occupied but mainly derelict, and often an intertwining maze of lanes and roads.
- Layout generally haphazard, but in some instances the houses/buildings are in a parallel alignment or, infrequently, around a small, ill-defined central area.
- Located mainly around the seaboard and hill margins in the north, west and south.
- Surrounding fields may be laid out in a regular, ladder or fan pattern, with little evidence of the infields. (For further detail see the Summer 2008 issue of *Archaeology Ireland*.)

Acknowledgements

Dr Jonathan Bell kindly made available to us a copy of his publication based on the Glens of Antrim Historical Society's Clachan Project, which involved a survey undertaken in conjunction with Mervyn Watson and with members of the Glens Society during the summer of 2006. We are also grateful to Dr Bell and Dr Matthew Stout for providing the illustrations contained in Fig. 1 and Fig. 2 respectively.

References

Aalen, F.H.A. (ed.) 1978 *Man and the landscape in Ireland*. London.

Bell, J. 2007 Rundale in the Glens of Antrim. *Ulster Folklife* **52**.

Doherty, C. 2002 Settlement in early Ireland. In T. Barry (ed.), *A history of settlement in Ireland*. London.

Evans, E.E. (ed.) 1957 *Irish folk ways*. London.

McCourt, D. 1971 The dynamic quality of Irish rural settlement. In R.H. Buchanan, E. Jones and D. McCourt (eds), *Man and his habitat: essays presented to Emyr Estyn Evans*. London.

Whelan, K. 1994 Decoding the landscape. In T. Collins (ed.), *Settlement patterns in the west of Ireland in the pre-famine period*. Galway.

Yager, T. 2002 What was rundale and where did it come from? *Béaloideas* **70**, 153–86.

This article was originally published in the Spring 2008 issue of Archaeology Ireland.

Section IV
Getting around

R oadways are not permanent. They can be the focus of ongoing repair, resurfacing, widening, straightening and other adjustments in response to a wide variety of influences, notably changing destinations, technology, responsible authorities and governing attitudes. A comparison of local roads today with those shown on the first-edition Ordnance Survey 6in. maps of less than two centuries ago will often show how much can change in half a dozen generations.

Interestingly, however, the general route from one part of the country to another tends to have survived, or to have changed more slowly. In this context, it is interesting to speculate on how old some of the specific routes we use today may be. The earliest evidence we have for what might be called national routes has survived in manuscript references from medieval times. Even before that, however, substantial wooden roadways were constructed across midland bogs during the Iron Age. Before the first bridges were built, fords across rivers were of critical importance. Reaching back to the earliest inhabitants of Ireland some 8,000 or 9,000 years ago, the absence of a road system would presumably have placed extra importance on other routeways—forest paths, river valleys, the margins of lakes and the seashore. Boats would have been useful—not only for maritime travel and fishing, but also as a mode of travel and transport on inland waterways.

Finds of prehistoric craft almost exclusively involve **logboats**. Most rudimentary at first sight, logboats were not simply hollowed-out logs. They were purposefully designed craft with crucial operational features built into the hulls. Logboats from as early as the Mesolithic and Neolithic periods have been found in Ireland and they continued in use into the latter part of the seventeenth century and seemingly later.

Paddle **currachs**, versatile craft, were in use from earlier times on rivers, lakes and coastal waters. They served a wide range of everyday purposes until they were superseded by rowing currachs from the early twentieth century. By the mid-twentieth century, large, improved fishing currachs were common on many parts of the west coast.

Five particularly well-known **early historical routeways** seem to have snaked through the Irish countryside. It would be nice to have scholarly unanimity on the geographical origins and alignment of these key routes of the early road system. However, as explained in the article below, two radically different perspectives have been advanced on this topic. **Historical bridges** were often built centuries after the roads they facilitated took shape. The construction of stone-built bridges evolved progressively from later medieval times onward, with two notable periods of bridge-building—one in the thirteenth century AD and another spanning the seventeenth and eighteenth centuries.

Currachs

Currachs were once made exclusively of natural materials, particularly cattle or horse hide over a frame of willows and hazel. Skin-covered boats seem to have emerged in the Iron Age and were used around Ireland from late prehistory, being well documented from early Christian times, throughout the medieval period and into more recent times.

Paddle currachs (sometimes termed coracles) were used on various rivers, notably the Boyne, in the nineteenth and twentieth centuries. Seagoing paddle currachs were once common around the Donegal islands from at least the mid-1700s. The paddle currach could be launched and landed almost anywhere and was used for multiple purposes, ranging from inland fishing to carrying turf and seaweed and ferrying passengers and even funerals between islands and the mainland.

The 1820s and 1830s heralded major innovations in currach design and construction, notably in Counties Clare and Mayo. The garrisons at signal towers and Coastguard stations played an important role in the adoption and spread of the new and improved currachs. The Kerry naomhóg has been described as the 'supreme achievement' of the currach-builders.

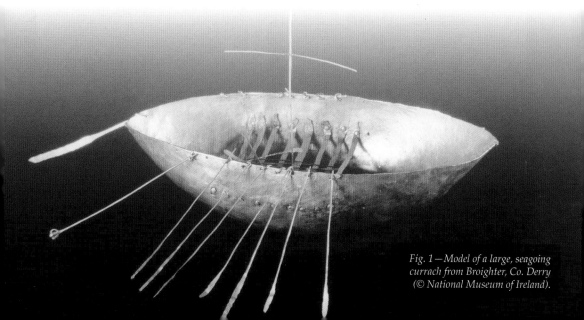

Fig. 1—Model of a large, seagoing currach from Broighter, Co. Derry (© National Museum of Ireland).

Hide and canvas boats

Currachs were boats that were once made exclusively of natural materials, in particular animal hides (usually cattle or horse) and a frame of willows and hazel. A transition to the more modern craft occurred from around the 1820s–30s, which marked, as outlined below, a notable period of currach innovation (Mac Cárthaigh 2008). As detailed by Breen and Forsythe (2004), logboats were dominant in prehistory (see *Archaeology Ireland*, Winter 2014), but the first evidence for skin-covered boats emerged in the Iron Age.

Archaeology

While no hide-covered boat survives in the Irish archaeological record, two well-known finds—the Broighter boat (Fig. 1) and the Bantry boat (Fig. 2)—provide invaluable representations of the craft.

Fig. 2—Carving of seagoing currach on a pillar stone at Kilnaruane, Bantry Bay, Co. Cork (courtesy of Con Brogan, National Monuments Service).

The model boat (Fig. 1) made of sheet gold found at Broighter (Co. Derry) has been dated to the first century BC. The general consensus is that it represents the earliest depiction of a skin-covered boat in Ireland (Breen and Forsythe 2004). The find is of particular importance, both nationally and internationally. It is the earliest representation of a boat in Ireland and it is also one of the earliest certain indicators of the use of a sail in northern Europe. The vessel has a single central mast, and 15 of the original 18 oars survive.

An important early depiction of a boat is carved on the Kilnaruane pillar stone overlooking Bantry Bay, Co. Cork (Fig. 2). The pillar has been dated to the eighth or ninth century AD, and the general view is that the boat more than likely represents a skin-covered craft, an early example of a currach (Breen and Forsythe 2004).

Historical records

Documentary evidence pointing to the use of skin-covered boats around Ireland since earlier times has been extensively covered in a number of recent books (Breen and Forsythe 2004; Mac Cárthaigh 2008; Ó Gibne 2012). Some important historical accounts concerning the use of currachs around Ireland are synopsised in Box 1.

Box 1	**Some reports on the historical use of currachs in Ireland**

- Early Irish literature is full of accounts of long sea journeys in large currachs during early Christian times, such as those of SS Brendan and Colmcille (Columba).
- The twelfth-century *History and topography of Ireland* by Gerald of Wales refers to a small currach paddled by two men in the vastness of the sea off Connacht.
- Accounts of Dónal Cam O'Sullivan Beara's epic march north in 1603 describe two hide-covered currachs built to ferry his followers across the quarter-mile-wide Shannon.
- In 1685 a currach of comparable proportions is recorded in the well-known colour-wash sketch of a large sailing currach by Thomas Phillips, a military engineer sent to Ireland to survey the harbours and fortifications.
- The 1800s heralded major innovations in currach design and construction (Box 2), culminating in large fleets of improved fishing currachs on many parts of the west coast.

Source: Mac Cárthaigh 2008

Fig. 3—Paddle currach, River Boyne, 1848—sketch by William Wakeman (courtesy of Críostóir Mac Cárthaigh).

Fig. 4—Paddle currach (right) and rowing currach (left), Tory Island (courtesy of Críostóir Mac Cárthaigh).

Predominant currach forms

Críostóir Mac Cárthaigh's *Traditional boats of Ireland* (2008) contains, in encyclopaedic detail, information on Irish skin-boats.

Paddle currachs

Paddle currachs (sometimes termed 'coracles') have been used on certain Irish rivers in the past (Mac Cárthaigh 2008; Ó Gibne 2012). The use of the paddle currach on the Boyne River is well established. It was reported in 1824 on the Blackwater close to Youghal, and in Cork Harbour in 1938. Paddle currachs have also been recorded on the Shannon and the Erne, and less certainly on the Bann and the Foyle.

The currach used on the Boyne (Fig. 3) is an oval-shaped boat with a framework of hazel. The size varied from 6ft to 6ft 6in. by 4ft. It would accommodate two people, one kneeling in front to paddle the currach and the other sitting towards the rear to tend to the fishing nets.

Seagoing paddle currachs were once common on Donegal islands such as Gola, Inishmere, Owey and Tory, and continued to be used in modern times around Kincasslagh and Owey (Mac Cárthaigh 2008). The paddler knelt in the bow, which allowed the craft to be manoeuvred around rocky inlets and in shallow water. Women from the islands used the craft. The little craft (Fig. 4) was the smallest of Ireland's working currachs, and closest in type to the Boyne currach (above). The earliest account of the Donegal paddle currach dates from 1752, when Richard Pococke observed a currach crossing the Clady River near Bunbeg, Co. Donegal.

The ancestor of the square-sterned paddle currach appears to have been an oval, basket-like craft closely resembling the twentieth-century currachs of the Boyne and Blackwater (Mac Cárthaigh 2008). Currachs were once common on northern rivers such as the Foyle, Erne and Bann, and Mac Cárthaigh wondered whether the tiny currachs of the Donegal islands might

Fig. 5—Four-man rowing currach off Inis Mór, Aran Islands, in 1895 (© Royal Society of Antiquaries of Ireland).

be descendants of the currachs on these rivers. This view was supported by the well-known ethnologist E. Estyn Evans, who noted that 'There are in Donegal several smaller paddling curachs [*sic*] eight or ten feet long which seem to start between the oval river baskets and the sharp pointed rowing curachs' (below). By the end of the nineteenth century the paddle currach (Fig. 4) had assumed a square-sterned, bath-like shape, which persists to modern times. Another fundamental change was the replacement of wicker with sawn timber throughout.

The paddle currach could be launched and landed almost anywhere. One man could carry the craft on his shoulders, and a woman could lift a small one. It was a multi-purpose vessel, used for local transport and for inshore hand-line and lobster fishing, and routinely carried sizeable loads of turf and seaweed, as well as coal and cement. They were commonly used as ferries and, where required, for funerals to burial grounds on the islands.

The small vessel gave way to larger paddle and rowing currachs. In his 1936 survey, Hornell (1937; 1938) reported the Tory and Bunbeg currach (which could be paddled or rowed) as being 12ft 6in. long, 43in. wide and 21in. deep.

Rowing currachs

The paddle currachs were, from the early years of the twentieth century, progressively superseded in most areas by rowing currachs (Fig. 5).

The 1820s–30s heralded innovations in currach design and construction (Box 2), and the transition to more modern craft (Mac Cárthaigh 2008). Chief among these developments were the following:

- Tarred canvas superseded the traditional animal-hide covering.
- Sawn timbers replaced hazel and willow in the construction of the hull.
- A double-gunwaled frame enabled the currach to be enlarged and to accommodate extra oarsmen.

Currachs exhibit distinctive regional characteristics, shaped by culture, environment and historical circumstances. Hornell identified 12 types of currach on the coast of Donegal, Mayo, Galway, Clare and Kerry, ranging from the short paddle currachs typical of the Rosses of Donegal to the more boat-like form of the Kerry naomhóg (Fig. 6).

Distinct forms of currachs were developed in Donegal, north Mayo and Kerry, among other locations. On Tory Island (Co. Donegal) a particular style of currach (Fig. 4) replaced the paddle currach, possibly early in the last century (Mac Cárthaigh 2008). It is a small craft, with a punt-like bow and a keel, using some traditional currach materials and techniques in its construction.

Another interesting example of a distinctive local currach was developed in Inishkea Island, off the Mayo coast (Mac Cárthaigh 2008). The single-gunwale, planked or 'boarded' currach, known as the 'skay', is an exceptionally light but robust craft, ideal for the rocky shores of Inishkea, especially with a two-man crew.

Fig. 6— Naomhógs at Dunquin, Co. Kerry (courtesy of Darina Tully).

Developments from the 1800s

County Clare appears to have been an important nexus of currach developments in the 1800s. The present-day Clare currach took shape during the first half of the 1800s and, as further detailed by Mac Cárthaigh (2008), owes much to the Royal Navy officers stationed at the signal towers (*Archaeology Ireland*, Summer 2012). The influence of their initiatives, allied to the Fisheries Board's incentives to local boat-makers to improve currach designs, was felt not only on the Clare coast and Galway Bay but also in north Mayo and south to Dingle Bay. By 1836 the majority of the technological changes outlined above had been fairly commonly adopted on the coast.

Mayo currachs underwent fundamental modifications and improvements (Box 2) in terms of size and construction during the nineteenth century (Mac Cárthaigh 2008; Mac Conamhna 2010). These were partly motivated by the improvements in currach design begun on the Clare coast in the early 1820s, gradually infiltrating north to Mayo. By the turn of the century, the Fisheries Board's 1827 design for an improved currach was well established in north Mayo.

According to Hornell, Belderrig was the centre for the north-Mayo currach. He recorded that the Belderrig five-man currach was 23ft long, 51in. wide and 27in. deep (Mac Conamhna 2010). A most informative plan of the currach, drawn in 1936 by Pádraig Mac Conghamhna for the Irish Folklore Commission, is shown in Fig. 7.

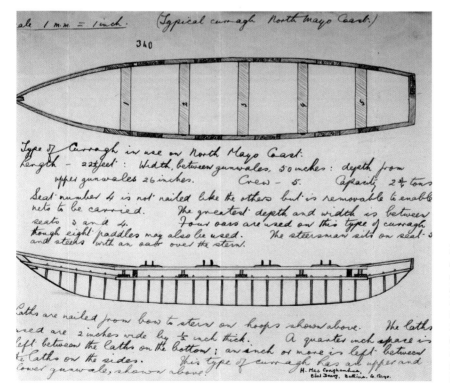

Fig. 7—*Plan of Belderrig currach, Co. Mayo, by Pádraig Mac Conghamhna, 1936 (courtesy of the National Folklore Collection, UCD).*

Based on a detailed appraisal, Mac Conamhna (2010) concluded that the Coastguard facilitated the adoption of the new, improved currach in north Mayo, influencing the design and evolution of the five-man Belderrig craft.

An interesting aspect of the rapid expansion of the improved Fisheries Board currach was that this development took place around the period of the Famine, when the capacity of the population to innovate and adopt technology was at a low ebb. Such a development would have required the encouragement and support of an agency such as the Coastguard (Mac Conamhna 2010). In a broader context, inadequate recognition is generally given to the remarkable contribution of the Coastguard Service to famine relief along the western seaboard (*Archaeology Ireland*, Winter 2013).

Hornell described the Kerry naomhóg (Fig. 6) as 'The supreme achievement of the currach builders …'. The new and more efficient design of currach, which was in widespread use in Clare in the 1830s, spread to the Kerry coast. By the 1890s, the naomhóg's area of use extended from the mouth of the Shannon to Portmagee on the south shore of Dingle Bay. The craft is closely identified with the Great Blasket Island. Today, the naomhóg is most in evidence in Brandon Bay on the north side of the peninsula, and at Dunquin.

Box 2	Diagnostic features
Paddled and rowed currachs	
Turn of the eighteenth century	Small, skin-covered, two-man craft, typically not exceeding 10ft in length and with wickerwood frame.
Rowing currachs	
From 1820s–30s	*Period of marked improvements (see text).*
Early nineteenth century	Increased currach size; sawn timber in the hull, double gunwale, and covered with tarred canvas.
1880s (for instance in County Mayo)	Traditional lattice framework replaced with flush planking; abandonment of indigenous lattice hull for boarded hull.
By mid-twentieth century	Large currachs for two-, three-, four- or five-man crews; approaching 20ft and up to 27ft long, 40–50in. wide, and from 20in. to 27in. deep.
Sources: Hornell (1937; 1938); Mac Cárthaigh (2008)	

Acknowledgements

The images received from Críostóir Mac Cárthaigh are most gratefully acknowledged. Darina Tully kindly made available to us a copy of her paper entitled 'The use and tradition of the currach in the 21st century', published in *Ships and maritime landscapes. Proceedings of the Thirteenth International Symposium on Boat and Ship Archaeology, Amsterdam 2012*, and also the image of the naomhógs at Dunquin, Co. Kerry. The publications brought to our attention by Conor McDermott have also been most helpful.

References

Breen, C. and Forsythe, W. (eds) 2004 *Boats and shipwrecks of Ireland*. Stroud.

Hornell, J. 1937a The curraghs of Ireland, Part I. *Mariner's Mirror* **23** (1), 74–83.

Hornell, J. 1937b The curraghs of Ireland, Part II. *Mariner's Mirror* **23** (2), 148–75.

Hornell, J. 1938a The curraghs of Ireland, Part III. *Mariner's Mirror* **24** (1), 5–39.

Hornell, J. 1938b *British coracles and Irish curraghs*. London.

C. Mac Cárthaigh (ed.) 2008 *Traditional boats of Ireland*. Cork.

Mac Conamhna, B. (ed.) 2010 *The Belderrig currach*. Sligo.

Ó Gibne, C. (ed.) 2012 *The Boyne currach: from beneath the shadows of Newgrange*. Dublin.

Tully, D. 2017 The use and tradition of the currach in the 21st century. In Gawronski, J., van Holk, A. and Schokkenbroek, J. (eds) *Ships and maritime landscapes. Proceedings of the Thirteenth International Symposium on Boat and Ship Archaeology, Amsterdam 2012*. Eelde.

This article was originally published in the Spring 2015 issue of Archaeology Ireland.

Early historical routeways

While Ireland would have had a wide variety of routeways in the first millennium AD, five major *slíghe* are said to have been especially prominent in the early road system. Direct archaeological evidence for these *slíghe*, in the form of significant expanses of road surface or boundaries, is missing, but there have been efforts to use the location of specific early monasteries, natural features and hubs of governance or commerce as a guide to narrowing down the route lines.

As originally speculated some three quarters of a century ago, the five routes are envisaged as radiating out of Dublin, with the *Slí Mór* ('Great Road') and the Esker Riada largely congruent but with some divergences (the Esker Riada is a natural and not entirely continuous series of ridges and mounds stretching across the country from Dublin to Galway Bay). According to more recent propositions, however, the five ancient roads are focused on Tara, and the only section of the Esker Riada to have coincided with the *Slí Mór* is between Ballinasloe and Clarinbridge.

The four remaining *slíghe* that made up the early road system were: (i) *Slí Mhidluachra*, the main Newry road running to Dunseverick, capital of Dal Riada, on the Causeway coast in County Antrim; (ii) *Slí Assail*, the main road to Connacht, with a focus on the royal site of Rathcroghan; (iii) *Slí Dála*, the route to west Munster; and (iv) *Slí Cualann*, the great main road to the south, leading to Old Ross and Waterford.

Fig. 1—Reconstruction photograph of the ninth-century (AD 840) wooden bridge crossing the Shannon on the southern side of the Clonmacnoise monastic site (courtesy of C. McDermott and A. O'Sullivan).

Travel in early medieval Ireland

Building on the pioneering study of roadways in ancient Ireland undertaken some three quarters of a century ago by Colm Ó Lochlainn (1940), further investigations have recently been published on the five major early routeways (O'Keeffe 2001; Doran 2004; Geissel 2006).

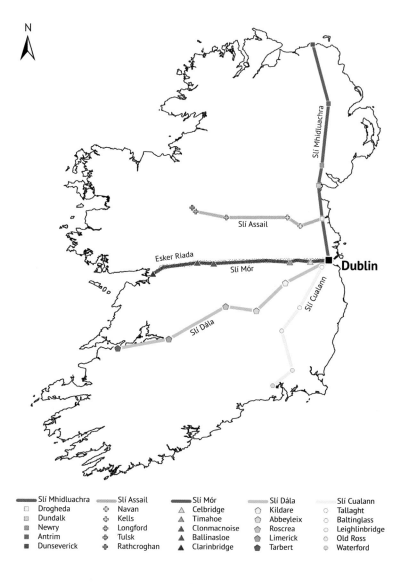

Fig. 2 — Representation of the routeways of the five major slíghe *identified by Ó Lochlainn (1940), including some prominent current centres (courtesy of M. Corcoran).*

Particular attention is given in this article to two radically different perspectives that have emerged in relation to key features of the routeways, focusing on (i) the hubs from which they are speculated to have radiated and (ii) the association between the *Slí Mór* and the Esker Riada.

Convergence on Dublin

The five major early routeways postulated by Ó Lochlainn (1940) are shown schematically in Fig. 2. The *Slí Mór* ('Great Road'), according to Ó Lochlainn, followed a route from Dublin across to Galway, passing through Clonmacnoise, and on to Clarinbridge.

The main Dublin to Newry road was reported by Ó Lochlainn as representing the *Slí Mhidluachra*. This routeway ran through Antrim to Dunseverick, and had a junction with Tara just north of Drogheda.

The *Slí Assail* seems to have been the main road from Meath to Connacht. Leaving the *Slí Mhidluachra* a little to the north of Drogheda, it ran on the high ground north of the Boyne via Navan (where there was a junction with Tara) and continued on through Tulsk to Rathcroghan.

A more recent investigation of the ancient routeways in Roscommon and Longford was undertaken by Doran (2004). In accordance with Ó Lochlainn, both the *Slí Mór* and the *Slí Assail* are taken to have commenced from Dublin. The *Slí Assail* is shown to have a clear focus on the early ritual site of Cruachain or Rathcroghan, as it is more often termed. It passed through Edgeworthstown, Termonbarry, Tulsk and on to Cruachain.

Ó Lochlainn reported that the *Slí Dála* was the road from west Munster to Tara. From Dublin, the route passed through Abbeyleix and Roscrea, and on to Limerick and Tarbert.

The *Slí Cualann* seems, according to Ó Lochlainn, to have been the great main road to the south-east. From Dublin it passed through Tallaght and Baltinglass and on to Old Ross and Waterford.

A reappraisal of the *Slí Mór* was more recently undertaken by Hermann Geissel (2006), in conjunction with Seamus Cullen. The route reported by Geissel broadly concurs with that of Ó Lochlainn, although some points of difference were discerned, as mentioned below.

Starting from Dublin, Geissel reported the *Slí Mór* as going in a general westerly direction towards Taghadoe, which could be easily recognised from a distance by its round tower. Following the present road west, the route continued towards Timahoe and on to Carbury. By way of coincidence, or maybe partial corroboration, several wooden trackways/toghers have been revealed under the peat in the Timahoe area. A pen picture of toghers is outlined in Box 1, and featured in Fig. 3 is an impressive togher/trackway excavated at Corlea, Co. Longford.

Carbury Hill was a major landmark on the *Slí Mór*. From Carbury the route runs parallel to the modern Edenderry Road, and on via Monasteroris to Rhode, both of which were identified by Ó Lochlainn as being located on the *Slí Mór*. Having crossed the bog on a togher, the route continues west towards Croghan Hill, which is another one of Ó Lochlainn's landmarks.

The route went on west to Durrow, which was an important historical centre and was again noted on Ó Lochlainn's map. West of Durrow, the route proceeded to Clara and on to Ballycumber. The ancient routeway here known as the Pilgrim's Road approaches Clonmacnoise from the east and is generally accepted as a part of the *Slí Mór*.

Clonmacnoise was founded at the crossroads of the *Slí Mór* and the Shannon, and, as noted by Geissel, several possible routes link the monastic site with the Ballinasloe road at Cloonfad. The modern road to Shannonbridge is the route marked by Ó Lochlainn on his map as the *Slí Mór* between Clonmacnoise and the ford at Shannonbridge.

Fig. 3—Togher/ trackway in County Longford dated to 2259 ± 98 BC, made of transverse split timbers and roundwoods, which ran for more than 750m across the bog (photo: Barry Raftery).

The Shannon could also once have been crossed from Clonmacnoise by a ninth-century wooden bridge (Fig. 1), which would have provided a continuation of the *Slí Mór* across the river. From Coolumber on the far side, the route headed for Cloonfad and on to Ballinasloe. Part of the main road through Ballinasloe coincides with the *Slí Mór*.

Box 1	Toghers

These are causeways or trackways in a bog, typically made of wood, although some historical examples are made with gravel, cobbles or stone slabs. The earliest Irish examples date from the mid-fourth millennium BC. They were constructed to give access into, within and across bogs. They can vary from small deposits of wood to trackways many hundreds of metres in length, providing a causeway from dryland to dryland. Most sites remained functional for no more than a number of years or decades.

In a small number of historical examples, such as at Lemanaghan and Bloomhill, Co. Offaly, a road was maintained and rebuilt with layers of wood and stone for up to 800 years. Although many roads crossing bogs today were constructed in recent centuries, some of these are likely to have earlier origins, such as the Togher of Croghan near Croghan Hill, Co. Offaly.

Source: Conor McDermott, pers. comm.; McDermott 2007

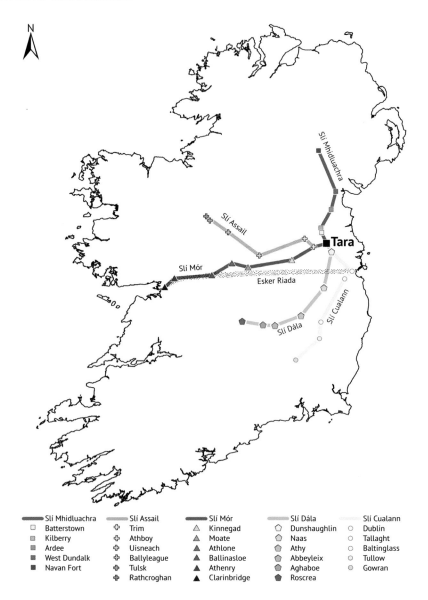

*Fig. 4—
Representation
of the routeways
of the five major
slíghe, showing
the Esker Riada,
according to
O'Keeffe (2001),
including some
prominent urban
centres of today
(courtesy of
M. Corcoran).*

━━ Slí Mhidluachra	▬▬ Slí Assail	━━ Slí Mór	▬▬ Slí Dála	━━ Slí Cualann
▢ Batterstown	✛ Trim	△ Kinnegad	⬠ Dunshaughlin	○ Dublin
▨ Kilberry	✛ Athboy	▲ Moate	⬠ Naas	○ Tallaght
▨ Ardee	✛ Uisneach	▲ Athlone	⬠ Athy	○ Baltinglass
■ West Dundalk	✛ Ballyleague	▲ Ballinasloe	⬠ Abbeyleix	○ Tullow
■ Navan Fort	✛ Tulsk	▲ Athenry	⬠ Aghaboe	◎ Gowran
	✛ Rathcroghan	▲ Clarinbridge	⬠ Roscrea	

According to Ó Lochlainn, the *Slí Mór* from Ballinasloe to Kilconnel went via Aughrim. Geissel favoured a more direct route, running in a westerly direction towards Kilconnel. He added, however, that the route between Kilconnel and Kiltullagh was most difficult to discern and required a more detailed fieldwork.

Having crossed the Athenry to Clarinbridge road, the *slí* follows a low ridge parallel to the road and on to a full-blown esker near Clarinbridge.

Convergence on Tara

Using his wide-ranging expertise in road engineering, O'Keeffe (2001) undertook a systematic investigation of the ancient road system. He mapped the probable lines of the five major routeways as radiating out from Tara (Fig. 4).

Slí Mhidluachra

According to O'Keeffe, the route of the *Slí Mhidluachra* ran from Tara Hill down to the Boyne at Dowdstown, and along the pre-1817 Dublin–Navan road. To reach Batterstown, the *slí* had to cross the Blackwater. From Ardee the route passes to the west of Dundalk and on to Navan Fort, which is two miles to the west of Armagh town.

Slí Assail

Starting from Tara Hill, a route due west would, as indicated by O'Keeffe, have encountered the great red bog which stretched from Delvin to Killyon. To skirt this formidable barrier, the route from Tara had to deviate north-west or south-west. Having passed around the bog boundary, the route changed direction to pass through the gap between Lough Ennell and Lough Owel. According to O'Keeffe, the route of the *slí* to the west had to run close to Uisneach and from there towards either Athlone or Ballyleague to avoid Lough Ree, which is 16 miles long. From Tara to Rathcroghan, the route shown in Fig. 4 went via Trim, Athboy, Uisneach, Ballyleague and Tulsk. Alternatively, the route from Uisneach could have proceeded via Athlone, Roscommon and Tulsk, and on to Rathcroghan.

O'Keeffe considers it most unlikely that the *Slí Assail* crossed the Shannon at the same location as the *Slí Mór*. Tullamore Ford, located 1.5 miles upstream from Clonmacnoise, was a common crossing place. The crossing at Termonbarry has also often been suggested as an ancient alternative to Ballyleague. O'Keeffe noted that Ó Lochlainn's *Slí Assail* misses both Tara and Uisneach, and also that it includes some links in the middle for which there is no evidence of an early road.

Esker Riada and the *Slí Mór*

O'Keeffe observed that most of the many papers and articles on the *Slí Mór* assume or seek to establish that it followed the Esker Riada. He mapped the lines of both the *Slí Mór* and the Esker Riada (Fig. 4) and showed that, in crossing the country from the east towards Clonmacnoise, they did not always coincide; from Ballinasloe to Clarinbridge, however, they appear to have been congruent.

According to O'Keeffe, the *Slí Mór* probably ran from Tara and passed through Kinnegad, Moate, Athlone, Ballinasloe, Athenry and Clarinbridge. The Esker Riada line comprised many prominent hills in the otherwise flat, boggy landscape on the route from Dublin, including Donadea, Rhode, Durrow and Ballinasloe, and from there the Esker Riada and the *Slí Mór* coincide.

Slí Dála

The terminal for this routeway is generally given as Roscrea (O'Keeffe 2001). The road believed to be the *slí* followed the country road through Ballaghmore from Clondeen, where it crossed the River Nore and went on to Aghaboe (Fig. 4). From there it ran on to Abbeyleix and into the ancient townland of Timahoe. The probable line from Timahoe went to Athy and on to Ballysax, which is close to Dún Ailline. The road passed through Naas, the seat of the early kings of Leinster, and thence to Clane, an ancient historical crossing place on the Liffey.

From there, the most likely line for the *Slí Dála* was north-east to Barberstown, and then north through Taghadoe Cross and on to Maynooth and into County Meath. As noted by O'Keeffe, William Larkin's 1817 map of County Meath shows a road line winding north to Dunshaughlin, with a junction at Ballylough, where it could have joined and followed the *Slí Cualann* to Tara Hill.

Slí Cualann

As stated by O'Keeffe, Pratt and Moll's maps of 1708 and 1714 show the road from Kileen to Dunshaughlin, Piercetown, Clonee, Castleknock and Áth Cliath (Fig. 4). From the south side of the ford, a road follows the top of an esker leading to Tallaght.

According to O'Keeffe, there is no evidence to indicate that the original *Slí Cualann* went beyond Oldbawn before AD 350. It appears, however, to have been extended southwards from Tallaght to Baltinglass, Tullow and Gowran during the period AD 351–800.

Conclusions

As mentioned above, contradictory perspectives have been documented in respect of (i) the convergence of the five major routeways either on Dublin or Tara and (ii) the extent to which the *Slí Mór* and the Esker Riada coincided.

According to Ó Lochlainn, the routes radiated out of Dublin (Fig. 2). This proposition, which otherwise has an air of hindsight about it, has been strongly supported by Geissel's detailed reappraisal of the route of the *Slí Mór*. Conversely, both O'Keeffe and Stout (unpublished) contend that the five ancient routes appear to have converged on Tara.

O'Keeffe and Geissel have advanced markedly different perspectives as regards the coincidence of the *Slí Mór* and the Esker Riada. According to O'Keeffe, only the western section of the Esker Riada, from Ballinasloe to Clarinbridge, coincided with the *Slí Mór*. Conversely, Geissel concluded that the *Slí Mór* and the Esker Riada were generally congruent but that they diverged between Dublin and Celbridge, and probably also in County Offaly between Rahugh and Durrow.

Given the diverse range of diagnostic features (Box 2) used in determining the routeways and, more particularly, the relative emphasis given to certain features by individual investigators, the emergence of conflicting perspectives was almost inevitable. In reality, Ireland would have featured a wide variety of routeways in the first millennium AD and scholarship has yet to contextualise this presumed reality against the semi-mythical routeways discussed here.

Box 2	**Diagnostic features**

- Place and townland names containing elements (often an Irish root word) relating to a road, routeway, esker, pass, weir, etc.
- Suitable topography, generally high ground with little soil cover, and avoiding poor drainage.
- Fording points and bridges.
- Ancient places of assembly and inauguration.
- Routes travelled by earlier saints and scholars.
- Movement of armies and sites of battles.

Acknowledgements

Conor McDermott's contribution to this article is gratefully acknowledged. Matthew Stout kindly made available to us his unpublished paper on early medieval roads, delivered at a Friends of Medieval Dublin Symposium in 2014. Our thanks are also due to Michelle Comber and Michael Corcoran.

References

Doran, L. 2004 Communication routes through Longford and Roscommon, and their associated settlements. *Proceedings of the Royal Irish Academy* **104**C, 57–80.

Geissel, H. 2006 *A road on the long ridge: in search of the ancient highway on the Esker Riada*. Newbridge.

McDermott, C. 2007 'Plain and bog, bog and wood, wood and bog, bog and plain': peatland archaeology in Ireland. In C. Green (ed.), *Archaeology from the wetlands: recent perspectives*. Edinburgh.

O'Keeffe, P. 2001 *Ireland's principal roads, 123 AD–1608*. Dublin.

Ó Lochlainn, C. 1940 Roadways in ancient Ireland. In J. Ryan (ed.), *Féil-sgríbhinn Eóin Mhic Néill: essays and studies presented to Professor Eoin MacNeill on the occasion of his seventieth birthday*. Dublin.

This article was originally published in the Autumn 2015 issue of Archaeology Ireland.

Historical bridges

Although an integral feature of any road system, bridges in Ireland were often erected centuries after the roadway they served initially came into shape. In many instances, fords and ferries would have preceded a bridge at a river crossing. The earliest record of the actual construction of a bridge in Ireland is from around AD 1000. Bridges evolved over the succeeding centuries, from timber structures to early stone ones, and later stone-arched bridges during the medieval period. By late medieval times, bridges were becoming more common in Ireland and William Petty's maps (surveyed in the 1650s) show 207 bridge locations on Irish rivers.

Two notable periods in the development of bridges in Ireland were: (i) the construction of stone-arched bridges in the thirteenth century, associated with the Anglo-Normans; and (ii) the erection of Tudor-style bridges at strategic locations on the major rivers in the seventeenth and eighteenth centuries. By 1714, most of the island's principal rivers had been spanned in many places.

The progressive evolution of bridge construction is well illustrated by the succession of bridges revealed recently in excavations at Bray, Co. Wicklow, beginning with a twelfth- or early thirteenth-century wooden bridge spanning the River Dargle and followed by a stone bridge mentioned in 1666, itself replaced by a four-arched stone bridge in 1735 and ultimately the current bridge, erected in the nineteenth century.

Fig. 1—Clapper bridge near Louisburgh, Co. Mayo (courtesy of Conor McDermott).

Crossing the river

From the Iron Age, if not earlier, Ireland seems to have evolved a functional system of routeways that involved the storied five major ancient routeways outlined in the Autumn 2015 issue of *Archaeology Ireland*. Although an integral part of roads, bridges were often installed centuries after the road first took shape (O'Keeffe 2001). The lines followed by earlier roadways were crucially determined by, among other landscape features, river crossings at fords, of which 124 have been identified by O'Keeffe.

The first record of the actual construction of a bridge in Ireland is from around AD 1000 (O'Keeffe and Simington 1991). Bridges evolved over the succeeding centuries, as outlined below, from timber to early stone bridges, and to stone-arched bridges from the medieval period. Six types of early bridges have been described (Box 1), three of which were timber constructions.

Box 1	Types of early bridges
Ces droichet	Wicker bridge
Cliath droichet	Hurdle bridge
Clar droichet	Wooden bridge
Cloch droichet	Stone bridge
Droichet clochaeltra	Bridge of stone and mortar
Droichet long	Bridge of boats
Source: O'Keeffe and Simington 1991	

The *ces droichet* was made primarily of wickerwork. The *cliath droichet* appears to have been a stronger bridge, with the wickerwork formed of hurdles. The *clar droichet* was made of planks and beams, in ancient times roughly worked with an adze, and in later times sawn and wrought. The piers of the *ces droichet* were, as indicated by O'Keeffe and Simington (1991), probably large baskets (*cessa*), woven from hazel, rowan or sally rods. The *cessa* or kishes would have been floated into position and filled with stones to form piers. In deeper water they were probably kept in position by large stones and/or, where possible, by stakes. The decks were probably 6–10ft long and composed of young trees laid longitudinally and tied securely to the kishes. The decking consisted of wickerwork sheets covered with twigs and scraggy sods (see Drumheriff Bridge, below).

Most bridges throughout Europe in the early medieval period were constructed of timber. As noted above, in Ireland the first record of the construction of bridges, as distinct from a reference to a bridge, is from around AD 1000 (O'Keeffe and Simington 1991). Some early references to timber bridges in the annals are synopsised in Box 2.

Box 2	**Early timber bridges referred to in the annals**

- **1000–1**: Bridges were made over the Shannon at Athlone and Lanesborough. The Shannon navigation reports suggests that some form of timber bridge was built at Athlone, where the bed is sandy clay, and that a *ces droichet* was built on the rocky bed at Lanesborough.
- **1000–14**: There was a timber/plank bridge at Cill Dalua on the east side of the Shannon.
- **1129**: A bridge at Athlone is referred to in the *Annals of the Four Masters*.
- **1154**: The wicker bridge at Athlone was destroyed; the wicker bridge at Ballyleague was constructed.
- **1155–9**: A wicker bridge was constructed at Athlone for the purpose of making incursions into Meath.
- **1158–9**: A wooden bridge over the Shannon at Curr Clawana is recorded in the *Annals of Clonmacnoise*.
- The pre-Norman bridges across the Liffey referred to in the annals are most probably of timber construction.

Source: O'Keeffe and Simington 1991

Drumheriff

The wooden bridge over the Shannon linking Drumheriff and Dereenasoo townlands, in Leitrim and Roscommon respectively, provides important insights into the traditional early form of bridges on large rivers in the late Christian period (O'Keeffe and Simington 1991).

It was described in the 1830s as 'one of these wicker bridges [that] stood over the Shannon above Carrick-on-Shannon and it was built of loose stone piers … placed close to each other; some rough black oak logs thrown across from pier to pier, and these covered with wicker-work in several layers, and gravel etc. strewn on these. It was very frail and the horse was unyoked from the cart and the latter pulled across by men.' The wooden bridge was used well into the 1800s to bring home turf and also for taking corn to a mill, the ruins of which are shown on the 1837 6in. Ordnance Survey map.

Wooden bridge at Bray

An excavation recently undertaken as part of the Dargle Flood Defence Scheme discovered a wooden bridge to the west of the nineteenth-century Bray Bridge in the centre of Bray town (John Purcell, pers. comm.). This was revealed just below sea level within what was formerly the river bed. The

Fig. 2—Medieval wooden bridge recently excavated in Bray, Co. Wicklow (courtesy of John Purcell).

remains of the bridge were remarkably well preserved and consisted of a large baseplate that had three upright timbers inserted into it (Fig. 2). The timbers of the bridge appear to have been laid directly onto the river bed. Rectangular mortises were cut through the baseplate to support the upright timbers.

The bridge timbers were identified as oak by Ellen O'Carroll and the wooden wedges were of holly and alder. Two of the oak timbers from the bridge have been dated by David M. Brown of Queen's University Belfast. One sample from the large horizontal timber had measured tree-ring series dates from AD 972 to 1084. A second timber from one of the uprights had measured tree-ring series dates from AD 933 to 1068. As further detailed below, stone bridges were also revealed at the site of the excavation.

Early stone bridges

The **clochan** bridge erected across the Camoge River at Knockainey, Co. Limerick, appears to have been typical of the first type of stone bridges built in Ireland (O'Keeffe and Simington 1991). It was a **clapper** bridge, consisting of a series of low stone piers erected across a shallow river bed and spanned by flat stone slabs or 'clappers' (Cox and Gould 2003).

Louisburgh, Co. Mayo, has the largest clapper bridge in Ireland (Fig. 1), which may date from medieval times (*ibid.*). The bridge has over 30 spans and the clappers or limestone slabs vary in length from 2.5ft to 5ft. A notable feature of the bridge is the openings in the parapet walls to allow water to flow through unimpeded during times of flood. Such bridges were, as indicated by Cox and Gould, constructed where the water depth was low during times of normal flow and were often associated with a nearby ford.

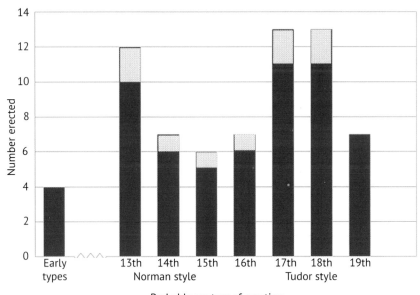

Fig. 3—Probable construction periods of 74 selected bridges and bridge groups (after O'Keeffe and Simington 1991).

Stone-arch bridges

Bridges were becoming more common in Ireland by the late medieval period. William Petty's maps, surveyed in the 1650s, showed 207 locations on rivers where there were bridges at that time (O'Keeffe 2001).

O'Keeffe and Simington (1991) have compiled a chronological listing of the probable periods when 74 selected bridges and bridge groups were erected. As shown in Fig. 3, two prominent construction periods were the thirteenth century and the seventeenth and eighteenth centuries.

Norman bridges

The Norman conquest heralded a notable period of bridge-building in Ireland. The construction of stone-arch bridges is typically associated with the Anglo-Normans. The reign of King John (1199–1216), who was generally regarded as a 'bridge-minded' monarch, marked a major milestone in bridge construction in Ireland. As shown in Fig. 3, upwards of 12 bridges were erected by the Normans in the thirteenth century.

The Shannon estuary posed an impregnable barrier to the development of through roads. As further detailed by O'Keeffe (2001), the first permanent crossing was King John's multi-span stone-arched bridge in Limerick, erected *c.* 1199. It survived, albeit with modifications and replacement of stone arches, until it was replaced in 1848. The impressive Thomond (Old) Bridge consisted of 14 stone arches and had gate towers at each end. The remains of some thirteenth-century stone bridges that have survived at least in part are outlined in Box 3.

Box 3	Remnants of some thirteenth-century stone-arch bridges

- Three-arch St Mary Magdalen Bridge (also called Maudlin Bridge) built across the Nanny River at Duleek, Co. Meath.
- Single arch survives of the once-massive 11-span Babes Bridge, built across the Boyne downstream of Navan—the oldest surviving authenticated bridge arch in Ireland.
- Six-arch masonry bridge, known as Mabe's, built across the Blackwater River less than a mile north-west of Kells, Co. Meath; rehabilitated by Meath County Council in the 1980s.
- Eight-arch bridge over the River Nore at Abbeyleix, known as Monks Bridge, has at least one thirteenth-century arch and pier.

Source: O'Keeffe and Simington 1991

The great period of construction of the Norman stone castles was in the twelfth–thirteenth century. Many towns grew up around these castles and markets were established, which led to increased traffic and a need for more durable and permanent bridges (O'Keeffe and Simington 1991). As noted by O'Keeffe and Simington, the pointed segmental arch (composed of two arcs) is almost invariably the hallmark of such bridges, including that at Trim (Fig. 4). The latter is recorded in the Down Survey (1657) as a fair stone bridge consisting of three or four stone arches. It was seemingly erected in the period 1330–50.

Fig. 4—Multi-span stone bridge at Trim, Co. Meath (courtesy of the National Monuments Service, Department of Arts, Heritage and the Gaeltacht).

A mid-seventeenth-century pictorial map of Galway (Fig. 5) shows the west bridge of Galway, built in 1442, and the outer gate, built in 1562, with a small adjoining mill. The bridge was replaced by the present William O'Brien Bridge in 1851.

Tudor period and later

The second half of the sixteenth century was marked by conquest and colonisation by the Tudors. A principal instrument of conquest was the erection of bridges at strategic locations on the major rivers (O'Keeffe and Simington 1991).

As shown in Fig. 3, the number of bridges erected in both the seventeenth and eighteenth centuries was seemingly twice the number built in each of the previous three centuries. Sir Henry Sidney, who was lord justice of Ireland for over 20 years from the mid-sixteenth century, attached great importance to bridges. He was instrumental in erecting about a dozen of them, including Ballinasloe, which still survives with its distinctive Tudor arches (ibid.). Ballinasloe Bridge seems to have been erected around 1570 and is still capable of carrying heavy traffic across the River Suck (Fig. 6) more than four centuries later. Other Tudor bridges, such as Islandbridge, Athlone, Belfast, Dungannon and Enniscorthy, were replaced in the eighteenth and nineteenth centuries.

In the seventeenth century, the export of both timber and iron by the landlords necessitated the building of roads and bridges. The earls of Cork were very active in this regard in the first quarter of the seventeenth century. By 1714 most of the principal rivers had been spanned in many places, as shown in *A new map of Ireland* by Herman Moll (ibid.).

The evolution of bridge construction over the centuries is well illustrated by the recent excavation at Bray, Co. Wicklow, referred to above. As further detailed by Purcell (2012), this revealed a succession of bridges built across the River Dargle. These comprised three distinctive bridge structures, ranging in date from the wooden bridge dated to the twelfth or early thirteenth century to a stone bridge referred to in 1666, which was replaced by a four-arch stone bridge in 1736. This collapsed in 1741 and a similar structure was built in its place. The current bridge spanning the River Dargle was constructed in the nineteenth century.

Fig. 5—Extract from a mid-seventeenth-century pictorial map of Galway, showing the west bridge and the outer west gate.

*Fig. 6—
Ballinasloe
Bridge, built
across the River
Suck originally
in the Tudor
period (courtesy
of the National
Monuments
Service,
Department of
Arts, Heritage
and the
Gaeltacht).*

| Box 4 | Diagnostic features |

- **Timber bridges**: decks of wickerwork sheets or wooden planks, supported by piers made of large woven baskets (*cessa*) filled with stones; some were hurdle bridges.
- **Early stone bridges**: the earliest types were typically clapper bridges, made of large flagstones, known as clappers, spanning rubble piers (Fig. 1).
- **Stone-arch bridges**: multi-span structures; those built in the thirteenth and fourteenth centuries are generally associated with the Anglo-Normans and have characteristic pointed segmental arches (composed of two arcs); many built in the seventeenth and eighteenth centuries have distinctive Tudor arches, some of which still survive.

Acknowledgements

We are grateful to John Purcell for making available to us the details of the excavation of the wooden bridge in Bray. The images provided by Joanna Nolan, Chris Randolph and Bob Lawlor are much appreciated, as are further images by Ann Burnell. The publications brought to our attention by Ian Doyle, Conor McDermott, Derry O'Donovan and Michael Corcoran are gratefully acknowledged.

References

Cox, R. and Gould, M. 2003 *Irish bridges*. Dublin.

O'Keeffe, P. (ed.) 2001 *Ireland's principal roads, 123–1608 AD*. Dublin.

O'Keeffe, P. and Simington, T. (eds) 1991 *Irish stone bridges: history and heritage*. Kildare.

Purcell, J. 2012 The discovery of early bridge remains in Bray. *Newsletter of the Institute of Archaeologists of Ireland* **2** (8), 4.

This article was originally published in the Winter 2015 issue of Archaeology Ireland.

Logboats

L ogboats were multi-purpose craft used over a protracted span of time as an everyday means of transport on lakes and rivers. They were also used offshore in reasonably calm conditions. A remarkable array of logboats dating from the early Bronze Age and the medieval period have recently been excavated in Lough Corrib (Co. Galway). Logboats were wooden-hulled dugout craft. However, they were not simply hollowed-out logs. They were purposefully designed vessels with a number of functional features built into their elongated hulls, such as rowlock-holders, seats and footrests, end-boards or transoms at the rear, and transverse bracing ridges. Some even had raised sides known as wash-strakes and, more rarely, a reinforced floor opening to receive the foot of the mast.

Logboats had a long history in Ireland, extending from the Mesolithic or very early Neolithic period, and they appear to have survived until the eighteenth century in Ireland, much longer than in parts of Britain and north-west Europe. They coexisted for many centuries with currachs.

Fig. 1—A logboat found near Annaghkeen, Lough Corrib (courtesy of Karl Brady, National Monuments Service, Department of Culture, Heritage and the Gaeltacht).

Dugout canoes

Logboats were one of several types of small craft used over the millennia for a diverse range of purposes (Fry 2000; Breen and Forsythe 2004; Forsythe and Gregory 2007; Mac Cárthaigh 2008). They coexisted for many centuries with skin-covered and plank-built small boats, but finds of prehistoric craft are almost exclusively confined to logboats. (Skin-covered boats, which also have a long history in Ireland, are considered in the Spring 2015 issue of *Archaeology Ireland*.)

Functions

Logboats were multi-purpose craft. They were an everyday means of conveyance, commonly used in lakes and as ferries stationed at critical points on unbridged rivers. They were also employed in the carriage of livestock and farm produce, and were used for fishing and wildfowling. The spectacular array of logboats recently revealed in Lough Corrib (Figs 2–4), outlined below, highlights their importance in lake transport over a protracted span of time.

Over 450 logboats have been recorded in Ireland and, as noted by Forsythe and Gregory (2007), they have predominantly been found in riverine and lacustrine environments. Only 2% of Irish logboats have been discovered in estuarine environments, in an obvious position to venture out to sea. Nevertheless, as further discussed by Fry (2000), logboats could have operated successfully offshore in reasonably calm weather. Some may have been capable of going to sea in the right hands and under the right conditions. The discovery (see below) of a logboat on the foreshore of Greyabbey Bay in Strangford Lough (Fig. 5) provides further evidence of the existence of maritime logboats in the Neolithic period (Forsythe and Gregory 2007).

Fig. 2—A well-preserved logboat with central floor spine and cross-ridges, found near Annaghkeen, Lough Corrib (courtesy of Karl Brady, National Monuments Service).

Fig. 3—Logboat lying on the bed of Lough Corrib near Rinnaknock (courtesy of Karl Brady, National Monuments Service).

Lough Corrib logboats

A remarkable array of logboats has recently been discovered in Lough Corrib, Co. Galway. As reported in *Current Archaeology* **292** (June 2014), a comprehensive investigation undertaken by the Underwater Archaeology Unit (National Monuments Service, Department of Arts, Heritage and the Gaeltacht) revealed a number of logboats, together with a range of artefacts that had lain for thousands of years at the bottom of the lake.

The craft dated from the early Bronze Age (*c.* 2500 BC) to the eleventh century AD. The oldest and largest vessel reported, a 12m-long dugout found near Annaghkeen, was radiocarbon dated to 2500 BC. It is well preserved and, as shown in Fig. 2, has a distinctive 2–3cm spine running the length of its floor. Four cross-ridges extend from this and appear to have divided the boat into a number of sections. It was an impressive craft that could be paddled by a crew of some ten to twelve, suggesting that it was perhaps primarily intended for formal or ceremonial purposes.

Two other logboats found in the lake were less well preserved. Just the base and lower parts of a 3,400-year-old craft located off Lee's Island survive. Only the base remains of a Bronze Age logboat found near Killbeg, but within the boat was a socketed bronze spearhead, containing fragments of wood that were radiocarbon dated to the ninth century BC. In addition, a complete spear carved from yew was found beside the craft.

A 6m-long logboat dated to the eleventh century AD was found near the townland of Carrowmoreknock. It appears to have been finely crafted and was probably intended for a high-status individual. Four of the craft's five thwarts—seats made from planks—were still in place. Unlike its Bronze Age counterparts, the Carrowmoreknock logboat was not paddled. It was rowed, as evidenced by the remains of four pairs of thole-pin holes, which held the craft's oars. As noted in *Current Archaeology*, this is probably one of the best-preserved logboats investigated in Ireland.

The boat may perhaps have been carrying warriors, as evidenced by the weapons found within, which included three battleaxes, an ironwork axe, two iron spearheads and the remains of what may have been a copper-alloy dagger pommel. A number of unusual items had been placed inside the hull, including a slab of red sandstone and a rock rich in fossils, perhaps intended as gifts for one of the many monastic communities located around the lakes.

More detailed investigations of the Lough Corrib logboats have been undertaken by the Underwater Archaeology Unit over the past year.

Fig. 4—
Logboat with two footrests projecting from the insides of the hull, found near Rinnaknock, Lough Corrib (courtesy of Karl Brady, National Monuments Service).

Greyabbey logboat

As previously indicated, the logboat (Fig. 5) discovered on the foreshore of Greyabbey Bay, Strangford Lough (Co. Down), further substantiates the existence of maritime logboats in the Neolithic period (Forsythe and Gregory 2007).

The boat was made of oak and has been dated to 3499–3032 cal. BC. It was a substantial vessel with a maximum potential load capacity close to 4,000kg and could have carried a crew of five. It exhibited a number of the functional features typically found in logboats (Box 1).

The original boat appears to have been at least 9.35m in length, with an average external width of 0.95m and an external height of up to 0.65m. Holes in the gunwales of the vessel are suggestive of side extensions known as wash-strakes (below). Another feature typical of logboats (Box 1) is the remains of a transverse ridge in the centre of the floor.

The Greyabbey logboat was built for stability and was capable of negotiating the challenges of Strangford's tidal environment. It would have been able to serve a variety of functions, from fishing to transporting people, their possessions and animals.

Design and performance

Logboats were not simply hollowed-out logs. They were, as detailed by Fry (2000), purposefully designed craft which were manoeuvrable and often quite versatile. The vessels had the ability to self-right, which was an integral feature of hull design.

The dimensions of the hull were of course largely determined by those of the tree trunk from which it was made. Thus the length of many ancient logboats tended to be somewhat disproportionate to their width. In addition, the height of the hull and the width of the beam were constrained by the diameter of the tree trunk from which the craft was fashioned. Thus logboats typically made in Ireland seldom exceeded 0.75m in either respect.

The height left in the hull limited the loading capacity of a logboat. A narrow hull also exercised an important restraint on the load that could be carried. Generally, the broader the hull, the more stable the boat. Further to this, Fry (2000) added that some builders occasionally extended the height of the sides with watertight sides or wash-strakes (see below).

Another important constraint arising from the dimensions of the parent tree was the difficulty of fashioning an effective keel. As a consequence, most logboats tended to become quite difficult to handle in water, especially when too much wind caught their sides.

Fig. 5—The remains of a logboat hull found partially exposed on the sandy intertidal zone of the sea lough at Greyabbey, Strangford Lough, Co. Down (courtesy of Wes Forsythe, Centre for Marine Archaeology, University of Ulster, Coleraine).

Logboat hulls seem to have shortened in length over time. In this regard, Fry observed that in Ireland very few late dugouts are exceptionally long-hulled; large craft are among the earliest recorded. The shift to shorter logboats may be attributed to a reduction in the size of oak logs from quite early times.

Functional features

Built into the hulls were a number of features crucial to the effective operation of logboats (Box 1). Rowlock-holders were clearly inherent features of rowing logboats. Seat features, in the form of ledges or slots in the sides of the hulls, have also been found in a number of logboats.

Sometimes at the rear extremity of the hull there was an end-board or transom stern in place of a solid chunk of tree.

Continuous low transverse ridges may be present in the floor and/or on the interior sides of the hull, resembling in appearance the ribs of planked vessels. They appear to have braced the interior of the hull. Less-continuous short ridges found in the floors of logboats appear to have served as footrests for paddlers or rowers. In some instances they were L shaped, apparently to assist paddlers standing up and using long-handled paddles to propel the craft through the water.

Plugged holes bored through various points in the floor have been commonly found. According to Fry, these are just the last few centimetres of gauging devices used by the builders to guide the hollowing out of hulls and to signal when the process should be stopped.

Although not a general feature of logboats in Ireland, planked extensions known as wash-strakes were sometimes used to raise the height of the sides of the hulls, so as to enlarge their carrying capacity and prevent the shipping of water.

The floors of a small handful of logboats from Ireland have reinforced openings, typically with a significant thickness of timber left standing proud at the circumference. These reinforced floor openings are generally regarded as mast-steps, provided to receive the foot of a mast.

Box 1   Some built-in functional features found in the hulls of logboats

- Rowlock-holders, sometimes known as thole-pin holes.
- Remains of seats for paddlers or rowers.
- An end-board or transom stern at the rear extremity.
- Transverse bracing ridges in the floor and/or the sides of the hull.
- Footrests for paddlers or rowers.
- Hollowing-out gauges in the form of plugged holes in the floor.
- Wash-strakes: planked extensions to the sides of the hull.
- Mast-steps: reinforced floor openings to receive a mast.

Source: Fry 2000

Usage periods

Logboats had a long history in Ireland, extending from as far back as the Mesolithic, or very early Neolithic, and continued to be used into the latter part of the seventeenth century and seemingly later (Fry 2000).

Logboats seem to have survived in Ireland for rather longer than in some parts of Britain and north-west Europe. Although long foreshadowed, their demise came gradually in the eighteenth century. This seems to have occurred for a variety of reasons, including the growing competition from much handier plank-built boats and the loss of big trees caused by forest clearance during the late sixteenth and seventeenth centuries; finally, the construction of more permanent bridges and river crossings reduced the need for small boats to act as ferries.

Box 2	Diagnostic features

- Wooden-hulled dugout craft.
- Canoe-shaped elongated hulls, typically narrow in width and low in height above the water-line.
- A number of functional features built into the hulls (Box 1).
- Generally found in riverine and lacustrine locations, and occasionally offshore.

Acknowledgements

The images of logboats provided by Karl Brady and Wes Forsythe are gratefully acknowledged. The publications brought to our attention by Conor McDermott have also been most helpful.

References

Breen, C. and Forsythe, W. (eds) 2004 *Boats and shipwrecks of Ireland*. Stroud.

Forsythe, W. and Gregory, N. 2007 A Neolithic logboat from Greyabbey Bay, County Down. *Ulster Journal of Archaeology* **66**, 6–13.

Fry, M.F. (ed.) 2000 *Coití: logboats from Northern Ireland*. Northern Ireland Archaeology Monographs No. 4. Antrim.

Mac Cárthaigh, C. (ed.) 2008 *Traditional boats of Ireland: history, folklore, and construction*. Cork.

This article was originally published in the Winter 2014 issue of Archaeology Ireland.

Section V
Local enterprises

Parallelling the advances in agriculture and food production, the medieval and especially the post-medieval period witnessed the progressive emergence of a diverse range of enterprises that heralded technological manufacturing processes of later centuries. The products of these frequently overlooked enterprises helped to keep the traditional rural economy functioning. Some of these enterprises and their surviving archaeological footprints are discussed in this section, while further examples are presented in other thematic sections to which they are especially relevant.

From the medieval period and well into the twentieth century in Ireland, two main forms of earth-covered kilns appear to have been used at **charcoal-production sites**, namely pit kilns and platform kilns. The platform production sites found in the Cummeengeera Valley near Lauragh (Co. Kerry) closely resemble those employed in the woods around Sheffield, where charcoal was produced from the medieval period up until recent decades.

Up until the post-medieval period, Ireland seems to have been largely dependent on imported salt. However, **salt-making** on an industrial scale became widespread with the importation of rock salt from the eighteenth century, and its stamp can be seen on many placenames that survive to the present.

Seaweed has been an important raw material for the chemical industry since the 1700s. Seaweed-harvesting and **kelp production** employed tens of thousands of people in the eighteenth and nineteenth centuries.

Turf-harvesting for fuel is said to have been almost universal in Ireland in the late 1600s. The making of charcoal from turf is also reported to have been remarkably common in the 1830s. The traditional harvesting practices developed in Ireland over the generations bear a number of striking parallels with those generally used in Wales in the nineteenth century.

Charcoal-production sites

A substantial number of charcoal-production sites have been recorded in Ireland. Charcoal pits are typically quite small in surface area and a number have been dated to the early and late medieval periods. The remains of charcoal platforms, however, are appreciably larger in surface and are dated normally from the late 1600s to the mid-1700s.

The relatively small size of the charcoal-production pits may indicate undertakings primarily concerned with meeting individual and/or local needs. The platform kilns, on the other hand, may have been involved in larger-scale production, associated with the fulfilment of industrial demands.

Fig. 1—Ovoid charcoal-production site in the Cummeengeera Valley, near Lauragh in the Beara Peninsula (courtesy of Brendan Riordan).

Making charcoal

Charcoal-production sites are neither picturesque nor well known, but they are increasingly being recognised as significant traces of industrial activity and are being revealed in substantially greater numbers in Ireland. Production sites in the woods around Sheffield, where charcoal was made for many centuries, perhaps from around AD 1300 up to the 1900s, have been classified by Ardon and Rotherham (1999) into the types outlined in Box 1, which may be of interest in the further investigation of such sites in Ireland.

Charcoal was the smelting fuel of the Bronze Age and Iron Age and was continually used in Europe for over 5,000 years, with the peak period of production occurring in the seventeenth and eighteenth centuries (Kelly 1996). Capable of achieving temperatures in excess of 1,000°C, charcoal was essential in metalworking, and indeed continues to be used in the metal and other industries today.

Charcoal is the carbon-rich substance produced when wood is partially burned under conditions where air is restricted and insufficient in supply to allow for complete combustion of the wood. During the charring process, the water in the wood is driven off, followed by a number of valuable by-products known as tarry liquors.

Box 1

Platform hearths (main forms)
- ovoid recessed
- revetted ovoid recessed
- subrectangular recessed
- revetted subrectangular recessed

Multi-feature hearths

Bowl hearths

Undefined hearths

Pits

Charcoal kilns

In previous centuries, and well into the twentieth century, two main forms of earth-covered kilns seem to have been predominantly used in charcoal production, namely **pit kilns** and **mound kilns**. Kilns were, as further detailed by Kelly (1996), progressively developed over time from the first method of production, which seems to have involved pit kilns. These were simple in form, consisting essentially of pits cut into the subsoil, carefully stacked with wood and covered with earth to exclude air.

As the demand for metal products grew, the more efficient mound kiln became a familiar feature of many woodlands in Europe (Kelly 1996). The traditional method of building the kiln involved stacking lengths of wood on end and facing inwards around a triangular wood flue or, alternatively, a central pole (Jones 1993). The stack was built to around 15ft in diameter and about 5ft in height, in the shape of an inverted pudding basin. The pile of wood was covered with straw, grass, bracken and turves, and finally with dust and ashes, so that the external air was largely excluded. Where the wood stack was built around a central pole, this was removed and red-hot charcoal, with a few dry sticks, dropped down the central flue. When the stack was alight, the flue was sealed and the fire allowed to spread through the stack. The charring process had to be very carefully controlled by the charcoal-burners.

To ensure their stability during the charring process, when the woodpile contracts, mound kilns were made on level sites, often referred to as charcoal hearths. As further detailed by Ardon and Rotherham (1999), charcoal hearths in the Sheffield area mostly occur as platform-like constructed features, formed by digging into a slope and bringing the excavated material forward to form a level surface, on which a stable mound kiln could be made and effectively managed. Platform hearths occur on slopes but are also found on level ground, where there was no need to create a flat surface. These hearths nearly always have more or less equal length and breadth.

Platform hearths are carefully engineered structures. The longer axis of an ovoid-shaped platform is generally aligned along the contours of a hillside. As noted by Ardon and Rotherham (1999), on steep slopes the construction of an oval platform may have limited the amount of excavation necessary, whilst also providing a more stable structure. In this regard, a noteworthy aspect of the platform charcoal sites recorded in Glendalough (see below) is the ratio of the short axis to the long axis. In almost half of the cases, this falls within the relatively narrow range of 0.75 to 0.85 (Fig. 2). The predominance of the ratios in this range is not likely to be due to chance, the chi-square (48.0685; df = 5; p = 0.000) being highly significant. Whether this reflects a practical rule of thumb employed where appropriate to construct a stable platform without unnecessary digging is uncertain.

Pit production sites

A substantial number of pits used in charcoal production have been excavated in Ireland in recent years during the course of large-scale development-led excavation projects. A comprehensive data source, comprising records of 100 excavated pit sites, has been compiled by Niall Kenny, who presented an analysis of the data at the 2009 National Roads Authority Seminar. Some of his overall conclusions are outlined below.

The charcoal-production pits generally consisted of simple earth-cut features with charcoal deposits and evidence of *in situ* burning. They occurred in circular, oval and rectangular forms and with roughly an equal proportion of each type. The pits ranged from under 1m to up to 4m in length and from under 1m to 2m in width (Fig. 3), and with few exceptions were less than 0.5m deep. Ten of them have been dated to the early and late

Shape of charcoal production platforms

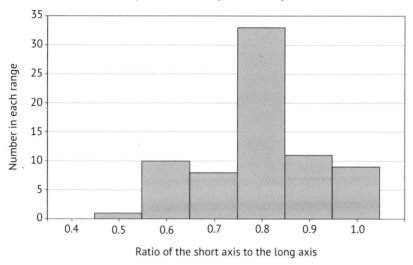

Fig. 2—Ratios of the short axis to the long axis of charcoal platforms in Glendalough (based on 72 sites recorded in Healy 1972).

Relative size of pit kilns and platform kilns

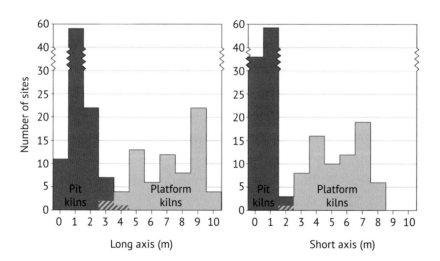

Fig. 3—Relative size of pit kilns and platform kilns recorded in Ireland (data from Kenny 2010 and Healy 1972 respectively).

medieval periods, in particular the ninth–thirteenth centuries. Later dates were obtained for a pit excavated in Cork, as well as another possible pit (AD 1280–1420 and 1420–1640 respectively).

Pits comparable in size and date to those referred to above have been recorded at two charcoal-production camps excavated in Kilkenny (Joanna Wren, pers. comm.). Both sites had similar oval pits containing constructed platforms of oak for the production of charcoal. The pits ranged in size from 1.8m by 1.4m to 1.4m by 1.05m, and varied in depth from 0.14m to 0.44m. Radiocarbon dates from charcoal recovered from pits from both camps ranged from the eleventh century to the mid-thirteenth century.

Platform production sites

Glendalough

The sizeable number of sites around Glendalough investigated by Healy (1972), together with those added more recently by Long (1996), provide an important source of information on upwards of 100 charcoal platforms recorded in Ireland. The surface dimensions of the majority of the sites measured by Healy fall within the range of 5–10m by 3–9m, with the larger sites being the more common (Fig. 3). Smaller platforms are few in number and tend to be more rounded. Platforms with surface dimensions greater than 10m by 9m are rare. Healy postulated that the charcoal-production platforms dated from *c*. AD 1680–1740.

Three of the platforms identified by Healy (1972) have recently been partly excavated (Fig. 4) by Conor McDermott and Graeme Warren (pers. comm.). The platforms, which are located in the townland of Lugduff, are cut into the hillside and form part of a dense scatter of such sites near the Upper Lake. Two of the sites are ovoid in shape (*c*. 12m by 7m and 10m by 5m respectively) and the other is much smaller and circular in shape (*c*. 3m by 3m). At least one site has a low wall constructed at the rear. The excavations confirm Healy's conclusion that the platforms are indeed charcoal-production sites, with extensive charcoal-rich deposits.

Historical references indicate that much of the valley may have been significantly deforested since at least the mid-seventeenth century. This suggests that the majority of the platforms in Glendalough are unlikely to be associated with more modern industrial activity. Charcoal analysis and

Fig. 4—Charcoal platform no. 77 at Glendalough, showing pre-excavation view and (opposite) excavated trench (courtesy of Conor McDermott and Graeme Warren).

radiocarbon dating will establish the dates of the platforms and will also provide insights into the type of woodland-management regimes associated with their use. Important information on the trees and woodlands in Wicklow over recent centuries has been documented by Carey (2009).

Beara Peninsula

Platform and other possible charcoal-production sites have been found in the Cummeengeera Valley near Lauragh, Co. Kerry (Connie Murphy, pers. comm.). A preliminary examination of the most prominent site, which has charcoal-impregnated soil and is located on the sloping valley hillside, indicates an ovoid-shaped charcoal-production platform. Its internal dimensions are around 9m by 8m and comparable to those in Glendalough (Fig. 1) and Sheffield. It is largely surrounded by a wall or bank surviving to around 0.5m or more at its highest point. The platform is supported on the downslope side by a fairly steep constructed bank, some 3m or more in height.

A second platform site occurs further on in the valley on more gentle sloping ground. It comprises a mainly grass-covered near-rectangular platform, around 11m by 7m in surface area and with fairly prominent upper and lower banks. On the lower ground approaching the end of the valley an ovoid grass-covered site may be found, with an approximate surface area of 10m by 9m. More systematic fieldwork in the valley and adjoining areas would be likely to reveal other charcoal-production sites.

Cummeengeera seems to have been well wooded prior to the early decades of the 1700s, when some 600 acres of trees in the adjacent Glenmore

Valley are said to have been felled to provide charcoal for the iron furnace operated in nearby Tousist (Kerry) from 1709 to 1735 (Mould 2002). By the end of the eighteenth century Cummeengeera was virtually treeless. Some of the hut sites found in the valley may have been associated with charcoal-burners and woodcutters.

It is interesting to compare the Cummeengeera sites to the typology of the Sheffield charcoal-production sites (see box). In particular, the ovoid and rectangular platforms in the valley closely parallel the ovoid recessed and the subrectangular recessed platform hearths in the Sheffield area. Whether the platforms in

Cummeengeera Valley have revetments has not been assessed, however. The ovoid surface site may be compared with the bowl hearths and/or undefined hearths in the Sheffield area.

In considering similarities between the sites in the two areas, it may be noted that a substantial number of English workers were engaged at the ironworks operating in the 1600/1700s at the head of the Kenmare River (McCracken 1971). A number of these were presumably well versed in the technology of charcoal production. Thus the production of charcoal in the Beara Peninsula and conceivably elsewhere may represent an important historical example of the transfer of technology into rural Ireland.

Conclusion

Pits and platforms, the two main archaeological features of charcoal production recorded in Ireland, differ not just in size and construction but also in the functionality of the kilns operated at these sites, and perhaps in many instances in their main periods of use.

The small size of charcoal-production pits is indicative of a small-scale rural enterprise, undertaken mainly to meet individual and/or local needs. The mound kilns, on the other hand, appear to have been involved in the larger-scale charcoal production required to supply industrial demands. Many ironworks operating in Ireland in the 1600s had large workforces of several hundred and more, such as the furnace in Kenmare (Kerry), and may be compared to more recent industrial developments in rural areas (McCracken 1971).

A number of pit production sites have, as outlined above, been mainly dated to the medieval period. Ironworks in Ireland were most prevalent between 1600 and 1800 (McCracken 1971), and many of the charcoal-production platforms may therefore be dated predominantly to the post-medieval period. Nevertheless, more extensive radiocarbon dating is required to provide an overall perspective of the relative chronology of pit and platform charcoal-production sites in Ireland.

Diagnostic features

Remains of charcoal-production sites of interest to archaeologists may be found in or adjacent to woodland areas. Some diagnostic features are summarised below.

- Ovoid, rectangular or circular earthworks, with charcoal deposits and blackened soil.
- They are recorded frequently as pits up to about 3m by 2m in surface area, or as platform-like earthen structures up to 10m by 9m in surface area that mostly occur on sloping hillsides.
- Sites may have less and/or different vegetation than the surrounding woodland flora, especially where prolonged and intensive charcoal production has taken place.

Acknowledgements

We are particularly grateful to Conor McDermott, Graeme Warren, Niall Kenny and Joanna Wren, who made available to us details of their recent investigations. The extensive information provided by Emmet Byrnes and the extracts from his book received from Michael Carey are much appreciated. The contributions of Connie Murphy, Brendan Riordan, Jim O'Donoghue, Eugene Hendrick and Katarina Domijan are also gratefully acknowledged.

References

Ardon, P.A. and Rotherham, I.D. 1999 Types of charcoal hearth and the impact of charcoal and whitecoal production on woodland vegetation. *Peat District Journal of Natural History and Archaeology* **1**, 35–47.

Carey, M. (ed.) (2009) *If trees could talk: Wicklow's trees and woodlands over four centuries*. Dublin.

Healy, P. 1972 *Supplementary survey of ancient monuments at Glendalough, Co. Wicklow*. Dublin.

Jones, M. (ed.) 1993 *Sheffield's woodland heritage*. Rotherham.

Kelly, D.W. (ed.) 1996 *Charcoal and charcoal burning*. Princes Risborough.

Kenny, N. (2010) Wood charring and fuel production in early medieval and late medieval Ireland—revelations from recent excavations. In M. Stanley, E. Danaher and J. Eogan (eds) *Creative minds: production, manufacturing and invention in ancient Ireland : proceedings of a public seminar on archaeological discoveries on national road schemes, August 2009*. Dublin.

Long, H. 1996 Medieval Glendalough: an interdisciplinary study. Unpublished Ph.D thesis, Trinity College Dublin.

McCracken, E. (ed.) 1971 *The Irish woods since Tudor times*. Newton Abbott.

Mould, D.P. 2002 The clachan of Cummeengeera. *Mizen Journal* **10**, 39–51.

This article was originally published in the Winter 2009 issue of Archaeology Ireland.

Salt-making and food preservation

L ittle is known of early salt-making in Ireland. Medieval references to the process are limited. However, there is some evidence of domestic salt production. With the importation of rock salt in the eighteenth century, salt manufacture developed on a relatively extensive scale throughout the country. Salt was widely used in the preservation of food products and was particularly necessary for the export of butter, fish and meat in the post-medieval period.

Rigorous in-process control was required to yield the different grades of salts and crystalline forms that met the specific preservation requirements of different food products.

Fig. 1—In situ *iron evaporation pan, exposed by storm action, at Ballycastle, Co. Antrim (photo: W. Forsythe).*

Production and use of salt

Although surrounded by sea, Ireland had neither the climate nor the coal resources to produce sea salt on a large scale (Ludlow 1949). Little is known of early salt-making in Ireland. Prehistoric remains of salt-making have not been detailed, and medieval references to the process are quite limited. With their large communities, monasteries would have required salt in considerable quantities for the preservation of meat, and more especially fish. They owned a remarkable number of medieval fish weirs; many were located in coastal areas, predominantly in estuaries (see *Archaeology Ireland*, Autumn 2009).

Scottish monasteries are known to have engaged in salt production, and there is some evidence that medieval Irish monasteries were also involved in the process. The project on 'The Archaeology of Salt Production in Ireland' (outlined below) refers, for example, to the likelihood of Mellifont Abbey, Co. Louth, being involved in salt-making, as reflected in the townland name of Salterstown on the coast between Drogheda and Dundalk. In an analogous vein, the foundation charter for Dunbrody Abbey, Co. Wexford, states that the monks will own 'lands fully …, according to their boundaries, in land, sea, in salt-pits, in fisheries, in fishing weirs, in ponds, both for land and grist mills …' (I. Doyle, pers. comm.). According to tradition, twelfth-century Cistercian monks engaged in salt-making at Mountcharles, on Donegal Bay. It is said that they produced salt by the natural evaporation of sea water in shallow pans, formed on the shore and lined with blue till, a local clay (Eamonn Monaghan, pers. comm.).

Mellifont, Dunbrody and Mountcharles were Cistercian foundations, which highlights the information gaps about salt-making elsewhere. Further investigation of the records of monastic orders could contribute to addressing the lack of information on salt-making in medieval Ireland. While the country remained largely dependent on imported salt, there is some evidence for the domestic production of salt in the seventeenth century, using turf as fuel (Ludlow 1949).

Sea-salt production

As further detailed by Greenwood (2011), successful commercial post-medieval sea-salt production in England depended on producing the optimum amount of salt without its becoming contaminated by bitter-tasting salts, known as 'bitterns', which are contained in the sea water. These include magnesium sulphate (Epsom salt) and sodium sulphate (Glauber's salt), as well as magnesium chloride. The sodium chloride (generally referred to as salt) had to be removed when it began to crystallise—otherwise it would become contaminated with bittern salts, to the detriment of its flavour and texture.

Controlling the evaporation process required considerable care, skill and know-how on the part of the salt-makers. It also involved the use of some interesting historical techniques (Greenwood 2011). To clarify the solution in the evaporation pans, and to draw off impurities from the salt crystals, various substances—such as beaten egg-whites, stale beer or ox blood—were added and the resultant scum skimmed off. The strength of the brine was monitored by testing its capacity to bear a new-laid egg, a technique known from the sixteenth century (*ibid.*).

In addition to ensuring the compositional purity of the salt, the other crucial dimension of salt-making that required careful in-process control was the temperature and speed of evaporation. These were varied to produce crystals of fine, medium or coarse salt: the quicker the evaporation, the finer the crystals (Fielding and Fielding 2006, 8–12).

Salt crystals generally occur in two different sizes, each with particular applications in food preservation (Greenwood 2011). **Large-grained** salt was produced by slow evaporation of brine, such as occurs naturally in the wholly solar evaporation areas, and was widely used in fish-curing. **Small-grained** salt was produced by the rapid boiling of brine. The dairy salt produced in this manner was generally used in the preservation of butter, but it appears to have been considered unsuitable for the curing of fish.

Rock-salt production

The discovery of rock salt in Cheshire in 1670 heralded the commercial salt manufacture of the post-medieval period. With the importation of rock salt in the early eighteenth century, salt-manufacturing developed on a relatively extensive scale in Ireland and became widespread throughout the country by the 1820s (Ludlow 1949).

In the first part of the nineteenth century, more than 200 salt-works were listed in trade directories and surveys (*ibid.*). In addition, there were a number of refineries in outlying areas not covered by these sources. As shown in Fig. 2, the salt-works were mainly located in the vicinity of prominent ports around the coast. A number were also listed in inland locations, mainly in counties south of a line from Dublin across to Galway.

The National Survey undertaken in the course of the 'Archaeology of Salt Production in Ireland' project (outlined below) identified the remains of over 400 post-medieval salt-works dotted around every coastal county.

The prevalence of salt-works in previous centuries can be seen from many placenames around the country, ranging from Salt Island on Strangford Lough to Salthill in south County Dublin, the Saltee Islands off the coast of Wexford, Salthill in County Galway and Saltpans townland in County Donegal.

Archaeological features

With the objective of identifying the remains of historic-era salt-works around the coast, an extensive project (https://saltarch.wordpress.com) entitled 'The Archaeology of Salt Production in Ireland' was initiated in 2014 (Box 1) by the Maritime Centre at the University of Ulster. The important outcomes of the project will feature in a future edition of *Archaeology Ireland*.

Box 1	'The Archaeology of Salt Production in Ireland'

Ireland's salt-production sites are predominantly coastal, reflecting the need to win salt from sea water in the absence of geological sources. This process was very inefficient, however, and required significant quantities of fuel, as the sea water had to be boiled in large pans, the water evaporated and the remaining salt skimmed off and set up to dry. In the eighteenth century the legal restrictions on importing rock salt were lifted, making production much more efficient; it could be added to sea water to make a brine that used less fuel. Typical sites would have included a pan house, stores for salt and fuel, a cistern to hold the water and accommodation for the saltmaster.

Source: https://saltarch.wordpress.com (courtesy of Wes Forsythe (pers. comm.))

As indicated above, over 400 sites were identified dotted around the coast. The survey of over 70% of these has provided a comprehensive perspective of the characteristic architecture and functional components of post-medieval salt-working sites (Box 3). In particular, the project has demonstrated the diverse form of the industry in Ireland, ranging from what appear to have been not much more than cottages through to the remains of purpose-built salt-manufacturing complexes, with rock-cut sea-water reservoirs (known as 'bucket pots'), evaporating pans accommodated in pan houses, stores, the homes of workers and sometimes foreshore landing places. With regard to both evaporation pans and bucket pots, the project has developed a much fuller understanding of the central importance of these two characteristic functional components in post-medieval salt-making.

The excavations undertaken at Ballycastle, Co. Antrim, the flagship site of the aforementioned project, revealed the last known

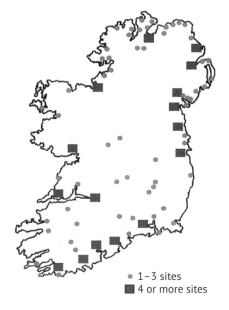

Fig. 2 — Geographic distribution of eighteenth- and nineteenth-century salt-works (after Ludlow 1949) (courtesy of B. Lawlor).

- 1–3 sites
- 4 or more sites

Fig. 3—Sea-water reservoir (or bucket pot) at Ballycastle, Co. Antrim, cut into intertidal bedrock (photo: T. Corey).

evaporation pans in Ireland (Fig. 1) and a bucket pot (Fig. 3), as well as the remains of a store, together with plentiful clinkers of coal, which was the main fuel used at the site.

The Slade salt-works on the Hook Peninsula, Co. Wexford (Box 2), which was the subject of a detailed conservation and management plan (Colfer and McElveen 2014), represents one of the most complete examples of a seventeenth-century salt-works site. As shown in Fig. 4, the salt-works comprised a series of corbelled vaults, as well as a pan house and a two-storey corbelled building that may have functioned as a dwelling.

Box 2   **Slade salt-works, Co. Wexford**

The salt-works at Slade was erected by William Mansell, who acquired the townland of Slade at the end of the seventeenth century. He may have developed the salt-works in order to supply the Newfoundland fishing industry, which depended on the area around Waterford Harbour for a lot of its supplies. The original salt-works appears to have had two pan houses, one with a possible windmill to pump sea water.

The salt was manufactured by boiling rock salt in sea water to produce a brine, and coal-fired evaporation pans were used to produce salt crystals from the brine. The rock salt used in Slade was imported by Mansell from Cheshire.

Sources: Colfer 2004; Colfer and McElveen 2014; Niall Colfer, pers. comm.

In order to economise on fuel consumption, many salt-works in Ireland combined rock-salt refining with lime manufacture (see *Archaeology Ireland*, Summer 2005). The remains of such a complex on the north side of Cork city in Gerald Griffen Street (formerly Clarence Street) are shown in Fig. 5.

Fig. 4 — Salt-works at Slade Pier, Co. Wexford (courtesy of N. Colfer).

Box 3 | Diagnostic features of post-medieval salt-works

- Purpose-built multiple structures
- Rock-cut salt-water reservoirs (known as bucket pots)
- Fire-heated evaporation pans
- House(s) to accommodate the pans
- Dwellings of the salt-works
- Landing sites on foreshores

Based on the 'Archaeology of Salt Production in Ireland' project

Fig. 5 — Remains of combined salt- and lime-works at Gerald Griffen Street, Cork city.

Food preservation

Salt-making was basically a relatively simple process, involving in essence the evaporation of water. Rigorous in-process control was, however, imperative for producing salt that met the specific preservation requirements of individual food products, especially in respect of the crystalline form of the salt, as outlined below.

Salt preserves food by dehydrating the micro-organisms responsible for food spoilage. The basic mechanism involved is the phenomenon known as osmosis, by which the salt draws the available water out of the microbial cells. The dehydration of the matrix of the food inhibits microbial growth and spoilage.

Fine-grained salt was traditionally preferred for the preservation of butter, whereas coarse-grained salt was considered to be required for the curing of fish. The differential preservation characteristics of the two forms of salt were, according to Greenwood (2011), known from at least the thirteenth century.

The preference for fine- rather than coarse-grained salt for the preservation of butter may have been to ensure that the salt would dissolve fully in the relatively low water content of butter, in order to prevent the butter from acquiring a grainy texture. The dissolved salt would have retarded the growth of bacteria, which can only occur in the moisture droplets of the butter. Fish has a higher water content and could perhaps have more readily dissolved the coarse-grained salt used in its preservation and also generally used for curing meat.

Salt-producers in Cheshire in the early decades of the 1900s made six different grades of salt to meet different market requirements: finer table salt without grinding; dairy or butter salt; common salt; coarse common salt for

Fig. 6—
Corbelled ceiling
of salt-works
at Slade Pier,
Co. Wexford
(courtesy of
N. Colfer).

curing etc.; no. 1 fishery salt; and no. 2 fishery salt (Fielding and Fielding 2006).

Salted food provisions

While salt was extensively used in the preservation of food from the post-medieval period, its usage for this purpose may have been much more limited in earlier times. Butter was a staple food of Ireland from prehistoric times; indeed, it is Ireland's oldest dated food product (see *Archaeology Ireland*, Spring 2006). A notable feature of the bog-butter samples that have been dated from the Bronze Age is the absence of salt. This may be interpreted as indicating that salt, which in earlier times was a relatively expensive commodity, may not have been widely used in butter-making in prehistory. Instead of using salt to control microbial degradation, butter made in earlier times may have been akin to the type of butter commonly known today as ripened cream butter (Downey 2010). The acidity produced during fermentation (ripening) of the cream prior to churning controls microbial growth in the butter, and hence salt is not required for its preservation.

This appears to imply that the salting of butter was not commonly practised in Ireland in earlier times. Based on references from the medieval period, however, Ó Sé (1949) states that heavily salted butter for longer keeping seems to have been made but that fresh-cream butter (unsalted butter) was more highly valued at the time.

From the medieval period onward, Ireland exported substantial quantities of salted food provisions. Salt, however, remained a relatively expensive commodity until the turn of the nineteenth century. For instance, the cost of salt per barrel of mackerel sent to America around that time (2/6d) amounted to almost one third of the cost of the fish, or almost as much as the cost of the barrel (Breathnach 2005).

Acknowledgements

We are most grateful to Wes Forsythe and Niall Colfer for information provided, together with the images of salt-works contained in the article. The contributions of Charles Ludlow, Paul Walsh, Ian Doyle, Derry O'Donovan and Bob Lawlor are also much appreciated. The additional information received from Tim Cogan, Frank Monahan, Michael O'Sullivan, Ann Burnell and Regina Sexton has been most helpful.

References

Breathnach, C. 2005 *The Congested Districts Board, 1891–1923: poverty and development in the west of Ireland*. Dublin.

Colfer, B. 2004 *The Hook Peninsula*. Cork.

Colfer, N. and McElveen, I. 2014 *Slade salt works: conservation and management plan*. Wexford.

Downey, L. 2010 How was butter made in earlier Ireland? *Ulster Folklife* **53**, 79–86.

Fielding, A. and Fielding, A. 2006 *The salt industry*. Princes Risborough.

Greenwood, J. 2011 The changing technology of post-medieval sea-salt production in England. Presented at 'Heritage, Uses and Representations of the Sea' conference, Porto, Portugal. http://www.citcem.org/encontro/pdf/new_01/TEXTO%20-%20Jeremy%20Greenwood.pdf.

Ludlow, C.G. 1949 Refining of imported rock salt in Ireland in the eighteenth and nineteenth centuries. *Journal of Salt History* **2**, 57–70.

Ó Sé, M. 1949 Old Irish butter making. *Journal of the Cork Historical and Archaeological Society* **54**, 61–7.

This article was originally published in the Winter 2016 issue of Archaeology Ireland.

Kelp production

B y the eighteenth and nineteenth centuries, harvesting seaweed
and burning it in kilns to produce kelp was extensively practised,
predominantly along the western and northern coasts of Ireland
and on offshore islands, but also in parts of the east. Over the centuries a
diverse range of chemicals have been produced from seaweed, including
alkali/soda (sodium carbonate), iodine and alginates.

Seaweed-harvesting and kelp production have left behind a
remarkable array of associated archaeological features in addition to the
kilns, including intertidal walls, kelp grids (seaweed farms), drying walls,
stacking platforms, trackways/wrack roads and kelp stores.

*Fig. 1—Intertidal wall, Coney Island,
Fergus estuary, Co. Clare (courtesy of
Aidan O'Sullivan).*

Harvesting seaweed

Introduction

The harvesting of seaweed and its use for various purposes appear to be quite ancient practices in Ireland. In addition to its long-standing role as a fertiliser and fodder for livestock, seaweed has been an important raw material for the chemical industry since the 1700s and possibly longer. By the eighteenth and nineteenth centuries, tens of thousands of people were employed in harvesting seaweed and producing kelp (Childs 2007).

Leaving earlier manifestations aside, the development of the Irish seaweed industry comprised three historical phases and a contemporary phase (Table 1). Kelp production was a vital source of income in many coastal areas—although, considering the cost incurred relative to the prices received, Nimmo (1814) queried whether the seaweed would not have been better employed as a fertiliser in agriculture.

The seaweed industry has left behind a remarkable range of archaeological features (Table 2), predominantly on the western and northern coasts and offshore islands, as well as in parts of the east.

Table 1	Milestones in the Irish seaweed industry		
Phases	**Main chemical produced**	**Main uses**	**Important seaweed sources**
Alkali phase (1700–1820)	Alkali/soda (sodium carbonate)	Soap, glass, alum for dyeing, paper-making, bleaching	*Laminaria digitata, L. hyperborea* and *Saccharina latissima*
Iodine phase (1820–1940)	Iodine	Medicine, photography	As above
Alginate phase (1940–continuing)	Alginates	Thickening agents in foods, cosmetics	*Ascophyllum nodosum* and *Laminaria hyperborea*
Contemporary phase	Sea vegetables—dulse, carrageen moss and other species Agro-chemicals—organic farming, horticulture Body products—algotherapy, thalassotherapy, cosmetic applications		
Sources: Childs 2007 and pers. comm.; Guiry 1997			

Table 2	Multifaceted array of archaeological features associated with seaweed-harvesting and kelp production		
Archaeological manifestation	Diagnostic features	Functions	Cited in text
Intertidal walls (Fig. 1)	Usually a single line of boulders on the foreshore, up to 20m in length, 0.5–1.5m in height and *c*. 1m wide.	Delineating seaweed rights; regulating rotational cutting	Strangford Lough; Fergus estuary
Kelp grids (seaweed farms) (Fig. 2)	Plots of stones on flat, sandy foreshores, up to 1m or more apart, occupying an area ranging from 0.25ha to considerably more than 1.5ha.	Cultivation of seaweed	Strangford Lough (17)
Drying walls (Fig. 3)	Found above the high-water mark on mainly wet/marshy shorelines and stretching 2–25m in length, often in a meandering line. Also found as groups of boulders set side by side, often in rectangular or arc formation.	Drying seaweed on wet/marshy shores	Rathlin Island; Aughris
Stacking platforms	Rudimentary enclosures defined by a man-made ditch and varying in shape and size. Subrectangular or curvilinear examples range from 6m x 6m to 19m x 9m.	Stacking dried seaweed in conical ricks awaiting burning	Aughris; Rathlin Island; Fergus estuary
Trackways/ wrack roads	Narrow tracks or roadways leading down to the foreshore in seaweed-harvesting areas.	Moving seaweed inland	Aughris
Kelp kilns (Fig. 4)	Rectangular, oval or circular settings of stones, open at the top and enclosing a pit, *c*. 1–1.25m long, 0.5–1m wide and 0.4–0.7m deep.	Burning dried seaweed	Rathlin Island (83); Strangford Lough (21)
Kelp stores (Fig. 5)	Purpose-built or reused structures, often surviving as buildings adapted for other purposes.	Storing kelp, grain, etc.	Rathlin Island; Rutland Island

Sources: Evans 1957; McErlean *et al.* 2002; Forsythe 2006; FitzPatrick 2007; O'Sullivan and Dillon 2009

Fig. 2—Kelp grid, Herring Bay, Strangford Lough, Co. Down (courtesy of Wes Forsythe).

Intertidal walls

Subdivision of the foreshore by small walls, erected to define seaweed rights and probably to regulate rotational cutting, are the most important imprints of kelp-making on the coastal archaeology of Strangford Lough (McErlean *et al.* 2002). Similar boundary walls (Fig. 1) have been recorded in the course of a recent intertidal survey of the channels and islands of the southern Fergus estuary, Co. Clare (O'Sullivan and Dillon 2009). The foreshore and grassy area above it were divided into sections known as **sciars**, the boundaries of which were marked by lines of stones.

Intertidal walls normally commence at or just below the high-water mark and continue down to the low-water mark. They are generally of drystone construction, built of a single line of medium-sized boulders. The intertidal walls at Strangford Lough range in height from 0.5m to a maximum of 1.5m, and are on average 1m wide. The longest walls in the Fergus estuary are around 20m in length. The intertidal walls recorded in both Strangford Lough and the Fergus estuary have no corresponding land counterparts and relate only to the foreshore.

Kelp grids

In a number of places, artificial stations—or seaweed farms, as they were sometimes called—were established to promote the growth of seaweed. This involved the placing of lines of heavy boulders on the shore. Turning and resetting the boulders at regular intervals seems to have facilitated seaweed growth. Good-sized plants developed in the course of a year and the seaweed was cropped on a rotational basis.

At Mill Bay, Co. Down, Evans (1957) described 'wrackbeds or plans' as 'half-acre rectangles set with rows of boulders a foot or so in diameter, but many beds are subdivided into "cuts" for sub-letting … the beds [having] the minutely fragmented appearance of land held in rundale'.

Fig. 3—Kelp-drying walls, Carravinally, Rathlin Island, Co. Antrim (courtesy of Wes Forsythe).

One of the more important aspects of the kelp industry in Strangford Lough was the extensive cultivation of seaweed as a crop in the intertidal zone, where some 17 kelp grids have been recorded around the foreshore (McErlean *et al.* 2002). These comprise plots of stones or boulders placed in parallel rows on flat, sandy foreshores and mostly located on the middle to lower shore. The average spacing between stones and rows is about 60cm.

The kelp grids recorded vary markedly in scale. One of the best examples, at Mill Bay in Carlingford Lough (referred to above), comprises over a square mile (2.6km²) of the intertidal sand flats laid out in rectangular plots composed of rows of spaced boulders. The kelp grid recorded at Herring Bay (Fig. 2) in Strangford Lough is also sizeable, occupying an area of approximately 2.2ha, and is composed of some 102 parallel rows of stones set from 0.9m to 1.7m apart. Other kelp grids recorded around the lough vary in extent from *c.* 0.25ha to 1.5ha. The kelp grids of Strangford Lough were in existence in the mid-1770s and are the subject of some of the earliest references to seaweed cultivation in Ireland, which was formerly quite widespread, especially along the western and northern seaboard. On Clare Island kelp grids were still in existence in the early 1900s, and as late as 1914 some 30 tonnes of burnt kelp were being exported annually from the island.

Evidence for kelp grids has not been recorded on the Donegal islands surveyed by Forsythe (2006) or in the Fergus estuary, where a number of features related to other stages of kelp-making, including oval settings of small boulders, have been found (O'Sullivan and Dillon 2009).

Drying walls and stacking platforms

Seaweed intended for kelp production was dried to prevent rotting, which would render it unsuitable for kelp-making; drying also allowed the seaweed to be burned more easily. The drying process resembled the process of haymaking.

Where the shore was wet and marshy, the seaweed was dried by draping it over stone field or sea walls. As shown in Fig. 3, drying walls were recorded on Rathlin Island (Forsythe 2006). They are roughly built of drystone boulders, sometimes augmenting natural bedrock outcrops, and have no particular orientation. They range in length from 2m to 25m and are good indicators of the presence of nearby kelp kilns. A well-constructed pair of drying walls called *síogáin* has been recorded on the coastline between Aughris and Easkey, Co. Sligo (FitzPatrick 2007).

The remarkable concentration of small platforms enclosed by a man-made ditch and found scattered along the coastal fields of the Aughris headland, Co. Sligo, were used for stacking dry seaweed in small cocks until it was carried away and burned to make kelp or spread on the land as fertiliser (FitzPatrick 2007). The enclosing ditch functioned as a drain, keeping the platform dry. The enclosures vary considerably in shape, orientation and size, with some conjoined and others overlapping. A number tend to be subrectangular or more rounded in shape. They range in size from 5.6m by 5.8m to 18.8m by 8.8m, as well as featuring anomalies in shape. A narrow track/roadway runs from the coastal fields containing the stacking platforms to Aughris village. This may have functioned as a 'wrack road' similar to those observed by Evans (1957) in the busy seaweed-harvesting townland of Ballynahatten on the County Down coast.

Kelp kilns

Typically these were very simple structures, consisting of rectangular, circular or oval settings of stones, open at the top and enclosing a shallow pit (McErlean *et al.* 2002). Rathlin Island had a substantial kelp industry in the mid-1800s, with up to 150 kilns, and, as further detailed by Forsythe (2006), the remains of 83 kelp kilns have been recorded on the island (Fig. 4).

Fig. 4—Kelp kilns, Ballycarry (left) and Craigmacagan (right), Rathlin Island, Co. Antrim (courtesy of Wes Forsythe).

Rectangular kelp kilns survived into the late 1800s and 1900s. The kelp kilns recorded by Forsythe in the Donegal islands ranged from 1m to 3.6m in length, from 0.41m to 1.5m in width and from 0.14m to 0.8m in depth. Very few kelp kilns are intact since, as mentioned below, the removal of kelp required the kiln to be broken open.

In Strangford Lough 21 surviving kelp kilns have been recorded (McErlean *et al.* 2002). They are all located on islands and most survive as a low spread or setting of stones (mostly about one stone high) on the shoreline just above the high-water mark. The eight kilns recorded on Salt Island are all subcircular to oval in shape, with maximum diameters ranging from 1.5m to 2.5m and heights of 25cm to 45cm. The eight kelp kilns on Chapel Island appear to be larger, much better preserved and oval in shape.

Burning seaweed to produce kelp was a slow process that had to be carefully controlled and involved arduous and filthy work. The kiln was lit at one end, and the dried seaweed was added slowly to the smouldering fire. The molten kelp coalesced at the bottom of the kiln and, upon cooling, hardened to a very dense, heavy block. This was broken down into manageable pieces using hammers, crowbars, picks, etc., a process that involved the removal of one of the long sides of the kiln. The kilns on Rathlin Island often have one terminal missing. During the burning, kilns gave off dense plumes of white, oily smoke, which clouded large parts of the coastline and drifted far inland.

Kelp stores

To prevent its rapid deterioration as a result of the leaching out of valuable components by rainwater, kelp immediately after production was brought to a dry structure for storage and to await shipment. Some of these were substantial, purpose-built structures, such as the kelp storehouse on Rathlin Island (Fig. 5). Some had weighing apparatus and were used to store grain

*Fig. 5—The kelp store, Church Bay, Rathlin Island; kelp hoof (**coran-cruisey**) and drag (courtesy of Wes Forsythe).*

Fig. 6—Design for an industrial-scale kelp kiln for Rutland Island, c. 1800 (courtesy of the Royal Dublin Society).

and other agricultural produce. On Rutland Island, Co. Donegal, the old fishing-station stores were reused as kelp houses.

In Strangford Lough only a small number of kelp storage houses have left visible remains. They are located on islands, with some surviving in an altered form as animal shelters or as ruined walls that have been used as shooting hides. The ruins of a relatively large stone-built kelp house, measuring approximately 13m by 3.5m, have survived on Chapel Island. Another on South Island consists of the ruins of a small, rectangular stone building measuring approximately 7.2m by 3.9m.

The number of kelp kilns found on Rathlin Island (83) and Strangford Lough (21), combined with the range of related archaeological features described above, highlights the importance of kelp-making from the 1700s.

This is further underlined by the industrial scale of the plans (Fig. 6) presented in 1800 to the Dublin Society for the construction on Rutland Island, Co. Donegal, of a reverberating furnace, at a cost of £300, for the manufacture of kelp (Hurley 2008).

Acknowledgements

We are particularly grateful to Wes Forsythe, Aidan O'Sullivan, Mike Guiry, Peter Childs, Livia Hurley and Arnold Horner for the articles and additional details provided. The information received from Críostóir Mac Cárthaigh, Ian Doyle, Beatrice Kelly and Brian Gilsenan is also much appreciated.

References

Childs, P.E. 2007 Seaweed and kelp: Ireland's forgotten industry. http://www.ul.ie/elements/Issue7/Seaweed.htm.

Evans, E.E. (ed.) 1957 *Irish folk ways*. London.

FitzPatrick, E. 2007 Interpreting a cultural landscape: a case for seaweed harvesting at Aughris, Co. Sligo. *Journal of Irish Archaeology* **16**, 11–33.

Forsythe, W. 2006 The archaeology of the kelp industry in the northern islands of Ireland. *International Journal of Nautical Archaeology* **35**, 218–29.

Guiry, M.D. 1997 *Research and development of a sustainable Irish seaweed industry*. Royal Dublin Society Went Memorial Lecture, 1996. Dublin and Cambridge.

Hurley, L. 2008 Public and private improvements in eighteenth-century Ireland: the case of the Conynghams of Slane, 1703–1831. Unpublished MLitt. thesis, Trinity College Dublin.

McErlean, T., McConkey, R. and Forsythe, W. (eds) 2002 *Strangford Lough: an archaeological survey of the maritime cultural landscape*, 334–58. Belfast.

Nimmo, A. 1814 *Fourth report of the Bogs Commission*. Dublin.

O'Sullivan, A. and Dillon, M. (eds) 2009 *Islands in time: the maritime cultural landscapes of the Fergus estuary's islands*. Clare.

This article was originally published in the Autumn 2010 issue of Archaeology Ireland.

Turf-harvesting

By the late 1600s, the harvesting and use of turf as a fuel in Ireland appears to have been widespread. Effective drying of the cut turf was of central importance. In this regard, it is interesting to note that the turf-stacking sites found in bogs around the western coast of Ireland (for example, on the Beara Peninsula) are remarkably similar to those recorded in Wales in the nineteenth century.

In addition to its use as a fuel for heating, turf was also widely used for the making of charcoal in Ireland. It was particularly common in the 1830s, especially in those locations where wood was scarce and turf readily available.

Fig. 1—Turf-stacking site on Crow Head in the Beara Peninsula (courtesy of Penny Durell).

From bog to fire

The harvesting of turf from bogs in Ireland over the centuries was a multifaceted operation, involving paring, cutting, drying, stacking and transporting. The archaeological imprint of this activity is elusive but identifiable.

The quality of the turf as fuel improved with the depth of cutting in the bog (Box 1). The brown fibrous matter cut from the higher levels of bogs, commonly called **turf**, was generally considered to be a poor fuel. The hard black matter cut deeper down in the bog was a better fuel and is generally referred to as **peat** in Britain and elsewhere.

Time-span

The earliest information relating to the use of turf as a fuel in Ireland is, according to Lucas (1970), contained in the *Senchus Mór*, the early law-tracts, which seem to have been first committed to writing at least as early as the eighth century.

From the fourteenth century onwards, the cutting, saving and transporting of turf formed part of the seasonal work levied on tenants by landowners in those areas with boglands on the estates. The dependence of the general population on turf for fuel increased with the shrinking of the area under woodland. This was accelerated in the sixteenth and seventeenth centuries by the growth of the trade in the export of pipe staves and the introduction of ironworks using wood charcoal as furnace fuel (see *Archaeology Ireland*, Winter 2009).

Writing in 1691, Petty stated that the use of turf for fuel was then almost universal (Lucas 1970). Further evidence for its widespread usage for fuel from the thirteenth century and on into the seventeenth century is illustrated in Fig. 2. This is based on over 180 dated references to the use of turf

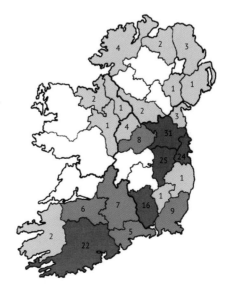

Fig. 2—Dated references to the use of turf as fuel in 24 counties from the thirteenth century to the seventeenth century, based on Lucas 1970 (no data reported for other counties) (courtesy of Bob Lawlor).

Fig. 3—Stacking of turf in the Phoenix Park during the Emergency (courtesy of Bord na Móna).

as fuel in 24 of the counties of Ireland. The most continuous set of data over these five centuries is for the counties of Dublin, Kildare and Cork. The most numerous dated references pertain to Leinster (particularly Counties Meath, Kildare and Dublin) and Munster (specifically County Cork).

From the available citations, Lucas (1970) concluded that in the thirteenth century turf was apparently an important source of fuel in Counties Louth, Meath, Dublin, Kildare, Kilkenny, Wexford, Waterford, Cork and Limerick. Data for County Kilkenny were fairly abundant from the fourteenth century, and for County Meath from the sixteenth century. The relatively small number of dated references to the Ulster counties relate predominantly to the seventeenth century.

The harvesting of hand-cut turf in Ireland appears to have reached a peak around 1926, when in excess of six million tons were produced (Feehan and O'Donovan 1996). During World War II, turf was the only fuel available to most people (Clarke 2010), and extensive stacks of turf (Fig. 3) were a common feature of the period.

Traditional practices

The raised bogs straddling the Shannon estuary in north Kerry and west Clare have been intensively harvested for domestic fuel for several hundred years (Mac Cárthaigh 2011). The cutting, storage and transport practices detailed by Mac Cárthaigh provide valuable insights into traditional turf-harvesting practices common in Ireland into the nineteenth century.

A number of west-Clare boglands were reported in 1814 to have been partly drained for turf-cutting to supply Limerick; particularly large volumes of turf were exported from west Clare to Limerick city and county.

Prior to cutting the bogs, the top layer of vegetation (termed **scraw**) was pared to a depth of about 8in. and thrown into the trench at the edge of the bank where the previous year's harvest had been cut. This provided a firm

Fig. 4—Turf-boat at Askeaton, Co. Limerick, c. 1890 (courtesy of Críostóir Mac Cárthaigh).

working foundation for those whose task it was to spread a portion of the cut turf on the lower surface of the bog.

The turf was cut vertically, starting at the right-hand side and working into the bank, and then cutting backward some 20 or 30 paces, before commencing on a second layer of sods. In deeper sections of the bogs, banks were cut to a depth of up to seven sods or **bars**.

Road access to the interior of the boglands was a vital requirement in turf-harvesting. As further detailed by Mac Cárthaigh (2011), massive ricks of seasoned turf were built by the roadside at the edges of the bogs in County Clare to supply turf-boats (Fig. 4). Cartloads of turf were transported by horse-, pony- or ass-drawn cart and tipped directly into the holds of waiting turf-boats at the quayside in Kilrush creek.

Effective drying of the cut turf was of central importance and could be a protracted process in damp climatic conditions, especially in the western counties. Having been allowed to dry on the ground for a week or two, a dozen or so sods of turf were typically collected or **footed** into small piles to catch the wind. The turf was turned periodically through the summer months, and was progressively built into larger heaps.

While no example of the turf-boats has survived, photographic evidence shows them to have been gaff-rigged vessels, 40–50ft long, with a beam in excess of 15ft (Mac Cárthaigh 2011). Their shallow draught enabled them to ply further up river creeks on the Limerick shore of the estuary than cargo vessels of equivalent size. Typically, the boats carried about 30 tonnes of turf, equivalent to 80 or 90 horse-loads.

The remains of a boat partially preserved in the mud at Blackweir, Poulnasherry Bay, Co. Clare (Fig. 5), was investigated by Mac Cárthaigh (2011) and other members of the West Clare Curragh Club. The vessel proved to be a large, flat-bottomed lighter, which older residents in the locality termed a **cot**, used to carry turf from the shore to the large turf-boats waiting in deeper water. It was one of the last of its type and was still in use in the 1930s.

Harvesting operations

The turf-harvesting practices painstakingly evolved in Ireland by earlier generations are rapidly fading from living memory. The successive stages of peat-harvesting in Wales in the nineteenth century (Owen 1970) exhibit a number of informative parallels to those in Ireland, particularly with regard to the drying process.

Drying was a fundamental dimension of the harvesting process. Having been allowed to dry on the ground 'to form a crust' in the summer breezes, stacking of the peat was begun as soon as possible. Stacks were generally built on the turbary on a dry spot accessible in the winter months, where the peats still wet could dry out. A foundation of large stones was sometimes constructed to keep the dampness of the bog from the dried peats. The same site tended to be used year after year, and the new stack was built over the peat dust remaining from previous years.

Remarkably similar turf-stacking sites can be found in Ireland, especially around bogs in the western counties and the offshore islands. These interesting archaeological features are, for instance, relatively common on the Beara Peninsula (Co. Cork), where they are known locally as *láithers*, a term which was also applied to hayrick sites (T. Ó Loingsigh, pers. comm.). The remains of turf-stacking sites typically comprise near-rectangular stone settings of varying dimensions, up to 20ft or more in length and around 6–8ft wide (P. Durell, pers. comm.). They are being increasingly overgrown (Fig. 1). *Láithers* are particularly plentiful on Dursey Island, along its northern side. Turf-stacking sites often occur in small groups around the peninsula, and

Fig. 5—Remains of a turf 'cot' at Blackweir, Poulnasherry, Co. Clare (courtesy of Críostóir Mac Cárthaigh).

Fig. 6—Turf-stacking site(s) on the Blasket Islands (courtesy of Críostóir Mac Cárthaigh).

can sometimes be found at relatively high locations in quite small patches of bog. As in Wales, stacks built in bogs in the Beara Peninsula were, in some locations, protected from damage by grazing animals.

Turf-stacking sites on the Blasket Islands seem to have been more enclosed structures (Fig. 6), apparently to protect the turf from the weather. Turf stacks made in Ireland could be up to 9ft high or more, and well-built stacks tended to throw off the rainwater. Moreover, it was usual in western Ireland to thatch the stack with rushes, with a coping of sods or stones added against the wind.

The transporting of peat or turf out of bogs clearly required access roadways and adjoining trackways. The historical development of these important features, which may be seen in abandoned turbaries in Ireland, tends not to be well documented. Many may originally have been opened by local farmers and others involved in turf-harvesting. By the 1900s the construction of access roads and tracks, as well as the organisation of drainage, was being undertaken by government agencies such as the Congested Districts Boards or the Land Commission, and in some instances by 'improving landlords' (Rotherham 2009). Information on turf-harvesting in the Beara Peninsula provided by a number of local residents indicates that in former decades the Board of Works and County Councils had relief schemes that involved the making of roadways and drains in bogs, as well as supporting turf-cutting operations. During World War II the army also became engaged in these tasks.

Turf charcoal

The making of charcoal from turf was, according to Lucas (1970), remarkably common in Ireland in the 1830s. He claimed that 'it was to be found everywhere in Ireland during the seventeenth and eighteenth centuries where facilities for making it existed', and that 'the use of charcoal by Irish smiths forms a continuum stretching from the Bronze Age to the closing decades of the nineteenth century'. Over the greater part of this long time-span, wood charcoal was, according to Lucas, probably the kind more generally used, but turf charcoal was commonly employed in those localities where wood was scarce and turf was available.

The turf charcoal was made by the controlled burning of dried turf in heaps, at the centre of which a fire was placed. They were allowed to burn until red and then quickly covered with clay to smother the fire. The charring of turf was also undertaken in pits in the ground, and the fire extinguished by covering with a fitted flag.

With the depletion of woods in Ireland in the 1700s, Robert Boyle, earl of Cork, appears to have pursued the possibility of using turf charcoal in his ironworks in Counties Kerry and Cork (Lucas 1970). In the mid-1800s peat charcoal was produced for a short time at Creevelea in Leitrim's coal-mining district (Feehan and O'Donovan 1996).

Box 1	Diagnostic features
Harvested from:	
Higher levels in the bog	Light brown fibrous turf—poor fuel
Deeper down in the bog	Hard, black, denser turf/peat—better fuel
Sources: Rotherham 2009; Clarke 2010	

Acknowledgements

The images received from Críostóir Mac Cárthaigh, Penny Durell and Bord na Móna are gratefully acknowledged. The insights on turf-harvesting in the Beara Peninsula provided by Noel David O'Sullivan, Tadhg Ó Loingsigh, J.B. Crowley and Paddy O'Sullivan are much appreciated. The information brought to our attention by Clodagh Doyle, as well as the contribution of Bob Lawlor to the article, has been most helpful.

References

Clarke, D. (ed.) 2010 *Brown gold: a history of Bord na Móna and the Irish peat industry*. Dublin.

Feehan, J. and O'Donovan, G. (eds) 1996 *The bogs of Ireland: an introduction to the natural, cultural, and industrial heritage of Irish peatlands*. Dublin.

Lucas, A.T. 1970 Notes on the history of turf as fuel in Ireland to 1700 AD. *Ulster Folklife* **15–16**, 172–202.

MacCárthaigh, C. 2011 Turf boats and turf cots of the Shannon estuary. *Béaloideas* **79**, 165–75.

Owen, T.M. 1970 Peat cutting in Wales: a socio-technical system. In A. Gailey and A. Fenton (eds), *The spade in northern and Atlantic Europe*. Belfast.

Rotherham, I.D. (ed.) 2009 *Peat and peat cutting*. Oxford.

This article was originally published in the Spring 2016 issue of Archaeology Ireland.

Other rural enterprises

A part from the four enterprises brought together here, a number of other rural enterprises are included in other parts of the book, as outlined below:

Enterprise	Section	Page
Making lime	I—Agriculture	63
Diet and production	II—Food processing	73
Medieval fisheries	VI—Coastal features	266

Section VI
Coastal features

There is something magical about the Irish coastline. Experiences of the shoreline are enhanced by the powerful impact of the uncontrollable sea and the diverse moods of weather and sky. The ghosts of past generations can be sensed in the ruins of ancient towers rising from headlands and the debris of enterprises along the seafront, whether recent or remote. Some of these remnants, like Martello towers or promontory forts, are reasonably well known. Others, such as signal towers or fish palaces, are encountered by walkers who may have difficulty recognising them or finding out about them. Others again are obvious landmarks such as lighthouses, with fascinating histories in their own right. What is presented below is no more than a sample of the many interesting traces left behind by generations past as they went about their lives at the interface between land and sea. In some cases, there is more to these sites than meets the eye.

For example, **shell middens**, which look like mere refuse dumps of discarded shells, might hold secrets to their complex uses and significance in prehistory. **Promontory forts**, again with individual and varying histories, are overtly defensive enclosures characterised by various combinations of earthen banks, ditches and stone walls running across the narrow necks of headlands.

Fish weirs were central infrastructural features of **medieval fisheries**. They were typically owned by manorial lords and a remarkable number were controlled by monasteries. Thriving pilchard fisheries existed along the south-west coast in late medieval times, the most prominent archaeological remains of which are medieval fish palaces.

The resumption of war with France in 1803 led the British military authorities to embark upon the construction of **Martello towers** at strategic locations, predominantly around the coast. Associated structures known as **signal towers** were built at stations around the coast in the period 1804–15. These were defensible guardhouses for naval signal crews and a military guard.

Dating mainly from the nineteenth century, **Coastguard stations** were imposing defensible structures, often supported by a signal station and hinterland. **Lighthouses** were progressively developed in the medieval period, gaining further momentum in the 1600s, and the nineteenth century witnessed major developments in lighthouses. The surviving remains of small, modest **lookout posts (LOPs)** erected at the outset of World War II at 83 strategic locations around the Irish coast belies their pivotal contribution to international intelligence-gathering throughout the war.

Shell middens

On the east coast of Ireland, shell middens are known to have begun forming as early as 5500 BC—well over a thousand years before the establishment of farming—and were in use in the north-east well after 4000 BC.

The significant diversity between sites in respect of size, location and seasonality of use points to middens being multi-functional focus points in the landscape—used for social gatherings, for the preparation and consumption of large quantities of food, and even as ancestral places of central importance.

Fig. 1—Shell midden, Rannagh, Arranmore, Co. Donegal (courtesy of Rosemary McConkey).

Eating shellfish

Some readers may have had the experience of walking along a beach and examining the isolated dark layers that tend to be visible on the vertical face of eroded sand. Generally, these dark lenses represent old surfaces, once grass covered but now buried and decayed. In the past, people walked along these surfaces, discarded or lost personal items on them, lit fires and dumped bones and seashells. Samples of this material are sometimes visible in the exposed dark layers. Occasionally there is so much organic material present that it survives not as a thin layer but as a mound known as a **midden**.

Middens are characterised by accumulated shells. They are usually found along shorelines. In addition to the shells, middens are generally made up of charcoal and burnt stones, and possibly bones of fish and other food sources. They may also contain the remains of hearths, tools made from stone, bone or shells, and sometimes human bone.

A noteworthy feature of middens is their extensive usage, in terms of both time-span and geographical distribution. They were formed from the Mesolithic up to the medieval period and occur over an extensive geographical area, including Ireland, Scotland, Denmark, Sweden, France and Portugal. Indeed, they are found as far away as Australia and New Zealand.

Location

Middens are generally situated in coastal areas, close to the high-tide mark on peninsulas, islands, estuaries and bays. At the time of formation, some middens may have been some distance—possibly up to half a kilometre—from the coast. They are typically sited on fairly level areas adjacent to a plentiful supply of shellfish, and are often found close to fresh water. In many of Ireland's southern and western coastal areas, late sea-level changes have reduced the likelihood of finding early midden sites. Moreover, because of their location, middens undergo progressive destruction during storms and high tides. They are sometimes found around rivers and swamps, as for example in Australia. Riverbank middens tend to be smaller than estuary or coastal middens. Such small sites may indicate short-term occupation or may even represent the debris of a single meal.

Time-span

Throughout much of north-west Europe, the sea was exploited during the Mesolithic era, and many middens started to form well before the end of the period. On the east coast of Ireland, shell middens are known to have begun forming as early as 5500 BC—well over a thousand years before the establishment of farming in Ireland—and these continued in the north-east until after 4000 BC. However, the vast majority of Irish shell middens are of much later date. The majority of the large number of shell middens noted on the west coast of Ireland date from the period after 2500 BC, from the early Bronze Age to the medieval period and probably later.

Some of the early Bronze Age middens recently excavated near Clifton, Co. Galway, contain accumulations of oyster and cockle shells. Later middens consist mainly of shells found on rocky shores, such as limpets and winkles. This has been interpreted as indicating that the large sandy beaches necessary for oysters and cockles had disappeared from the area by the early Christian period, suggesting coastal changes in the area during the intervening period.

Structure

Middens vary markedly in form and size. In Ireland they range from small scatters of shell to mounds a few metres across, up to 100m or more long and some 2m thick. Middens in Australia and Denmark are much larger than the Mesolithic shell middens found in Ireland.

In addition to the characteristic shells and burnt stones, middens may contain items such as human bones and structural features in the form of hearths, pits and hut foundations, visible as stones arranged in rough arcs.

European late Mesolithic cemeteries are typically associated with shell middens. In these cemeteries burials are typically laid out in single graves, but people were also buried in groups. However, only a small percentage of known Mesolithic sites have produced human burials or even fragmentary human remains. In general, Mesolithic deposition practices associated with middens involved the incorporation of fragments of human bone, notably parts of the skull and teeth, as well as bones from the hands, feet and legs. It has been suggested that, at least in some instances, bodies were exposed on the middens until the flesh rotted off, and that when the bones were being gathered subsequently for transport elsewhere, small hand and foot bones simply fell away into the

Fig. 2—Shell midden at the foot of Knocknarea, Strandhill, Co. Sligo (courtesy of Aidan O'Sullivan).

Fig. 3—Shell midden at Site 4, Ferriter's Cove (courtesy of P.C. Woodman).

shell heaps. It is possibly even more likely that the presence of individual bone specimens represents deliberate incorporation. Mesolithic human remains are known from shell middens at Rockmarshall, Co. Louth, and Ferriter's Cove, Co. Kerry, dated to the centuries before 4000 BC.

Artefacts
A wide range of artefacts have been found at Irish midden sites, including polished stone axes, lithics (mostly blades, flakes and cores), sherds of food-vessel pottery, an alder-wood basket (dated to *c.* 3500 BC) and burnt grains of cereals (barley and oats), as well as a range of typical crop weeds.

Formation
The marked variation in the size of middens indicates that they were formed in different ways. The smaller middens may have arisen from a significant one-off event or from groups of people consuming shellfish over many seasons for generations. The larger middens may have been formed by larger gatherings of up to 100 people over a protracted time-span. In Denmark, some of the larger middens at Ertebølle were used for some one thousand years. As previously indicated, some of the middens in Ireland seem to have been formed over many centuries. It has been suggested that middens with well-structured hearths may have been used over extensive periods and for the consumption of larger quantities of shellfish than those with poorly formed hearths, where usage may have been more intermittent.

Function
Middens are poorly understood archaeological features. The perception that they are simply refuse dumps of discarded shellfish remains may

Fig. 4—
Seashells,
Rainy Island,
Strangford
Lough, Co.
Down (courtesy
of Wes Forsythe).

not adequately reflect their complexity, function and significance. Given the significant diversity between sites, in terms of date, size, location and seasonality of use, middens are unlikely to have had one individual function.

They might be described as significant multifunctional focal points in the landscape, used for social gatherings. As one of the special features created by human activity over hundreds of years, sometimes involving the deposition of human bones, middens may have been seen as ancestral places of central importance to the identity of the family, community or society. Studies of twentieth-century hunter-gatherers suggest that Mesolithic people may have met a number of times a year to exchange knowledge and resources and to arrange marriages and burials. These gatherings might typically have involved the preparation and consumption of large quantities of food. Burnt stone is, as previously mentioned, a characteristic feature of shell middens. Accordingly, it might be worth considering whether some midden sites might be compared with *fulachta fiadh*, similarly enigmatic features.

Checklist of diagnostic features

- Mounds or spreads characterised by accumulated shellfish remains, admixed with charcoal and burnt stones.
- Varying markedly in form and size, ranging in Ireland from small scatters of shells to mounds a few metres across and up to 100m or more long and some 2m thick.
- Generally located in coastal areas, adjacent to the high-tide mark, usually on fairly level sites and often close to fresh water.

References

Cross, S. 2001 Competitive feasting in the Neolithic. *Archaeology Ireland* **15** (1), 11–13.

McCormick, F., Gibbons, M., McCormac, G. and Moore, J. 1996 Bronze Age to medieval shell middens near Ballyconneely, Co. Galway. *Journal of Irish Archaeology* **7**, 77–84.

O'Sullivan, A. 2002 Living with the dead among hunter-gatherers. *Archaeology Ireland* **16** (2), 10–12.

Woodman, P. 2001 Mesolithic middens—from famine to feasting. *Archaeology Ireland* **15** (3), 32–5.

This article was originally published in the Spring 2005 issue of Archaeology Ireland.

Promontory forts

The very exposed locations of many coastal promontory forts indicate that they may have been constructed mainly as places of refuge in times of grave danger. On the other hand, several promontory forts are built on a large scale and, some very impressive in appearance, are visible from a distance and designed to dominate the adjacent countryside. These characteristics combined with the Gaelic *dún* element common in their names—as in Dunabrattin, Dún an Óir, Doonsheane and Downpatrick Head—suggest that these monuments had quite complex roles in ancient times, including prestige and ceremony.

With few examples scientifically excavated, producing inconclusive results, promontory forts are tentatively dated to the Iron Age. Some may possibly be older, while medieval remains have been recorded at other sites.

Fig. 1—Promontory fortified with single bank and ditch at Dundoilroe, Co. Clare.

Life on the edge

The coastal promontory fort is an enigmatic type of archaeological complex. Seemingly defensive in nature, it occurs on selected coastal headlands, especially those with a narrow neck of land giving access to the promontory from the mainland. Many are bounded on two or three sides by natural precipices falling to the sea below. On the mainland side, promontory forts are bounded by various combinations of earthen banks, ditches and stone walls running across the narrow neck of the headland. The headlands enclosed by these fortifications vary considerably in size, from relatively small spurs or long narrow necks of lands to substantial areas of 30 or more hectares.

Have you seen a promontory fort?

The occurrence of the Irish word *dún* or its anglicised version 'doon' in a placename associated with a headland, even a very small one, is often a guide to the presence of a promontory fort. Some promontory forts occur at well-known scenic or historical locations. Those who have travelled around Slea Head from Ventry, for example, may remember Dunmore Head, the smooth grass-covered headland reaching out towards the Blasket Islands near Dunquin, and may even have noticed the remains of the fortification across the neck of the promontory. Further around the scenic route is Dún an Óir, a seemingly eroded promontory fort linked with an infamous sixteenth-century massacre. Those who have visited Céide Fields in north Mayo will be familiar with Downpatrick Head and the associated sea stack Dún Briste, the location of yet another promontory fort. On the north coast of County Antrim, the promontory fort at Dunseverick looks out towards the Scottish isles, an appropriate reminder of its legendary status as the capital of proto-historic Dal Riada. Then there is Drumanagh in north County Dublin, the subject of controversial claims in the 1990s that Ireland had, after all, been invaded by the Romans. Less controversial is the idea that the Norman invasion began with the establishment of a bridgehead at Baginbun, a promontory fort on the Hook Peninsula in County Wexford, from which the embattled foreigners reputedly broke out behind a herd of stampeding cattle.

In all, close to 300 promontory forts have been recorded around the Irish coast, predominantly along the west, south and north coasts, with relatively few along the east coast. Many were discovered by the antiquarian Thomas Johnson Westropp, whose name is closely linked with this monument type.

Fig. 2—
Ramparts of
a promontory
fort, west Cork,
showing a length
of ditch with
causeways.

Fortifications

Of the various combinations of earthen banks, ditches and stone walls cutting across the necks of coastal headlands, the following arrangements are the most readily characterised.

- **Closely spaced stone walls:** Several promontory forts feature two or more closely spaced (less than 10m apart) stone walls cutting off the headland.
- **Main rampart with subsidiary defences:** In many cases the main line of defence is augmented to varying degrees by a number of banks and/or ditches that are usually of a weaker nature.
- **Combination of stone walls and earthworks:** In some cases the defences involve the combined use of stone walls and earthworks, comprising one or more stone walls, outside which are various arrangements of banks and ditches.
- **Bank-and-ditch or wall:** The simplest and most common form of defence consists of a bank (with ditch) or a wall, and even occasionally just a ditch.
- **Closely spaced earthen banks:** Some promontory forts have several closely spaced earthen banks, each with an external ditch, and are reminiscent of multivallate ringforts.

The necks of land giving access to promontory forts vary from broad strips to precarious pathways with precipices falling away on either side. The defensive ramparts are usually pierced by one or more entrances or causeways, sometimes lined with upright slabs, which occasionally support lintels. Small chambers within the thick stone walls are also known, as are buttresses on the inner side and even terraces or walkways.

Rows of hollows, several metres wide and approximately a metre deep, are known at certain promontory forts. Known also at promontory forts in Wales and Brittany, they appear to be ditches with causeways. It is interesting that a somewhat similar phenomenon occurs at the hillfort on Baltinglass Hill in County Wicklow.

When were promontory forts built?

The traditional answer to this question, coloured by medieval myths and more recent ideas about the Celts, would have pointed towards the Iron Age, the millennium prior to the arrival of Christianity in Ireland, when heroic figures were supposedly engaged in great military enterprises. Nowadays the answer is less clear cut.

Part of the difficulty is that hillforts, also traditionally seen as Iron Age defences, have proved under excavation to have been occupied from the late Bronze Age, some hundreds of years earlier than anticipated. Furthermore, some promontory forts appear to be related to cliff-top forts like Dún Aonghusa, a site that was excavated by Claire Cotter on behalf of the Discovery Programme and was found also to have originated in the later part of the Bronze Age. The activity recorded at these sites is more industrial and ceremonial than martial.

Unfortunately, few promontory forts have been scientifically excavated, and even then the results have proved inconclusive. A burnt hazel stump located beneath a rampart wall during Terry Barry's excavations at Dunbeg on the Dingle Peninsula yielded a tentative Iron Age date, but a large hut standing within the fort was dated to the tenth century AD. Medieval remains

View along the interior of the rampart wall, Dunbeg promontory fort, Dingle Peninsula, showing stepped construction.

have also been recorded at the sites of other promontory forts. Dunluce Castle, not far from the Giant's Causeway in County Antrim, and Black Castle near Wicklow town are classic examples. On the other hand, pre-Christian features like ring-barrows are occasionally found in the vicinity of promontory forts.

Not all promontory forts, it should be emphasised, need have been built in the same era. Inland, to take a parallel situation, enclosures from various times in the past are known. Even in the case of hilltop forts, some date from the Neolithic, some from the Bronze Age or Iron Age, and some from the early medieval period. It is also likely that a promontory fort, once built, would have been reused in later times. The only reasonably safe date for the construction of a promontory fort is one derived from the ramparts themselves.

Function

Explanations for the building of promontory forts tend to revolve around two likely purposes, namely habitation/refuge and prestige/ceremony. Their overtly defensive character and exposed locations, allied to the admittedly scarce excavation evidence, suggest that they might have been built as temporary refuges for use in times of grave danger. On the other hand, assuming that defence was the purpose, the cliff-top location suggests a fight to the death rather than a safe refuge. Assuming that human nature does not change radically from one era to another, one potential explanation for the location is prestige. Several promontory forts are built on a large scale and some are very impressive in appearance, especially those with closely spaced walls or banks. These may have been status sites, visible from a distance and designed to dominate the adjacent countryside. The spectacular locations, unspoiled sea views, occasional associations with royalty, pagan deities or

Fig. 4—Circular hut, interior of Dunbeg promontory fort, Dingle Peninsula.

St Patrick, and even the element 'dun' combine to suggest that the social role of these monuments in ancient times may have been quite complex. Without further excavation, the circular huts known at a number of promontory forts do not throw any meaningful light on the function of the sites.

Possible diagnostic features
- Coastal location.
- Closely spaced walls.
- Main rampart augmented with subsidiary banks and / or ditches.
- Rows of hollows associated with the defences.

References
Redmond, M. 1995 A survey of the promontory forts of the Kerry peninsulas. *Journal of the Kerry Archaeological and Historical Society* **28**, 5–63.

Redmond, M. 1998 On the promontory forts of the Kerry peninsulas. In T. Bartlett (ed.), *History and environment*. Dublin.

In addition, readers are referred to the county archaeological inventories for coastal counties, and to the Dingle and Donegal surveys.

This article was originally published in the Summer 2004 issue of Archaeology Ireland.

Medieval fisheries

Fish weirs and fish palaces are amongst the archaeological remains of fisheries from the past. In-season fish weirs could take good catches of a wide variety of fish. A sizeable number were erected on rivers but generally the more impressive fish weirs were constructed in coastal waters, particularly estuaries. The scale and distribution of fish weirs varied considerably during medieval times. Those on Strangford Lough were massively built, measuring in the range 300m to 1,600m. Smaller weirs were constructed in the Shannon estuary, although, again, the remains of some are quite substantial.

The Strangford Lough and Shannon estuary fish weirs provide dates in the range AD 450–1300, with many dating from the thirteenth century. Fish traps were again constructed, and on a significantly larger scale, in the late eighteenth and early nineteenth centuries. Fish weirs presented a serious obstruction to navigation and went out of use in the late 1800s.

Pilchard, a smaller fish in the herring family, were processed in fish houses or 'fish palaces', as they were commonly known. Processing the pilchards was a two-stage operation, involving firstly curing of the fish with salt. Following this the fish were placed in barrels and the oil pressed out using pilchard presses. The oil, used for lighting and other purposes, was a more valued commodity than the pressed fish, which were packed in hogheads and exported to a number of European countries in the 1600s and 1700s. The remains of fish palaces have been recorded at a number of places along the south-west coast. Ancillary buildings included salt stores and coopering yards. Memories of these fish palaces may be found today in various placenames, notably on the Beara Peninsula.

Fig. 1—A medieval wooden fish weir at Bunratty 6 on the Shannon estuary, radiocarbon dated to AD 1164–1279, showing the fencing funnelling to a V-shape where the remains of the basket trap occur (courtesy of Aidan O'Sullivan).

Catching and processing

Fisheries were a major feature of the medieval economy. As further detailed below, they were a mainstay of exports and were also of central importance in local trade. Fisheries prospered in the 1400s and 1500s, but by the early 1700s they were in serious decline.

Fish weirs

The archaeology of fish weirs is a subject of growing world interest, investigated in North America, Australia, New Zealand and Europe. Neolithic and Bronze Age wooden structures potentially associated with fishing activities have been documented in Britain, and stone-walled fish weirs have been recorded in Scotland.

In Ireland, the pioneering studies published some 50 years ago by Went (1945; 1955; 1960; 1964) have been greatly extended in recent years, notably by the impressive weirs well documented on Strangford Lough and in the Shannon estuary (McErlean and O'Sullivan 2002; O'Sullivan 2003; 2005).

Construction

Fish weirs were typically V-shaped wooden or stone structures, with post-and-wattle fences and a gap or eye at the apex (Fig. 2), into which the fish were funnelled and trapped in baskets of varying size and construction (Went 1964; O'Sullivan 2003; 2005). Medieval fish weirs were erected on rivers: for instance, a sizeable number have been recorded on the River Lee in Cork (Went 1960). The generally more impressive structures located in coastal waters, particularly estuaries, are the main focus of this article. Erected between the tidemarks, most estuarine fish weirs caught fish during the ebbing tide. Some were oriented to trap fish on the flooding or falling tide.

Fish weirs, although often abandoned for hundreds of years, exhibited a striking degree of continuity of form across generations as well as locations but could vary markedly in size (O'Sullivan 2003; 2005). The fish weirs on Strangford Lough were massively built, with post-and-wattle fences often measuring from 300m to 1.6km in length and with fish traps comprising rectangular or box-like pounds, nets on post rows or fish-tight fences. These impressive constructions greatly contrast with the smaller Shannon estuary fish weirs (Fig. 1), which were not much more than 30–40m in length and trapped the fish in long narrow baskets placed at the end of post-and-wattle fences.

The Strangford Lough fish weirs usually had two long wooden or stone fences. At least 15 wooden and stone-built fish traps have been recorded on Strangford Lough (McErlean and O'Sullivan 2002). Two so-called **salmon walls** in Doonbeg Bay, Co. Clare, have been described by Went (1964). Each structure or weir comprised a very long wall, up to 5ft in height and built from loose stones on the flat strands. Weirs made of post-and-wattle were not very durable and may not have lasted much longer than 20–30 years (O'Sullivan 2003). According to Went (1964), some seem to have been transformed into stone weirs in the 1800s. These were more efficient and led to legislation being enacted to preserve salmon stocks.

Location

The scale and intensity of medieval fisheries around the coast varied considerably and this is reflected in the archaeology and distribution of fish weirs (O'Sullivan 2003). Medieval fishing communities had a well-informed understanding of fish movements and availability, and weirs were accordingly erected at locations to maximise catches. They were usually built on the lower foreshore, crossing creeks and channels—often with freshwater streams carrying nutrients that attracted the fish. Also, sites were selected that allowed sufficient time between tides to recover the fish and to maintain and repair weirs.

Fish weirs from different periods were frequently located beside each other. In this regard, O'Sullivan (2005) observed that on the Shannon estuary 'every time we identified a medieval fish trap there were nearly always post-medieval fisheries beside them'. This indicates that eighteenth- and

Fig. 2— Simon Dick's reconstruction showing the main structural features of a medieval fish weir, with wattle-and-daub fences, a long woven basket and men and women at work (courtesy of Aidan O'Sullivan).

nineteenth-century fishing communities learned the location of good fishing grounds by observing the remains of older fish weirs.

Medieval fish weirs were extensively used on Strangford Lough as well as at Castlebellingham, Co. Louth, and Clontarf in Dublin. Whether the concentration of weirs from the River Slaney over to the River Shannon recorded by Went (1964) reflects more intensive medieval fisheries along the south and south-west coasts is uncertain.

Dating

The use of medieval coastal fish weirs in Ireland and Britain seems to have peaked in the seventh and eighth centuries, and perhaps again between the twelfth and fourteenth centuries (O'Sullivan 2003; 2005). The Shannon estuary and Strangford Lough weirs mostly range in date from around 450 to 1300. The earliest known fish weir is a small post-and-wattle fence, approximately 8m in length, on the Fergus estuary, Co. Clare (a tributary of the Shannon estuary), dated to between 442 and 644. A number of fish weirs in the Shannon estuary and on Strangford Lough date from 1200 to c. 1300.

Many fish weirs constructed from wooden material may, as previously mentioned, be older than stone-walled weirs. On Strangford Lough, late medieval stone-walled fish weirs were constructed directly over the wooden fish traps that pre-dated them by hundreds of years and had been abandoned for generations (O'Sullivan 2003).

In the late eighteenth and early nineteenth centuries fish traps were again being constructed, and on a significantly larger scale. Fish weirs were a serious obstruction to navigation, and all but two were declared illegal in 1863 (Went 1964). The remaining two weirs, one near Bunratty Castle, Co. Clare, and the other at Buttermilk Castle in Wexford Harbour, went out of operation in the late 1800s and early 1900s.

Economic importance

Medieval fisheries were an important source of food, income, wealth and power (O'Sullivan 2003). Fish weirs provided food for domestic consumption, and fish for sale at local markets and fairs. The fish could also have been preserved by salting, smoking or drying, and then exported. With meat consumption forbidden for 100 and more days each year, fish was a necessary part of the medieval diet. Weirs could in season take good catches of a wide variety of fish. Salmon were in constant demand by wealthy households and religious orders. Eels, which could be kept alive for relatively long periods in special boxes with running water, were also highly valued (Went 1955).

Many manorial lords and important townspeople owned fish weirs. Monasteries, however, controlled a remarkable number of fisheries, which were among their more valuable possessions. In this regard, Went (1955) estimated that the total combined income that religious houses could have derived from fishery sources (excluding tithes) may have been in the order of £100,000 to £150,000 per annum in 1955 equivalent values. This could

Fig. 3—Fish palace at Crookhaven, Co. Cork, showing the remains of buildings and press walls with holes for the beams (from Went 1945, courtesy of the Cork Historical and Archaeological Society).

amount to around €3–4.5 million in 2008 monetary terms. The commercial scale of monastic fisheries is evident from Strangford Lough, where some of the large wooden and stone fish traps, which may have been the property of the Cistercians, are much more substantial than those associated with the secular settlements on the Shannon estuary (McErlean and O'Sullivan 2002; O'Sullivan 2003; 2005).

While ownership of medieval fish weirs resided mainly with monastic orders, bishops and local lords, the operation of weirs, as well as their maintenance, was undertaken by local people, who may have combined this activity with farming and other work. As further detailed by O'Sullivan (2003; 2005), the tenth- and eleventh-century fish weirs on the Shannon estuary might have been worked by **betaghts** (from the Irish word *biatach*, meaning 'food provider'). They may have lived in or near Anglo-Norman manors, working as farmers, unfree tenants and labourers, ploughing land, harvesting crops and herding cattle. The combined occupation of fishing and farming may have been common. The communities involved could be envisaged as being engaged in an agri-fish economy, such as prevailed in many coastal areas well into the mid-1900s. Various placenames on the Shannon estuary seem to be associated with farming activities (O'Sullivan 2005).

Pilchard fisheries

Ireland had valuable pilchard fisheries in the late medieval period, notably along the south coast (Went 1945). Fishing was undertaken with seine nets, using two boats to enclose the pilchard shoal in a purse-like net.

There were thriving pilchard fisheries at various locations along the Cork and Kerry coasts (Went 1945). In the 1600s pilchards were the predominant export from the south-western ports (Breen 2007). Bantry Bay was one of the most important pilchard fisheries, and the town itself may indeed owe its existence to the prosperity of these fisheries (Went 1945). In the early decades of the 1700s Bantry Bay abounded with pilchards.

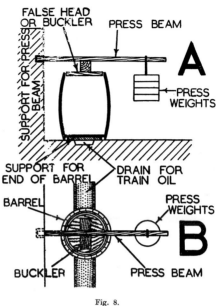

Fig. 8.

A.—Elevation of pilchard press. Barrel and support
for press beam shown in section. Contents of barrel
omitted.

B.—Plan of pilchard press.

*Fig. 4—
Diagrammatic
representation of
a pilchard press:
(A) elevation
and (B) plan
(from Went
1945, courtesy
of the Cork
Historical and
Archaeological
Society).*

Enormous hauls of up to 600 barrels are said to have been taken in a single net, and several thousands of pounds' worth of pilchards were exported to Spain, Portugal and Italy.

Fish palaces

As soon as possible after being brought ashore, pilchards were processed in fish houses or 'fish palaces', as they were also known. These were a common feature of seventeenth-century pilchard fisheries. The remains of fish palaces have been recorded at a number of places along the south-west coast, such as Crookhaven (Fig. 3) and Baltimore, Co. Cork (Went 1945; Breen 2007). They are among the more prominent archaeological features of medieval pilchard fisheries. Footprints of fish palaces may also be seen in the placenames Palace or Pallice associated with a number of locations in the Beara Peninsula.

As further detailed by Breen (2007), the original buildings may have been simple stone or wooden structures. A number may have consisted of little more than stone walls, sometimes using the walls of existing buildings or perhaps rock faces. More elaborate structures seem to have evolved later in the seventeenth century, with the advent of the pilchard-pressing operations outlined below. Ancillary buildings such as salt stores and coopering yards may also have existed at some pilchard-processing sites.

Curing and pressing

The curing of pilchards with salt was carried out, as described by Went (1945), at a number of locations along the south coast, from Ardmore in Waterford to Ballinaskelligs in Kerry. Alternate layers of fish and salt were built up in the fish palaces, where they were held for around two to three weeks, during which time some of the excess salt and blood were drained off. The fish were then washed and taken to a yard or building for pressing in barrels.

The process involved a long beam or pole, one end of which was placed in a hole in the press wall (Fig. 4). The barrels, with a round piece of timber or plank (termed 'buckler') on top of the fish, were placed in a row against the press wall. The pilchards were pressed down by means of the beam, and the barrels were topped up and re-pressed until they could hold no more. The fish could then be stored or exported immediately in barrels.

In the course of the salting process, and especially during the pressing operations, quantities of oil mixed with water and blood etc. were collected in specially constructed tanks or sumps. The mixture was transferred into barrels and the water and blood were drained off. The oil retained in the barrels was repeatedly washed with water until it was moderately clean. This oil, known as 'the train' or 'train oil', was a valued commodity, used for lighting, preparing leather and other purposes.

Diagnostic features

In walking foreshores and adjacent coastal areas, remains of earlier fisheries, of interest to archaeologists, may be encountered. Some diagnostic features of medieval fish weirs and fish palaces are summarised below.

- Remains of wooden fish weirs usually comprise V-shaped or angular protruding fence stumps, stretching across the intertidal zone of a bay or estuary (Fig. 2).
- Remains of stone fish weirs may be seen at low tide as long walls (sometimes of mainly loose stones) built up on a flat foreshore and unconnected to any land features.
- Remains of fish palaces may be found adjacent to the foreshore as ruined buildings (Fig. 3), with sloping floors and walls with holes (possibly oblong), which were used to support the press beams; in some instances, the holes may be cut into an almost vertical natural rock face.

Acknowledgements

The permission of the Cork Historical and Archaeological Society, Dr Aidan O'Sullivan and Connie Murphy to use the illustrations contained in this article is gratefully acknowledged. The invaluable information provided by Dr O'Sullivan and Brendan Riordan is also much appreciated.

References

Breen, C. (ed.) 2007 *An archaeology of southwest Ireland, 1570–1670*. Dublin.

McErlean, T. and O'Sullivan, A. 2002 Foreshore tidal fishtraps. In T. McErlean, R. McConkey and W. Forsythe (eds), *Strangford Lough: an archaeological survey of its maritime cultural landscape*. Belfast.

O'Sullivan, A. 2003 Place, memory and identity among estuarine fishing communities: interpreting the archaeology of early medieval weirs. *World Archaeology* **35**, 449–68.

O'Sullivan, A. 2005 Medieval fish traps on the Shannon estuary, Ireland: interpreting people, place and identity in estuarine landscapes. *Journal of Wetland Archaeology* **5**, 65–77.

Went, A.E.J. 1945 Pilchards in the south of Ireland. *Journal of the Cork Historical and Archaeological Society* **50**, 137–57.

Went, A.E.J. 1955 Irish monastic fisheries. *Journal of the Cork Historical and Archaeological Society* **60**, 47–56.

Went, A.E.J. 1960 The fisheries of the River Lee. *Journal of the Cork Historical and Archaeological Society* **65**, 24–39.

Went, A.E.J. 1964 The pursuit of salmon in Ireland. *Proceedings of the Royal Irish Academy* **63**C, 191–244.

This article was originally published in the Autumn 2009 issue of Archaeology Ireland.

Martello towers and signal towers

Martello towers were circular gun-towers erected between 1804 and 1815 at strategic locations and generally augmented by adjacent gun placements or batteries. The entrance to a tower was placed at first-floor level, where living accommodation was provided for the garrison. The interior of a Martello tower at ground level housed the powder magazine, ammunition and food stores. The circular gun platform on the flat roof was surrounded by a massive parapet. Many Martello towers were decommissioned after the Napoleonic Wars ended; some were rearmed in the early 1850s as a precaution against Russian attacks during the Crimean War.

Signal towers supported coastal defence by signalling information about the movement of shipping to the naval and military authorities. They were square in plan, generally with two storeys and an entrance at first-floor level. These structures provided accommodation for the signal crew and military guard, which could amount to some ten men or more at each station. The towers were generally positioned within rectangular enclosures with an extension on the seaward side, where the signal mast was located. Most signal towers had small ancillary buildings within their enclosures.

Following the end of the Napoleonic Wars, most signal towers were abandoned. Some were reused as admiralty signal stations during the Second World War. It was at the onset of the Second World War that coastal lookout posts were erected in the vicinity of signal towers.

Fig. 1—Martello tower, Baginbun, Co. Wexford, showing machicolation (courtesy of Colin Rynne).

Strategic defence

With the renewal of war with France in 1803, the British military authorities embarked upon the construction of extensive fortifications in Ireland, including Martello and signal towers. This article draws extensively on the comprehensive documentation of these fortifications by Paul Kerrigan in *Castles and fortifications in Ireland, 1485–1945* (1995).

Martello towers

Martello towers (Fig. 2) were circular gun-towers of which fewer than 50 were erected in Ireland between 1804 and 1815 (Kerrigan 1995; 2003). They generally had one gun but some had two or three. Where possible, towers were sited to give mutual support to each other and to overlap in their field of fire.

Martello towers were predominantly erected around the coast at strategic positions where they might be necessary for defence. Concentrations of towers (Fig. 3) were built on the Dublin coast (27) from Balbriggan to Bray, along the Wexford–Waterford coast (3), and at various locations around Cork

Fig. 2—Typical Martello tower. Note the absence of machicolations in this case.

Harbour (5), Bere Island (4) and Galway Bay (3). Several towers were erected on the north coast, along the shores of Lough Swilly and at the entrance to Lough Foyle. Inland, two Martello towers were erected at the middle reaches of the River Shannon.

The towers generally had ancillary fortifications, including batteries (see below). Notable features of the tower on Tara Hill overlooking Killiney Bay (Fig. 4) were the surviving guardroom, artillery storey and dry moat; the three-gun walled battery area surrounded by a steep glacis; and a gunner's cottage and gunpowder store alongside.

Fig. 3—
Geographical
distribution of
Martello and
signal towers.

Martello towers
Signal stations
Shannon River

0 20 40 60 80 100 kilometres

An 1862 plan of the site is shown in Fig. 5. The impressive restoration of the fortifications at this site provides a unique insight into what went on within and around Martello towers.

The typical external features of Martello towers are summarised in Box 1 below. In some locations, however, the towers had important variations in design and layout. While the walls generally slope inwards, the Martello towers in Cork Harbour have vertical walls and are drum shaped in form. Moreover, they have no machicolations over the doorway (Fig. 1), a characteristic shared with other towers built during the last five years of the Napoleonic Wars, such as those at Galway Bay, Banagher and Duncannon. The thin wall of the machicolation would have been more vulnerable to cannon fire, compared with the much thicker walls of the tower and parapet. This potential risk may have influenced the design of these later towers. The Dalkey Island tower also has no machicolations and is larger than the other towers, having a gun platform more than 10m in diameter, in contrast to the average of less than 6.5m. The larger size may reflect the extra space required to accommodate two guns; it is termed a double tower.

The Martello towers at Finavera and Aughinish in Galway Bay and at Meelick on the Shannon are cam shaped in plan. The gun platform at the Meelick tower is trefoil in plan to provide for three guns. The towers at Banagher, Rosaveel and inland of Duncannon fort are elliptical or oval in plan, with a thicker wall on the seaward side.

The interior of the Martello towers at ground level consisted of the powder magazine, ammunition and food stores. The first floor provided

Fig. 4—Martello tower and guardhouse on Tara Hill, Killiney, Dublin (courtesy of Niall O'Donoghue).

living accommodation for the garrison. The garrison intended for a one-gun tower was a sergeant and 12 men, and twice that number for a two-gun tower.

The circular gun platform on the flat roof was surrounded by a massive parapet. The gun carriage was mounted on a revolving traversing platform or slide carried on a perimeter iron track and a smaller central track. Access to the gun platform and to stores and powder magazines on the lower floor was by means of a narrow spiral staircase in the wall thickness. Built into the parapet was a shot furnace for heating the 18- and 24-pounder shot; red-hot shot was capable of setting fire to the wooden sailing-ships of the period.

Batteries

Martello towers were often strengthened by adjacent gun placements or batteries. The garrison intended for a tower and battery fortification was an

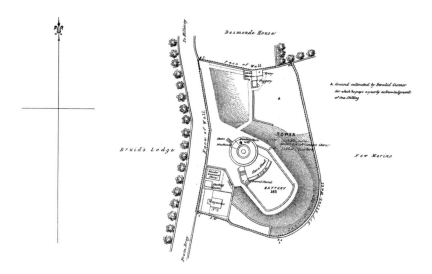

Fig. 5—1862 plan of the fortification at Tara Hill Martello tower, Killiney, Dublin (courtesy of Niall O'Donoghue).

officer and up to 30 or 40 men. Militia or other infantry may have assisted the artillery men at a tower and battery in manning the guns.

Of the fourteen Martello towers south of Dublin, eight had adjacent batteries. No batteries were constructed with the towers north of Dublin, which seem to have been less vulnerable to attack.

The armament at the Martello towers and batteries south of Dublin comprised three to five 24-pounders as well as an 18-pounder and, in some instances, a 10-inch mortar (or mortars). The tower at Sandycove (now the James Joyce Museum) had a battery a short distance from it; there were five 24-pounders mounted on traversing platforms and two 10-inch mortars.

Batteries were constructed in the vicinity of Martello towers positioned at other strategic locations, including the cluster of four in the eastern part of Bere Island in Bantry Bay. The armament here in 1811 was six 24-pounders at the four Martello towers and a further eight 24-pounders at the four batteries. At the conclusion of the war with France in 1814, the Office of Ordnance advised that the four batteries under the protection of the towers might be dispensed with.

The Martello towers around Dublin Bay were decommissioned in the 1840s but were rearmed in the early 1850s as a precaution against Russian attack during the Crimean War.

Signal towers

Signal towers (Fig. 6) were defensible guardhouses for naval signal crew and military guard, built at stations around the coast of Ireland between 1804 and 1806. As shown in Fig. 3, a chain of 81 signal towers was erected and numbered from Dublin southwards, along the south coast, up the west coast to Donegal and over to Malin Head.

While they vary somewhat in detail, a standard design seems to have been generally employed in the construction of signal towers. The typical architectural features of the towers are summarised in Box 1. Although built a few centuries later, they share a number of features with tower-houses (*Archaeology Ireland*, Summer 2009), such as the vertical profile, the use of machicolations and the positioning of the doorway at first-floor level.

Signal stations were intended to play a central role in coastal defence in conjunction with the Martello towers and batteries (see above). Their function was to signal information about the movement of shipping to the naval and military authorities. As well as communicating with adjacent signal stations, the crew were able to communicate with naval vessels offshore and to pass information by messenger to the military guard inland.

Following the arrival of the French expeditionary fleet in Berehaven (Cork) in 1796, and in the expectation of further invasions, priority seems to have been given to the construction of signal towers on the west-Cork coast. The absence of signal stations along the coast from Malin Head to Dublin reflects the prevailing views of the military authorities at the time that invasion was unlikely on the north-east and along the east coast from Belfast to Drogheda.

The towers provided accommodation for the signal crew and military guard. At Kerry Head signal tower, the first floor was divided by a partition to provide a room for the lieutenant. The remaining space at this level was a passageway with access to the ground floor, where the military guard were accommodated. It also provided access to the flat roof above. The accommodation seems not to have been too inviting. Many of the towers were damp in wet weather. Slating or rough rendering to the walls was used to prevent excess dampness penetrating the towers.

The signal-station enclosure had in some instances a graded slope or glacis exterior, providing a defensive perimeter for the military guard. Most towers had small ancillary buildings within the enclosure on the landward side of the signal tower. Roads were an essential infrastructural element of signal stations. The road surviving today at Blackball signal tower on the Beara Peninsula (Cork) is remarkably wide. Other interesting features of this signal station are the regular array of substantial cultivation ridges and low earthen-bank enclosures, as well as sizeable, well-formed, deep depressions (possibly water reservoirs) in the lower ground leading up to the signal tower.

The signalling system involved the use of a rectangular flag, a blue pendant or narrow rectangular flag and four black balls made of hoops covered in canvas. To convey signals, these were hoisted in various arrangements on a signal post. This consisted of an old topmast (15m long with a cap), cross-trees and a fid (conical wooden pin) to secure the 9m flagstaff. The pendant and canvas-covered balls were hoisted by means of a graff or spar (9m) set at an angle to the mast. Naval vessels offshore used flags to communicate with the signal stations.

The signal crews were drawn from what were known as the Sea Fencibles, a form of naval reserve made up of local fishermen and merchant seamen commanded by naval officers, including signal lieutenants. The Sea Fencibles were organised into 21 districts and manned most of the signal stations. The composition of signal-station crews included a signal lieutenant, a midshipman and two signalmen of the Sea Fencibles. Military guards of some five to seven yeomanry or infantry were also located at signal stations, amounting to around ten men at each station.

Fig. 6—Signal tower, Old Head of Kinsale, Cork (courtesy of Colin Rynne).

Following the end of the Napoleonic Wars, most of the signal stations were abandoned. Some were used as admiralty signal stations during the First World War. At the onset of the Second World War, coastal watching posts were erected close to the signal towers. Most of these were small concrete buildings, the remains of which can still be seen on many headlands.

Box 1	Diagnostic features

Martello towers
- Generally circular in plan (diameter around 12m at ground level). Parapet about 7.6m above the ground. External wall often sloping inwards but in some locations vertical. In plan some towers are elliptical or cam shaped.
- Entrance at first-floor level on landward side. Many, but not all, have a machicolation above the doorway at parapet level.

Signal towers
- Square in plan (some 4.5m square internally), generally with two storeys (up to *c*. 9m in height) and an entrance at first-floor level on the seaward side. Walls are about 0.6m thick and were originally faced with weather-slating.
- Machicolations occur in the parapet directly over the doorway and two more at the landward corners of the tower.
- Windows are found in side walls at ground- and first-floor levels, and fireplaces and chimneys are built into the splayed rear wall.
- May be sited in rectangular enclosure with a semicircular or fan-shaped extension on the seaward side, where the signal mast was located.

Acknowledgements
The contributions of Niall O'Donoghue, Rob Sands, Ted O'Sullivan and Colin Rynne to the composition of this article are gratefully acknowledged.

References
Kerrigan, P.M. 1995 *Castles and fortifications in Ireland, 1485–1945*. Cork.

Kerrigan, P.M. 2003 Signal towers on the west Cork coast. *Mizen Journal* **11**, 29–45.

This article was originally published in the Summer 2012 issue of Archaeology Ireland.

Coastguard stations

By 1860 there were 200 Coastguard stations dotted around the Irish coast. Those built from the mid-1800s typically consisted of a defensible terrace of stone- or brick-built houses, usually two storey, with a characteristic watch-tower at one end.

In the early twentieth century the navy divested itself of 52 Coastguard stations and, instead, concentrated on constructing what are termed signal stations. These were generally positioned to provide a wide perspective of the surrounding seascape and adjoining countryside. Some were reused as lookout posts during the First World War.

Coastguard stations are most commonly seen today in remote coastal areas as conspicuous ruins with a prominent walled enclosure, possibly containing the remains of terraced houses, a well and perhaps also a boat-house, as well as a slipway and the footprint of a flagstaff.

Fig. 1—Terrace of houses at the former Coastguard station at Ballycrovane near Eyeries, Co. Cork (courtesy of B. Riordan).

Coast protection

Coastguard stations are conspicuous features of many coastal areas, often seen as prominent ruined structures, although some have been converted to more modern uses. They date mainly from the 1800s and were imposing, defensible constructions (Figs 1 and 2).

Development of the service

The Coastguard Service was established in Ireland in 1824 and its initial purpose was primarily revenue protection. This changed radically in 1856 with its transfer to the Admiralty, which saw the force as providing the basis for a naval reserve (Symes 2002/3). Under the control of the Admiralty, the Coastguard was effectively an integral part of the Royal Navy (Murray 1998).

Coastguards were frequently seen by coastal communities as the 'eyes and ears' of the establishment. As shown in Box 1, however, the Coastguard Service in Ireland undertook a wide variety of notable duties.

The most prominent figure in the formation, development and direction of the Coastguard Service in Ireland was James Dombrain (Symes 2003), who was centrally involved in its establishment and in instigating its diverse range of functions (Box 1).

Fig. 2—Front view of the remains of the Coastguard station at Ballycrovane near Eyeries, Co. Cork (courtesy of B. Riordan).

Box 1	Main functions undertaken by the Coastguard Service in Ireland

Control of smuggling

By the 1830s smuggling, which had been extensive around the coast, had been curtailed by the Preventive Water Guard (the forerunner of the Coastguard Service) within some two decades of its introduction into Ireland in 1819 by Dombain.

Saving of life at sea

During the nineteenth century, countless ships were rescued and many thousands of lives were saved by the Coastguard Service, particularly before the advent of steam.

Famine relief

In virtually all periods of distress from 1831 until the end of the nineteenth century the Coastguard Service was involved in the distribution of famine relief along the western seaboard.

Naval reserve

From the mid-1850s, the primary role of the Coastguard Service began to be the defence of the coasts and the manning of the navy in the event of war or an emergency.

Fisheries

Many of the reports on the state of Irish fisheries in the nineteenth century were compiled from, among other sources, the surveillance information collected by coastguards.

Receivers of wrecks

Coastguards had the unenviable task of trying to protect from pillage vessels wrecked on the coast. Communities on parts of the coast regarded a wreck as a welcome bounty; indeed, it was not unknown for ships to have been deliberately directed onto hazardous coasts.

Other duties

The prevention of gunrunning was added to the duties of coastguards. In the early decades of the twentieth century the Coastguard Service began to undertake more political duties. Consequently, relations with local communities had deteriorated by the outbreak of the War of Independence in 1919.

Sources: Symes 2002/3; Murray 1998

Construction of stations

By 1860 there were 200 Coastguard stations around the coast (Symes 2002/3) (Fig. 3). Up to the late twentieth century, Coastguard stations typically consisted of a terrace of cottages/houses, a watch-tower, a boat-house, an

*Fig. 3—
Distribution
of Coastguard
stations around
the Irish coast
(based on
Kerrigan 1980/1;
map courtesy of
B. Lawlor).*

equipment store, earth-closets, wash-houses and outhouses.

Senior officers were generally provided with larger houses, built separately or placed at the end of the terrace. These sometimes contained a watch-room, perhaps with a canted bay window from which a watch could be maintained. In the early decades of the 1800s, the Coastguard Service appears to have built 'permanent watching posts', watch-towers and lookouts. These were sometimes built within the stations, but many were separate constructions sited at intermediate locations between stations.

From the mid-1800s the Board of Works was responsible for the construction and maintenance of Coastguard stations, and generally more substantial buildings were erected. As described by Symes (2002/3), the stations generally consisted of a terrace of stone- or brick-built houses, usually two storey, with the characteristic watch-tower at one end. Each house had a living room and scullery on the ground floor, and upstairs a main bedroom and two or three smaller bedrooms. There were privies, coal sheds and a communal washing area at the rear of the terrace.

During the 1850s the Board of Works built over 60 new stations in Ireland (Symes 2002/3). Because of the disturbed state of the country in the second half of the nineteenth century, many of the stations had defensive features such as oriel windows with gun loops at each side. Exterior doors were strongly reinforced, and the upstairs windows could be protected by iron shutters.

Following the transfer of the Coastguard Service to the Admiralty in the mid-1800s, signalling and communications became an increasingly important role of the coastguards from the late nineteenth century. In the early twentieth century, the navy divested itself of 52 Coastguard stations and detachments in Ireland (Symes 2002/3). Instead, it concentrated on providing a small, well-trained force to man the signal stations (see below) attached to some Coastguard stations.

Archaeological features
Early in the 1920s isolated Coastguard stations, particularly on the south-west and north-west coasts, were attacked by IRA units seeking arms and

ammunition, and in 1920 14 stations were reported to have been destroyed (Symes 2002/3). Further stations were destroyed during the Civil War. Among these were the Coastguard stations near Eyeries and Allihies in the Beara Peninsula (Co. Cork), the archaeological remains of which are outlined below.

Eyeries

The ruins of the Coastguard station at Ballycrovane (Figs 1 and 2), which was constructed in 1899, are an important feature of the landscape near the village of Eyeries (Co. Cork). The prominent walled enclosure and terrace of houses exhibit a number of the characteristic aspects of the stations described by Symes. Evident on the ground floors are the remains of the living rooms and small kitchens, and overhead were the bedrooms, with fireplaces.

The house at the western end of the terrace is apparently larger than the others and has a bay-window-like opening in the front wall, giving it wide views over the surrounding seascape. It exhibits a number of features of the houses that were provided for senior officers (see above).

The back wall of the terrace contains the entrances to the individual houses. Positioned on either side of each doorway are the remains of small, one-storey attachments. One of these may have been used for the storage of coal and other items, while the other may have been a privy or washing unit.

In front of the houses is a large covered well (Fig. 2) with a square opening on its seaward side. The upstanding stone structure with the rounded top attached to the wall may perhaps have held a water-pump. Other notable aspects of the Coastguard station still evident today are its surrounding walls, boat-house and slipway.

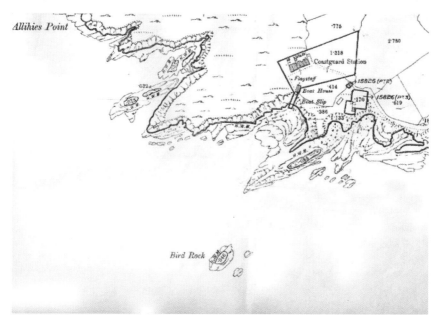

Fig. 4—Plan of Coastguard station at Allihies, Co. Cork (courtesy of Ordnance Survey Ireland/ Government of Ireland) (copyright permit no. MP0009113).

Allihies

As further detailed by MacMahon (2012), the Coastguard station near Allihies was located at the northern end of Ballydonegan Bay, a few hundred metres to the west of the modern pier. The station had a terrace of around six houses, with some small buildings at the rear, shown as surveyed in 1898 and published in 1899 (Fig. 4).

The architect Enoch (Edward) Trevor Owen was assigned in 1874 by the Board of Works to commission the Coastguard station at Ballydonegan (J. Ryan, pers. comm.). It was described as a terrace of cottages, and a tower with pyramidal roof, oriel windows and batter to walls. Extra houses were commissioned at the station in 1905.

The surrounding walls (Fig. 4) are the most striking aspect of the Allihies station evident today. Among the other features still surviving is a properly lined well, 36ft deep (MacMahon 2012). The remains of the boat-house and slipway, as well as what seems to be a portion of the flagstaff, can still be found today.

The view from the Allihies Coastguard station of the surrounding sea and adjoining countryside is somewhat limited. Thus the station may have been provided with an auxiliary lookout post, which could have been located at the site of the signal station outlined below.

Signal station

Positioned a few miles inland of the Coastguard station and close to the top of Knockroe West Hill is what appears to have been a signal station. It was surveyed in 1898 and is marked on the 1899 Ordnance Survey map (OSI Historic 25in. Sheet CK 127-06) as a signal station with a flagstaff. The location provides a panoramic perspective of the seascape over the approaches to Bantry and Kenmare Bays, as well as the surrounding countryside (Fig. 5).

The most prominent surviving remains at the site are two upstanding constructions (Figs 5 and 6), which appear to have been large water tanks.

Fig. 5— Panoramic view from the signal station on Knockroe West Hill, Co. Cork (courtesy of B. Riordan).

Fig. 6—Water tanks at the remains of the signal station on Knockroe West Hill, Co. Cork (courtesy of B. Riordan).

Close to these is possibly a dugout water reservoir. The large rectangular feature lying on the ground near the tanks (Fig. 6) may have been the base of an earlier building. This could possibly have housed a steam engine used to pump water from the possible reservoir up into the tanks.

The site at Knockroe West continued to be used for coast-watching into the twentieth century. Invaluable local insights indicate that the site had a flat-roofed building with a fireplace within living memory (P. O'Sullivan, pers. comm.). A lookout post manned by coastguards was located at the site during the First World War. This seems to have been demolished around the 1930s, but a temporary lookout, seemingly in the form of a tent, was put up there at the start of the Second World War.

Famine relief

In the mid-1800s the Coastguard Service had 77 stores at or near stations, stretching from Cork to Donegal, which were engaged in the distribution of food (Symes 2003). James Dombrain instructed his officers to issue free food to starving families on a doctor's certificate. He was publicly rebuked by the authorities in London for giving the food away without official sanction.

The most spectacular and best-documented incident involving the Coastguard in famine-relief operations along the western seaboard occurred in 1879/80 (Murray 1998). The US frigate *Constellation* was met on arrival in Cork Harbour in April 1880 by a flotilla of cruisers under the command of the duke of Edinburgh. The cargo, which included 1,600 barrels of potatoes and corn, was transferred onto smaller gunboats for immediate delivery to islands and coastal locations extending from Cork along the west coast and up to north Donegal.

Box 2	Diagnostic features

- Defensible terrace of some six or more nineteenth-century houses in coastal locations, often with a tower at one end of the houses; usually found in a ruined condition, but some restored.
- Other typical features may include prominent enclosing walls, as well, perhaps, as a boat-house, with a slipway running down to the sea.
- Most commonly found in remote coastal areas as conspicuous ruins.

Acknowledgements

The insightful contributions of Brendan Riordan, Paddy O'Sullivan, Joe Ryan and Seán MacMahon are gratefully acknowledged.

References

Kerrigan, P.M. 1980/1 Irish Coastguard stations, 1858–67. *Journal of the Military History Society of Ireland* **14**, 103–5.

MacMahon, S. 2012 The strange tale of the Ballydonegan Coastguard station. *Allihies Echoes* (2012).

Murray, J.P. 1998 The Coastguard in famine relief on the west coast. *Journal of the Galway Family History Society* **5**, 64–8.

Symes, E.P. 2002/3 The Coastguard in Ireland. *Journal of the Military History Society of Ireland* **23** (92), 201–10.

Symes, E.P. 2003 Sir James Dombrain and the Coastguard. *Dublin Historical Record* (Spring 2003), 56–70.

This article was originally published in the Winter 2013 issue of Archaeology Ireland.

Lighthouses

In the later medieval period, lighthouses were built on Hook Head (Co. Wexford) and at Youghal (Co. Cork) that had towers with fire beacons at the top. They were operated respectively by monks and nuns.

In the mid-1600s, the original tower on Hook Head was enlarged and the fire beacon was replaced by a large oil lamp. In addition, what are known as cottage lighthouses were erected on Howth Head (Co. Dublin), Copeland Island (Co. Down), Loop Head (Co. Clare) and on the Old Head of Kinsale, where the best-preserved example survives today. These were simple seventeenth-century family cottages equipped with a coal-burning open beacon.

Some 40 of Ireland's principal lighthouses were established in the period between 1810 and 1870. An estimated 80 to 100 lighthouses were in operation by Irish Lights towards the end of the twentieth century.

Fig. 1 — Hook Head lighthouse, Co. Wexford.

Navigation lights

The display of navigation lights on the Irish coast reaches back to the fifth century at least. Early navigation lights were little more than fire beacons on prominent headlands. As further detailed below, they were progressively developed during the early modern period from what were known as cottage lighthouses to the tower lighthouses common today.

Medieval lighthouses

During medieval times, religious communities were centrally involved in the establishment of navigation beacons (Wilson 1968; Long 1993; Taylor 2004; Colfer 1984–5).

Hook Head

In search of solitude, St Dubhán of Wales is reputed to have settled near Hook Head in the fifth century; the site of his cell or oratory can be seen at Churchtown, about 1km from the tower. To warn mariners of the perils of the coast, Dubhán established a beacon fire consisting of a large iron basket or 'chauffer' suspended from a strong mast sited near the edge of the cliff (Long 1993).

In order to guard the entrance to Waterford Harbour, the Normans replaced the original fire beacon with the first tower of Hook. It appears to have been instigated by either William Marshal, earl of Pembroke and lord of Leinster, or one of his sons, but was seemingly built by monks in the first quarter of the thirteenth century (Colfer 1984–5). The massive tower with the beacon at its top was vested in the custody of the monks of Churchtown, the nearby site of Dubhán's original oratory.

The tower at Hook is a three-storey structure (Fig. 1). A survey undertaken by William Colfer in 1984 detailed a number of archaeological features dating from the monastic origins of the tower. In particular, the second floor seems to have been used as the main residence by the monks in medieval times. It appears to have comprised one large mural chamber, which seems to have been the main living area, and six alcoves, with a number of small box-like openings in the walls that could have been used for storing personal possessions.

Except for a break in the seventeenth century, the tower has served as a lighthouse for some 800 years and, as noted by Colfer (1984–5), may be the only early thirteenth-century secular building in the country still serving its original purpose.

Youghal, Co. Cork

In 1190 a lighthouse was established and endowed at Youghal by Maurice Fitzgerald (Wilson 1968). It was built on the same site as the present lighthouse and was put into the care of the nuns of St Anne's Convent, who maintained it until the dissolution of the monasteries in 1542. In his 1644 tour of Ireland, M. Boullaye le Gouz referred to the lighthouse as being 'formerly part of a convent of nuns of which there remains a tower called the Nunnery, upon which they used to light torches to enable vessels to come into the harbour during the night' (*ibid.*). The original building was replaced in the mid-1800s by the current lighthouse and adjoining dwelling house.

Early modern lighthouses

The establishment of lighthouses in Ireland gained momentum in the mid-1600s, and over subsequent centuries three builders were foremost in lighthouse developments (Box 1). The increasing recognition of the crucial importance of lighthouses was heralded in 1665, when Robert Reading was granted a franchise by King Charles II to establish six lighthouses at strategic locations around the coast (Wilson 1968; Long 1993; Taylor 2004).

Box 1	Builders of early modern lighthouses	
Builder	**Date**	**Location**
Robert Reading	Second half of 1600s	Re-established the fire beacon on the tower at Hook Head; established a number of cottage lighthouses
Thomas Rogers	Late 1700s and early 1800s	Refurbished the old tower at Hook Head; built a number of new lighthouses, including on Howth Head, the Old Head of Kinsale, Loop Head and Cape Clear (forerunner of the Fastnet)
George Halpin Sr	First half of 1800s	Prolific designer and builder; rebuilt, refurbished or established over 60 lighthouses, notably the Tuskar
Sources: Wilson 1968; Long 1993; Taylor 2004		

Hook Head tower lighthouse

The second phase in the history of the Hook Head lighthouse (Fig. 1) involved the re-establishment of the beacon on the tower, some time in 1665–7. Though it is not certain, Reading seems to have been responsible for the construction of a special 'lantern' to house the beacon fire on top of the tower (Long 1993). This had a special brick dome constructed to withstand the tremendous heat of the fire, with a flue to help conduct the smoke clear of the flame and give the mariners a much brighter light. It was replaced by a lamp in 1677 (Wilson 1968).

The original tower was enlarged by the construction of a new wall outside the old wall, and with a stone stairway built between the two. By

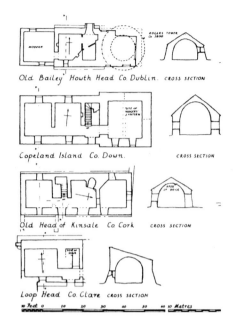

Old Bailey Howth Head Co. Dublin. CROSS SECTION

Copeland Island Co. Down.   CROSS SECTION

Old Head of Kinsale Co Cork   CROSS SECTION

Loop Head Co. Clare CROSS SECTION

Fig. 2—Plans of four cottage lighthouses by Michael Costello (formerly of Irish Lights).

1677 the new lighthouse was operational and a large oil lamp had replaced the fire beacon.

Towards the end of the eighteenth century the tower had fallen into disrepair. In 1791 Thomas Rogers was contracted to maintain and staff Hook lighthouse. He refurbished the old tower and installed what, for the time, was state-of-the-art lighting equipment (Long 1993).

Cottage lighthouses

These were simple cottages with an open, coal-burning beacon (Long 1993; Taylor 2004). Cottage lighthouses, in which the keepers lived with their families, are significant archaeological features that reflect the progressive development of lighthouses in Ireland.

The cottage lighthouses were established around 1667, under franchise by Reading, at the Old Baily, Howth Head, Co. Dublin, Copeland Island, Co. Down, and the Old Head of Kinsale, Co. Cork. Another was established at Loop Head, Co. Clare, by a special commissioner appointed by the Queen Anne Act 1704. Informative drawings of those four cottage lighthouses have been produced by Michael Costello, formerly of Irish Lights (Fig. 2).

At **Howth Head**, the cottage lighthouse (Fig. 3) established about 1667 by Reading had a coal-burning beacon on top of a squat tower positioned against the eastern gable of the cottage (Long 1993; Taylor 2004). In 1790, over

Fig. 3—Drawing of cottage lighthouse at Baily Green, Howth, 1665–1790, by Michael Costello (formerly of Irish Lights).

a century later, the next lighthouse on Howth was built by Thomas Rogers on the same site as the old cottage lighthouse. He replaced the coal-burning light with a conventional tower and lantern (Taylor 2004). As noted by Long (1993), the lighthouse was a very advanced design by the standards of the time.

In common with a number of other lighthouses constructed around that time, the light was often obstructed by mist or cloud owing to its high position on the hill. In 1814 a new tower and keepers' dwellings, designed and supervised by George Halpin Sr, was established lower down on the headland at Little Baily or Duncriffan, where almost 2,000 years earlier King Crimthan reputedly had his fortress (Taylor 2004).

At **Copeland Island**, Co. Down, the cottage lighthouse had, as shown in Fig. 2, a square tower, 12m high (Long 1993). In 1796 Thomas Rogers added a 1.8m-diameter lantern to a corner of the tower and changed the light from coal to oil (Taylor 2004). In 1815, a new 16m-high tower and lantern with a fixed oil-fired light, designed and built by George Halpin Sr, was established alongside the old tower. Prior to the Copeland light, there had been a lighthouse, probably a cottage type, also on Islandmagee, near Carrickfergus, which had a short life of four to five years (Long 1993).

On the **Old Head of Kinsale**, the first lighthouse proper was a cottage type (Fig. 2), established by Reading in 1665 (Long 1993; Taylor 2004). The light was exhibited from a fire platform built on a pillar projecting through the roof. The keeper and his family lived in the cottage. The remains of the cottage lighthouse (Fig. 4) can still be seen on the headland today (O'Donovan 2003).

Fig. 4—Remains of cottage lighthouse on the Old Head of Kinsale.

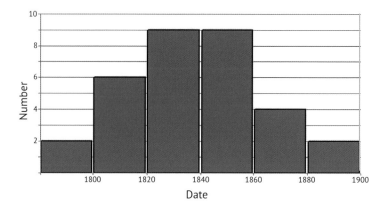

Fig. 5—
Lighthouses first
established in the
1800s (derived
from Wilson
1968).

In 1804 Thomas Rogers was contracted to replace the old fire-burning beacon on the rooftop with a temporary 1.8m-diameter lantern with 12 oil lamps and reflectors. In 1812 the cottage lighthouse was replaced with a 13m-high tower lighthouse designed by George Halpin Sr, similar to one then under construction at the Baily, Howth (O'Donovan 2003). In 1853 it was replaced by the present lighthouse, located on the extremity of the peninsula (*ibid.*). The general type of dwelling provided for keepers and their families during the 1800s is shown in Fig. 6.

At **Loop Head**, Co. Clare, the first lighthouse on the headland was a cottage type with a coal-fire beacon, built around 1670 (Fig. 2). It was replaced in 1802 by a more conventional lighthouse built by Thomas Rogers. The tower was about the same height as the present one, with four rooms and a lantern (Taylor 2004). To accommodate a better lantern, it was replaced in 1854 by a new tower designed by George Halpin Sr.

Fig. 6—Typical
lighthouse
dwelling, built
and designed
by G. Halpin
Sr, in the 1800s
(courtesy of the
Commissioners
of Irish Lights).

The nineteenth century saw major developments in lighthouses. Wilson (1968) has listed the dates on which some 40 of the principal lighthouses were first established at various locations around the coast; as shown in Fig. 5, they were predominantly established from around 1810 to 1870. The extent of lighthouse construction during the period was indeed somewhat higher when the rebuilding of previously established lighthouses is taken into account. In addition, not all of the lighthouses established around the coast of Ireland are contained in Wilson's list. In total, something from over 80 to around 100 lighthouses were operated by Irish Lights towards the end of the twentieth century.

Box 2	Diagnostic features

Cottage lighthouses

Simple seventeenth-century family cottages, equipped with a coal-burning open beacon. The best-preserved example occurs on the Old Head of Kinsale (Fig. 4). At Loop Head a small part of the remains of the old structure may be seen near the keepers' dwellings, as well as the pillar on which the fire platform was built. The remains of the fuel used for the coal fires have been found at some sites.

Tower lighthouses

In the medieval period, lighthouses at Hook Head and Youghal had towers with a fire beacon at the top. More modern conventional tower lighthouses have a lantern in the form of a glass structure near the top, which houses the source of illumination. Dwellings were generally built nearby for the keepers, but in a few lighthouses (e.g. the Fastnet) they lived in the tower.

Sources: Wilson 1968; Long 1993; O'Donovan 2003; Taylor 2004

Acknowledgements

The informative contributions of Frank Pelly (formerly of Irish Lights) to this article are gratefully acknowledged. Our appreciation is also due to Robert McCabe, Joe Varley, Derry O'Donovan, Bob Lawlor and Brendan Riordan.

References

Colfer, W. 1984–5 The Tower of Hook. *Journal of the Wexford Historical Society* **10**, 69–78.

Long, B. (ed.) 1993 *Bright light, white light*. Dublin.

O'Donovan, D. (ed.) 2003 *Ballinspittle and de Courcy country: historic landscapes*. Bray.

Taylor, R.M. (ed.) 2004 *The lighthouses of Ireland*. Cork.

Wilson, T.G. (ed.) 1968 *The Irish lighthouse service*. Dublin.

This article was originally published in the Autumn 2014 issue of Archaeology Ireland.

Coastal lookout posts

Eighty-two World War II lookout posts were hastily built in the winter of 1939–40. The final one was opened on the side of Dingle Bay in early 1942. The huts are said to have been damp, smoky and cramped.

Seven men led by an NCO manned individual LOPs and were paid at army rates. The basic operational equipment at the LOP huts consisted of binoculars, a telescope and charts, a logbook and, most crucially, a telephone (provided in later years).

While LOPs were spartan, they provided a vital intelligence network—very little could happen around the coast without the knowledge of the coast-watchers. The 'EIRE' signs erected close to the LOPs provided a simple navigation aid for incoming US planes.

Fig. 1—Aughris Head LOP, Sligo, March 1940 (National Archives of Ireland).

World War II

Several different types of structure are found on headlands around the Irish coast, ranging from Martello towers and lighthouses to signal towers and lookout posts, not to mention cliff-top castles and forts. Some are well-known local landmarks but the modest appearance (Fig. 1) of World War II lookout posts (LOPs), the remains of which (Figs 2, 3 and 4) are still to be seen on various headlands (Fig. 5), belies their pivotal contribution to intelligence-gathering during the war.

The comprehensive account presented in the book on the Coast-Watching Service (1939–45) published in 2008 by Michael Kennedy (*Guarding natural Ireland*), on which this article is based, testifies to the importance attached to the information recorded by LOPs, not just in Ireland but also in Britain and the United States.

Among the notable endeavours undertaken by LOPs were the systematic recording and tracking of aircraft and marine activities, particularly along the west coast but also associated with the bombing of Belfast and Dublin and the ferrying of US aircraft across the Atlantic. Some important aspects of these activities are summarised in Box 1.

Other major events with which the LOPs were associated include, as detailed by Kennedy, the systematic tracking along the Mayo coast (during the night of 25/26 May 1941) of the two flying boats from Castle Archdale (Northern Ireland) that succeeded in locating the German battleship *Bismarck*, culminating in its sinking on 27 May. This was a defining point in the Atlantic war. Although not as centrally involved as Blacksod Lighthouse (Co. Mayo), perhaps the most historic event to which information gathered by the LOPs, in particular Erris Head (Mayo), made a significant contribution was the provision of weather reports that enabled Eisenhower's meteorologists to forecast a period of favourable conditions for the launch of the D-Day invasion in June 1944.

Coast-Watching Service

With a European war on the horizon and the Irish coast undefended, the Coast-Watching Service (CWS) was officially established in April 1939 (Kennedy 2008). It was a volunteer land-based force deployed in strategically positioned LOPs located some 5–15 miles apart along the coastline (Fig. 5). The LOPs were numbered from Ballagan Head (no. 1) in County Louth around to Inishowen Head (no. 82) in County Donegal, with the final one

Box 1	LOP reports

West coast

With the Battle of the Atlantic being waged off the west coast after the fall of France in 1940, LOPs monitored increased submarine and aircraft activity off the west coast from June onward. From July 1940, the logbooks of the Donegal LOPs showed a sharp increase in convoy traffic off the north coast.

Belfast bombings

Luftwaffe raids on Belfast were heralded by increased German flights along the east coast, which were regularly recorded in LOP logbooks from the spring of 1941. The first raid on the city took place on the night of 7/8 April. Reports of aircraft along the border between Cavan and Tyrone were transmitted from the Irish observers to British air-defence services.

On the afternoon of Easter Monday (15 April), the LOP at Hook Head (Wexford) observed a German reconnaissance aircraft crossing into Irish territory. The following night (15/16 April), a second and much larger bombing raid was made on Belfast. In total, 747 people were killed and 430 seriously injured.

The logbook at Ballagan Point LOP (Louth) recorded on the night of 4/5 May 1941 a large number (some 200) of Luftwaffe aircraft flying north. On the night of 5/6 May, 150 people were killed in what turned out to be the final raid on Belfast by the Luftwaffe.

Before midnight on 30 May, LOPs along the coast reported incoming aircraft off Carnsore Point (Wexford), heading for Belfast. The raid was aborted and on the return leg Dublin was bombed.

Dublin bombing

The German aircraft, bound for Belfast (above), turned over Northern Ireland and flew south along the coast. Bombs were dropped on the North Strand, Dorset Street and what is now the residence of the President of Ireland (Áras an Uachtaráin) on the night of 30/31 May 1941. One woman subsequently died in hospital and fourteen people were seriously injured. Infrastructure in the area was damaged and two houses were demolished.

The bombing of the North Strand by the Luftwaffe provides an important example of 20 LOPs linked into Air Defence Command and engaging in collaborative monitoring. An examination of the LOP logbooks and reports from Air Defence Command indicate that Dublin was not the intended target, nor was Dublin mistaken for Belfast (Kennedy 2008).

Atlantic ferry flights

By the autumn of 1941, the majority of inland flights over the west and north of Ireland were US aircraft. They were regularly observed by LOPs in the last stages of their crossing. By 1942 overflights by aircraft of the newly formed Ferry Command became one of the main aerial activities along the Irish coast. This could be seen as the apogee of the Coast-Watching Service.

added in Foileye (no. 83) in County Kerry. The LOPs generally overlooked likely landing points on the shores. Some were constructed in the vicinity of the pre-1922 Coastguard sites, or of earlier coastal fortifications such as signal towers (Fig. 4) built during the Napoleonic Wars (*Archaeology Ireland*, Summer 2012).

The LOPs were not intended to be a deterrent to any invasion of Ireland. Rather, they were to function as observation posts. Any belligerent vessel that entered Irish coastal waters or any aircraft that flew through Irish airspace was to be tracked and recorded and the appropriate details transmitted to the headquarters of military districts, to military commandants and to the Defence Forces General Headquarters in Dublin for analysis.

When fully established, the CWS was to comprise approximately 700 men. Seven men led by an NCO manned each of the eighty-three LOPs, which were grouped into eighteen districts. Each district was overseen by a district officer, whose duty was to inspect the LOPs at frequent and irregular intervals by day and night, to ensure that the coast-watchers were on duty at all times. The volunteers recruited were generally men who knew the sea and coast in the vicinity of their LOPs, and preferably those who had some seafaring experience. They were typically young men (17–30 years old) who resided within a few miles of their LOPs.

The coast-watchers were paid at army rates: two shillings a day for a fourth-class private, two shillings and sixpence a day for a first-class private and four shillings a day for a corporal. The men also received an allowance of three shillings a day in lieu of army rations, as they lived at home. Coast-watchers worked in pairs on eight- or twelve-hour shifts. One man remained

Fig. 2—Dursey Head LOP, Cork, October 2003 (courtesy of Michael Kennedy).

in the LOP hut with responsibility for the phone while the other patrolled outside, and they alternated during the shifts.

The primary duties of the CWS were passive defence and information-gathering, keeping a constant watch along the coastline for air and naval activity and enemy forces likely to invade, as well as anyone who sought to assist invaders. Training was provided during the spring of 1940, and by the summer the type and accuracy of the information recorded by LOPs had improved. There were problems but with the belief that a German invasion was likely, if not imminent, coast-watchers felt a certain sense of duty in fulfilling their crucial role in the LOPs.

In under a year the CWS had been built up as a new wing of the Defence Forces. It became the first service to report aircraft crossing the coast and was in effect Ireland's frontline force. Clearly there were initial teething problems, particularly in regard to accommodation for the men and the lack of telephone communication, both of which required priority attention.

LOP huts

At the outset, coast-watchers had to operate in the most difficult conditions, with many LOPs offering very inadequate shelter. The army bell-tents provided initially as temporary accommodation were ill suited to the exposed locations of many LOPs. They were often blown down in winter storms, requiring the men to resort to improvised shelters, involving in one instance a disused water tank and in another an upturned boat.

Huts were built at LOP sites very quickly; as one coast-watcher put it, 'they went up like mushrooms …'. Eighty-two of the huts were constructed in the winter of 1939/40. The final one (no. 83), built at Foileye on the south side of Dingle Bay, opened in January 1942. Only in the most remote locations were pre-1922 buildings reconditioned.

The huts were built from pre-cast blocks and conformed to a standard design. Their structural features are outlined in Box 2. Owing mainly to their hasty construction, often during inclement weather, the huts were beset with continuing problems throughout their operational life. They were prone to let in wind and rain, and during stormy weather the walls and windows could leak. The small fireplace was said by coast-watchers to have been of little use for burning turf, and in many instances the chimneys smoked. The huts tended to be damp, smoky and cramped, and quite uncomfortable for the men on duty.

The basic operational equipment available in LOP huts consisted of binoculars, a telescope, charts and a logbook. The most crucial item, however, was the telephone, as further detailed by Kennedy (2008).

With the possibility of an invasion looming, telephones were installed at most LOP huts during the summer of 1940. Prior to this, coast-watchers' reports had to be conveyed by bicycle or by foot, often over 4–8 miles, to the local Post Office. In December 1939, delays of an hour or more were involved in dispatching messages to command headquarters. In some locations no telephone connection was possible until the Post Office opened.

Fig. 3—'EIRE' sign at Erris Head LOP, Mayo, April 2003 (courtesy of Michael Kennedy).

Installation of the telephones enabled the Coast-Watching Service to maintain more effective communications with command headquarters and general headquarters in Dublin, and well as with other LOPs. They also provided a morale boost to the coast-watchers themselves, particularly in the small hours of the morning. They were no longer carrying out their duties in isolated LOPs but were part of an interconnected countrywide system.

While LOPs were spartan, they constituted a vital intelligence network—very little could happen around the coast without the knowledge of the coast-watchers.

'EIRE' signs

In the 12 months up to March 1944, over 20,000 aircraft were reported near or over Ireland, and overflights rose to 16,000 in 1943/4 (Kennedy 2008). This was attended by a growing number of forced landings and crashes caused by crews losing their bearings or aircraft running low on fuel.

To assist crews operating near or over the coast of Ireland, especially the huge increase in aircraft crossing Irish territory on delivery flights from the United States (Box 2), it was decided in mid-1943 to construct markers reading 'EIRE' close to LOPs to indicate to aircrews that they were passing over Ireland—a neutral country. At the request of the United States air force, the number assigned to each LOP (Fig. 5) was added to the signs. This turned them into a simple aerial navigation aid, enabling aircrew to plot their position along the Irish coast and alter or maintain their course as appropriate.

Some of the signs initially erected were found to be too small and were replaced in 1944 by larger signs, built to a standard format of 12m by 6m and surrounded by a wide, rectangular stone border (Fig. 3). The signs were sizeable constructions, requiring, in some instances, up to 150 tons of stone, which was embedded in concrete and whitewashed to increase visibility.

Their strategic importance is underlined by the aerial inspection of the signs undertaken at the outset by General Hill, who commanded the

Fig. 4—
Knockdoon Head
LOP, Cork,
August 2006,
with Napoleonic-
period signal
tower in the
foreground
(courtesy
of Michael
Kennedy).

American air force in Northern Ireland, and the chief of staff in the south, General McKenna. This was followed by ongoing inspections for the remainder of the war. While the records of some LOPs refer to a 'fire signal', there is no evidence to indicate whether the signs were illuminated at night.

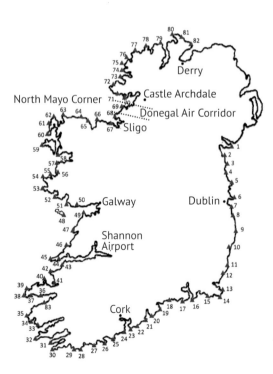

Fig. 5—
Geographical
distribution of
LOPs around the
coastline (after
Kennedy 2008).

Briefing instructions from the Office of the Commanding General of the Headquarters of the United States Strategic Air Force in Europe explained how 'A system of marking the coastline of Eire to orient pilots flying in that district as to their location had been put into effect …'. With the aid of this information and a bearing from Derrynacross Beacon, the aircrew could set their course for Nutts Corner near Belfast or another assigned landing ground.

Despite the signs, a number of United States aircraft landed or crashed on Irish territory in 1944. Nevertheless, it was noticeable that, following the erection of the signs, United States aircraft that had to land on Irish territory tended to do so at Shannon Airport, though some still crashed in poor weather conditions.

At the end of the war many of the signs were removed and the stones were often used in wall-building by farmers. Few of the 'EIRE' signs still exist or are still visible. Most of the remaining signs are on the west-Mayo coast (Fig. 3), and a few are still visible in Donegal. Some have been defaced by tourists who have used local stones to add their names to a sign of considerable historical significance.

In highlighting some of the crucial contributions to international intelligence-gathering made by the LOPs during World War II, it should be noted that there was no formal British–Irish dimension to the operations of the Coast-Watching Service. Nevertheless, close intelligence cooperation between the two countries developed progressively during the course of the war (Kennedy 2008).

Box 2	Diagnostic features

- Small, angular-shaped LOP hut, 13ft long by 9ft wide, built of pre-cast blocks and located along the coastline, usually on prominent headlands (Figs 1 and 2).
- Large bay window at the seaward side of the hut, with two central windows facing directly out ahead; on either side, two sets of windows looking out to the left and right.
- Door in right-hand wall; inside, a small fireplace in the centre of the rear wall.
- 'EIRE' sign made of stones surrounded by a wide, rectangular stone border (Fig. 3) may be found at some LOP sites, mainly on the west coast.
- Some sites have the remains of telegraph poles beside the hut, and a number of western sites have ruins of small bunkers used for storing turf.

Acknowledgements

The photographs provided by Michael Kennedy are much appreciated, as is the preparation of Fig. 5 by Bob Lawlor. Thanks are due to Ian Doyle for bringing Kennedy's book to our attention.

References

Kennedy, M. (ed.) 2008 *Guarding natural Ireland: the Coast-Watching Service and military intelligence, 1939–1945*. Dublin.

This article was originally published in the Summer 2013 issue of Archaeology Ireland.

Other coastal features

Section VII
Ritual and ceremony

The term 'ritual' encapsulates the religious and mythological beliefs of a society, and is a useful umbrella term for monuments of various well-known and lesser-known functions touching on this elusive aspect of life. The relationship between ritual practices and the monuments at which they were conducted can be quite complex, and the ritual monuments themselves can have uses that extend well beyond the standard understanding of ritual. An ancient monastery, for example, can be classified as a ritual site but it is also a place where monks lived, where students were taught, where land was farmed, where crafts were practised and where local trade was conducted. Conversely, as we know, even mundane places like traditional farmhouses and outhouses had many associated ritual practices, from the incorporation of special objects 'for luck' to the tracing of a cross on the back of a cow before milking. Nevertheless, the sites described here fall broadly within the realm of ritual.

The more ancient ritual sites range from reasonably explicable monuments like megalithic tombs and other structures featuring human burial to spectacles of an inherently mysterious nature, such as stone circles, stone rows and rock art. At the other end of the spectrum, holy wells, mass rocks and children's burial grounds are more recent and more familiar. Ogham stones help to bridge the gap: we can decipher the characters to learn the names of the individuals commemorated on the stones but we seldom know why the stones were set where we find them or precisely what function they were primarily intended to fulfil.

There are enormous gaps in the list of monument types provided here. We feature passage tombs and wedge tombs, for example, but not court tombs or portal tombs, nor indeed other types of burial structure built through the ages. More obviously, the ubiquitous 'cill', referring to an ancient ecclesiastic site and giving rise to many a modern placename—such as Kildare, Kilcoole, Kilquane and Kiltrassy—has not yet been the subject of an article in the series. This is but one of many placename components that have their roots in ancient sites arising from human activity in the distant past. Sometimes an obvious archaeological feature survives, but closer inspection may be required in order to throw further light on its age and significance. To take one example, standing stones are known from the Neolithic period, the Bronze Age, the Iron Age and historical times, but there are identifiable traits that often differentiate standing stones of one period from those of another. In these cases an informed observer can enjoy the challenge of tackling the identification puzzle.

Enigmatic **rock art**, found on natural outcrops and boulders in the landscape, provides a tantalising link with the minds and souls of prehistoric people. Cupmarks hollowed into the rock face are the most common elements, followed by cup-and-ring motifs and a lower incidence of linear/rectinlinear forms. **Passage tombs**, mostly built in the centuries before 3000 BC and spectacularly represented at Newgrange, for example, are often repositories of **megalithic art** and sometimes feature solar alignments. The greatest of the passage tombs are of gigantic proportions, but more typically the monuments are relatively moderate structures of less than 30m across. **Summit cairns**, located on mountaintops, are among the most visibly prominent prehistoric monuments. They share a number of important features with passage tombs and some are associated with passage-tomb clusters.

Earthen embanked enclosures are the most prevalent type of **henge** in Ireland. They are usually found in special prehistoric landscapes associated with a succession of ritual activity that may at some sites have extended over more than two millennia. Several different types of **burial barrows** (circular earthen mounds) were constructed in prehistoric times and they were especially current during the Bronze Age and Iron Age. Ring-barrows seem to have been the most numerous type.

Wedge tombs are key monuments for the understanding of life and death in Bronze Age Ireland. The unassuming scale of many wedge tombs masks their significance as the most prevalent class of megalithic tomb in Ireland and belies their practical, symbolic and cultural importance, especially in the transition from the Neolithic period to the Bronze Age. **Stone circles** are sacred sites used in the Bronze Age and thought to have served various purposes, including ceremonial practice, burial events and other community gatherings. Astronomical sightlines seem to have been important functions of **stone rows and stone pairs**, and have also been recorded at many stone circles and wedge tombs. **Boulder burials** were formed during the Bronze Age in the form of boulders overlying burial deposits, seemingly as memorials.

Ogham stones first appeared at the beginning of the Christian period, or just before it, and a large number appear to have served as memorials, possibly marking burials or other culturally significant locations. The language in ogham inscriptions is habitually Irish. However, many of those in Britain are termed 'bilingual' because the Irish inscriptions are accompanied by contemporary equivalents in Latin or Roman characters, while a number of the ogham inscriptions in Scotland are in Pictish or possibly Old Norse.

Medieval writings in Latin and Irish associate **holy wells** with the blossoming of early Irish Christianity, while references in ancient mythology suggest their cultural origins may be in prehistory. Mass sites, although popularly associated with the Penal Laws, appear to have emerged even earlier. They may have come into use some time after the suppression of the monasteries in the mid-1500s. Burial of children, and several other classes of people deemed ineligible for burial in consecrated ground, in *cillín* sites proliferated in the post-medieval period.

Rock art

Rock art appears to have flourished in Ireland some time between the later fourth and later third millennia BC. Carvings of simple cupmarks seem to have appeared initially at an earlier date and continued over a much longer duration.

The location of rock art was influenced by a range of landscape features, including the availability of suitable rock faces and, most strikingly, by the suitability of the soil for farming. Major concentrations of rock art occur in Donegal, Louth/Monaghan and Kerry. Panels of carving may be found in one of two configurations. Regional clusters of carved panels feature in the major rock-art concentrations, while dispersed individual panels are scattered across the overall rock-art distribution in Ireland.

Fig. 1—Petroglyphs on an earthfast rock face, Drumirril, Co. Monaghan (photo: Blaze O'Connor).

Mysterious markings

'Rock art' describes the cup-and-ring and related carvings found in the landscape on natural rock surfaces (Figs 1 and 2). Megalithic art, commonly associated with passage tombs, is generally taken to be a different tradition in the Irish context. Increasingly, however, overlapping features between the two traditions are being highlighted and, on the European scale, the distinction is considerably blurred. In Ireland and Britain both may be found on standing stones, for example, or on the stones of other megalithic monuments. The recent discovery of a spiral on a rock surface overlooked by Mount Brandon near Dingle highlights the extent to which motifs may be shared between the traditions.

The in-depth investigations undertaken by Blaze O'Connor have made important contributions to our knowledge of rock art, notably the landscape dimensions of rock-art sites and their spatial relationships to settlements and agriculture. This article is considerably informed by O'Connor's published work and her Ph.D thesis, which was prepared for publication on-line through the UCD School of Archaeology website.

Fig. 2—Rock-art panel showing nested circles with a radial line extending from a central cupmark, Loughadoon, Dingle Peninsula, Co. Kerry.

Dating

According to the present state of knowledge, the most likely period in which rock art flourished in Ireland lies some time between the later fourth and later third millennia BC. Carvings of simple cupmarks located out of context are not limited to this period, having appeared initially at an earlier date and continued over a much longer duration.

With a view to developing a fuller understanding of rock-art sites and what went on around them, a pioneering excavation in the context of rock art in Ireland was undertaken at the Drumirril complex in County Monaghan (O'Connor 2003). A number of archaeological features were revealed, including an oval enclosure and a terrace-like structure with four rock panels at its centre. Among the artefacts recovered were pottery sherds, a quartz hammer-stone, a small flint scraper, blue glass bead fragments and burnt bone with some fragments of farm animal bone.

The finds of early and middle Neolithic pottery and the round scraper are, as noted by O'Connor (2006), consistent with the emergent theory that rock art may have been practised at various times from the Neolithic onwards. Further support is offered by recent pre-development excavations in County Monaghan. A settlement considered to be earlier Neolithic (*c.* 4000–3000 BC) has been uncovered at Monanny, Carrickmacross, which is located 6km east of the Drumirril rock-art cluster, while evidence for a Neolithic settlement has been revealed at Tankardsrock, some 700m from the Drumirril site.

Based on these excavations, combined with the extensive investigation of rock-art panels outlined below, O'Connor (2006) concluded that 'the carving of quintessential rock-art motifs onto living rock surfaces … began as early as the Middle Neolithic (possibly even earlier) and continued at least into the later Neolithic and possibly into the early Bronze Age'.

Regional distribution

Rock art occurs mainly in the peninsulas and coastal areas of Ireland (Fig. 3). The major concentrations are located in Donegal, Louth/Monaghan and Kerry. Rock art has also been recorded in the west of Ireland in Mayo and Sligo, and along the eastern seaboard in Waterford, Kilkenny, Wicklow and Meath. Further inland, it has been found in Carlow, Kildare, Westmeath, Cavan and Fermanagh. Sites are also known in the northern counties of Derry, Tyrone and Down.

Regional clusters

The major rock-art concentrations feature locations with significant clusters of carved panels, three of which were investigated by O'Connor (2006), namely the Isle of Doagh on the Inishowen Peninsula in Donegal, the townland of Drumirril on the Monaghan border, and Loch an Dúin on the Dingle Peninsula in Kerry. The clusters generally occur within distinctive topographical locations. Within the regional clusters, O'Connor identified focal points in terms of panel numbers or a central nexus of panels. At the Drumirril cluster, for instance, 11 panels are located within a few metres of one another at the centre of the distribution and on the most visually distinctive natural outcrop in the area.

Regional clusters may have been places to which generations of people returned, with the rock carvings accumulating over time. They could have become regional focal points at which people gathered at particular times of the year or for important events, analogous to the role envisaged for major complexes of Neolithic tombs.

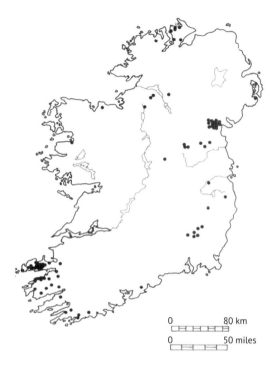

Fig. 3— Distribution of rock-art sites in Ireland (after Johnston 1991).

0   80 km

0   50 miles

Dispersed panels

Dispersed panels are scattered individually or in small groupings across the rock-art distributions and seem to have played a somewhat different role in relation to local settlements, in terms of both proximity and access. A degree of restricted access may have been a characteristic of regional rock-art clusters. Landscape features may have separated them from the surrounding dispersed panels. The distribution of dispersed panels seems to reflect more closely the perception of rock art as located along well-travelled routeways through the landscape. Reaching regional clusters from surrounding areas would have involved a journey through the landscape. The Louth/ Monaghan rock-art concentration, with its linear distribution, may have been associated with a ritual routeway, leading, perhaps, to the megalithic tombs in the mountains of the Cooley Peninsula. There is also merit in the suggestion that the decorated outcrops at Drumirril were effectively natural monuments that may not have been differentiated in the prehistoric mind from built megalithic cairns (O'Connor 2007).

Dispersed rock-art panels appear to be located variably throughout the Irish countryside, with regional concentrations. In summary, the spatial distribution articulated by O'Connor may be envisaged as comprising three concentric configurations of carved panels, namely (i) the major rock-art concentrations themselves, such as the Louth/Monaghan group, (ii) an inner cluster, such as Drumirril, and (iii) a central focal point or nexus of panels at the core of the inner cluster.

Regional motifs

Rock art typically comprises three basic motifs. Simple cupmarks are the predominant form, followed by cup-and-rings and a lower incidence of linear/rectilinear motifs. The full range of motifs is much more diverse and complex, however. O'Connor (2006) isolated 100 different design elements of rock-art motifs, of which a selection are illustrated in Fig. 4. A pen-picture of the predominant motifs in the major rock-art concentrations is presented in Box 1.

Certain motifs seem to be preferentially sited in particular locations (O'Connor 2006). For instance, parallel-groove motifs (Fig. 4) are considered to be a distinctive feature of the Isle of Doagh (Inishowen Peninsula). Rare examples are also known from Argyll in Scotland. The Louth/Monaghan region features a prevalence of motif truncation, in addition to the extensive use of natural cups, cups positioned in ring gaps and enclosed dimples (Fig. 4). A distinctive feature of rock art in the Dingle Peninsula is the prevalence of multi-ring motifs and the adoption of pecking within the inner ring of cups.

The significance of these regional distinctions in motif types in other parts of Ireland needs to be investigated. In this regard, rock markings recently noted in the Beara Peninsula (Cork) on one of the stone pairs at Finaha, a short distance north-west of Castletownbere (see *Archaeology Ireland,* Summer 2011), are reminiscent of the parallel-groove motifs, which, as indicated above, are with few exceptions considered to be distinctive to the rock art in the Isle of Doagh.

Landscape dimensions

Bedrock geology and the availability of suitable outcrop surfaces were important determinants of the general location of rock art across Ireland. The rock had to be right in terms of having durable surfaces amenable to carving as well as the appropriate texture, colour and form.

Agriculture

A range of landscape features influenced the siting of rock art, including proximity to rivers, streams and lakes. Among the most striking, however, is the correlation between soil type and rock-art location. Over half of rock-art sites are located on soils suitable for arable farming or pasture (Johnston 1991; O'Connor 2006). Many of the soils now considered as marginal for agricultural purposes may in earlier times have been more productive. If this were taken into account, the correlation between soil quality and rock-art sites would be even more definitive. The strong affinity between rock-art sites and soils suitable for agriculture is also significant from the perspective of settlement locations (Johnston 1991).

Settlements

Rock-art sites tend to be perceived as isolated locations on the margins of the settled landscape, and with little or no evidence of human activity. The association of rock-art sites with productive farming land, however, allied to their proximity to water resources, is indicative of a functional relationship with settlements. Indeed, the coincident distribution of rock art with soils suitable for agriculture suggests that proximity to settlements and accessibility were typical features of many rock-art sites. Further to

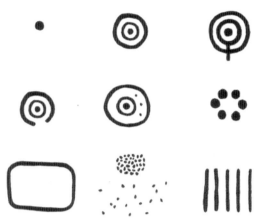

Fig. 4—Selection of the 100 basic design elements identified in Irish rock art by O'Connor (2006).

this, the Drumirril excavation undertaken by O'Connor (outlined above) suggests that a range of settlement-related activities appear to have been undertaken in the vicinity of rock-art sites over substantial periods from the Neolithic onwards. As already indicated, this is further evidenced by the pre-development excavations undertaken in County Monaghan not too far distant from the rock-art cluster.

The spatial relationship between rock-art locations and agricultural land parallels that of megalithic tombs (*Archaeology Ireland*, Winter 2010) and indicates that detailed investigations of rock-art sites could further our understanding of prehistoric settlement and society.

Conclusions

Further excavations, combined with more definitive dating, are essential for advancing our understanding of what went on at rock-art sites, and, in particular, what were the motivations underlying the widespread practice of rock-carving in prehistory.

Ancient graffiti found in a wide range of regions across the ancient world, and featured notably at Pompeii, shares a number of parallels with contemporary graffiti, such as visibility and clustering built up over time (Baird and Taylor 2011). Rock art and the form of graffiti inspired by the 'street artist' Banksy have been understood by some as representing aspects of the same phenomenon, and, indeed, modern graffiti has been linked to prehistoric antecedents.

Graffiti is commonly viewed as an illicit, largely urban occurrence, which defaces property and is in some circumstances considered to be inherently subversive. A better-informed understanding is, however, required of the motivations that lie behind what may be described as 'graffiti art', with its characteristically complex designs and skilful compositions. In addition to display, its practitioners may be involved with what could be seen as the personalisation of the urban landscape, developed equivalents of carving names on trees in the countryside. Motivations distinctive in character but perhaps not entirely unrelated could possibly underlie the creation of rock-art sites in the rural landscape. Whether this can be reconciled with the interpretation of rock-art sites as ritual locales is another matter.

Box 1	Diagnostic features (see motifs, Fig. 3)

Inishowen Peninsula—mainly on rock outcrops
Wide range of motifs, including high frequency of cupmarks and complex motifs and compositions, panels with irregular arrangements of dispersed motifs, and those with a prominent single central motif. Distinctive parallel-groove motifs are associated with the Isle of Doagh cluster.

Louth/Monaghan—mainly on rock outcrops
Fairly homogeneous corpus, including panels with dense, closely set and/or interconnecting motifs, those with a prominent central motif and surfaces with a simple arrangement of typically one or two motifs.

Dingle Peninsula—mainly on erratic boulders
High proportion of panels with dense, closely set and/or interconnecting motifs, and rocks with a simple arrangement of typically one or two motifs.

Iveragh Peninsula
Features some of the most complex compositions, including the frequent occurrence of paired multi-ringed motifs. Some designs occur on a mutually exclusive basis (e.g. cup-and-ring versus cup-and-ring with radial). Individual groupings of panels within the valleys exhibit distinctive motifs, such as the rosette and keyhole.

Sources: O'Connor 2006; Purcell 2001

Acknowledgements

Many individuals have contributed to our understanding of Irish rock art, notably Eoin MacWhite in the 1940s, but we hope we will be forgiven for underlining Dr Blaze O'Connor's impressive scholarship in particular. Her untimely death in 2009 was an immense loss to research in rock art and to archaeology more generally.

References

Baird, J.A. and Taylor, C. (eds) 2011 *Ancient graffiti in context*. New York and London.

Johnston, S. 1991 Distributional aspects of prehistoric Irish petroglyphs. In P. Bahn and A. Rosenfeld (eds), *Rock art and prehistory*. Oxford.

O'Connor, B. 2003 Recent excavations in a rock art landscape. *Archaeology Ireland* **17** (4), 14–16.

O'Connor, B. 2006 Inscribed landscapes: contextualising prehistoric rock art in Ireland. Unpublished Ph.D thesis, University College Dublin.

O'Connor, B. 2007 Carving identity: the social context of Neolithic rock art and megalithic art. In D.A. Barrowclough and C. Malone (eds), *Cult in context: reconsidering ritual in archaeology*. London.

Purcell, A. 2001 The rock-art landscape of the Iveragh Peninsula, County Kerry, south-west Ireland. In G. Nash and C. Chippendale (eds), *European landscapes of rock art*. London.

This article was originally published in the Winter 2011 issue of Archaeology Ireland.

Passage tombs and megalithic art

Passage tombs tend to be aligned according to solar events along the horizon and often to distant cairns or other passage tombs but, in many respects, the most intriguing and challenging feature of the structures is the fact that they are important repositories of megalithic art.

The largest assemblage of megalithic art in Europe is concentrated in the Boyne Valley. Remarkably, however, the Boyne Valley corpus is atypical of Irish megalithic art as a whole. Its most distinctive feature is what is termed 'plastic' art.

Radiocarbon dating indicates that the construction and primary use of passage tombs in Ireland fall into the middle Neolithic period (3400–3000 BC). Carvings of rock art also appear to have begun around that time or possibly even earlier. The relationship between megalithic art (in the tombs) and rock art (in the landscape) is uncertain, but some degree of commonality appears to be indicated.

Fig. 1—Carnbane West at Loughcrew, with standard-sized cairns surrounding the larger Cairn L.

Stone Age ambition

Passage tombs are the most common European megalithic monuments. They consist basically of a passage leading to an internal burial chamber, and are generally covered by a cairn with, in Ireland, a kerb of boulders normally occurring around the edge.

The greatest passage tombs are of gigantic proportions, such as the renowned Newgrange monument. Typically, however, they are moderate structures (Fig. 1), usually less than 30m in diameter, and the overall length of some chambers and passages can be little more than 4–5m.

Passage tombs occur at altitudes ranging from sea level to more than 800m, and a significant number are positioned on the summits of ridges or mountains. Many are aligned on solar events, and often on distant cairns or other passage tombs. The best-known solar alignment is at Newgrange, with its remarkable roof-box through which the beam of the rising sun at midwinter projects along the passage into the back of the chamber.

Summit cairns have certain affinities with passage tombs, some obviously containing such monuments and others inviting reclassification (*Archaeology Ireland*, Autumn 2011). At this juncture, the total number of passage tombs in Ireland is uncertain but seems to be in the region of 200 sites.

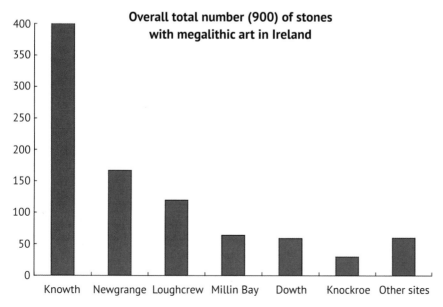

Fig. 2— Histogram showing the predominant locations of the total numbers of stones with megalithic art, based on a definition that goes beyond the traditional norm.

The typical architectural features of passage tombs are synopsised in Box 1. Passage tombs are the repositories of megalithic art. This is, in many respects, the most intriguing and challenging feature of these monuments and is the primary focus of the article. They also contain the bones of Neolithic people, resting communally in association with diagnostic artefacts.

Box 1	Typical diagnostic features

- Passageway connecting the entrance of the tomb to an internal burial chamber.
- Generally covered by a circular cairn of earth and stones, often denuded or unfinished, and usually surrounded by a kerb of large stones.
- Burial chambers may be polygonal, rectangular or oval in shape, varying in diameter from 1–2m to up to 6–7m, and roofed with horizontal overlapping stones forming a corbelled vault; many have a pair of side chambers and an end chamber, resulting in a cruciform plan.
- Passages, built with orthostats, run from 1–2m to over 30m in length and are roofed with lintels.
- The entrance area may be decorated with quartz and perhaps water-rolled nodules of granite.
- Repositories of megalithic art, typically comprising geometric motifs arranged in distinctive styles.

Location

The overwhelming majority of megalithic art in these islands is located in Ireland, with important pockets across the Irish Sea in Anglesey, Wales and Merseyside, as well as Orkney.

Overall, a total of some 900 decorated stones have been recorded in Ireland (O'Sullivan 2002), occurring predominantly in six concentrations, with the remainder spread across various other sites from north Antrim to west Cork (Fig. 2). This total is based on a broader definition of megalithic art than previously employed. The definition includes aspects of picking and linear ornament that transcend the traditional geometric motifs. Of the total number of decorated stones from various contexts in the Boyne Valley and Loughcrew, some 30% have no recognisable geometric motifs that can be discerned.

County Meath is the major focus of megalithic art. The Boyne Valley contains the largest collection of such artwork in Europe, with several hundred decorated stones at the Newgrange, Knowth and Dowth complexes. The next-largest assemblage in Ireland is located at Loughcrew, relatively close to the Blackwater, a major tributary of the Boyne. Within the past 25 years a new corpus of megalithic art has been recorded at Knockroe in County Kilkenny (below).

While the vast majority of the megalithic tombs in Ireland are located in the eastern half of the country, sites are also known in the west of Ireland, with some new recordings in Sligo (below). A sizeable number of decorated stones occur in the north, in particular in the Millin Bay complex at the tip of the Ards Peninsula, Co. Down.

Passage-tomb art

Megalithic art is commonly associated with larger and more complex passage tombs or nearby smaller structures. The motifs, produced by picking and incision, occur on the structural stones of the tombs. In Ireland they are usually found on the orthostats, corbels, roof stones and enclosing kerbstones. The kerb is a uniquely Irish feature of passage tombs and it is significant that some of the more innovative examples of megalithic art in Europe occur on the kerbstones in the Boyne Valley.

Fig. 3— Depictive art on orthostat in a cairn at Loughcrew, Co. Meath.

Irish passage-tomb art is composed of geometric motifs, including cupmarks, circles, spirals, arcs, chevrons, lozenges/triangles, squares, radial motifs, scalariform (ladder-like) motifs and meandering. As further detailed below, standard megalithic art in Ireland is based on the depiction of a small range of basic elements that are varied and combined with considerable imagination. Two generic styles are known, described as depictive art and plastic expressions of megalithic art (O'Sullivan 2002).

Depictive art comprises seemingly two-dimensional arrangements of standard geometric motifs on the surface of a stone (Fig. 3). A standard style occurs throughout the distribution of megalithic art, not just in Ireland but also in Britain. **Plastic art** is characterised by the remarkable sympathy shown to the configuration of the surface on which it occurs (Fig. 4). Other distinctive features of plastic art include its tendency to be superimposed on standard depictive art and its restriction to surfaces that were accessible after the tombs were built.

A schematic representation of the design structure of Irish megalithic art is illustrated in Fig. 5. This comprises three progressive dimensions, starting with six basic geometric elements. In the middle part of the diagram, a number of known variations of each identified element are shown. In the lower part, designs incorporating combinations of these essential elements are depicted. Even at this seemingly basic level, there appears to have been considerable significance in the choice and mixing of geometric elements. The association of cupmarks with circles, which is also common in rock art (*Archaeology Ireland*, Winter 2011), seems to have been a frequent practice.

Boyne Valley

The largest assemblage of megalithic art in Europe is concentrated in the Boyne Valley, although the corpus is atypical of Irish megalithic art as a whole (O'Sullivan 2002). Plastic art is confined almost exclusively to the three major tumuli in the Boyne Valley. Depictive art, found throughout the megalithic art distribution, also occurs in the valley. The plastic art is superimposed on top of the other artwork. It overlies the standard art on certain surfaces and usually displays a remarkable disregard for the presence of the previously existing motifs. It simply cuts through them, without taking the trouble either to avoid them or to remove them completely. What sets the Boyne Valley artwork apart is the fact that the megalithic art continued to be applied after the initial wave of standard artwork.

As previously indicated, the pattern of plastic art conforms to the surface on which it is formed. Indeed, the style would make little sense if separated from the shape of the particular stone on which it occurs.

The Boyne Valley plastic art occurs in a number of manifestations (O'Sullivan 2002).

- Linear artwork based on standard geometric motifs, but applied on a larger scale, more boldly defined and showing an obvious empathy with the form and surface of the stone (e.g. the Newgrange entrance stone).

Fig. 4—Plastic art on kerbstone directly across from the entrance of Newgrange, Co. Meath.

- Linear artwork in which the standard geometric elements are absent or seemingly incidental (e.g. the east and west entrance stones at Knowth). Some of the designs are tightly organised, while others are fluid, almost cursory, in appearance.
- Concentrated blanket picking, in which large areas are picked away, and again there is an obvious awareness of the modulations of the stone itself (e.g. orthostats along the passages at Newgrange).
- Diffuse or scattered picking, in which no discernible design can be recognised but surfaces appear to have been modified or marked in an orchestrated way (e.g. the chamber of the west tomb at Knowth).

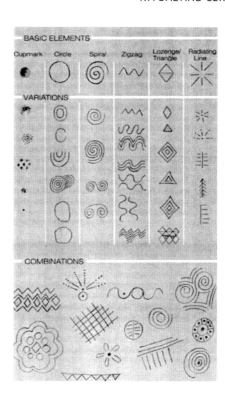

Fig. 5— Geometric elements in Irish megalithic art, showing the motifs arranged in three orders: (i) basic geometric elements; (ii) variations of these basic elements; and (iii) various combinations of the elements.

While plastic megalithic art is distinctive to the Boyne Valley, parallels can be drawn elsewhere. Linear designs similar to those outlined above are found (Fig. 6) on two orthostats in the western passage tombs at Knockroe (below), although there is no evidence of superimposition in the artwork, and at a number of sites in Brittany, France.

Some recent discoveries

Kilkenny

The passage tomb excavated at Knockroe is the most ornate Irish passage tomb outside County Meath. It is located relatively low on the side of a south-facing valley. On a level platform two tombs were constructed, one opening towards the south-east and the other to the south-west. For convenience, they are termed the **east tomb** and **west tomb** respectively. The tombs are set within a broadly circular cairn, measuring approximately 20m across and featuring a megalithic kerb.

The west tomb is built from larger stones and is much higher in profile than the east tomb. Two of its orthostats, as well as two kerbstones in the façade, are pillar stones. The tomb is aligned on the setting sun at the winter solstice. The east tomb has a lower profile, with smaller structured stones, and may perhaps also be aligned on the rising sun on midwinter day.

Fig. 6—Chamber of the west tomb at Knockroe, showing plastic art (left) and standard depictive art (right) respectively on two adjoining orthostats.

A notable feature of the Knockroe passage tomb is the occurrence of approximately 30 decorated stones, divided evenly between the east tomb, the west tomb and the kerbs. The artwork in the west tomb is generally more obvious, compositionally more varied and aesthetically more sophisticated than that in the east tomb. The decorated stones in the east tomb have just a single recognisable element, namely circles. These are sometimes ovoid in outline, occur individually or in small clusters, and are so lightly carved that they are almost invisible.

The artwork on the kerbstones is confined almost exclusively to the southern side of the cairn. It has an extensive array of curvilinear designs, one stone bearing a distinctive arrangement of snake-like lines. As already mentioned, the kerb is a unique feature of Irish passage tombs. In this regard, it may be noted that Knockroe contains the most extensively decorated kerb in Ireland, apart from the three great tumuli of the Boyne Valley. Both depictive and plastic art occur side by side at Knockroe (Fig. 6) but on separate stones, and there is no evidence that either was later than the other.

Although much smaller in scale, the cairn at Knockroe has many elements in common with the large tumulus at Knowth. Accordingly, it is not surprising that some of the best comparisons for the Knockroe art can be found at Knowth. The artwork at Knockroe may perhaps be regarded as a remarkable outlier of the megalithic art concentration in the Boyne Valley.

Sligo

Using innovative survey techniques, new recordings of megalithic passage-tomb art, some previously known, have recently been reported in the north-west of Ireland (Hensey and Robin 2011). The motifs have been recorded in County Sligo in cairns at Listoghil, Heapstown and Carrowhill. They include nested arcs, chevrons, circles, vertical lines and anticlockwise spirals. One of the carvings at Listoghil, originally described as a 'three-armed figure', was re-examined and is now considered to be of late prehistoric origin rather than Neolithic.

The motifs recorded and their positioning in the monuments are typical of passage-tomb art. Accordingly, the investigators note that passage-tomb art is clearly not exclusively an Irish Sea phenomenon.

Origins

As further detailed by Shee Twohig (1981), Iberia, Brittany and the Atlantic archipelago of Ireland, Britain and Orkney each appear to have a core selection of motifs distinctive to each individual region. This indicates that megalithic art was not developed in one of the regions and then spread to the others.

Calibrated radiocarbon determinations for the construction and primary use phase of excavated passage tombs in Ireland appear to fall into the middle Neolithic period (c. 3400–3000 cal. BC). Based on an extensive investigation of rock art in Ireland, Blaze O'Connor concluded that the carving of rock art began as early as the middle Neolithic (and possibly even earlier) and continued at least into the later Neolithic and possibly into the early Bronze Age (*Archaeology Ireland*, Winter 2011). The relationship between megalithic art and rock art is uncertain but some degree of commonality seems to be indicated.

The geometric motifs of megalithic art are different from the typical rock-art motifs, but some variations of cupmarks and circles, as well as picking, occur in both traditions. Moreover, motifs normally associated with passage-tomb art are known on rock panels and on the structural stones of burial cists.

In Iberia and elsewhere, the best analogies for Irish megalithic art are sometimes to be found in rock art. The occurrence of megalithic art in rock-art domains indicates a degree of overlap between the two traditions. Indeed, in Iberia, for example, there is a case for the notion that megalithic art is a specialised rock-art tradition.

The meaning of megalithic art has so far defied single-code interpretation. There is no equivalent to the Rosetta Stone that could provide a basis for elucidating the 'meaning' of megalithic art. On the other hand, patterns of location in the tomb structure from one site to another indicate that the artwork was originally invested with complex meanings. This is underlined by the many other meaningful references in passage tombs, from solar alignments to left/right discrimination and subtle patterns of stone choice.

References

Hensey, H. and Robin, G. 2011 More than meets the eye: new recordings of megalithic art in north-west Ireland. *Oxford Journal of Archaeology* **30**, 109–30.

O'Sullivan, M. 2002 The Boyne and beyond: a review of megalithic art in Ireland. In R. Joussaume, L. Laporte and C. Scarre, *Origins and development of megalithic monuments in western Europe*. Bourgon.

O'Sullivan, M. 2012 South Kilkenny—a mythically enriched Neolithic landscape. In D. Ledwidge, J. Eogan and P. Friel (eds), *Monuments, maps and memories: discovering Kilkenny's landscape heritage*. Kilkenny.

Shee Twohig, E. (ed.) 1981 *Megalithic art in western Europe*. Oxford.

This article was originally published in the Spring 2012 issue of Archaeology Ireland.

Summit cairns

The origin of summit cairns can be traced to the Neolithic period. They are associated with burial practices from that period and they continued into the Bronze Age.

Summit cairns vary widely in scale and design. They share certain features with passage tombs, including proximity in some cases and often intervisibility. In addition, some cairns exhibit architectural features that are familiar in the passage-tomb tradition and, in addition to known passage-tomb cairns on the summits of many hills and mountains, a number of apparently blank summit cairns may also contain passage tombs.

Fig. 1 — Maeve's Cairn (Miosgán Meadhbha) on the summit of Knocknarea Mountain, Co. Sligo (Stefan Bergh, National University of Ireland, Galway).

Marking special places

Summit cairns are among the most visibly prominent prehistoric monuments in Ireland. They occur mainly in upland locations, usually sited on the summits of mountains and hills (Figs 1–3), and are generally found as loose mounds of stones or slabs of varying sizes. Summit cairns are not, however, haphazard collections of stones. As further detailed below, they are erected monuments, deliberately sited for maximum visibility and often aligned on other monuments (Bergh 2002; Coyne 2006; Prendergast 2010). Some have been shown to have archaeological features associated with the passage-tomb tradition.

Typology

Over 2,000 cairns have been recorded in Ireland. The Archaeological Survey of Ireland Database compiled by the Department of Arts, Heritage and the Gaeltacht (National Monuments Service) details some 1,600. Close to 300 of these are classified into 8 defined types (see Box 1) but these are unlikely to capture the entire range. The majority are recorded in the database as **unclassified cairns**. In addition to these there are indications, for example, that the nineteenth-century Ordnance Survey engineers sometimes altered or constructed cairns for survey purposes.

Fig. 2—Cairn on top of Mullyash Mountain, Co. Monaghan (Sylvia Desmond).

Fig. 3— The Paps of Anu, located between Killarney and Macroom, are neighbouring summits marked with cairns (Frank Coyne, Aegis Archaeology Ltd).

Four of the defined cairn types appear to be prehistoric in origin. These are classified as **burial cairns** and **ring-cairns**, which are found countrywide, and as **radial cairns** and **cairn circles**, which have more limited distributions. The radial cairns are largely confined to Cork and Kerry, with single examples recorded in Waterford, Tipperary and Galway. Those defined as cairn circles are confined to Waterford. Some of these types of cairn may also be included among the unclassified cairns.

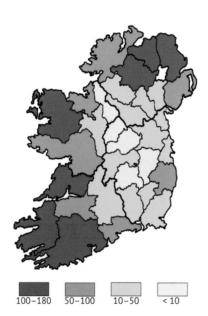

Fig. 4— Geographical distribution of cairns, showing density by county.

100–180	50–100	10–50	< 10

The other four defined cairns include types from relatively recent centuries as well as those that may date from the prehistoric era onwards. **Clearance cairns** have a widespread distribution. While **cairnfields** were recorded only in the south-east, they are known in the south-west and presumably also in other locations. Both types could date from any period from the prehistoric onwards, especially peat-covered examples. **Boundary cairns** are relatively modern constructions, dating from the nineteenth century onwards. They are associated with the Griffith Boundary Commission. The number of boundary cairns recorded may not be representative of their wider prevalence. **Wayside cairns** are also relatively modern, probably dating from the seventeenth–twentieth centuries. They may have resulted from the funeral tradition of placing a stone on a cairn in memory of the deceased.

Distribution

The geographical distribution of cairns presented in Fig. 4 combines the 1,311 unclassified cairns recorded in the database described above and the 559 records relating to cairns compiled by the Northern Ireland Environment Agency.

The cairns are predominantly concentrated in the seaboard counties, stretching in a crescent from north-east Ulster across to Donegal, down the coast of Connacht and extending into south-west Munster. Cairns also occur in counties in the south and east of the country, notably Waterford and Wicklow.

Visibility

Visibility is a distinguishing design feature of prehistoric summit cairns. The positioning of cairns on well-selected summit sites can be a more crucial determinant of their visual impact than actual size. Some cairns seem to have been sited so as to be more prominently visible in the landscape from one side of a mountain.

An innovative investigation recently undertaken by Prendergast (2010) shows that a significant number of triangulation stations, erected on mountain summits by the Ordnance Survey of Ireland in the first half of the nineteenth century, occur at sites with recorded cairns or passage tombs. The degree of overlap between the positioning of prehistoric cairns/passage tombs and the sites identified by engineers as optimal for the erection of triangulation

Fig. 5—Slieve Donard, Co. Down, showing paired cairns (Crown copyright, Northern Ireland Environment Agency).

stations testifies to the spatial and technical understanding applied by the societies that erected these monuments so as to ensure their distant visibility, and indeed intervisibility.

Pairing of summit cairns seems to have been common in prehistory, as shown for instance by the relative proximity of the two extant cairns (Fig. 5) on Slieve Donard, Co. Down (Prendergast 2010). The larger of the pair may have been a passage tomb destroyed in 1828 to make way for an Ordnance Survey station (Fig. 6). At the other end of the island, the two cairns crowning the summit of the Paps of Anu (Fig. 3) are another example of cairn pairing.

The quantitative and geographical occurrence of passage tombs with entrances aligned on higher and distant mounds/cairns, documented by Prendergast (2010), is much more prevalent than previously recorded. The passage tomb at Rush, Co. Dublin (now destroyed), and the cliff-top tombs on the north-Antrim coast are respectively aligned on Lambay and Rathlin Islands. In this regard, Prendergast makes the interesting observation that both islands were important production sources of polished stone axeheads in the Neolithic. Lambay, it should be noted, is crowned by the Knockbane prehistoric cairn.

Construction

Summit cairns exhibit a wide variety in scale and design, ranging from the massive Maeve's Cairn (Fig. 1) to the somewhat more modest form shown in Fig. 2. Some have stone kerbings and revetments to retain the stones and prevent collapse and slippage of the cairn. Cairns may be ranked in terms of importance according to the ground covered by the monument (Bergh 2002).

Fig. 6—Great cairn on the summit of Slieve Donard, Co. Down (Crown copyright, Northern Ireland Environment Agency).

Maeve's Cairn on the flat summit of Knocknarea Mountain, Co. Sligo (Fig. 1), is probably the most spectacularly positioned prehistoric monument in Ireland. The conspicuous landmark has a basal diameter of 60m and a height of 10m and can be seen with the naked eye in favourable viewing conditions at a distance of 47km (Prendergast 2010). As indicated by Bergh, the monument is a passage-tomb cairn. It shares the summit of the mountain with seven other passage tombs. Two hut sites on the north-east side of the mountain were dated to *c.* 3000 BC.

Upwards of 23 circular hut sites were discovered by Bergh on the southern part of the mountain, as well as an interesting system of banks on the eastern side, with evidence of intensive activity during the Neolithic period. Knocknarea and the Cúil Irra Peninsula were among the major cultural and ritual areas in Neolithic Ireland.

Mullyash hilltop cairn (Fig. 2) has an overall diameter of approximately 17m and a height of 2.5m. The monument is a two-tiered kerbed cairn, with the large bulk of stones contained within two levels of drystone masonry. Depressions on the top of the cairn suggest a possible chamber (or chambers), and the collapse in the western portion may indicate the presence of a passage tomb. The possible existence of such structural features, allied to the prominent visibility of the mountain from monuments in the wider landscape, may invite reclassification of the cairn as a passage tomb. Mullyash Mountain is a Lughnasa site (see below), which continued to be visited by many people into the mid-1900s.

The Paps (Fig. 3), with their two summit cairns and unmistakable profile, are distinctive features of the Kerry landscape south-east of Killarney (Coyne 2006). The cairn on the eastern Pap is the more impressive of the two monuments. A modern structure has been erected on its top but otherwise the monument survives in relatively good condition. Some internal collapse on its western side may, according to Coyne, suggest that the interior of the cairn could be hollow along that side, possibly marking a passage or internal chamber.

The cairn on the western Pap is the smaller of the two. As it survives today, it measures 14m north–south by 14m east–west, with a maximum height of 2m. The cairn is damaged, especially on its south-eastern side, where a shelter has been cut into the monument. A rescue excavation undertaken by Coyne showed that the original cairn was circular, with a diameter of 10m, which is half that on the eastern Pap. A likely entrance was located on the northern side of the monument and is now well hidden under cairn slippage.

The construction technique used in building the pair of cairns is similar. They have architectural elements known in passage-tomb construction, but may also have elements from the Bronze Age (Coyne 2006). They may contain burial monuments of the Neolithic period and possibly passage tombs. The cairns were the focus of ritual activity in prehistory. They continue to be visited today, especially on the feast of Bealtaine.

Origins and symbolism

Summit cairns are among the most common monuments found throughout Ireland whose origins may be traced to the Neolithic period (Coyne 2006). They are associated with burial practices from the Neolithic and continued into the Bronze Age. Cairns have been found covering megalithic tombs, as well as cists, pits and urn burials. They contain Bronze Age features, with some having architectural components associated with the passage-tomb tradition. Although speculative, the proportion of summit cairns erected in the Neolithic may be greater than generally envisaged. Like Maeve's Cairn, discussed above, the cairn on the summit of Slievenamon, Co. Tipperary, and the one designated Site D at Loughcrew, Co. Meath, are identified as Neolithic only by their association with known passage-tomb clusters, while it was archaeological excavation that showed the cairn on Baltinglass Hill, Co. Wicklow, to be a passage-tomb structure.

Mountaintops and hills held special significance for prehistoric societies in Ireland. The regard for sacred places may have been a feature of Irish life from the Mesolithic onwards (Cooney 2000). Their persistent influence is still echoed today in the celebration of pre-Christian festivals such as Lughnasa. The extent of the overlap between Festival of Lughnasa assembly sites and hilltop passage tombs and cairns documented by Prendergast (2010) affirms the enduring symbolic fascination with summit sites.

Box 1	Diagnostic features

Burial cairns: mounds of stones with definite evidence of burial.

Ring-cairns: low, wide ring or bank of stones (inner and outer faces may be kerbed) surrounding an open, roughly circular area, usually about 13m in diameter but ranging from 3m to 28m.

Radial stone cairns: mounds of stones delimited by a series of spaced stones, set with their long axes aligned towards the centre of the cairn.

Cairn circles: low circular mounds of stones with a circle of non-contiguous upright stones at its edge or emerging some distance from it.

Boundary cairns: mounds of stones located at boundaries.

Clearance cairns: mounds of stones resulting from field clearance for agricultural purposes.

Cairnfields: three or more clusters of clearance cairns.

Wayside cairns: mounds of stones erected by the side of a road or thoroughfare.

Unclassified cairns: mounds of stones not defined as any specific cairn type.

Source: Department of Arts, Heritage and the Gaeltacht (National Monuments Service)

Conclusions

Summit cairns have certain affinities with passage tombs, including possible proximity, intervisibility and alignment. Allied to these spatial associations, some cairns contain architectural features resembling the passage-tomb tradition. Clearly, more extensive investigations are required to reveal the full architectural and other distinctive characteristics of summit cairns. A significant number may be shown to contain passage tombs and merit reclassification.

Even if only a relatively small proportion (say 10% or less) of the sizeable number of summit cairns were reclassified as passage tombs, important questions would arise concerning the spread of early settlement and agriculture in Ireland. Such issues would pertain in particular to the south-west, where there is a relatively high incidence of summit cairns (Murphy 2009), a small number of known passage tombs and few earlier Neolithic monuments.

Acknowledgements

We are particularly grateful to Frank Prendergast for making available extracts from his recently completed Ph.D thesis. The details on cairn recordings in Ireland provided by Paul Walsh and Rhonda Robinson were important contributions to the article. The publication on Mount Brandon and the Paps by Kerry County Council drawn to our attention by Ian Doyle was most informative. The photographs received from Frank Coyne and Gail Pollock are much appreciated.

References

Bergh, S. 2002 Knocknarea: the ultimate monument; megaliths and monuments in Neolithic Cúil Irra, north-west Ireland. In C. Searra (ed.), *Monuments and landscape in Atlantic Europe: perception and society during the Neolithic and early Bronze Age*. London and New York.

Cooney, G. (ed.) 2000 *Landscapes of Neolithic Ireland*. London and New York.

Coyne, F. (ed.) 2006 *Islands in the clouds: an upland archaeological study on Mount Brandon and the Paps, County Kerry*. Kerry.

Murphy, C. 2009 The prehistoric archaeology of Beara. In W. Walsh (ed.), *Local worlds: early settlement landscapes and upland farming in south-west Ireland*. Cork.

Prendergast, F. 2010 Linked landscapes: spatial, archaeoastronomical and social network analysis of the Irish passage-tomb tradition. Unpublished Ph.D thesis, University College Dublin.

This article was originally published in the Autumn 2011 issue of Archaeology Ireland.

Henges

Henges are typically relatively large enclosures more than 100m in diameter; some are particularly massive constructions ranging up to 160m or more. Henge-like enclosures are often found near traditional *oenach* sites. Almost half of all known henges in Ireland are concentrated in County Meath, particularly the Boyne Valley.

Henges have been associated with ritual activity over a period extending from the middle or late Neolithic through the Bronze Age and sometimes even into the Iron Age. Indeed, their role as focal points within a local landscape seems to have lasted up until the early medieval period and beyond.

Fig. 1—Stackallan henge, Co. Meath (Leo Swan).

Enclosures from the third millennium BC

A number of different forms of henge monument, usually associated with ritual activities, are found in special prehistoric landscapes in Ireland. As outlined below, **earthen embanked enclosures** (Fig. 2) belong to the most common class of henge monuments known in Ireland.

Increasing attention has been paid in the past two decades to Irish henges, and recent analysis of LiDAR images has both revealed previously undiscovered sites and provided a fuller understanding of the topographical context of these monuments (Stout 1991; Condit and Simpson 1998; Hicks 2009; O'Sullivan *et al.* 2012).

Morphology

Earthen embanked henges are circular/subcircular or oval in plan and are typically relatively large constructions (see scale, Fig. 2). The internal profile of the monuments is often saucer shaped, akin to a shallow bowl; others have dome-shaped internal profiles. The surrounding banks are sometimes broad and commonly broken by a single entrance, but in some cases by two possible

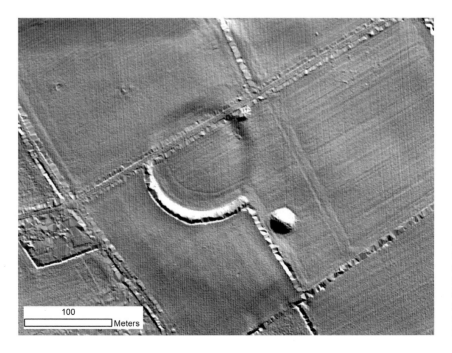

100
Meters

Fig. 2—LiDAR image of embanked enclosure at Micknanstown, Co. Meath (courtesy of Steve Davis).

entrances. The henges were generally constructed by scarping and scooping the soil from the interior to create a bank. Alternatively, they may have been built by digging a ditch immediately inside the bank. The Giant's Ring in County Down, defined by a massive bank, is visually the most impressive henge in Ireland.

Chronology and ritual

Several types of ritual enclosure, ranging in date from the Neolithic to the Iron Age, are to be found in Ireland. One important form of these is the henge, which appears to have had its roots in the Neolithic. These monuments have been associated with ritual activities over a period extending from the middle or late Neolithic to the Bronze Age and sometimes the Iron Age. Indeed, their role as foci within the landscape seems to have persisted, in some cases to the early medieval period and beyond. The most commonly occurring pottery at these sites is Grooved ware, Beaker and late Bronze Age coarseware, and sometimes all three types at once. The available evidence points to a succession of activities at some sites, extending over two millennia or more.

In some cases the henges appear to be situated within or perhaps central to landscapes featuring contemporary or slightly earlier or later archaeological activity (below). Again, this is consistent with henges having ritual functions. The earthworks, however, constitute only one element of the protracted and complex history of these sites.

Several scholars have speculated that the extensive internally ditched enclosures at royal sites, notably Ráith na Ríg at Tara and Emain Macha (Navan Fort), might have originated as henges. Hicks (2009) noted that henge-like enclosures are frequently found near traditional *oenach* sites associated with Lughnasa or other calendrical festivals. As further detailed by Hicks, the term *oenach* implies an enclosed space or structure, seemingly quite extensive, which might have functioned as a natural amphitheatre where people gathered. The assemblies held at *oenach* sites in many ways resembled historical fairs but with ritual and political overtones. Henges are often described as enclosures demarcating areas set aside for ritual purposes and are also sometimes described as amphitheatres.

One of the most interesting examples of an association between henges and *oenach* sites occurs near Lough Gur, notably the hill of Knockainey overlooking the area. *Oenach* sites have been identified at or near the concentrations of henges shown in the geographical distribution outlined in Figs 3 and 4. If not a coincidence, the association between henges and *oenach* sites would represent an extraordinary continuity from the Neolithic to modern times.

Number and distribution

Over 50 henges have been catalogued in Ireland and classified into three forms, termed **embanked enclosures** (71%), **internally ditched henges** (23%) and **variant henge forms** (7%) (O'Sullivan *et al.* 2012). Not included in these

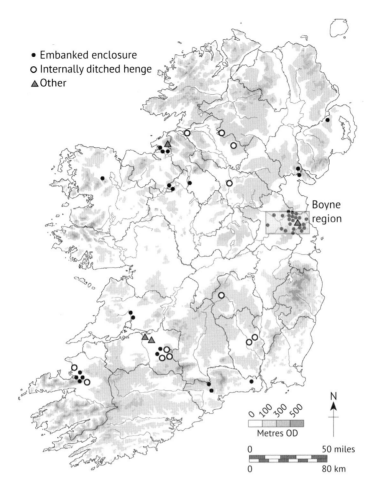

• Embanked enclosure
o Internally ditched henge
▲ Other

Boyne
region

N

0 100 300 500
Metres OD

0   50 miles

0   80 km

Fig. 3—
Geographical
distribution
of earthen
embanked
henges in Ireland
(courtesy of
Geraldine and
Matt Stout).

are other henge forms such as timber- and pit-defined or water-filled circles. The predominant form of henge in Britain has internally ditched banks, which define the monuments. The majority of earthen embanked henges in Ireland have no obvious ditch on the inside of the bank, although a sizeable minority have such a feature.

The spatial distribution of known henges in Ireland is depicted in Fig. 3. They occur principally in the eastern part of the country and also in Counties Sligo, Roscommon, Clare and Limerick, with further sites elsewhere. The Boyne region (Fig. 4) features a notable concentration of henges, virtually none of which have an obvious internal ditch in their surrounding banks. Internally ditched henges are, however, well represented among the sites distributed throughout the rest of the country.

Meath henges

Close to half of the total number of henges recorded in Ireland (56) are concentrated in County Meath (Fig. 3), notably in the Boyne Valley (Fig. 4). The monuments are predominantly located along the Boyne, as well as the

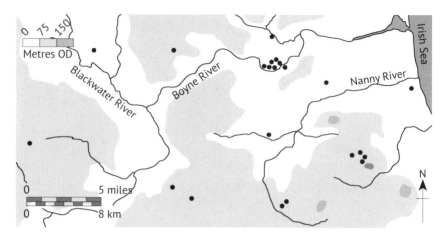

Fig. 4—Spatial distribution of Boyne Valley henges, Co. Meath (courtesy of Geraldine and Matt Stout).

Nanny and Delvin Rivers. Their distribution is apparently related to that of earlier prehistoric sites, such as passage tombs (below), and of watercourses. Thirteen of the henges were catalogued by Stout (1991). Recent analysis of LiDAR data has identified a number of other possible sites, with a particular concentration in Brú na Bóinne, as well as potential henges distributed elsewhere, such as Rathcarran and Julianstown.

The best-preserved example of a 'Boyne'-type henge is Site P (Fig. 5), which lies adjacent to the Boyne to the south of Newgrange. This is a massive site (*c.* 160m in external diameter) with substantial remaining banks, up to 2m high in places and exceptionally broad (*c.* 35m). In the majority of Boyne Valley henges (Fig. 4) the remaining bank section is considerably less imposing, often under 0.5m in height.

A pen picture of the typical forms of the Boyne henges is presented in Box 1. This highlights the notable differences between the main group of Boyne henges and the Dowth henge, as well as a number of other comparable

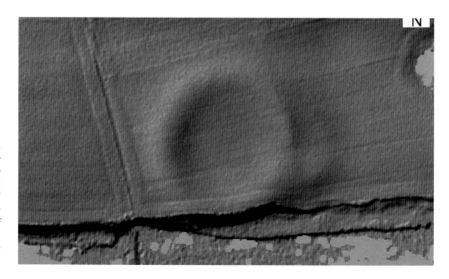

Fig. 5—LiDAR image of Boyne Valley-type henge, known as Site P, located beside the Boyne to the south of Newgrange, Co. Meath (courtesy of Steve Davis).

sites. In essence, the main group of Boyne henges are typically circular/ subcircular in plan, have a saucer-like profile and are not internally ditched. They are generally low lying and overlooked by the surrounding landscape.

The Dowth henge is substantially different (Fig. 6). It is ovoid in plan, domed in profile and not internally ditched; it occupies an elevated location and is not overlooked. The banks are not flattened and are interrupted by two breaks. Whether these represent two entrances is uncertain.

Box 1	Typical forms of Boyne henges	
Main group (listed below)[1]	**Dowth henge** (comparable sites listed below)[2]
Circular/subcircular in plan	Ovoid in plan
Saucer-like in profile	Domed in profile
Not internally ditched	Internally ditched
Low-lying location	Elevated location
Generally overlooked	Not overlooked
[1] Including Sites A & P, Rathcarran, Fourknocks/Micknanstown, Julianstown and Carranstown	[2] Henges with some resemblance to Dowth include Heathtown, Stackallan, Irishtown and Kilbrew

Within the Boyne henges, the closest parallel for Dowth is the largely destroyed site at Heathtown. Like the Dowth henge, it is noticeably domed towards the centre and occupies a small rise in otherwise low-lying ground. A notable feature of the Heathtown site, as opposed to the main group of Boyne henges, is the presence of a *bona fide* internal ditch, suggesting a genuine parallel with British henge monuments. The ditch was highlighted by a recent magnetometric survey. Conversely, no ditching of any description was detected at Garranstown, one of the henges in the main group of Boyne monuments (Box 1). The survey revealed an archaeological quiet space, with the interior of the henge showing even less activity than the exterior.

Other Meath sites with some resemblance to the Dowth henge are Stackallan and the monuments at Irishtown/Kilbrew (Box 1). Like Dowth, the Stackallan site is somewhat ovoid in form; it occupies a position just off the crest of a rise, and its interior is almost totally hidden from external viewpoints.

The two henges at Irishtown and Kilbrew also occupy moderately high ground and are not overlooked by other areas in the vicinity. While the exterior banks of the Irishtown and Kilbrew henges are intervisible, there is no visual connection between the interiors of the enclosures.

Adjunct structures

The monuments at Sites A and P are unusual in that they have a second, associated enclosure in the form of an alcove abutting the main henge. The annexe-like feature encompasses the one clear entrance at Site P.

The main central henge at Site A is surrounded by up to three smaller enclosures. One of these appears to be an additional annexe. The other two could themselves be classified as embanked enclosures. At Dowth henge (Fig. 6) a low-profile enclosure, just inside the south-western entrance, is visible through the coverage. The presence of these smaller enclosures at Site A and Dowth may represent a site type preceding the large henges.

Clusters

Clusters of embanked enclosures are most notable in Brú na Bóinne. Fourknocks, the Lee Valley (Kerry) and the Boyle area of Roscommon all feature clusters of three or more sites. They are generally located within perhaps 2km of each other and sometimes much less, for example at Brú na Bóinne. Clustering does not, however, appear to be a universal phenomenon, with many sites standing in apparent isolation.

Passage tombs

As previously mentioned, some henges are focused on areas of significant earlier Neolithic activity, e.g. the Boyne and Fourknocks sites. A number are located within some 2km of passage tombs (*Archaeology Ireland*, Spring 2012). Monknewtown was constructed less than 200m from a passage tomb in the same townland, and the Tralee group is located in proximity to the supposed passage tomb at Ballycarty. It is debatable, however, how important proximity to passage tombs was in determining the location of henges. Numerous significant clusters of passage tombs, in particular upland clusters, lack any recognisable embanked enclosure in their vicinity. Accordingly, the presence of a passage tomb (or tombs) was perhaps not the only defining factor in determining the location of henges. Nevertheless, shared concerns may have been important in influencing the juxtaposition of these monument types.

Landscape settings

As already indicated, many henges occupy locally high ground or encompass a low rise, thereby restricting views to the interior of the sites while maximising views from the exterior. This is by no means always the case, however. The locations chosen for a number of henges, including some sites referred to above (Site A and P and Brú na Bóinne), appear to be low lying, at the base of a river terrace (Fig. 4). The henge at Tonafortes, Co. Sligo, is located at the centre of a natural amphitheatre defined by surrounding mountains, thus creating an inward-looking situation analogous to some of the Boyne henges listed in Box 1. This henge is atypical of such Irish monuments. It is enclosed by two banks, with an intervening ditch.

Conclusion

As already indicated, henges vary markedly in form and context and defy convenient generalisations. Some of the more prominent features of the monuments recorded in Ireland are highlighted in Box 2.

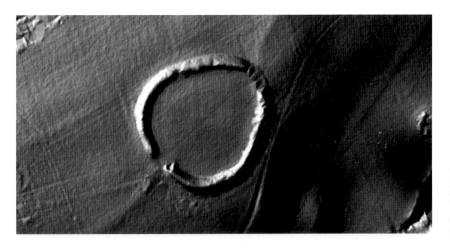

Fig. 6—LiDAR image of Dowth henge, Boyne Valley, Co. Meath (courtesy of Steve Davis).

Box 2	**Diagnostic features**

- Circular/subcircular or oval enclosures with surrounding banks, often less than 0.5m in height and sometimes broad and broken, commonly by a single entrance or two possible entrances.
- Characteristically large enclosures in excess of 100m in diameter; a number are appreciably smaller, while others are massive constructions (up to *c.* 160m in diameter or more).
- The interior of henges may be saucer-like or dome shaped in profile, and the majority, but by no means all, are not internally ditched.
- Tend to be found in the neighbourhood of other ritual monuments and sometimes occur in clusters.
- Found in the landscape in low-lying locations, often along river valleys, and also on moderately high ground, where they are typically not overlooked.

References

Condit, T. and Simpson, D.D.A. 1998 Irish hengiform enclosures and related monuments: a review. In A. Gibson and D.D.A. Simpson (eds), *Prehistoric ritual and religion*. Stroud.

Hicks, R. 2009 Some correlations between henge enclosures and *oenach* sites. *Journal of the Royal Society of Antiquaries of Ireland* **139**, 35–44.

Ó Ríordáin, S.P. (ed.) 1953 *Antiquities of the Irish countryside* (3rd edn). London.

O'Sullivan, M., Davis, S. and Stout, G. 2012 Henges in Ireland: new discoveries and emerging issues. In A.M. Gibson, *Enclosing the Neolithic: recent studies in Britain and Europe*. Oxford.

Stout, G. 1991 Embanked enclosures of the Boyle region. *Proceedings of the Royal Irish Academy* **91**C, 245–84.

This article was originally published in the Autumn 2012 issue of Archaeology Ireland.

Burial barrows

The distribution of burial barrows is widespread in Ireland but notable concentrations occur in Munster and Connacht, with a remarkable number known in the lower Shannon basin. The prevalence of burial barrows increased from around 40% of burial sites in the second half of the Bronze Age (1300–400 BC) to 60% during the Iron Age (400 BC–AD 400).

The chronology of different types of burial barrows seems to range from earlier Neolithic and Bronze Age forms to the ring-barrows of the later Bronze Age and Iron Age. Few securely dated barrows are known to have been constructed after AD 400.

Fig. 1—Ring-barrow at Cooga (Co. Tipperary), which exhibits typical characteristics of this class of monument, namely a circular mound, enclosing ditch and outer bank (Con Brogan, National Monuments Service, Department of Arts, Heritage and the Gaeltacht).

Mounds and rings

B arrows were predominant funerary monuments in prehistory, and the burials placed in them were typically cremations. As outlined below, they are widely distributed in Ireland, with notable concentrations in Munster and Connacht.

Several different types of burial barrows were used during the Bronze Age and Iron Age. As shown in Box 1, burial barrows have been classified into seven different types in the database compiled by the Archaeological Survey of Ireland. Ring-barrows (Figs 1 and 2) are the most common type in most areas of the country, and have accordingly received relatively greater emphasis in this article.

An impressive barrow (Fig. 2) recently excavated by O'Brien (2012) near Killumney, west of Cork city, comprised a C-shaped earthen enclosure (27m in overall diameter) with characteristics typical of ring-barrows (Box 1). It contained a level central area surrounded by a flat-bottomed ditch (1m in depth), and the material quarried from it was used to form a low external bank. The barrow was built for the funeral of a presumably important individual and the enclosing bank and ditch served to demarcate the sacred space, allowing the monument to be used for ceremonial observance during the burial and for some time afterwards (O'Brien 2012).

Landscape context

A Discovery Programme project undertaken in the lower Shannon basin during the 1990s documented a remarkable number of burial barrows, as well as some important spatial features of the monuments in terms of clustering, ceremonial enclosures and geographical distribution (Grogan 2005).

Over 1,600 barrow-type monuments were recorded in the study area, of which the vast majority (close to 80%) are termed barrows/ring-barrows and the remainder ring-ditches. Around 1,000 of the barrows are concentrated in east Limerick and the adjacent parts of west Tipperary, particularly along the river valleys, principally on the extensive floodplains of the Camoge River.

The most emphatic manifestations of barrow clustering are cemeteries, which can contain anything from three to 70 sites. One of the most impressive is at Mitchelstowndown West, Co. Limerick, where the main part of the cemetery consists of 53 barrows, amounting to just under 3 barrows per hectare. The cemeteries may represent the funerary sites of large communities. Occurrence in cemeteries is a key feature of this monument type and, as further detailed by Cooney (2009), the development of large cemeteries might be taken to convey a sense of lineage and ancestries.

The siting of barrows in the interior of ceremonial enclosures is another notable spatial feature of those recorded in east Limerick and west Tipperary (Grogan 2005).

A third spatial feature of barrows is their preferential geographical distribution (Fig. 3). As previously mentioned, a remarkably high concentration of barrows occurs in east Limerick and west Tipperary. The distribution of barrows extends across into Leinster and up into Connacht, with a distinctive concentration in the Sligo area (below). Conversely, barrows are not generally common in Ulster, apart from south Antrim.

Some interesting patterns can be discerned in relation to the preferential geographical distribution of different barrow types (Box 1). Ring-barrows are, as previously mentioned, the more common type in most areas of the country (Fig. 4). The related monument type known as ring-ditches

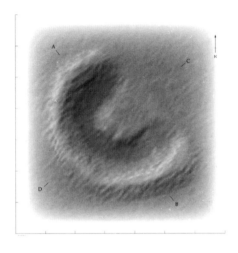

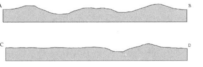

Fig. 2—
Excavation at
Knockateenane
barrow, near
Kilumney, Co.
Cork (courtesy of
W. O'Brien).

(defined below) occur in significant numbers in east Limerick and west Tipperary, across to the east coast and north-wards to Louth (Grogan 2005). Other barrow types (Box 1) are comparative-ly uncommon in Ireland, apart from Sligo, and with some also located across the north midlands and in north Tipperary.

Sligo features a not-able diversity of barrow types. Over 200 barrows have been recorded in the county, including 29 bowl-barrows (Fig. 5) and a pond-barrow. The areas around Ballymote and

Fig. 3—Geographical location of burial barrows relative to fulachta fiadh *(courtesy of the Discovery Programme).*

overlooking Ballysadare Bay have sizeable numbers of barrows, including an unusually high proportion (some 10–20%) of bowl-barrows. The distinctive nature of these barrow types suggests a regional characteristic, particularly in Sligo and the north midlands area.

As noted by Grogan, barrows and *fulachta fiadh*, the two largest monument groups recorded in later prehistory, exhibit contrasting distribution patterns (Fig. 3). *Fulachta fiadh* are predominant in the southern third of the country. Conversely, burial barrows are more prevalent in the other counties.

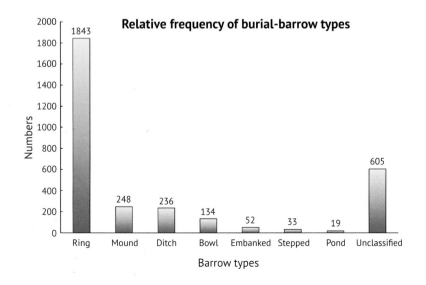

Fig. 4—Numerical distribution of the different types of burial barrows classified in the national database, compiled by the Archaeological Survey of Ireland.

Fig. 5—Two
bowl-barrows
in a cemetery
at Rathdooney
Beg (Co. Sligo),
together with
a low-profile
ring-barrow,
discernible
behind the
smaller bowl-
barrow (Con
Brogan, National
Monuments
Service,
Department of
Arts, Heritage
and the
Gaeltacht).

Bronze Age and Iron Age burials

The available information from the 108 burial sites most securely dated to the late Bronze Age and Iron Age (*c.* 1300 BC–AD 400) has furthered our understanding of late prehistoric burials in Ireland (McGarry 2009). The vast majority (80%) of the sites had curvilinear ditches, which, as indicated by McGarry, are very similar to the surviving monuments like ring-barrows described by Newman (1997). The burial monuments were overwhelmingly earthen constructions, some with central mounds partly formed from material excavated from rock-cut ditches.

They were predominantly annular in form; approximately 40% were penannular, having at least one gap (2m wide on average), possibly representing an entrance in the circuit of the ditch. The external diameters of barrows generally ranged from less than 7m to 25m, averaging 11m.

The majority of barrow sites contained fewer than five individual burials; about half of the sites produced the documented remains of only one person. The primary burial appears to have normally been in the central area of the sites and often in pits beneath the mound. Nevertheless, almost as many sites produced cremated burials from the ditch fills as from central contexts. The burials and rituals associated with the barrows are likely to have been perceived as 'sacred' (McGarry 2009).

Barrow classification

Burial barrows have been differentiated into distinctive types in the seminal publication by Newman (1997). As previously indicated, the Archaeological Survey of Ireland has, over the past decade, progressively compiled a national database of burial barrows in Ireland. The barrows are classified into seven types (Box 1), largely on the basis of the morphological features visible on the surface.

Box 1	Classification of burial-barrow types recorded in Ireland Basic surface features		
Type (number in brackets)	Central area—circular or oval	Enclosing ditch	Outer bank
Ring-barrows (1,843)	Raised generally up to 1m above the external ground or level with it	✓	✓
Bowl-barrows (134)	Mound like an inverted bowl, generally over 1m above the external ground	✓	Sometimes
Ditch-barrows (236)	Level or slightly raised (<1m) above the external ground; less than 20m in diameter; often found in association with other barrow types	Defined by a ditch	
Mound-barrows (248)	Earthen or earth-and-stone mound with no external features; found in association with other barrow types		
Pond-barrows (19)	Shallow, man-made circular depression enclosed around its rim by an earthen bank		✓
Embanked barrows (52)	Raised area generally less than 20m in diameter; enclosed by a continuous bank; bank size large relative to the small internal diameter		✓ Level or concave interior
Stepped barrows (33)	Raised platform; flat-topped or rounded central area; 'stepped' profile		Some sites on outer edge of platform
Unclassified barrows	605 sites recorded		

Source: Archaeological Survey of Ireland

Ring-barrows (Figs 1 and 2) are by far the most common type recorded in the database (Fig. 4). They exceed, by orders of magnitude, the number of each of the other six classified types. Of the total number of ring-barrows (1,843) in the database, the highest concentration is in County Limerick (above), with almost half of the total number recorded.

As further detailed in the 'scope note' prepared by the Archaeological Survey of Ireland, the classic definition of a barrow is a mound of earth or stones erected over human remains. The term 'barrow' has, however, been extended to include monuments containing and/or covering burials, as well as monuments with funerary associations—including, for example, ring-barrows—where no burials were found upon excavation. Barrows do not require a mound as an essential component but all barrows are of earth or earth-and-stone construction, and the typical barrow is less than 30m in diameter.

Barrows frequently occur in clusters (above) and in Bronze Age/Iron Age archaeological landscapes. They are often associated with other monuments of these periods. This association can be crucial in identifying some monuments as barrows, particularly embanked barrows and ditch-barrows, as these can morphologically resemble other monument types such as hut sites or ring-ditches.

The classification 'ring-barrow' (Box 1) applies to barrow types with both level and raised interiors enclosed by a ditch and outer bank. Over 700 ring-ditches have been recorded by the Archaeological Survey of Ireland. They are defined as circular or near-circular ditches, usually less than 10m in diameter and visible as crop-marks/soil-marks on aerial photographs. Ring-ditches may be the remains of ploughed-out barrows but in many cases they represent other types of structures and, individually, their date is problematic pending excavation.

Chronology

The appearance of barrows in Britain during the later Neolithic has been seen as a departure from the long-standing tradition of large collective burial monuments in favour of single burials (Newman 1997). Barrows continued to be used in Britain throughout the Bronze Age and into the Iron Age. In Ireland, burial practices appear to have evolved along much the same lines and, as outlined below, the tradition of barrow construction appears to have continued into the Iron Age. They became more common during the course of late prehistory, increasing from around 40% of burial sites in the period

Chronology of burial barrows

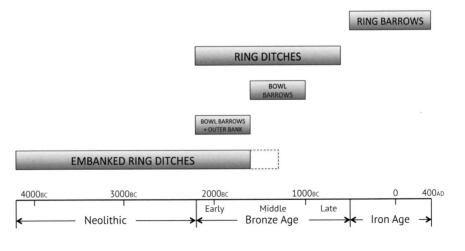

Fig. 6—Schematic representation of the indicative date ranges of burial barrows and ring-ditches (based on Newman 1997). Although slightly over-simplified, this is a useful general guide.

c. 1300–400 BC to 60% during *c.* 400 BC–AD 400 (McGarry 2009). The surface expression of the burial sites may have varied over time and, as indicated by McGarry, a barrow-like form was most dominant during the Iron Age.

While emphasising the uncertainties involved, given the dearth of innovations, Newman (1997) has described some broad general trends apparent in the date ranges of the different types of burial barrows. The indicative date ranges shown schematically in Fig. 6 are outlined below.

The monument type termed 'embanked ring-ditches' seem to range in date principally from the Neolithic and earlier Bronze Age, and may have continued in use into the middle Bronze Age. Bowl-barrows may date principally from the middle Bronze Age, while those with an outer bank may possibly date from the earlier Bronze Age. In the excavation at Rathdooney Beg, Co. Sligo (Fig. 5), the larger bowl-barrow was dated to the Neolithic and the small form produced an Iron Age date (*Archaeology Ireland*, Autumn 1998). Most excavated ring-ditches date from the earlier and later Bronze Age. As noted by Newman, ring-barrows appear to be principally an Iron Age type of burial monument.

The burial-barrow types recorded in the database compiled by the Archaeological Survey of Ireland (Box 1) appear to date principally from the Bronze Age–Iron Age (*c.* 2400 BC–AD 400); ditch-barrows usually date from this period but may date from the Neolithic. Few securely dated barrows are known to have been constructed after AD 400 (McGarry 2009).

Following the various regional studies of recent decades, the classification, chronology and wider social function of burial barrows remain elusive, and the type is in serious need of a coherent, in-depth and island-wide analysis.

Box 2	Diagnostic features

- Circular or oval enclosures of earth or earth-and-stone construction, typically less than 30m in diameter, some with one entrance.
- Ring-barrows (Figs 1 and 2) exhibit three characteristic surface features, namely a central area (mound or flat) and enclosing ditch, with a surrounding outer bank.
- Bowl-barrows (Fig. 5) have a central raised mound (over 1m) like an inverted bowl, an external ditch and sometimes an outer bank.
- Ditch-barrows have a level or slightly raised (less than 1m) central area defined by a ditch and generally less than 20m in diameter. They are often found in clusters or in association with other barrow types.
- The other four defined types, namely mound-, pond-, embanked and stepped barrows, have no enclosing ditch. They may be distinguished from each other by their characteristic central area and outer bank (Box 1); mound-barrows have no external features.
- Ring-ditches, the related monument type, are relatively simple morphologically, and may be found as a circular/near-circular enclosure defined by a ditch.

Acknowledgements

The invaluable information and knowledgeable insights received from Paul Walsh are gratefully acknowledged. The background documents provided by Gabriel Cooney are also much appreciated.

References

Cooney, G. 2009 Tracing lines across landscapes: corporality and history in later prehistoric Ireland. In G. Cooney, K. Becker, J. Coles, M. Ryan and S. Sievers (eds), *Relics of old decency: archaeological studies in later prehistory. Festschrift for Barry Raftery*. Bray.

Grogan, E. (ed.) 2005 *The North Munster Project, Vol. II. The prehistoric landscape of North Munster*. Discovery Programme Monograph 6. Bray.

McGarry, T. 2009 Irish prehistoric ring-ditches. In G. Cooney, K. Becker, J. Coles, M. Ryan and S. Sievers (eds), *Relics of old decency: archaeological studies in later prehistory. Festschrift for Barry Raftery*. Bray.

Newman, C. (ed.) 1997 *Tara: an archaeological survey*. Discovery Programme Monograph 2. Dublin.

O'Brien, W. 2012 *Iverni: a prehistory of Cork*. Cork.

This article was originally published in the Winter 2012 issue of Archaeology Ireland.

Wedge tombs

The majority of wedge tombs appear to have been built between 2500 and 1800 BC, with some possibly dating from within a few centuries of this range.

Those who built and used wedge tombs played an integral role in the development of the farmed landscape and the distribution of these tombs may represent a significant agricultural settlement in the south-west of Ireland. Many wedge tombs occur in areas where prehistoric copper mines have been discovered and, in the Cork/Kerry region, the majority of the tombs were apparently built by metal-using communities.

In addition to being repositories for human remains, wedge tombs might also have functioned as territorial markers and symbolic expressions of belief systems, ritual authority and access to the supernatural.

Fig. 1 — Labbacallee wedge tomb, Co. Cork, from the side (courtesy of the National Monuments Service, Department of the Environment, Heritage and Local Government).

Last of the megalithic tombs

Wedge tombs are the most numerous type of megalithic tomb in Ireland, accounting for over 500 or one third of the total. They are key monuments for the understanding of life and death in Bronze Age Ireland. The unassuming scale of many wedge tombs does not reflect their practical, symbolic and cultural importance, as further detailed below.

Architecture

The central feature of wedge tombs is a **chamber** or gallery that lowers and narrows towards the rear (Fig. 1). Based on chamber size, wedge tombs may be differentiated into two groups: (i) single wedge-shaped, box-like constructions and (ii) long, low galleries, as shown in Fig. 2 and Fig. 3 respectively.

The simplest wedge tombs consist of no more than a wedge-shaped chamber. Many also have a small antechamber or portico at the western end, in front of the main chamber. Less commonly, they have a small closed chamber or cell at the eastern end or rear of the main chamber. The two side

Fig. 2—Parknabinnia wedge tomb, Co. Clare (courtesy of the National Monuments Service, Department of the Environment, Heritage and Local Government).

Fig. 3—
Labbacallee
wedge tomb, Co.
Cork, from the
rear (courtesy
of the National
Monuments
Service,
Department of
the Environment,
Heritage
and Local
Government).

walls of the chamber are built of one or more upright slabs, which directly support large roof stones or capstones. Wedge tombs differ markedly in size, with the galleries varying from as little as 2m in length to almost 14m (Fig. 3) in the case of the large, well-known site at Labbacallee, Co. Cork. A consistent feature of the Irish wedge tombs is the orientation of the chamber axis towards the western or south-western horizon. This alignment on the setting sun seems to be a central element of the symbolism of wedge tombs (below).

Cairns or covering mounds occur in some larger wedge tombs, varying from round to short oval or D shaped (Fig. 4), and occasionally with a kerb feature. Many small wedge tombs also have traces of a small cairn or mound. Some tombs, however, may never have had covering cairns.

Cupmarks or circular hollows, averaging 5cm in diameter, have been recorded on many wedge tombs and are generally found on the capstones. In this regard, the wedge tomb at Kilmackowen in the Beara Peninsula, Co. Cork, is atypical. It has some nine cupmarks inside the chamber, located on the orthostat on the left side of the chamber (Fig. 5). Six of the cupmarks are laid out in a broadly S-shaped pattern, with others on either side of this. There is a large standing stone a short distance downhill from the wedge tomb, and a line of stones protruding from the bog runs between the two monuments. At Ballyedmunduff, Co. Dublin, the cupmarked stone is too small to be a roof lintel.

Cists and pits containing cremations are sometimes found within the chambers or outside wedge tombs. In some instances the cists are later insertions, while in others they seem to be contemporary with the building of the tomb.

Dating and origins

It has been suggested that the majority of wedge tombs were built between 2500 and 1800 BC, a period often known as the Chalcolithic, with some possibly dating from within a few centuries of this range. The first wedge tombs appeared in many parts of Ireland during the centuries from *c.* 2500 to 2100 BC, the final Neolithic, when inter-regional contacts were expanding through networks associated with the spread of Beaker pottery (below) and related artefacts. The building of wedge tombs appears to have petered out during the later stages of the early Bronze Age, *c.* 1900–1600 BC.

Fine-quality Beaker ware, found widely throughout Europe from about the mid-third millennium BC onwards, may have been used as a type of prestige drinking vessel. In areas such as Brittany, Beaker pots were commonly placed in a tomb as an accompaniment to burials, which took place long after the construction of the tomb. Beaker pottery, with its distinctive fabric and form, appeared in Ireland around 2500 BC and has been found in approximately one third of excavated wedge tombs.

Gallery tombs were being built in northern France probably as early as 3200 BC. This Atlantic gallery-tomb tradition may have contributed to the origins of Irish wedge tombs, which are generally believed to be derived from or influenced by the late Neolithic gallery graves of Brittany, known as *allées couvertes*.

Geographical distribution

Wedge tombs exhibit a marked western distribution (Fig. 6). Over half (56%) are concentrated in north and south Munster. Further concentrations occur in the Sligo/Mayo area and extend northwards into mid-Ulster. The simple wedge tombs (Fig. 2) are typically found in north-west Clare and south Munster, while the long, low gallery forms (Fig. 3) occur principally in the northern half of the country, although examples do occur elsewhere.

Fig. 4—
Ballyedmunduff
wedge tomb, Co.
Dublin.

The siting of wedge tombs was influenced by the suitability of the area for settlement, combined with various economic and social concerns. As outlined below, agriculture and copper were two important determinants of the location of wedge tombs.

Agriculture

Several studies have demonstrated an apparent correlation between the siting of megalithic tombs and agricultural land (de Valera and Ó Nualláin 1961; O'Brien 1999). The suitability of areas for settlement and farming has been identified as the primary 'pull' factor that influenced the location of megalithic tombs in County Leitrim (Cooney 1979). Wedge tombs in the Mizen Peninsula are generally located on or in proximity to good agricultural soils (O'Brien 1999). Excavations undertaken at Roughan Hill in the south-east Burren, Co. Clare, have revealed farms and field systems with wedge tombs from the Beaker period (Jones *et al.* 2010).

Wedge tombs formed an integral part of the development of the farmed landscape. They represent the first significant agricultural settlement in the south-west of Ireland and a long-term change in settlement patterns brought about by an increasing dependence on agriculture. The introduction of agriculture to Ireland probably involved some element of migration, possibly by small population groups in the centuries around 4000 BC. Its adoption as the mainstay of the economy was a slow process, however, marked by much regional variability.

While many have been lost over the intervening centuries, the relict remains of wedge tombs in the modern landscape provide invaluable indicators of the early adoption of agriculture in Ireland, especially in western counties.

Fig. 5— Cupmarks on a chamber orthostat at Kilmackowen wedge tomb, Co. Cork (courtesy of Connie Murphy).

Fig. 6—
Distribution of
wedge tombs
(after Walsh
1995).

Copper

Many wedge tombs occur in copper-rich areas, where Bronze Age copper mines have been discovered. In the Cork/Kerry region, with its proliferation of megaliths, the majority of the tombs were built by metal-using communities. The appearance of wedge tombs in the region and the introduction of metallurgy after 2500 BC involved external contacts. The mining of copper by various wedge-tomb communities in west Cork seems to have consisted of relatively small-scale, short-lived ventures, probably under local control and undertaken in response to the limited needs of these small communities.

Multifunctionality

Wedge tombs were not simply burial structures or grave markers. Megalithic tombs seem to have served a variety of functions, ranging from the practical to the symbolic, for the societies that built and subsequently used them. They were as much 'monuments for the living as monuments for the dead' (Walsh 1995).

Burials

At a purely functional level, these megalithic tombs were repositories for human remains and the focus for associated funerary practices. The majority of wedge tombs were sealed, although some were built to allow ongoing access involving recurrent burial. With a few exceptions, wedge tombs had generally fallen out of use for human burial by the later Bronze Age, and by

1500 BC single-burial sites had been widely adopted in different forms across Ireland.

Territorial markers

Wedge tombs were monumental markers in the landscape and might have been used to demarcate boundaries and resource ownership. They may have been a focus around which territorially based descent groups were formed, fostering the development of a wider community identity. This may have led to individual wedge-tomb communities becoming virtual corporate entities in terms of the proprietary rights to land and other resources, such as copper ores, fishing or hunting grounds.

Symbolism

Megalithic tombs were symbolic expressions of ideological beliefs, ritual authority and access to the supernatural. The wedge tomb was at the centre of a community of individuals who shared certain beliefs and values. The ancestors may have been regarded as spirits whose function was to communicate with higher spirits in order to further the prosperity of the group. The rituals associated with wedge tombs helped in the symbolic construction of the community.

White-vein quartz held a special significance during the Neolithic and Bronze Age and has been found at Toormore and Altar wedge tombs in the Mizen Peninsula, Co. Cork. The spread of white quartz pebbles excavated at Toormore and the discovery of an early metal deposit in close proximity to the site might be indicative of a symbolism relating to copper-mining.

Settlement patterns

In spite of the concentration of wedge tombs in the south-west of the country and their association with agriculture and mining, there is a general dearth of settlement archaeology for the prehistoric period in the region. O'Brien (1999) has postulated that Neolithic and early Bronze Age settlements may have comprised dispersed household units rather than the agglomerated village-style settlements that characterise the Neolithic in central Europe. This view is further supported by recent research in the Beara Peninsula, where there is a widely spaced distribution of wedge tombs in the Castletownbere/Eyeries/Ardgroom area. Though no contemporary habitation sites have been found, these monuments may be regarded as proxy indicators of the final Neolithic/early Bronze Age farming settlement in that area. The prevailing distribution of these monuments is consistent with a pattern of dispersed settlement in parts of the region that were optimal for human settlement. In marked contrast, Roughan Hill in the Burren is characterised by the densest concentration of wedge tombs in the country, with many little more than 30m apart (Jones 2004)—seemingly a response to increasing competition and subdivision of fields that had been cleared and farmed over a very long time.

Box 1	Diagnostic features

- Generally wedge shaped in both plan and profile, and consisting of a main chamber or gallery, many with a small portico or antechamber at the western end, and occasionally a small closed chamber at the eastern end.
- Two forms: (i) single wedge-shaped, box-like constructions and (ii) long, low galleries.
- Axis of the main chamber aligned on the western or south-western horizon and the setting sun.

Acknowledgements

The informative publications and other information provided by Dr Paul Walsh, Dr Carlton Jones, Professor William O'Brien and Mick Monk are gratefully acknowledged. The illustrations kindly provided by the National Monuments Service (Department of the Environment, Heritage and Local Government) and by Connie Murphy are also much appreciated.

References

Brindley, A. and Lanting, J.N. 1991–2 Radiocarbon dates from wedge tombs. *Journal of Irish Archaeology* **6**, 19–26.

Cooney, G. 1979 Some aspects of the siting of megalithic tombs in County Leitrim. *Journal of the Royal Society of Antiquaries of Ireland* **109**, 74–91.

de Valera, R. and Ó Núallain, S. 1961 *Survey of the megalithic tombs of Ireland, Vol. I: Clare*. Dublin.

de Valera, R. and Ó Núallain, S. 1982 *Survey of the megalithic tombs of Ireland, Vol. IV: Cork, Kerry, Limerick and Tipperary*. Dublin.

Jones, C. (ed.) 2004 *The Burren and the Aran Islands*. Cork.

Jones, C. (ed.) 2007 *Temples of stone: exploring the megalithic tombs of Ireland*. Cork.

Jones, C., Carey, O. and Hennigar, C. 2010 Domestic production and the political economy in prehistory: evidence from the Burren, Co. Clare. In E. Fitzpatrick and J. Kelly (eds), *Domestic life in Ireland*, special supplement to *Proceedings of the Royal Irish Academy* **110C**.

O'Brien, W. (ed.) 1999 *Sacred ground: megalithic tombs in coastal south-west Ireland*. Bronze Age Studies 4. Galway.

O'Brien, W. 2002 Megaliths in a mythologised landscape. In C. Scarre (ed.), *Monuments and landscape in Atlantic Europe*. New York.

O'Brien, W. (ed.) 2009 *Local worlds: early settlement landscapes and upland farming in south-west Ireland*. Cork.

Shee Twohig, E. (ed.) 1990 *Irish megalithic tombs*. Princes Risborough.

Walsh, P. 1995 Structure and deposition in Irish wedge tombs: an open and shut case? In J. Waddell and E. Shee Twohig (eds), *Ireland in the Bronze Age. Proceedings of the Dublin Conference, April 1995*. Dublin.

This article was originally published in the Winter 2010 issue of Archaeology Ireland.

Stone circles

Stone circles occur in three major geographical distributions. Distinctive concentrations occur in south Munster and mid-Ulster, while the third group is spatially more dispersed and generally consists of an earthen bank with a circle of large stones set against its inner face. This third group appears to be a type of henge.

It would appear that agricultural settlement influenced the siting of stone circles. Some were built in land used previously for farming. Astronomical alignments with the sun, and possibly the moon, are features associated with many stone circles, but their core purpose is unclear. The belong to a new range of freestanding megaliths that proliferated in the Cork/Kerry region from around 1500 BC. In other cases, notably mid-Ulster and the famous example surrounding Newgrange, at least some of the stone circles may have been erected in the Neolithic period and into the early Bronze Age.

Fig. 1—Multiple-stone circle at Derreenataggart, Co. Cork (Connie Murphy).

Multifunctional enclosures

The two concentrations of distinctive stone circles in south Munster and mid-Ulster, as well as the more dispersed group of embanked stone circles, are detailed below, together with an outline of their multifunctionality.

South Munster group

The distinctive type of stone circles occurring in Cork and parts of south-west Kerry are composed of an uneven number of spaced orthostats, varying from five to an estimated nineteen (Ó Nualláin 1984; 1991; Walsh 1993; Burl 2000; Murphy 2009). The entrance is towards the north-east and is marked by the two tallest stones (portal stones) of the circle. Directly opposite is the notable recumbent or axial stone. Characteristically, the stones decrease in height from the entrance down to the recumbent stone, which is normally the lowest stone of the perimeter.

Based on the number of stones forming the rings, the south-Munster stone circles have been differentiated into five-stone circles and those with a greater number of stones marking the perimeter, namely multiple-stone circles.

Five-stone circles (Fig. 2) constitute just over half the total number. Multiple-stone circles (Fig. 1) have from 7 to 19 stones in the rings, most commonly 11 or 13. The majority of the circles are between 7m and 10m in diameter, and up to 17m in the largest at Kenmare and Cashelkeelty, Co. Kerry. An unusual feature of the multiple-stone circles in the region is that ten of them enclose one or more boulder burials. A few of the multiple-stone circles are surrounded by a bank or by a bank and ditch, which, as outlined below, is a characteristic feature of embanked stone circles.

Over 95% of the stone circles in south-west Ireland are concentrated south of a line from Kenmare Bay to the Boggeragh Mountains (Walsh 1993). Multiple-stone circles predominate along the Beara Peninsula.

Mid-Ulster group

Unlike other regions in Ireland and Britain, the rings in the mid-Ulster group of stone circles are composed of numerous stones, mainly small in size. The monuments are also characterised by normally occurring as a multiplicity of rings set in clusters, which may also include cairns, cists and monoliths (Mallory and McNeill 1991; Ó Nualláin 1991; Donnelly 1998; Burl 2000).

This distinctive concentration of stone circles is centred on Tyrone and the neighbouring areas of Fermanagh and Derry. Over 100 circles are known in Ulster; with nearly 150 reported in the Sperrins (Burl 2000), however, the total number is seemingly much higher.

About half of the circles have more than 20 stones, and indeed up to 45 and more close-set stones make up almost half of the inland rings. Few of the stones are more than half a metre in height, and the majority are much lower.

The profusion of multiple rings, notably in Counties Tyrone and Derry, is an intriguing feature of the mid-Ulster group. The vast majority (80%) of stone circles in Tyrone are in clusters, with a number comprising four or five rings, and some as many as nine. The best-known assemblage of stone circles and other monuments in Ulster is at Beaghmore, near Cookstown, Co. Tyrone (Fig. 3). Excavations of the bog have revealed seven subcircular stone circles, as well as ten stone rows and a dozen cairns. The stone circles occur in pairs, apart from one whose interior is filled with almost 900 upright, sharpish small stones known as 'dragon's teeth'.

Embanked stone circles

These are composite monuments comprising stone circles and earthen banks or ditches. They are relatively uncommon and are dispersed monuments. Notable groups occur at Lough Gur, Co. Limerick, west Wickow/Kildare and Cong, Co. Mayo (Ó Nualláin 1984; 1991; Burl 2000).

With embanked stone circles, the stones are set in the bank, as distinct from circle-henges, in which the stones of the circle stand independently inside the henge.

The best-known embanked stone circle is at Grange, beside Lough Gur, where the great earthen bank is lined internally by continuous stones (Fig. 4).

Fig. 2—Five-stone circle, Dromatouk, Co. Kerry (Con Brogan, Photo Unit, Department of the Environment, Heritage and Local Government).

*Fig. 3—
Beaghmore
stone circle
and row, Co.
Tyrone (Crown
copyright,
Northern Ireland
Environment
Agency).*

Ó Nualláin (1991) envisaged embanked stone circles as representing localised but important episodes of the late Neolithic/early Bronze Age in Ireland. As indicated below, they may have drawn their inspiration from contact with north-west Britain, where in Cumbria stone circles with banks and entrances are also known (Burl 2000).

Dating and ancestry

To date a stone circle using diagnostic material or organic samples collected on the ground within or near it, or from the sockets of the stones themselves, is to risk arriving at false conclusions. This, however, this is the only evidence at our disposal until some researcher succeeds in applying the latest thermo-luminescence-dating techniques to the buried ends of the standing stones. This may explain why the dating of stone circles has long been contentious; nevertheless, caveats aside, there has been some progress in the area. In the Cork/Kerry region, according to O'Brien (2002), a new range of free-standing megaliths, including stone circles, appeared from around 1500 BC onwards, with some examples built as late as 800 BC. As further documented by Lynch (1999), four stone circles in the region have construction dates in the range of 1600–800 BC.

At least some of the stone circles in mid-Ulster may have been built during the Neolithic period (Mallory and McNeill 1991). Late radiocarbon dates from the Beaghmore complex (Fig. 3) and from the secondary ring-cairn at Dun Ruadh of *c.* 1875–1750 BC indicate second-millennium BC activity at many rings in the Sperrins (Burl 2000). Outside the mid-Ulster group, the stone circle at Ballynoe, Co. Down, seems to have involved several different building phases, beginning in the Neolithic and continuing into the early Bronze Age.

The ancestry of stone circles in Ireland, relative to their counterparts in Britain, has been extensively explored by Burl (2000). The parallel traits synopsised in Box 1 seem to reflect the exposure of stone circles in Ireland to influences from England and Scotland. As noted by Walsh (1993), however, stone circles and related monuments adopted from outside can be given a new and independent formal expression, in effect producing an apparent regional variation.

Box 1	Parallels between stone circles in Ireland and their counterparts in Britain	
Ireland	Britain	Parallels
Cork	Scotland	Recumbent stone circles but exhibiting distinctive differences
Ulster	Cumbria	Ballynoe stone circle (Co. Down) almost a duplicate of that at Swinside (Cumbria)
Wicklow	Cumbria	Large Wicklow stone circles exhibit weak Cumbrian traits
Number of counties	Cornwall	Stone circles with centre stones
Source: Burl 2000		

Multifunctionality

Stone circles were used for a multiplicity of purposes, both cultural and practical, including burials and ceremonial rites, religious practices and community gatherings, as well as acting as places of exchange and trade; possible astronomical uses have also been suggested (Lynch 1981; Ó Nualláin 1991; Walsh 1993; Ruggles 1999; Burl 2000, O'Brien 2002).

Burial and ceremonial sites

Stone circles were associated with the cult of the dead and mortuary practices. They were repeatedly used for rituals and as places where people congregated to participate in ceremonial rites. Their use to hold burials, mainly cremations, generally took place early in the history of the monuments. While these functional uses were reflected in the design of stone circles, their consistent execution over a wide geographical area suggests a deeper religious significance (O'Brien 2002).

Symbolism

The architecture and orientation of stone circles were inherently symbolic, reflecting in a fundamental way a sense of spirituality and belief in the Otherworld. They were sacred sites. Many may have been the focus for ancestral veneration, housing the remains of individuals who were important to the collective memory of the community.

Exchange and trade

The correlation between regions of early stone circles and stone-axe factories and their distribution is well attested in Britain (Burl 2000). Stone circles close to trackways may have indicated depots for the acquisition and distribution of stone axes and their transfer to rich settlement areas. Substantial numbers of axes from County Antrim have been found in Scotland. Axes from the mountains of Antrim have also been recovered on the Knockadoon Peninsula at Lough Gur, Co. Limerick. It would be interesting to determine whether stone circles were as important in the exchange and distribution of stone axes and trading in Ireland as they seem to have been in Britain.

Astronomical orientation

Solar or lunar alignments are features of many stone circles (Ó Nualláin 1984; Ruggles 1999; O'Brien 2002). The astronomical purpose(s) of such alignments can be a contentious issue, however.

Recumbent stone circles in the south-Munster group have a general orientation between west and south. The respect for the sunset horizon in the darker months of the year is consistent with the funerary function of these monuments. This is further emphasised by the presence of white quartz in a number of stone circles.

Astronomical alignments have been reported for several stone circles in Ireland, some involving outliers and/or cupmarked stones. The Beltany stone circle in County Donegal is claimed to have a number of solar alignments, the best of which is from the great pillar at the south-west to the cupmarked stone (Burl 2000).

The orientation of monuments was considered important by prehistoric societies. By marking the approach of the winter solstice and the returning sun, stone circles, properly aligned, may have acted as calendrical symbols in the farming cycle, for instance, as well as in the seasonal timing of ceremonies. Whether, however, stone circles functioned as astronomical observatories, as is often postulated, has been questioned based on a reappraisal of the alignment data reported in respect of a variety of monuments, including a diversity of stone circles in Britain. In this regard, Burl (2000) contends that 'Whatever astronomical purpose it [the monument] contained was only a part, perhaps minor, of its function.'

Settlement

Agricultural settlement influenced the siting of stone circles. Some were built on land previously used for agriculture. At Beaghmore (Fig. 3), for instance, monuments were constructed on land where agriculture had taken place in the Neolithic. In the south-west of Ireland, the earliest activity at Cashelkeelty (Co. Kerry) involved period(s) of cereal cultivation and possibly pasture farming (Lynch 1981). With its decline, the land was chosen as a site for funerary activities involving the building of stone circles and alignments. One of the major aims of the extensive investigation undertaken at Cashelkeelty was to locate the habitation sites associated with the stone circle/alignment complex and the ancient field boundaries. No trace of a settlement was located, however.

The appearance of stone circles and related monuments in south-west Ireland by 1500 BC has generally been seen as marking an emphatic break with the past through the arrival of a new people or new ritual practices (O'Brien 2002). Nevertheless, the generally common orientation of wedge tombs and stone circles reflects certain shared elements of belief. This continuity of belief is further emphasised by the complementary regional distribution of these monuments and is suggestive of stable settlement patterns in the long term.

Box 2	Diagnostic features

- Circular or subcircular rings of upright stones of uneven height, with the tallest two stones marking the entrance and located directly opposite the recumbent stone, which is normally the lowest stone of the perimeter.
- The stone circle concentration in south Munster comprises five-stone and multiple-stone monuments, some containing boulder burials and monoliths.
- The mid-Ulster stone circles are characterised by the numerous small stones making up the ring, and by their tendency to occur in clusters that may contain cairns, cists and monoliths.
- Embanked stone circles are dispersed monuments comprising earthen banks in which the stones are set.

Fig. 4—
Embanked stone circle at Grange, Lough Gur, Co. Limerick (Con Brogan, Photo Unit, Department of the Environment, Heritage and Local Government).

Acknowledgements

The published articles and other information kindly provided by Ann Lynch, Claire Foley, Kerri Cleary, Connie Murphy, Paul Walsh, Billy O'Brien, Paul Logue and Ian Doyle have been most helpful in compiling this article. The photographs provided by Con Brogan (Photo Unit, Department of the Environment, Heritage and Local Government) and Connie Murphy are also much appreciated.

References

Burl, A. (ed.) 2000 *The stone circles of Britain, Ireland and Brittany.* London.

Donnelly, J.C. 1998 *Historic monuments of Northern Ireland: an introduction and guide.* Belfast.

Lynch, A. (ed.) 1981 *Man and the environment in south-west Ireland.* British Archaeological Reports, British Series 85. Oxford.

Lynch, A. 1999 Excavation of a stone row at Maughanasilly, Co. Cork. *Journal of the Cork Historical and Archaeological Society* **14**, 1–20.

Mallory, J.P. and McNeill, T.E. (eds) 1991 *The archaeology of Ulster: from colonisation to plantation.* Belfast.

Murphy, C. 2009 The prehistoric archaeology of Beara. In W. Walsh (ed.), *Local worlds: early settlement landscapes and upland in south-west Ireland.* Cork.

O'Brien, W. 2002 Megaliths in a mythologised landscape. In C. Scarre (ed.), *Monuments and landscape in Atlantic Europe.* New York.

Ó Nualláin, S. 1984 A survey of stone circles in Cork and Kerry. *Proceedings of the Royal Irish Academy* **84C**, 1–77.

Ó Nualláin, S. 1991 Stone circles, stone rows, boulder burials and standing stones. In M. Ryan (ed.), *Irish archaeology illustrated.* Dublin.

Ruggles, C. (ed.) 1999 *Astronomy in prehistoric Britain and Ireland.* London.

Walsh, P. 1993 In circle and row: Bronze Age ceremonial monuments. In E. Shee Twohig and M. Ronayne (eds), *Past perceptions: the prehistoric archaeology of south-west Ireland.* Cork.

This article was originally published in the Spring 2011 issue of Archaeology Ireland.

Stone rows
and stone pairs

S tone rows are relatively simple structures comprising linear settings of freestanding stones, usually of megalithic size. Rows and pairs of such freestanding stones are sometimes interpreted as route or territorial-boundary markers. However, their astronomical alignments suggest a calendrical function, which some have related to the seasonal timing of agricultural practices, claiming them to be 'farming calendars'.

Two strikingly different concentrations of prehistoric stones rows are known, one in the south of Ireland (mainly Cork and Kerry) and the other in mid-Ulster (Tyrone, Fermanagh and Derry). The stone rows in the southern group have been dated to the period from *c*. 1650 BC to 800 BC, while dates from the late Neolithic period to the late Bronze Age have been reported in respect of the stone circles and stone rows in the Beaghmore complex in County Tyrone.

Fig. 1 – Two stone pairs at Finaha, to the north-west of Castletownbere, Co. Cork.

Aligned standing stones

In the public perception, the astronomical sightlines built into many megalithic monuments are amongst the most interesting features of sites such as Newgrange and Stonehenge. The astronomical interpretations and functions attributed to megalithic alignments, however, have been a most contentious issue in archaeology (Ruggles 1999; Burl 2000).

The alignments built into wedge tombs and stone circles were outlined respectively in the Winter 2010 and Spring 2011 issues of *Archaeology Ireland*. This article focuses on stone rows and the possible functions of their associated alignments.

Prehistoric astronomy

The study of the practice of astronomy in ancient times, termed 'archaeo-astronomy', is a hybrid endeavour between archaeology and astronomy, requiring formidable statistical capability (Ruggles 1999). A synopsis is presented below of the contributions of three knowledgeable pioneers who, from the early 1900s, applied their wide-ranging technical expertise, including knowledge of archaeology and astronomy, to megalithic alignments.

Norman Lockyer (1836–1920) was the first to put speculation on megalithic alignments on some sort of scientific footing (Ruggles 1999). He was director of the Solar Physics Laboratory, a distinguished physicist and astronomer, as well as founding editor of *Nature*, one of today's most prestigious scientific journals. Having carried out careful measurements at dozens of stone monuments from Cornwall to Aberdeenshire, Lockyer concluded that there were many significant alignments on the sun, moon and stars at a variety of British megalithic monuments. Further to this, he contended that the monuments were built to observe and mark the rising and setting places of heavenly bodies.

Boyle Somerville (1863–1936) was an important and distinguished Irish archaeologist (see the Summer 2009 issue of *Archaeology Ireland*). Using his considerable surveying skills, he undertook pioneering investigations of megalithic monuments in Ireland as well as Britain, and published a substantial body of research. He is recognised internationally as one of the founders of archaeo-astronomy.

Born in Castletownsend, west Cork, Somerville was a much-travelled Royal Navy surveyor. He rose up through the ranks to become vice-admiral shortly before retirement. While engaged in a hydrographical survey in

Lough Swilly, Co. Donegal, he carried out detailed investigations of ancient monuments in the vicinity, with a view to determining their associations with astronomical events.

Among Somerville's noteworthy contributions to archaeology was the establishment of significant alignments at the well-known Beltany stone circle (Co. Donegal), including one pointing to the sunrise on the May festival (Bealtaine) and another aligned on the winter-solstice sunrise. He undertook similar surveys in other parts of Ireland, including west Cork. Based on extensive investigations over a number of decades in Ireland and Britain, Somerville concluded that the monuments surveyed were laid out 'with definite intention, to the point of the horizon where sunrise or sunset took place on certain special days of the year …'.

Alexander Thom (1894–1985) was a professor of engineering at the University of Oxford and, following retirement, became one of the most influential twentieth-century figures in archaeo-astronomy. By the middle of the century Thom had accumulated a substantial volume of survey data covering several megalithic monuments in Britain. He subjected the data to rigorous statistical analysis and published articles in a wide range of academic journals, demonstrating the alignment of monuments upon the sun and moon.

Some archaeologists were prepared to consider that some monuments might possibly have been planned in relation to a celestial phenomenon. As further detailed by Ruggles (1999), however, the more far-flung contentions of Thom that stone circles and rows of standing stones were (i) laid out using precisely defined units of measurement and particular geometrical constructions and (ii) that the monuments were used to carry out meticulous observations of the sun, moon and stars led to a polarisation of views between archaeologists and astronomers. The ensuing protracted public debate was, as outlined below, coloured by assertions made in relation to the precision of the alignments, and the consequent astronomical uses attributed to them.

Stone rows: Munster and mid-Ulster

Linear settings of freestanding, regularly spaced stones were erected in prehistory in prominent locations (Ó Nualláin 1988; Lynch 1999; Burl 2000). Stone rows are also common in Britain and Brittany.

Over 200 stone rows have been recorded in the south of Ireland. They are differentiated into two categories, namely stone rows (also sometimes called 'alignments'), consisting of three to six stones, and stone pairs, comprising just two stones. The stones are of megalithic proportions, intervisible and set in short lines. They exhibit a general south-west/north-east alignment. A significant number are aligned on astronomical events, including the solstices and equinoxes, and the lunar standing positions (Lynch 1999).

The vast majority of stone rows in the south of Ireland (Fig. 2) are concentrated in Cork and Kerry. Single rows also occur in the adjoining counties of Clare, Limerick and Tipperary, and in the nearby counties of

Fig. 2 —
Stone row at
Maughanasilly,
Co. Cork
(National
Monuments
Service,
Department of
Arts, Heritage
and the
Gaeltacht).

Kilkenny and Waterford. They comprise no more than six stones, and the rows tend to be relatively short (around 2–13m). Those with three stones are by far the most common, followed by rows of four stones. In many cases the stones are roughly graded in height, with the tallest stone at one end and, more often than not, at the south-west.

Stone pairs in the south of Ireland are predominantly confined to Cork and Kerry. In the majority of cases they consist of a taller and a shorter stone (Fig. 3), typically around 2–4m in height and similar in size and shape to those in the stone rows. The gap between the two orthostats of stone pairs usually ranges from 0.5m to 4m (Fig. 1). Those with wider gaps are termed 'anomalous pairs'.

Some stone rows and pairs are sited close to five-stone circles (Fig. 4), boulder burials, cairns and enclosures. They are, however, more usually found in isolation.

Mid-Ulster stone rows are concentrated in Counties Tyrone, Fermanagh and Derry, and are distinctly different from the rows in Munster. They are characteristically composed of large numbers of low stones set close together and seldom exceeding 1m in height. The rows are frequently set tangentially to stone circles, and can extend for 30m or more in length, as is evident at the Beaghmore complex, Co. Tyrone (*Archaeology Ireland*, Spring 2011). A number of short rows of three or four tall stones also occur at the site, again set tangentially to the circles. The Ulster rows are sometimes accompanied by cairns, cists and monoliths.

The striking morphological differences between the Munster and Ulster rows may be indicative of different cultural traditions (Lynch 1999).

Dating

Excavations undertaken by Lynch (1999) indicate a date range of 1650–*c*. 800 cal. BC for two stone rows (Maughanasilly and Cashelkeelty) in the Munster group (Figs 2 and 4). Dates ranging from the late Neolithic to the late Bronze Age have been produced for the complex of stone circles and rows at Beaghmore. Burl placed stone rows in Britain and Ireland in the period 1800–1200 cal. BC. He suggested that stone circles are generally earlier than stone rows, with stone pairs presenting the final manifestations of a linear tradition.

Function

The astronomical precision implied for the alignments associated with stone monuments seldom existed (Burl 2000). The 'accuracy' of the alignments could be as coarse as ±5°, and would have militated against their use as 'astronomical observatories' for solar or lunar observations and prediction of eclipses, as postulated by some proponents of archaeo-astronomy.

Burl, however, considers the possible calendrical interpretation of the alignments as valid, but notes that 'the evidence for it is weak'. Based on a reappraisal of alignments reported from a diverse range of sites in Britain, he concluded that eight declinations seemed to emphasise risings and settings of the sun around ±16° and ±24°, coinciding with the major 'Celtic' festivals. The two solstices were strongly emphasised, with midwinter being recorded almost twice as heavily as midsummer. Consequently, he noted that 'the turning points of the year, particularly the time of change from darkness and cold to light and warmth, were of very great importance to prehistoric people'.

Fig. 3—Stone pair, Clogherane, Co. Kerry (National Monuments Service, Department of Arts, Heritage and the Gaeltacht).

By heralding the approach of such seasonal changes, megalithic monuments, properly aligned, could have fulfilled important calendrical functions.

Astronomical alignments seem to have served multiple functions, but one vital use may have applied to the seasonality of farming and its operation at community level. Agrarian societies observed the movement of heavenly bodies as indicators of the changing seasons and the availability of food supplies (Lynch 1999). Seasonal timing is today a widely recognised imperative in crop cultivation and cattle-breeding and husbandry. Indeed, in recent decades, a 'farming calendar' has been strongly advocated by agriculturalists as an invaluable husbandry tool. Even by observing seasonal changes in biodiversity, time-critical annual farming practices could hardly have been carried out successfully and consistently by prehistoric communities without advance notice of the approaching growing season and a reliable means, even if crude, for the calendrical scheduling of the farming cycle. Thus it may not be too speculative to consider that the alignments built into certain monuments may, among other purposes, have been used in prehistory for the timely undertaking of seasonal farming practices. In essence, they may be seen as an early agricultural technology and perhaps what Burl (2000) refers to as a part 'of the Neolithic mixed farming tool-kit'. Further to this, he observes that a line of stones for computation would be more efficient than a stone circle.

The use of stone circles for burial, ceremonial rites, religious practices and community gatherings has been well articulated. The purpose(s) behind the construction and location of stone rows is much less clear. Nevertheless, given their relatively simply structure and notwithstanding suggestions of a symbolic *axis mundi* in prehistoric alignments, a utilitarian function of stone rows, and perhaps even more so stone pairs, may have been calendrical.

Astronomical alignment is a common feature of wedge tombs, stone circles and stone rows. The intrinsically different architecture of the three monument types may reflect the inherent purpose for which each was originally constructed. Although an oversimplification that masks overlapping layers of intention, their respective design functions, in the transition from the Neolithic into the Bronze Age, could perhaps be envisaged as extending from burial repositories and associated symbolism in the case of wedge tombs to ceremonial enclosures for stone circles, and to seasonal calendrical functions, route and territorial boundary markers for stone rows.

Fig. 4—Stone row and five-stone circle with internal cist grave at Cashelkeelty, Co. Cork (Connie Murphy).

| **Box 1** | **Diagnostic features** |

- Deliberate placement of freestanding, spaced, intervisible stones.
- The Munster stone rows typically comprise relatively short lines of three to six stones of megalithic proportions and exhibiting a general south-west/north-east alignment; the majority occur in isolation but they are found sited close to stone circles, boulder burials, cairns and enclosures.
- The mid-Ulster stone rows consist of large numbers of low stones set close together and often running tangentially to stone circles for up to 30m or more in length; some short rows of three to four tall stones also occur. The rows and circles are often set in clusters accompanied by cairns, cists and monoliths.

Acknowledgements

The information and insights kindly provided by Ann Lynch, Brian Lacey, Paul Walsh and Connie Murphy are gratefully acknowledged. The photographs provided by the Department of Arts, Heritage and the Gaeltacht (National Monuments Service) and by Connie Murphy are much appreciated.

References

Burl, A. (ed.) 2000 *The stone circles of Britain, Ireland and Brittany*. London.

Lynch, A. 1999 Excavation of a stone row at Maughanasilly, Co. Cork. *Journal of the Cork Historical and Archaeological Society* **14**, 1–20.

Ó Nualláin, S. 1988 Stone rows in the south of Ireland. *Proceedings of the Royal Irish Academy* **88**C, 178–256.

Ruggles, C. (ed.) 1999 *Astronomy in prehistoric Britain and Ireland*. London.

This article was originally published in the Summer 2011 issue of Archaeology Ireland.

Boulder burials

The large coverstone (or boulder) that characterises most boulder burials rests on a nest of three or four much smaller stones, which act more as props for the coverstone than as walls defining a chamber. Some boulder burials cover a pit containing possible fragments of cremated bone and/or some charcoal or burnt soil. They date in the region 1500–800 BC.

With few exceptions, boulder burials occur in south-west Cork and Kerry, suggesting a localised tradition. The majority occur as single monuments in their own right, with some clustering in pairs or in groups of three or four, but they are also often found in association with other Bronze Age monuments common in the south-west—sometimes with one or more boulder burials enclosed in a stone circle or located close by.

Fig. 1—Boulder burial, Uragh townland, Co. Kerry. This monument is located in a stone circle overlooking Inchiquin (sketch by Margaret Kennedy).

Monumental boulders

The so-called boulder burial consists of a single large coverstone (or boulder) resting on a nest of three or more very much smaller flat-topped supporting stones, which often scarcely protrude above ground level (Fig. 1). The evidence to hand suggests that these monuments were built during the Bronze Age as memorials over burial deposits.

Structural details

The coverstone is typically about 1–2m long by 1m wide and 1m thick, although greater dimensions are known. The supporting stones seldom protrude more than 0.25m above ground level. Sometimes small wedge-stones placed between the coverstone and the supporting stones position the coverstone in such a way that its upper surface forms a level plane. At first sight in some instances the coverstones of boulder burials might be mistaken for the capstones of megalithic tombs, especially the Carrowmore type of passage tomb or even a small portal tomb (dolmen). What sets the boulder burial apart, however, is the low stature of the supporting stones and the fact that they act more as props for the coverstone than as walls of a formal chamber. Boulder burials stand above the ground and, unlike the megalithic tombs, there is no evidence that they were covered by cairns or mounds.

What was their purpose?

Some boulder burials have been found to cover a pit containing possible fragments of cremated bone and/or some charcoal or burnt soil. From this it has been inferred that boulder burials may have been intended as memorials over formal or token burial deposits. This interpretation is reinforced by their occasional association with other ceremonial or quasi-ceremonial monuments, such as stone circles, stone rows, lone standing stones (gallauns) and radial stone settings (Fig. 2).

Where are they found?

Boulder burials are, with few exceptions, located in south-west Cork and Kerry, where they are mainly concentrated in coastal areas. About 80% of all known boulder burials occur in these two counties, suggesting that the tradition was a localised one. A large number occur on the Beara Peninsula, reflecting their close association with copper-bearing areas. The general distribution coincides broadly with the occurrence of distinctive Bronze Age

Fig. 2 — A pair of boulder burials and a standing stone (right foreground), Derrynamucklagh townland, Co. Kerry (photo: Connie Murphy).

features in south-west Ireland, such as gallauns, stone circles, stone rows, wedge tombs and rock art. Of the 80 or more boulder burials known in the 1990s, the majority (50) were single monuments, although there were six pairs, two groups of three and three groups of four (Figs 2 and 3). There appears to have been a link with the so-called multiple-stone circle, although the precise nature of the link is unclear. The multiple-stone circle is distinguished from a more coherent stone circle subgroup, the so-called five-stone circle, by the proliferation of stones along the perimeter. Ten multiple-stone circles, all in the Kenmare/Bantry region, enclose one or more boulder burials, while a further three occur adjacent to boulder burials. We do not have sufficient evidence at this stage to state definitively which came first.

How old are they?
A generation ago it was taken for granted that boulder burials and the various other ceremonial monuments with which they appeared to be associated could be assigned to the early Bronze Age. Archaeological excavation and the application of radiocarbon dating have challenged this perception and it is now suggested that many of these monuments belong to the middle and later part of the Bronze Age, the boulder burials dating from about 1500–800 BC.

Diagnostic features
- Single large boulder resting on a nest of smaller stones that seldom constitute a formal chamber.
- Usually occurring alone but occasionally in pairs or clusters, or within a multiple-stone circle, or adjacent to a stone row or other monument.
- Normally found in Counties Cork and Kerry.

Fig. 3 — Group of four boulder burials, townland of Derrymihan West, Castletownbere, Co. Cork (photo: Connie Murphy).

References

O'Brien, W. 1992 Boulder-burials: a Late Bronze Age megalith tradition in south-west Ireland. *Journal of the Cork Historical and Archaeological Society* **97**, 11–35.

Ó Nualláin, S. 1978 Boulder-burials. *Proceedings of the Royal Irish Academy* **78**C, 75–114.

Ó Nualláin, S. 1991 Stone circles, stone rows, boulder-burials and standing stones. In M. Ryan (ed.), *The illustrated archaeology of Ireland*. Dublin.

Ó Ríordáin, S.P. 1979 *Antiquities of the Irish countryside*. London.

Waddell, J. 2000 *The prehistoric archaeology of Ireland*. Bray.

Walsh, P. 1993 In circle and row: Bronze Age ceremonial monuments. In E. Shee Twohig and M. Ronayne (eds), *Past perceptions: the prehistoric archaeology of south-west Ireland*. Cork.

This article was originally published in the Autumn 2003 issue of Archaeology Ireland.

Ogham stones

Ogham stones in Ireland are concentrated mainly in Counties Kerry, Cork and Waterford, but they are also known in many other parts of the country. The inscriptions occur predominantly on stones located at ecclesiastical sites or built into the fabric of souterrains. From their context, it is surmised that a large number of ogham stones served simply as grave markers. They might also, however, have marked a sacred place, a burial ground, a grant or title for land, a tribal boundary, a church foundation or a hermitage.

The use of ogham is identified with the early centuries of Christianity in Ireland and is thought to have been especially prevalent from the fourth or fifth century AD to the seventh century. It appears to have fallen out of fashion as the more standard form of writing took hold at the dawn of Old Irish, the ancestor of Modern Irish.

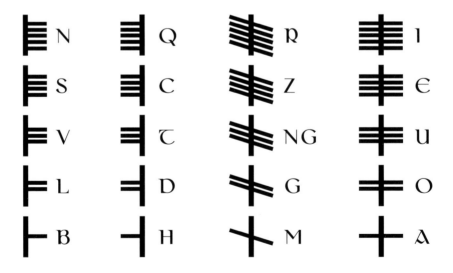

Fig. 1—Ogham alphabet used in inscriptions
(courtesy of the Ogham in 3D Project).

Earliest writing in Ireland

Ogham inscriptions are of great antiquity and have been described as Ireland's oldest documents, surviving from an otherwise undocumented age. While we may never know with any certainty precisely when, where or why this uniquely Irish inscription system was devised, the outline below indicates some notable advances in our understanding of how the ogham system operated, its functions, archaeological dimensions and relative chronology (McManus 1991; 2004; Swift 1997; Moore 2010).

The innovative Ogham in 3D Project (McKenna and Kelly 2010), based in the School of Celtic Studies at the Dublin Institute for Advanced Studies, which is being undertaken in collaboration with the Discovery Programme and the National Monuments Service, has opened up new horizons in the recording, study and conservation of ogham inscriptions (Box 1).

Box 1	Ogham in 3D Project

Using 3D technology, the project will capture inscriptions in greater detail (Fig. 2) and facilitate the reading of the weathered and worn ogham characters, including where possible the digital reconstruction of broken ogham stones (Fig. 3).

Up to 70 ogham stones have so far been digitised and are freely available on a dedicated searchable website (http://ogham.celt.dias.ie). This allows the inscriptions to be searched by personal and tribal names, formula words, site types and the presence of a cross on the stone, as well as by relative chronology of linguistic features. The 3D models also have the potential, for example, to facilitate the determination of whether crosses on ogham stones pre-date the inscriptions or vice versa.

Following the launch of the project, a number of new ogham discoveries have been reported, as well as the rediscovery of a 'long-lost' ogham stone in County Kerry.

Source: Nora White (pers. comm.)

Inscriptions

The ogham alphabet (Fig. 1) utilised for inscriptions on stones comprised a series of twenty characters arranged in four groups, each group made up of one to five scores/lines disposed to the right or left of, or diagonally across, a stem-line (McManus 2004). For vowels a system of mere notches was often

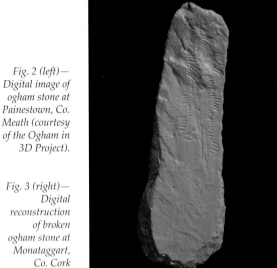

Fig. 2 (left)—Digital image of ogham stone at Painestown, Co. Meath (courtesy of the Ogham in 3D Project).

Fig. 3 (right)—Digital reconstruction of broken ogham stone at Monataggart, Co. Cork (courtesy of the Ogham in 3D Project).

used. The stem-line is usually the natural edge of the stone, but sometimes it may be actually carved on the stone.

Ogham inscriptions were generally carved by starting at the bottom left-hand side of the stone face. Thus the ogham is usually read upwards along the left-hand edge of the stone and sometimes across the top and then down the other side.

The letters in the alphabet (Fig. 1) can be shown to have been of great historical antiquity and were themselves meaningful words in the language (McManus 2004). The largest single semantic category of letter names was an arboreal one, such as *beithe* (birch tree), *dair* (oak tree), *fern* (alder tree), *onn* (ash tree) and *sáil* (willow tree).

In establishing the meaning of the names of the letters and the original value of the symbols reflected in the initial sound of the name, McManus underlined the great importance of Old Irish 'keenings' (Irish funeral songs accompanied by wailing). The name of the third symbol in the alphabet was *fern* ('alder tree' in Old Irish) and the keenings point to the use of alder for the making of shields and vessels for containing liquids.

The ogham system has much in common with the primitive tally and operates by marking position to a fixed series of sounds (McManus 2004). Orthodox bilingual (Latin/Roman and Irish ogham) inscriptions in Wales, the Isle of Man, Devon and Cornwall provide the key for the majority of the sounds, and the later manuscript tradition fills in the gaps. The inscriptions follow a limited number of formulae. As explained by Moore (2010), they usually took the form of 'X *maqi* Y', meaning 'X son of Y'. They can also read

'X *avi* (grandson of) Y' or 'X *maqi mucoi* (descendant of) Y', where *mucoi* refers to an ancestral deity or eponymous figure. Female names are rare; *inigena*, 'daughter of', occurs on one stone in Wales. *Niotta*, 'nephew of', is found on one stone at Garraunddarragh near Castleisland, Co. Kerry (Moore 2010).

The language of the inscriptions in ogham is invariably Irish; many of those in Britain, however, are accompanied by contemporary equivalents in Latin and in Roman character (Fig. 4), and are accordingly generally termed 'bilinguals' (McManus 2004). A number of the inscriptions in Scotland also use the ogham script but differ from those above in using a language other than Irish, namely Pictish or possibly Old Norse.

Archaeology

An estimated 360 ogham stones have been recorded in Ireland, and in conjunction with those in Britain the total number exceeds 400 (Moore 2010).

The distribution of ogham stones in Ireland has a marked southern bias. They are concentrated predominantly in Munster (70% of total), notably in Counties Kerry, Cork and Waterford. The ogham stones in Wales, Scotland and the Isle of Man are generally found in areas of Irish settlement during the period of decline of the Roman Empire.

The location of ogham stones recorded at various archaeological sites commonly found in Ireland has been analysed by Moore (1998). They occur predominantly at ecclesiastical sites and in souterrains. Ogham inscriptions are also found on an appreciable number of lone standing stones, with fewer at other archaeological site types.

The distribution of ogham stones recorded at various types of archaeological sites in Munster is shown in Fig. 5. This highlights the relatively high concentrations found both at ecclesiastical sites and in souterrains, and, to a lesser extent, on standing stones of probable prehistoric date (Moore 1998).

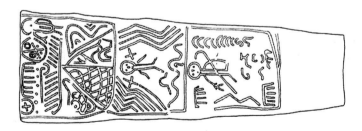

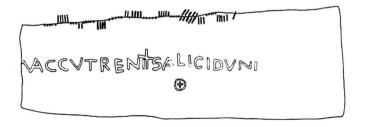

Fig. 4—Bilingual inscription in Latin and ogham at Tre Castle, Wales (courtesy of F. Moore and K. O'Brien).

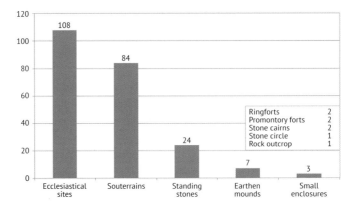

Fig. 5—Ogham stones recorded at various types of archaeological sites in Munster (from Moore 1998).

Functions

A large number of ogham stones served simply as grave markers. The existence of ogham stones at a variety of site types (Fig. 5) indicates, however, that they may have had a broader function. This is further underlined by their location on geographical and political boundaries and by their prominent position within a number of church sites (Moore 1998).

Early Irish legal texts refer to ogham inscriptions, giving them official recognition as documents confirming title to land (McManus 2004). Thus it appears that ogham stones may have had an important function in asserting land ownership and fixing territorial boundaries (Moore 2010).

Moore (1998) suggests that a close examination of the siting of ogham stones may make it possible to determine instances where an ogham stone could have marked a sacred place, a burial ground, a grant or title for land, a tribal boundary, a church foundation, a hermitage or, indeed, a combination of some of these. The presence of ogham inscriptions on what would otherwise be regarded as prehistoric monuments, such as standing stones and stone rows (*Archaeology Ireland*, Summer 2011), may, as indicated by Moore, imply that there was a continuity of function from prehistoric times into the early medieval period in relation to these particular sites. Alternatively, it may simply reflect the reuse of a prominent landscape feature.

In addition to these functions, McManus (2004) alluded to the view that ogham was designed as a vehicle for the Irish language and may perhaps have been invented as an exclusive system with the intention that it should be the preserve of the learned. The system was, according to McManus, the framework for the study of Irish letters from the Old Irish period (seventh–ninth centuries) until the demise of the native schools of Classical Modern Irish (seventeenth century) and, as previously mentioned, was regarded as uniquely Irish.

Origins and dating

According to the explanatory myth found in manuscripts, the Biblical narrative of the creation of linguistic diversity inspired the invention of the ogham system of writing and the Irish language (McManus 2004). McManus also mentions a separate tradition that ascribes the invention of ogham to Ogma Mac Elathán of the Tuatha Dé Danann.

Absolute dating of ogham stones is not possible and archaeological evidence points generally to the early medieval period. McManus (1991; 2004) utilised relative linguistic analysis of the inscriptions to propose that they belong to the period from the fourth/fifth century to the seventh century. While the period of the creation of the alphabet cannot be determined with any certainty, there is reason to suppose that it belongs to an earlier period than that of the first inscriptions on memorial stones (Swift 1997).

Using dating evidence for the linguistic evolution of Primitive and Archaic Irish developed by McManus (1991), the vast corpus of ogham stones has been categorised by Swift (1997) into four subgroups. The characteristics of the inscriptions in the individual subgroups and the understanding of their relative chronology are summarised in Box 2.

The use of ogham belongs to the Christian period and it appears to have fallen out of fashion at the dawn of Old Irish (McManus 1991; 2004). This view is further substantiated by Swift's analysis, outlined below. The four subgroups categorised in Box 2 reveal strong indicators of the presence of Christianity. The Christian feature of the Maltese cross group (Fig. 6) is clearly evident. The use of the word *ANM* in the second subgroup (Box 2) is thought to derive from Christian burial formulae using the word *nomen*; five of the twenty examples are ornamented with crosses (Swift 1997), and at least two of the six stones with Latin names have associated crosses. The word $> < 01$ in ogham is seemingly derived from another Christian formula, using the phrase *HIC IACET*, and at least two of the stones have crosses (Swift 1997). McManus suggested that $> < 01$ may be a word for locality and that it is analogous to the use of *HIC IACET* on Latin memorial stones in Britain.

In respect of the two earlier subgroups of Irish ogham (Box 2), Swift observed that those which commemorated men with Latin names and those which incorporated the $> < 01$ formula seem to parallel Roman practice most closely.

Box 2   Diagnostic features

- Ogham stones with Maltese crosses (Fig. 6) appear to be later sixth and early seventh century and continued to be used for Latin inscriptions until the eighth century.
- Ogham stones with an inscription beginning with *ANM* seem to belong predominantly to the later sixth or even the early seventh century.
- Ogham stones with Latin names appear to belong to the earlier half of the dating range for ogham, possibly from the fifth to approximately the first half of the sixth century.
- Ogham stones incorporating the element $> < 01$ may also be assigned to the fifth century and the first half of the sixth century.

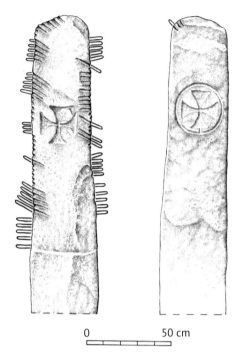

Acknowledgements

The informative publications received from Fionnbarr Moore, Damian McManus and Fergus Kelly are much appreciated. The outline of progress in the Ogham in 3D Project provided by Nora White is gratefully acknowledged, as are the contributions of Bob Lawlor and Dick Coveney.

Fig. 6—Ogham stone with Maltese cross at Arraglen, Mount Brandon, Co. Kerry (courtesy of F. Moore and K. O'Brien).

0   50 cm

References

McKenna, M. and Kelly, F. 2010 The Ogham in 3D Pilot Project: a report on work in progress. *Celtica* **31**, 200–4.

McManus, D. 1991 *A guide to ogham*. Maynooth.

McManus, D. 2004 *The ogham stones at University College Cork*. Cork.

Moore, F. 1998 Munster ogham stones: siting, context and function. In M.A. Monk and J. Sheehan (eds), *Early medieval Munster: archaeology, history and society*. Cork.

Moore, F. 2010 The ogham stones of County Kerry. In G. Murray (ed.), *Medieval treasures of County Kerry*. Tralee.

Swift, C. 1997 *Ogham stones and the earlier Irish Christians*. Maynooth.

This article was originally published in the Summer 2014 issue of Archaeology Ireland.

Holy wells

Holy wells are a common feature of the Irish countryside, sometimes located beside or within an ancient ecclesiastical site, and are often associated with a venerated tree or a venerated stone. These elements, very much associated with local expressions of Christianity, are important symbolically in age-old Irish mythology. The tradition of the venerated tree (a *bile* in medieval Irish) and its uncommon powers, notably of healing, pre-dates the arrival of Christianity. The venerated or healing stones found at some holy wells comprise three 'functional' types, namely stones as heads, stones as tables and stones as beds or seats. The stone as head seems to be the most prevalent and it is interesting in this regard that drinking the water from a specific local holy well is often believed to provide a cure for headaches.

With the coming of Christianity, the venerated springs of prehistory were transformed into holy wells. It would seem, however, that this was a gradual and incremental process over the centuries.

Fig. 1—Holy well (marked by the standing stone in the foreground) in Killamery churchyard, Co. Kilkenny, with a decorated high cross in the background. This site may have been linked with the Gobán Saor.

Folk shrines

Holy wells provide an opportunity to observe and study sacred sites and practices, many of which may have their origins in the prehistoric period. The practice of visiting holy wells was one of the three main expressions of Catholic devotion in pre-Famine Ireland. The other two were (i) the household-based 'stations', which were a response to the restrictions of the Penal Laws and appear in the documentary records in the 1780s, when the patterns at holy wells were declining, and (ii) the chapel-based practice, which achieved dominance in the nineteenth century (Ó Giolláin 2005).

Location

With virtually every townland having at least one holy well, and with some counties having 100 or more, estimates put the total number of holy wells in Ireland at more than 3,000. While they also occur in cities and towns, the majority are in the countryside, many near the ruins of medieval parish churches or on the sides of hills or mountains or by the seashore. According to Brenneman and Brenneman (1995), the three main topographical locations of holy wells are: (i) generally in meadows or boggy areas at the centre of bowl-like formations; (ii) less frequently in rocky or mountainous areas, often on mountain passes, and associated with the cure of bones or teeth; and (iii) on the seashore, sometimes a few yards inland, or at the very edge of the shore and occasionally within the tidal surf. They are also found on islands, either offshore or in lakes. These contexts may be symbolically important. Several large finds of votive deposits have been uncovered that indicate the ritual use of wells and other water bodies.

Names

Holy wells are usually dedicated to saints, mostly Irish saints of local or national importance (Ó Giolláin 2005). The two most prevalent dedications in all four provinces are to St Brigid and St Patrick. Other common dedications are to Mary, Christ or God. The wells of universal saints are much less numerous than those of native saints. Some wells are called after priests who lived in relatively recent times. The names of others reflect their curative attributes, such as *Tobar na Súl* (Well of the Eyes), *Tobar na Deilge* (Well of the Thorns) or *Tobar an Ailt* (Well of the Joints).

Oral legends are a characteristic feature of holy wells. The origin of the well is sometimes attributed to the saint being thirsty or letting a tear fall on the spot, from which a well sprang up. In other legends, an existing well was sanctified by a saint and a wonderful cure took place there. There are numerous legends of wells that moved because they were profaned.

Cures

Catholics went to holy wells to obtain a cure for some physical ailment or for release from sin and its associated punishment (Ó Giolláin 2005). The most common ailments for which cures were sought included mental illness, sickness in children, eye diseases, tooth-, head- or backaches, sprains, wounds, rheumatism, barrenness and the safe delivery of children. The patron saint was also believed to keep plagues and influenza from a district. A piece of coloured cloth or sometimes a tassel of a shawl was left at the well, often attached to a venerated tree, as outlined below.

Visits to wells were also believed to heal animals. In a number of counties, cattle are reported to have been driven to holy wells on the saint's feast day. Also, the swimming of horses in lakes and their presence at holy wells were common at Lughnasa festivals.

Structural features

The spring, a venerated tree (termed the *bile*) and venerated stones are the three prominent features of holy-well sites, and each is important symbolically in ancient Irish mythology (Brenneman and Brenneman 1995). All three features need not occur at every well site. It is estimated that possibly half contain all three and another third have just two of the components. A minority of sites contain only the spring.

Venerated trees, in terms of their longevity and self-renewal, are important symbolic features of holy wells, although they do not occur at all

Fig. 2—St Kieran's Well, Cooleeshill, Co. Tipperary.

Fig. 3—Holy well at Kilkieran, Co. Kilkenny, with adjacent bullaun stone. The well is located beside the churchyard, with a La Tène-type phallic stone standing between the well and some decorated high crosses. Note the ladle hanging on the fence.

sites. Like the water, which was believed not to boil, the branches of the *bile* overhanging holy wells were also believed not to burn. At many sites the venerated tree is festooned with pieces of coloured cloth, which are believed to contain the illness, pain or sins of the wearer. The *bile* takes upon itself the accumulated illnesses or sins of the parish, or, in earlier times, of the *tuath*.

Venerated trees, and the attribution to them of healing or other powers, pre-date the arrival of Christianity in Ireland. Trees that were important in the Celtic calendar, such as ash, hazel and whitethorn, are still found at some holy-well sites. However, the most common trees at holy wells today are whitethorn and hawthorn.

Venerated or healing stones, often found at holy-well sites, have been subdivided into three functional types, namely stones as heads, stones as tables and stones as beds or seats (Brenneman and Brenneman 1995). While these three structural features may be found at wells, the stone as a head seems to be the most prevalent. It functions symbolically as a head and is generally associated with fertility. Often the head stone is mounted upon a pillar stone. For example, at Olan's Well in Aghbulloge, Co. Cork, the head stone sits upon an ogham-inscribed pillar. Touching or inscribing the head stone was said to cure headaches. Two other forms of head stones, again associated with fertility, are **egg-shaped stones** and **butter stones**. A bullaun stone with indentations containing worn oval pebbles, termed **butter lumps**, was used in the Easter Pattern ritual at Tousist, Co. Kerry. The water in the hollows of stones associated with holy wells was often believed to be curative.

Stone tables most commonly comprise a large flagstone raised a few feet above the ground by four pillar stones. They are sometimes compared to small dolmens and are thought to have symbolically similar functions. The ritual of crawling under the table stone was believed to cure backaches.

The **stone bed or seat**, which was also said to have the power to heal backaches, may be found in the form of a container or trough, possibly embedded in the ground. Alternatively, it may function as a seat, as for example the large stone at Earl's Well (Co. Kildare) known as the Chair of Kildare, upon which the earls of Kildare were inaugurated. A similar stone sits at the inauguration site of the earls of Thomond, Magh Adhair near the town of Quinn in County Clare. In other cases, stones with indentations considered to be the marks of the saint's feet or knees are found in the general vicinity of holy wells.

Patterns

The festival celebrated at holy wells or other sites such as ecclesiastical ruins, usually on the patron saint's feast day, is known as the **Pattern** (or **Patron**) **Day**. While holy wells were visited by individuals at all times of the year, the water was believed to be most efficacious on the patron saint's feast day. Many accounts exist of the well-attended religious practices, festive and other events that took place at patterns held throughout Ireland in previous centuries.

The distinctive feature of the religious practices performed at Irish holy wells is the rounding ritual (Ó Giolláin 2005). Those performed at different sites were broadly similar, but with distinct local variations. A number of circuits or rounds, often an odd number, were made around the well and other features of the site, such as a cross or venerated stone, at which the pilgrims knelt and prayed, frequently reciting the rosary. The rounds were usually made in a clockwise direction and in some instances a small stone was dropped each time around. They were often undertaken barefoot, taking some hours to complete, and many accounts detail the severe mortification sometimes involved.

While pagan origins have been assumed for the rounds performed at holy wells, direct evidence of ritual activity at wells in pre-Christian times or in the times of the early saints is limited; neither are rounding rituals mentioned in medieval accounts of the Irish church (Ó Giolláin 2005). However, patterns at holy wells seem to have been well established by the seventeenth century, and there are occasional earlier references to rounding and stations. Some contend that the tradition of making rounds developed in the post-Reformation, Tridentine period. The legitimisation of holy-well cults by local clergy was an important factor in their popularity. The hierarchy seemed to support patterns, as long as superstitious practices formed no part of them, and the potency of the well was attributed to the patron saint.

Those attending were drawn from the local parish(es), but many travelled long distances to important patterns, which usually went on for a few days. Many patterns had a secular as well as a religious aspect, and were the occasion for various types of entertainment.

The period 1760–1830 saw a marked decline in the popularity of patterns, and by 1850 many wells had fallen into disuse (Ó Giolláin 2005). In recent years many holy wells have been tidied up and made accessible. The pattern is still a tradition in many parts of the country. While usually held on the saint's feast day, it may also take place at the time of important Christian festivals, such as Easter Sunday, midsummer or St John's Eve. Most patterns are held in the summer and autumn, especially in July.

Origins

Extensive medieval writings in Latin and Irish link holy wells to early Irish Christianity, and indeed early mythology, where the origins of many of them may be found (Brenneman and Brenneman 1995; Ó Giolláin 2005).

There are holy wells close to many ancient sites, such as Tara and Rathcroghan, and some wells retain much of their pre-Christian character. At sites associated with St Kieran of Saighir, for example, phallic-shaped standing stones occur in the general vicinity of the holy well.

Ancient features associated with holy wells, such as the venerated or healing stones, have been incorporated into the practices or rituals still performed there. Some wells are associated with night-time pilgrimage. Some are linked with the festival of Lughnasa, a pre-Christian ritual associated with the Celtic god Lug. A large number of patterns at holy wells, in particular those located on mountainsides, still take place at the time of the old Lughnasa feast, now usually celebrated on the last Sunday of July and often known as Garland Sunday. In addition to these mythological associations, the location of springs at all surviving inauguration sites points to the importance of sacred springs in the inauguration of kings. One of the most prominent sites in this regard is Doon Well (Kilmacrennan, Co. Donegal), which was the O'Donnell inauguration site up to the seventeenth century.

Fig. 4—Bullaun stone located beside the holy well in Kilkieran churchyard, County Kilkenny.

With the coming of Christianity, the venerated springs of prehistory were transformed into holy wells. This was a gradual process that took place in increments over centuries, and the combination of holy well, sacred tree and sacred stone provided the primary symbolism around the transformation from paganism to Christianity.

Checklist of diagnostic features

- The predominant structural features of holy-well sites are the spring, the venerated tree and stones. Many of the sites contain all three or at least two of these features, with a minority containing only the spring.
- Holy wells are predominantly found in meadow or boggy areas, at the centre of a bowl-like formation. Those in rocky/mountain areas, often in mountain passes, are less common. Some are found on the seashore, near the edge or within the tidal surf. Many holy wells are located at ancient ecclesiastical sites or near medieval parish churches.

References

Brenneman, W.L. Jr and Brenneman, M.G. 1995 *Crossing the circle at the holy wells in Ireland*. Charlottesville and London.

Ó Giolláin, D. 2005 Revisiting the holy well. *Éire-Ireland: An interdisciplinary journal of Irish studies* **40** (1–2), 11–41.

This article was originally published in the Spring 2006 issue of Archaeology Ireland.

Mass rocks

Around 300 Mass-rock sites have been recorded in Ireland. Their distribution exhibits a western bias, with notable concentrations in the Cork/Kerry area and northwards to Galway/Mayo and the Shannon region.

In general, Mass rocks are relatively large, earthfast boulders ranging up to 2m in height. They were sited in remote areas away from main roads, but generally at well-known local landmarks such as ringforts or elevated places, sometimes commanding a good view of the approaches.

In later penal days, Mass sites seem to have been gradually improved. In some locations, a temporary shelter and perhaps a permanent roof was erected over the altar. This might ultimately have led to the subsequent formation of a Mass house, transitioning in some cases to a modest chapel and, occasionally perhaps, in later years, to the first post-penal church.

Fig. 1—'A Christmas Mass in the Penal Days' by John Dooley, reproduced in the Christmas 1884 issue of the United Irishman *(courtesy of the National Library of Ireland, Dublin).*

Clandestine worship

Mass sites are generally seen as being a consequence of the Penal Laws, which were in operation from 1695 until 1829. The origins of the sites can, however, be traced from the previous century; they appear to have come into use after the suppression of the monasteries in 1540 (Nugent 2013). The Cromwellian persecutions of the mid-1600s imprinted the Mass-site tradition on Irish culture (Fig. 1), and many of the Mass sites seem to have been in use in that period (McCarthy 1989).

Box 1	Pen-picture of the main restrictions on Catholics under the Penal Laws

Religion

Keeping of church registers; exercise of the religion; attendance at Catholic worship; guardianship of children. Compelled to attend Protestant worship.

Education

Receiving education; teaching of children by a Catholic parent; having children educated by a Catholic teacher or sending them abroad for education.

Property

Land ownership, leasing and mortgaging; buying land from a Protestant; receiving land as a gift or as an inheritance from a Protestant; renting land that was worth more than 30 shillings a year; reaping a profit from land that exceeded a third of the rent; owning a horse of greater value than five pounds; and holding a life annuity.

Business

Engaging in trade or commerce; entering a profession; living in or within five miles of a corporate town.

Franchise

Voting, holding public office and keeping arms for self-protection.

Source: Murphy 2013

From 1695 a new set of Penal Laws were progressively introduced, two of which, enacted in the early years of the 1700s, defined the circumstances

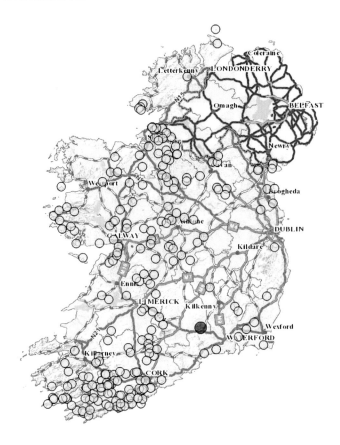

*Fig. 2—
Geographical
distribution
of Mass sites
(courtesy of
the National
Monuments
Service,
Department of
the Environment,
Heritage and the
Gaeltacht).*

under which clergy were allowed to operate (Box 1), as further detailed by Nugent (2013) and Murphy (2013). The Act of Registering the Popish Clergy, introduced in 1704, required all priests and bishops to register at their local court and to provide security of 100 pounds, to be forfeited if they engaged in non-peaceable behaviour. They were barred from practising outside of their designated parish. In 1709 the crown decided that all registered priests would now have to take the Oath of Abjuration, which effectively demanded that they renounce their religion (Murphy 2013). Just 33 priests in Ireland swore the oath. Consequently, all other priests were operating outside the law.

The crown offered a bounty for the apprehension of Catholic clergy 'of 50 pounds and 20 pounds for each regular clergyman or non-registered secular clergyman so discovered and 10 pounds for each popish schoolmaster, usher or assistant'. Notably, the local people were forced to pay the bounty (Murphy 2013).

The bounty payments were very attractive relative to the annual wage of a skilled tradesman, such as a carpenter, which was just £15. As extensively documented by Murphy (2013), this led to the proliferation of what was commonly known as 'priest-catching'. From 1709 onwards, the Catholic clergy were vigorously pursued by priest-hunters, a number of whom developed fearsome reputations.

Fig. 3—Mass rock in the townland of Glanalin overlooking Bantry Bay, Co. Cork (courtesy of the National Monuments Service, Department of the Environment, Heritage and the Gaeltacht).

Geographical distribution

The database compiled by the National Monuments Service, Department of the Environment, Heritage and the Gaeltacht, Dublin, records 272 Mass rocks and 36 penal Mass stations. The Mass rocks show a western distribution (Fig. 2), with notable concentrations in the Cork/Kerry area (Figs 3–5), extending north into Galway and Mayo and along the Shannon region (Fig. 6).

In Northern Ireland over 30 Mass rocks/sites have been recorded by Built Heritage (Historic Monuments Unit) of the Northern Ireland Environmental Agency.

The two extensive surveys outlined below have made important contributions to our understanding of Mass sites, and their gradual development over the centuries.

Fig. 4—Mass rock in the townland of Carhoo South, Co. Cork (courtesy of the National Monuments Service, Department of the Environment, Heritage and the Gaeltacht).

Diocese of Clogher

A landmark survey of what were termed 'field altars' in the parishes of Clogher was published by R. Ó Gallachair in 1957. A total of 141 sites were recorded, which have been classified into four main forms (Box 2). As outlined below, the survey has provided important insights into the improvement of Mass sites over time.

The first reference to Mass sites in the diocese of Clogher dated, according to Ó Gallachair, from the time of James I (1603–25), when Catholic religious practices became treasonable and were conducted surreptitiously on field altars in remote places. Many of the earlier field altars surveyed were marked on the 1609 maps of the Ulster confiscated counties, and 44 were recorded again in 1733.

In the later penal days, Mass sites in Clogher seem to have been gradually improved. As further detailed by Ó Gallachair (1957), in some locations a temporary shelter (*scalán*), and perhaps later a permanent roof (*bothóg*), was erected over the altars. These could possibly have led to the subsequent formation of a Mass house. Some five or more of these were recorded in the diocese in the 1730s/40s. This may have been followed by the transition in some areas to a modest chapel, and in later years the first post-penal church could have been built in some places. This progressive development is likely to have varied between localities; indeed, earlier Mass sites appear to have continued in use in various places.

County Cork

Over 160 Mass sites were recorded in the county by McCarthy (1989; 1991), of which some 100 are classified as Mass rocks, or *carraigh an aifrinn* sites.

The sites recorded were mainly concentrated south of a line from Cork city to Millstreet, with some extending to around Newmarket and Kanturk. No Mass rocks or altars were found in the valley of the Blackwater from Dromagh to Mallow, an area with much of the best land (McCarthy 1991). The vast majority of the known sites were on poor-quality land, which was

Fig. 5—Bullaun stone in the townland of Inishfoyle, Co. Kerry, which, according to local tradition, was used as a Mass rock in penal times (courtesy of the National Monuments Service, Department of the Environment, Heritage and the Gaeltacht).

Fig. 6—Mass rock consisting of a drystone slab of red sandstone, supported by a drystone-built pier, in the townland of Bridgecartron or Derrycashel, Co. Roscommon (courtesy of the National Monuments Service, Department of the Environment, Heritage and the Gaeltacht).

neglected by landlords. Many were on wetland or in rough wooded glens. Mass rocks and altar sites were located away from main roads but generally at well-known local landmarks, such as old forts. Mass sites were sometimes located close together, thereby allowing the altar to be shifted so as to provide some shelter for the priest and people in adverse weather conditions.

The number of potential Mass-rock sites in the diocese of Cork and Ross has recently been extended to 181, a number of which were previously unrecorded (Hilary Bishop, pers. comm.). Some of the Mass rocks in County Cork are located in ringforts, for example the site at Drombeg, Clonakilty. Inscribed crosses have been recorded at a number of others, including those at Kilnadur and Curraheen.

While the survey was not intended to include Mass houses, McCarthy (1989) noted that a number of these were listed in County Cork in the early decades of the 1700s. What was often termed a Mass-house, however, was frequently only a shelter for the priest, leaving the congregation out in the open. In this regard, the 1731 Report on the State of Popery noted 'That in the parishes of Dromaleague and Caheragh … there are two reputed mass houses (one in each) which are only small shedds or cabbins [*sic*] covering an altar and in the parish of Dromaleague has been often removed from place to place'.

The Mass houses listed in County Cork were dated to 1714–23 (McCarthy 1989). Interestingly, those noted by Ó Gallachair (1957) were from around the same period—the 1730s/40s. Whether this may be interpreted as pointing to a broadly comparable pattern of development at Mass sites in the north and south of the country in the early part of the 1700s merits further investigation.

Form

Four forms of Mass site have been described, namely Mass rocks, field altars, Mass gardens and what is termed a *bothóg* or *scalán*. While the differentiation between some of the forms may in certain respects be somewhat tenuous, the main morphological features that typify these sites are synopsised in Box 2.

Other interesting features that may be seen at some Mass sites are inscriptions, such as a chalice or cross on a rock surface (Ó Gallachair 1957; McCarthy 1989; 1991). Crosses occur at a number of Mass sites, many of which were erected over the past century. Some Mass sites are located within existing ritual landscapes. The wedge tomb at Srahwee, near Killadoon in south-west Mayo, locally called *Altóir*, has a small cross incised on the surface of the roof stone (*Archaeology Ireland*, Summer 2000).

| **Box 2** | **Diagnostic features that typify different forms of Mass sites** |

Mass rock

A rock or earthfast boulder, typically large and varying in height from upwards of 3–5ft to 5–9ft, some being about 9ft long and around 4ft wide.

Field altar

Built of earth and stone, or with small flat stones, and some made of stone and lime.

Mass garden

A lone bush often sited within a hollow in a secluded place, and commonly known as the Mass, Holly or Thorn Bush.

Bothóg/scalán

A roof erected over the altars at some Mass sites.

Source: Ó Gallachair 1957—based largely on sites in the diocese of Clogher

Acknowledgements

The information provided by Paul Walsh, Grace Maloney, Edith Logue, Donogh McCarthy, Kevin Bartley, Mary Sleeman, Hilary Bishop, Joanna Nolan, Chris Corlett, Brendan Riordan, Ned Culleton, Barry O'Reilly and Jack Flynn is gratefully acknowledged. The photographs provided by Con Brogan, National Monuments Service, Department of the Environment, Heritage and the Gaeltacht, are much appreciated.

References

McCarthy, D. 1989 Mass rocks and altar sites of County Cork. *Times Past* (1989–90), 25–37.

McCarthy, D. 1991 *Seanchas Duthalla* (1991), 83–97.

Murphy, C.C. (ed.) 2013 *The priest hunters*. Dublin.

Nugent, T. (ed.) 2013 *'Were you at the rock?' The history of mass rocks in Ireland*. Dublin.

Ó Gallachair, R. 1957 Clogher's altars of the penal days. *Clogher Record* **2** (1), 97–130.

This article was originally published in the Spring 2014 issue of Archaeology Ireland.

Cillíní

The spatial segregation of children's burials in one section of a cemetery may have emerged in early medieval times.

Cillín burials are frequently perceived as having been secretive and unaccompanied by ceremony, often involving rapid disposal of the dead. However, excavations at Tonybaun (Co. Mayo) revealed that many of the bodies were interred in wood coffins, which, together with the grave-goods recovered, indicate the care and religious observances associated with these burials.

Fig. 1—Children's burial ground at Filane West, Co. Cork (photo: Connie Murphy, reproduced courtesy of the National Monuments Service, Department of Arts, Heritage and the Gaeltacht).

Children's burial grounds

*C*illín burial grounds are generally associated with stillborn and unbaptised children. Several other classes of people, however, were also deemed ineligible for burial in consecrated ground and were generally interred in *cillín* sites. Among these were suicides, the mentally disabled, the shipwrecked, criminals, famine victims and strangers—and also, it seems, women who had not been 'churched' after childbirth (Nolan 2006; Donnelly and Murphy 2008; Murphy 2011).

Children's burial grounds are well known in many parts of the country. Around 1,394 have been recorded in the database compiled by the Archaeological Survey of Ireland. They show a marked western distribution, with high concentrations in Counties Galway and Mayo, as well as Counties Clare and Roscommon (Fig. 6). The extent to which this may reflect the relatively comprehensive field surveys undertaken in some of these counties is uncertain. It may be noted, however, that the townland name Cealtragh, generally explained as 'burial ground' and sometimes used to denote *cillíní*, is an element chiefly found in the western half of Ireland (C. Ó Crualaoich, Placename Branch, Department of Arts, Heritage and the Gaeltacht, pers. comm.).

Location

Cillín sites occur in a diverse range of landscape settings, including deserted churches and graveyards, ancient monuments, natural landmarks and boundary ditches, seashores, lakeshores and crossroads. As further detailed by Murphy (2011), the documentary and archaeological evidence indicates that specific locations were deliberately selected as suitable sites for use as *cillíní*. The preferred sites tend to be prominent places in the landscape that would not be forgotten or disturbed. Children's burial grounds were often developed around abandoned ecclesiastical sites, reflecting their former religious significance. The *leacht* or altar cairn revealed (Fig. 5) by Nolan's (2006) excavation at Tonybaun, Co. Mayo (below), and also found at other burial grounds, points to the possible presence at *cillín* sites of features relating to their earlier use.

Topographical features

The main characteristics of *cillín* burials are outlined below (Nolan 2006; Donnelly and Murphy 2008; Wilkins and Lalonde 2008). In many instances, individual burials were deliberately marked by small stones placed around the margins of the graves and the remains interred in what may be described as a cist-like structure (Murphy 2011). Wooden coffins were often used, which appear to have been held together by the iron nails found at a number of excavations. Some individuals were wrapped in shrouds fixed with pins, one or two of which have been recovered at various *cillín* excavation sites. Quartz pebbles are a common feature at *cillíní*.

The construction (often showing the expenditure of considerable time and effort) of stone-lined graves, combined with interment in coffins and shrouds, demonstrates the respect paid in many instances to the individuality of children and others buried in *cillín* sites. In some respects, the mourning practices adopted at *cillíní* may be compared to those of contemporary consecrated burial grounds. Most of the people buried in consecrated ground in the post-medieval period would not have been able to afford elaborate or inscribed headstones. Indeed, the simple stone grave markers still seen today in many old graveyards are not markedly different from those in *cillín* burial sites. As observed by Murphy (2011), the real difference between the grave memorials found within a *cillín* and those of individuals of the same class within graveyards of the period is essentially the consecrated nature of the latter.

Dating

A review of the dating evidence associated with 16 *cillíní* excavated from 1966 to 2004 indicates that this site type proliferated in the post-medieval period (Donnelly and Murphy 2008; Murphy 2011). They were used during the past 400 years, particularly in the eighteenth and nineteenth centuries, and continued in use well into the twentieth century. The spatial segregation of children's burials in the post-medieval period is well attested by the excavation undertaken in 2003 at Tonybaun, Co. Mayo (below). The practice

Fig. 2— Children's burial ground within the ruins of Teampall in Comeen, Allihies, Co. Cork (courtesy of Connie Murphy).

*Fig. 3—
Examination
of the* cillín *at
Tonybaun, Co.
Mayo (courtesy
of Chris
Randolph).*

may be traced to the early medieval period, however, as is evident from the excavation, outlined below, undertaken in 2008 at Carrowkeel, Co. Galway (Wilkins and Lalonde 2008).

Tonybaun, Co. Mayo

An important perspective on children's burial grounds has been provided by the excavation of the known *cillín* in Tonybaun townland, south of Ballina (Fig. 3), on behalf of the National Roads Authority and Mayo County Council. Some 248 burials were identified at the site, of which 147 or close to 60% of the total were infants, and a further 23 (9%) were children of 2 to 6 years. Radiocarbon dating established that none of the burials pre-dated the fifteenth century, and indicated a period of use beginning in the late fifteenth century and ending in the mid-twentieth century.

As described by Nolan, 100 stone settings were recorded at Tonybaun, but only 25 of them closely corresponded with underlying burials (Fig. 4). The grave settings were roughly rectangular and were made up of generally uniform-sized stones. The head (west) and foot (east) ends were sometimes marked by large stones laid flat. The north and south sides of the burials were delimited by rough, parallel rows of stones.

Many of the bodies were interred in wooden coffins, typically 0.7m long and 0.2m wide at the head (west) and seemingly made of Scots pine. As previously noted, most of the burials were of infants, but the presence of older age groups, including 55 adults, reflects the practice of interring in these burial sites other individuals who were not considered eligible for burial in consecrated ground.

Cillín burials are frequently seen as having been secretive and unceremonious, often involving rapid disposal of the dead. As Nolan observed, however, some of the excavated grave-goods, such as shrouds, pins, buttons, wool and fabric, as well as a small crucifix, indicate the care and religious observances associated with these burials.

A second layer of burials underlying those described above has been interpreted as representing the earliest phases of the site (Nolan 2006). Notably, no infant remains were present at this level, nor any material such as coffin nails or timbers.

The excavation revealed the presence at the site of an altar-like structure (Fig. 5), known as a *leacht* or outdoor altar cairn, which is indicative of some form of spiritual or commemorative activities at the site (Nolan 2006). These structures occur in many early medieval burial grounds and some have been dated to the first millennium AD. The small, water-rolled stones, mainly quartz or quartzite, scattered on the ground surrounding and within the *leacht* may

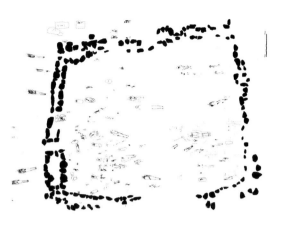

Fig. 4—Plan of the upper layer of burials in the cillín *at Tonybaun, Co. Mayo (courtesy of Mayo County Council).*

have been brought by mourners and left as part of a ritual round or *turas*, with accompanying prayers for the dead.

It is gratifying to record that the skeletons excavated at Tonybaun were reburied in the local Ballynahaglish cemetery, Knockmore, Ballina, after a funeral service in the parish church. In addition, a memorial plaque giving details of the burials and the excavation was erected by Mayo County Council in the graveyard, and another on the site of the *cillín*.

Carrowkeel, Co. Galway

Excavations undertaken in 2005/6 at an enclosure and cemetery site at Carrowkeel, Co. Galway, provided evidence for the segregation of children's burials in Ireland during the medieval period, possibly indicative of an emerging burial practice at that time (Wilkins and Lalonde 2008).

The Carrowkeel site comprised a substantial early medieval enclosure ditch with a cemetery contained in its eastern half. The human remains recovered from the excavated area of the site represent a total of 158 individuals, with the burials ranging over 800 years from the seventh to the fifteenth century. A notable feature of the burials is the predominance of children's remains.

The remains of 37 individuals were recovered from the earlier phase of the cemetery, dated to the period *c.* AD 650–850. Over 70% of these individuals were non-adults, subdivided into foetus (14%), perinate (8%), infant (16%), younger child (16%), older child (11%), and adolescent (5%).

During the following period (*c.* 850–1050), the cemetery appears to have been used almost exclusively for the burial of non-adults. The 75 individuals recovered from this period contained the largest proportion of very young children. Of these, close on two thirds (64%) were below one year of age at death (foetus 27%; perinate 7%; neonate 4%; infant 27%).

The Carrowkeel burials were all uniformly simple in nature, with little evidence of lining of graves, grave markers or grave-goods, and were, with some exceptions, aligned roughly east–west. River-rolled quartz pebbles and some animal bones were found in a number of burials. The cemetery appears to have begun to fall out of use from around 1050–1250. Only two individuals were retrieved from the cemetery for the subsequent period (*c.* 1340–1450). Both were of a very young age, suggesting that the site may have been used at that time as a *cillín* (Wilkins and Lalonde 2008).

The predominance of very young children in the burials at Carrowkeel from around 850 to 1050 provides securely dated evidence for the deliberate spatial segregation of children's burials during the medieval period. In this regard, Wilkins and Lalonde (2008) refer to excavations in the past decade at Cashel and Raystown (Co. Meath) that have found clusters of non-adult burials within larger cemeteries. They suggest that this segregation of children in one section of a cemetery may be a precursor to the *cillín* tradition that proliferated in the post-medieval period.

As a multi-period settlement/cemetery site, the majority of which have been identified in Leinster, Carrowkeel seems to be the first of the type west of the Shannon where a combined stratigraphic excavation and radiocarbon-dating programme has been undertaken (Wilkins and Lalonde 2008).

Box 1	Diagnostic features

- Relatively small sites, characterised by numerous low-standing stones, marking graves.
- Generally located in prominent places in the landscape, typically abandoned ecclesiastical sites, and often within church ruins. They are also found in close association with ancient monuments (ringforts etc.), at natural landmarks and boundary ditches, as well as seashores and lakeshores. Others occur in less prominent positions, such as the corner of a field.
- Some may be found within large enclosures that were used for both occupation and burial purposes.
- Sites may be enclosed, within boundary walls, while others are unenclosed or partly enclosed.

Fig. 5—Leacht excavated at Tonybaun, Co. Mayo (courtesy of Mayo County Council).

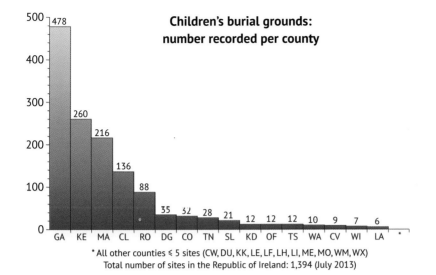

Fig. 6—Geographical distribution by county of children's burial grounds, based on database compiled by the National Monuments Service, Department of Arts, Heritage and the Gaeltacht.

Acknowledgements

The important publications brought to our attention by Paul Walsh, Eileen Murphy and Ronan Swan are gratefully acknowledged. The photographs and illustrations provided by Joanna Nolan, Connie Murphy and the National Monuments Service (Department of the Environment, Heritage and Local Government) are much appreciated, as is the preparation of Fig. 6 by Conor McDermott.

References

Donnelly, C.J. and Murphy, E. 2008 The origins of *cillíní* in Ireland. In E.M. Murphy (ed.), *Deviant burial in the archaeological record*. Oxford.

Murphy, E.M. 2011 Children's burial grounds in Ireland (*cillíní*) and parental emotions towards infant death. *International Journal of Historical Archaeology* **15**. http://dx.doi.org/10.1007/s10761-011-0148-8.

Nolan, J. 2006 Excavation of a children's burial ground at Tonybaun, Ballina, Co. Mayo. In J. O'Sullivan and M. Stanley (eds), *Settlement, industry and ritual*. Dublin.

Wilkins, B. and Lalonde, S. 2008 An early medieval settlement/cemetery at Carrowkeel, Co. Galway. *Journal of Irish Archaeology* **16**, 57–84.

This article was originally published in the Autumn 2013 issue of Archaeology Ireland.

Table of monuments

Topic	Time-span	Originally published in *Archaeology Ireland*
Section I—Agriculture		
Ancient fields	From the Neolithic period to the Bronze Age.	Autumn 2004
Fieldscapes	Enclosure of arable strips seems to have started in the Middle Ages and appears to have been well under way by the eighteenth century, at least in certain areas.	Winter 2007
Post-medieval fieldscapes	Adopted in the seventeenth century; widely practised in the late eighteenth and early nineteenth centuries, especially in disadvantaged areas.	Autumn 2008
Booleying	Thought to have been especially used from the mid-eighteenth century to the early nineteenth century; associated with rundale farming in disadvantaged farming areas.	Winter 2003
Post-medieval farming	Field enclosure: from the seventeenth century, throughout the eighteenth century and into the nineteenth century.	Winter 2008
Cultivation	Ridge and furrow: from Neolithic times onward; became more prevalent in the medieval period; increased further in prevalence with widespread land cultivation from *c.* 1780 to 1840.	Summer 2007
Agricultural drainage systems 1	Traditional drains and ditches: introduced in the late eighteenth century; more widely used in the earlier part of the nineteenth century; continued in some areas into the twentieth century.	Spring 2010

Agricultural drainage systems 2	Early modern drains: from the early nineteenth century through much of the twentieth century.	Summer 2010
Making lime	Lime kilns: from the mid-eighteenth century to the early nineteenth.	Summer 2005

Section II—Food processing

Diet and production	Historical food products: from as far back as the Neolithic period until more recent times, corn and milk being the mainstay of the general diet; butter recovered from bogs has yielded radiocarbon dates ranging from the early seventeenth century BC to the late eighteenth century AD.	Summer 2016
Fulachta fiadh	Most in use during the Bronze Age, particularly in the period 1800–800 BC.	Spring 2004
Grinding grain	Quern stones: in use from Neolithic to relatively recent times, as follows: • Saddle querns: Neolithic period and Bronze Age. • Beehive querns: Iron Age (second century BC–fourth century AD). • Disc querns: first and second millennium AD. • Pot querns: medieval times to recent decades.	Summer 2006
Drying grain in days of old	Corn-drying kilns: the majority are dated to between the fourth and the thirteenth century AD, but kilns were widespread up until the mid-1800s.	Autumn 2005
Watermills	Ranging from the middle of the first millennium AD to the thirteenth century, with a prominent construction period encompassing the eighth–tenth centuries AD.	Autumn 2006
Windmills	First seen during the Anglo-Norman period but mainly erected in the seventeenth and eighteenth centuries, with many falling into disuse during the early decades of the nineteenth century.	Summer 2015

Section III—Settlement

Hillforts	Current during the late Bronze Age, with excavations revealing beginnings around the twelfth or thirteenth century BC.	Spring 2013
Rath, lios and cashel	Generally constructed in the period AD 600–900, with platform ringforts lagging slightly and current from the mid-eighth to the mid-tenth century AD.	Autumn 2007

Souterrains	Mainly from around AD 750 to AD 1250, with some earlier and later examples also known.	Winter 2004
Crannogs	Primarily the early Middle Ages (AD 400–1000), with indications of settlement and construction in the first millennium BC at certain sites and evidence of usage into the late Middle Ages (thirteenth-fifteenth century BC) in other cases.	Winter 2005
Early church sites	From about the sixth to the twelfth century AD.	Spring 2017
Mottes	Constructed mainly in the twelfth and thirteenth centuries AD, with some beyond 1300, and continued in use into the fourteenth and in some cases even the fifteenth century.	Spring 2007
Moated sites	Dating evidence is limited, with indications of construction in the late thirteenth or early fourteenth century AD.	Winter 2006
Deserted medieval towns	Thrived from the late twelfth to the fifteenth century AD, with some towns possibly surviving as late as the seventeenth century and then abandoned for a variety of reasons.	Autumn 2016
Tower-houses	Mostly erected between AD 1450 and 1620; many were built even before the mid-fifteenth century and some before the end of the fourteenth century.	Summer 2009
Clachans	Emerged during the eighteenth century and widespread in the early nineteenth century, with a small percentage inhabited until the present.	Spring 2008

Section IV—Getting around

Currachs	Emerged in the Iron Age and widely used throughout the medieval period, followed by a transition to modern modern versions.	Spring 2015
Early historical routeways	Seemingly current in Ireland from the Iron Age, if not earlier; amongst a wide variety of routeways, five major *slíghe* have been postulated.	Autumn 2015
Historical bridges	The first recorded bridge construction occurred around AD 1000 and bridges became more common during the high medieval period, with notable phases of bridge building in the thirteenth and then the seventeenth and eighteenth centuries.	Winter 2015

Logboats	Current from Mesolithic or early Neolithic times and continued in use until the seventeenth century AD, declining in the eighteenth century.	Winter 2014

Section V—Local enterprises

Charcoal-production sites	Pits: early and late medieval times, especially ninth–thirteenth century AD, with some in use during the thirteenth–seventeenth century. Platforms: predominantly post-medieval times, possibly current in the seventeenth and eighteenth centuries	Winter 2009
Salt-making and food preservation	Current during the medieval period at some monastic centres; commercial salt manufacture became widespread in the early decades of the nineteenth century and continued into the twentieth century.	Winter 2016
Kelp production	From the eighteenth century and possibly earlier; widely practised around the coast in the eighteenth and nineteenth centuries.	Autumn 2010
Turf-harvesting	During the medieval period; dependence on turf increased in the sixteenth and seventeenth centuries, continuing into modern times and reaching a peak in the early part of the twentieth century.	Spring 2016

Section VI—Coastal features

Shell middens	Already forming from Mesolithic times onward; continued to appear, possibly intermittently, from the late Neolithic to relatively modern times.	Spring 2005
Promontory forts	Tentatively dated to the Iron Age, although some could possibly be older, while others were in use in medieval times.	Summer 2004
Medieval fisheries	Many dated from around AD 450 to 1300 but some were constructed as late as the late eighteenth or early nineteenth century.	Autumn 2009
Martello towers and signal towers	Martello towers: erected AD 1804–15; many decommissioned after the end of the war with France in 1814. Signal towers: built AD 1804–6, with most abandoned after the end of the Napoleonic Wars and some used again during World War I and World War II.	Summer 2012

Coastguard stations	Mainly the nineteenth century and early twentieth century, with signal stations developed in the vicinity of a number.	Winter 2013
Lighthouses	Some originally built in the twelfth and thirteenth centuries; the establishment of lighthouses gained momentum in the mid-seventeenth century and many were also developed in the nineteenth century.	Autumn 2014
Coastal lookout posts	Constructed mainly during 1939 and 1940.	Summer 2013
Section VII—Ritual and ceremony		
Rock art	Long antiquity in Europe and may have been current by the middle Neolithic period in Ireland, continuing into the later Neolithic and even the early Bronze Age.	Winter 2011
Passage tombs and megalithic art	Constructed mainly during the middle Neolithic period (3500–3000 BC).	Spring 2012
Summit cairns	Some present from the Neolithic period and some appeared during the Bronze Age.	Autumn 2011
Henges	From the middle or late Neolithic period to the Bronze Age, sometimes with Iron Age and even early medieval activity present.	Autumn 2012
Burial barrows	First appeared during the Neolithic period but various forms flourished during the period 1700–400 BC and again during the Iron Age (400 BC–AD 400).	Winter 2012
Wedge tombs	Emerging from the final Neolithic period, the majority were built between 2500 and 1800 BC, petering out during the following centuries.	Winter 2010
Stone circles	Cork/Kerry group: from around 1500 BC, with some as late as perhaps 800 BC. Mid-Ulster group: at least some constructed during the Neolithic period and the Bronze Age.	Spring 2011
Stone rows and stone pairs	Current in Britain and Ireland from about 1800 to 1200 BC. Munster: mid-seventeenth century BC to c. 800 BC (Maughanasilly and Cashelkeelty). Mid-Ulster: late Neolithic period to late Bronze Age (complex of stone circles and rows at Beaghmore, Co. Tyrone).	Summer 2011
Boulder burials	The second half of the Bronze Age (1500–800 BC).	Autumn 2003

Ogham stones	Inscriptions apparently belong to the period from the fourth to the sixth and possibly even the seventh century AD.	Summer 2014
Holy wells	Many still venerated today, holy wells have been a feature of Irish Christianity from early times; many were probably transformed from prehistoric sanctuaries.	Spring 2006
Mass rocks	Associated with the Penal Laws in Ireland (AD 1695–1829), especially the earlier century.	Spring 2014
Cillíní	Particularly the eighteenth and nineteenth centuries and well into the twentieth century.	Autumn 2013

Index of sites